ESSENTIAL PAPERS IN PSYCHOANALYSIS

ESSENTIAL PAPERS ON COUNTERTRANSFERENCE

Benjamin Wolstein
Editor

New York University Press
New York and London
1988

Library of Congress Cataloging-in-Publication Data

Essential papers on countertransference.

(Essential paper in psychoanalysis)
Bibliography: p.
Includes index.
1. Countertransference (Psychology)   I. Wolstein,
Benjamin.   II. Series.
RC489.C68E77   1988   616.89'17   88-9887
ISBN 0-8147-9220-0
ISBN 0-8147-9221-9 (pbk.)

New York University Press books are Smyth-sewn
and printed on permanent and durable acid-free paper.

Book design by Ken Venezio

For Jim,
who went to
the widow-maker

Contents

Acknowledgments

We wish to gratefully acknowledge the following copyright holders: Sigmund Freud Copyrights Ltd., the Institute of Psycho-Analysis, the Hogarth Press, and Basic Books for permission to reprint "The Future Prospects of Psychoanalytic Psychotherapy" from *The Standard Edition of the Complete Psychological Works of Sigmund Freud,* translated and edited by James Strachey.

Dover Publications for permission to reprint excerpts from *The Development of Psychoanalysis* by Sandor Ferenczi and Otto Rank, pp. 28–44, 1923.

Psychiatry for permission to reprint the following: Janet MacKenzie Rioch, "The Transference Phenomenon in Psychoanalytic Therapy, Vol. 6, pp. 147–56, 1943; Mabel Blake Cohen, "Countertransference and Anxiety," Vol. 15, pp. 231–43, 1952; Edward S. Tauber, "Exploring the Therapeutic Use of Countertransference Data," Vol. 17, pp. 331–36, 1954.

Farrar, Straus & Giroux for permission to reprint chapter 23 from Theodor Reik, *Listening with the Third Ear,* 1949, © 1948 by Theodor Reik, renewal © 1975 by Arthur Reik.

Grune & Stratton for permission to reprint chapter 4 from Benjamin Wolstein, *Countertransference,* pp. 79–123, 1959.

Samiksa and the Indian Psycho-Analytical Society for permission to reprint Ralph M. Crowley, "Human Reactions of Analysts to Patients," Vol. 6, pp. 212–19, 1952.

International Universities Press for permission to reprint from *Journal of the American Psychoanalytic Association* the following: D. Orr, "Transference and Countertransference: A Historical Survey," Vol. 2, pp. 647–62, 1954; L. Tower, "Countertransference," Vol. 4, pp. 224–55, 1956, and L. Stone, "The Transference-Countertransference Complex." In Stone, *The Psychoanalytic Situation: An Examination of Its Development and Essential Nature,* pp. 66–83, 1961.

American Journal of Psychotherapy for permission to reprint Clara Thompson, "The Role of the Analyst's Personality in Therapy," Vol. 10, pp. 347–59, 1956.

Psychoanalytic Quarterly for permission to reprint H. Racker, "The Meanings and Uses of Countertransference," Vol. 26, pp. 303–57, 1957.

Journal of Nervous and Mental Disease for permission to reprint H. Searles, "The Schizophrenic's Vulnerability to the Therapist's Unconscious Processes," Vol. 27, pp. 247–62, © Williams & Wilkins, 1958.

The British Psychological Society for permission to reprint D. W. Winnicott, "Counter-Transference," *British Journal of Medical Psychology,* Vol. 33, 17–21, 1960.

Contemporary Psychoanalysis for permission to reprint the following: L. Epstein and A. Feiner, "Countertransference: The Therapist's Contribution to the Treatment: An Overview," Vol. 15, no. 3, pp. 489–513, 1979; M. Gill, "The Interpersonal Paradigm and the Degree of the Therapist's Involvement," Vol. 19, no. 2, pp. 202–37, 1983; B. Wolstein, "The Pluralism of Perspectives on Countertransference," Vol. 19, no. 3, pp. 506–21, 1983.

Introduction

A historical review of the conceptual and clinical study of countertransference offers convincing evidence of the integrity of psychoanalysis as an ordered structure of psychological inquiry. Over the past seventy-five years, the empirical definition of *countertransference* has gradually been corrected and enlarged; its systematic analysis has been coordinated within a body of knowledge that remains largely provisional and cumulative; and the interpretive views of its clinical psychoanalytic meaning continue to be viewed as open and pluralistic.

I consider these three orders of inquiry the distinctive marks of a science, and could not otherwise refer to psychoanalysis or any other field of inquiry equally subject to empirical, systematic, and interpretive reconstruction, without doing serious epistemological injustice. At least since Breuer and Freud's 1895 *Studies on Hysteria,* observations of transference and countertransference have become increasingly clarified in the various interpretive perspectives. They give strong support for the reconstructible foundations of the field of psychoanalytic inquiry.

The papers singled out for this collection were written between 1910 and 1983, and were chosen for their critical value in delineating the major changes in psychoanalysis during those years. As these papers will show, early practicing psychoanalysts sought to keep all evidence of countertransference out of the actual clinical inquiry. Currently, most choose to work directly with it using many different interpretive and procedural approaches. Yet between these seemingly divergent positions lies a discordant but coherent historical context of development for the study of countertransference. The evidence for this emerged unexpectedly as my editorial work progressed, especially after arranging these papers chronologically by date of original publication.

Countertransference, it is now clear, has undergone a remarkable career in the history of psychoanalytic ideas. It was once even discounted and yet came back to the center of attention. At the same time, other notions, once seen as critically important, have been assigned to obscurity. The early view toward the concept of anxiety offers a striking comparison to countertransference. Once construed as undischarged libido and the focus of much attention, that concept of anxiety is now considered obsolete and quite useless. In contrast, countertransference, which Freud expressly held from direct consideration in the psychoanalytic inquiry, was not initially a focus in analysis. It is thus most extraordinary that, more than seventy-five years later, the tables have so completely turned that a collection of papers such as this is justified.

Why, then, did classical psychoanalysts initially give countertransference such short shrift? And, perhaps more importantly, what later clinical developments made possible, even necessary, such a complete about-face in the response to countertransference? While it is true that answers to questions of this sort can only suggest probable and not definitive explanations, they can nonetheless shed light on future directions of psychoanalytic research and practice.

I

In 1910, Freud strongly recommended that practicing psychoanalysts keep all countertransference out of their clinical work. He and his followers believed quite seriously that any direct consideration of countertransference as it arose during the actual psychoanalytic inquiry would threaten the viability of the whole field. Later Freudians, attempting to follow his recommendation to the letter (interestingly enough, it was nowhere modified in his own writings), strove to restrict their procedure solely to the interpretation of transference. Freud had recommended that psychoanalysts act like a mirror or a surgeon, like a blank screen or uninvolved expert. Freud and later classical analysts adhered rigidly to interpretation as the single parameter of procedure. They struggled long and hard to remain free of the countertransference of individual psychic differences, and thus took a position of neutrality without, however, seeing their way clear to a workable statement of it. They eventually lost the struggle. How did this come about?

It seems evident from a fair-minded reading of Freud's case studies that he consistently ignored his own recommendation to be like a mirror or a surgeon. Instead, he brought his personal strivings, beliefs, and values fully into his therapeutic efforts. Witness such cases as Dora, the Rat Man, or the Wolf Man. I am not suggesting that he should have followed his recommendation, but rather remarking that he even thought it possible to act like a mirror or a surgeon. It seems clear he himself did not behave this way. Many have neglected the fact that Freud, in his work with patients, exercised his personal imaginative powers to their fullest, without internal reservation, at the same time that he called for the repression of countertransference within the actual clinical inquiry. Freud made his speculative interpretations based on his own self-analysis, which had resulted in his unique perspective of instinctual-libidinal myth and metaphor. This perspective was absolutely unabridged by either the perspectives of his patients or those of his colleagues, such as Adler, Jung, Rank, and so on.

As we know, Freud originally uncovered the psychic sources of his interpretive metapsychology through his self-analysis, in an attempt to make some sense out of the anomolous and personally difficult features of his own psychosexual history. Only later, in the grand manner of nineteenth-century German philosophical idealism, did he seek to extend his speculative life and death instincts into a universal philosophy of human psychic suffering. Others, such as Adler, Jung, and Rank, created alternative views on interpretation, and their myths and metaphors were at least equally useful to Freud's, if not more so. As we know, most were later drummed out of the then-fledgling field. Like Freud, they were unaware how exclusionary their views were. No one even suggested that their individual countertransferences were probably deeply embedded in their differences of interpretive belief and value, which were manifest in all their clinical psychoanalytic inquiries.

Some implications of the contradiction between Freud's proffered view and his practice remain unarticulated. For example, to require that all psychoanalysts exclude their countertransference is to require, in effect, that all except Freud do so. The metapsychology he had proposed to interpret his own dynamic psychic experience was supposed to guide interpretation in every psychoanalytic therapy. As I have noted, he often brought countertransference into his own clinical work. Freud's metapsychology was the major source of support for the myth and metaphor with which he explained both his and everyone else's countertransference. Freud had it both ways: Not only did he not exclude his singular interpretation of countertransference from his own practice, but he also thought it would dominate the practice of all other psychoanalysts. It thus follows that he thought other psychoanalysts should both keep their own countertransference in check and pattern theirs after his. No other approach could appear in the Freudian field of therapy, I am suggesting, because it was a field he constructed from his point of view.

This suggests that for each psychoanalyst and each patient, the meaning of their own personal suffering and misery was laid out long in advance of their own psychoanalytic inquiries by Freud's interpretive and speculative psychic determinism. This approach leaves no room for individual differences in temperament or character. Classical psychoanalysts, of course, genuinely believed that their interpretive metapsychological absolutism would alone provide the primary source of psychic healing. At the time, there was practically no consideration of the two-way field of experience in which the therapy took place, nor any direct reference to the intuitive and distinctly exploratory activities from both sides, even though they were as much a part of the psychoanalytic inquiry as the interpretive and speculative activities. According to classical psychoanalysts, only through making instinctual-libidinal interpretations, and in their subsequent acceptance by the patient, could success be assured. Patients who did not accept these interpretations were seen as resisting, and, in response, psychoanalysts counterresisted them by, as Freud put it, conquering or overcoming that resistance. But he never treated this conquest of resistance as part of interpretive psychoanalysis proper. Nor did he ever change his mind about it—not, at least, in print. Instinctual-libidinal interpretation was, for him, always the focus; for some, it remains so.

There are a number of aspects neglected in discussions of the classical approach to countertransference. First, Freud's self-analysis was conducted without the interference of anyone's countertransference. Through it, he came to terms with the burden of psychic baggage to which he was heir, and interpreted it in terms of the biology of instinct, libido, and id. These psychoanalysts who still call themselves classical or traditional Freudians do so by taking over this core of interpretive metapsychology lock, stock, and barrel. Even though they do not personally get it through the same method of self-analysis as Freud, they defend it to the absolute exclusion of all other views, perhaps even their own. They practice psychoanalysis from an attitudinal standpoint, as the impersonal conduits for the beliefs and values nested in Freud's personal myths and metaphors. The truths of their dynamic psychology come to reside in some else's head, and fail to originate in their own.

There is an implicit question here, that often escapes critical notice: Why don't psychoanalysts who follow Freud to the letter take up Freud's psychic activity as their model instead; why don't they undergo the process of direct psychic inquiry he followed, and, by that means, but according to their own unique gifts of curiosity, arrive at the myths and metaphors of their own interpretive metapsychology? They could then, like him, responsibly present to patients their own deeply held interpretive perspective on both life experience in general and on psychoanalytic therapy in particular. And why don't their patients again, like him, exercise the same freedom to speculate about their own myths and metaphors of interpretation? It seems to me that the inner psychic journey as direct experience, no matter what interpretive metapsychological guidelines frame it, define the striving for psychoanalytic self-knowledge.

A final point concerns the narrowly restricted perspective from which Freud initially recommended psychoanalysts exclude any consideration of countertransference from clinical experience, which relates to his early perspective of libido. In 1910, Freud's perspective of libido was narrowly restricted when compared to his tripartite statement of the middle 1920s. His focus was limited to the instinctual-libidinal, which excluded any interpretive reference to the ego or the superego or to a psychology of the self that remained outside the Freudian purview. His early view of libido is the unaddressed reason for withholding countertransference from the experiential field of therapy, and exploring it instead within the confines of his own personal analysis. Through conscious will, he thought he could shut down his personal analysis, and the stream of consciousness from which it arose, during his therapeutic efforts with patients. Yet he did not consider that his patients would seek to explore their own intuitions, observations, and inferences about their psychoanalyst's countertransference. In fact, this was their personal analysis. In any case, in 1910, neither psychoanalyst nor patient had the clinical awareness or knowledge with which to explore the direct emergence of countertransference. Freud thought it derived solely from libido, and his patients, who knew nothing of his metapsychology, were unable to use it for their analysis.

One could, of course, also consider dealing with the countertransference of libido derivatives by expressing or enacting sexual impulses directly. This approach was not open to him and no classical psychoanalyst worth his salt, certainly not Freud, would have considered it.

In sum, during this early period, Freud construed psychoanalysis as a direct interpretive discipline that covered the oedipal period of psychosexual development, in which all interpretation was made in the instinctual-libidinal mode and which, without the benefit of ego or superego, had to exclude the direct consideration of countertransference. This purposeful exclusion did not make countertransference disappear from the psychoanalytic experience. Psychoanalysts and patients may choose not to talk about it, but talking is not the only way to communicate it. Although concealed, Freud's countertransference was nevertheless communicated in therapy. The procedure he recommended only repressed, dissociated, or split it off—effectively stopped psychoanalyst or patient from considering it as it arose, which curiously enough, put it beyond their permissible verbal limits, but not beyond their communicational field.

II

A new approach to countertransference developed during the 1950s. Countertransference had become a generally unavoidable, if occasionally unworkable, concern in all perspectives of psychoanalysis, even in those urging psychoanalysts to adopt an attitude of neutrality or anonymity. This decade recorded a sudden outpouring of books and monographs, papers and reports, symposia and lectures on practically all variations of this theme imaginable. This seemingly unprecedented and certainly unanticipated new interest in countertransference appeared to have sprung up from nowhere. Yet an enduring historical fact is, perhaps for polemical reasons, less frequently noticed than is deserved. Namely, the focus of serious clinical interest on countertransference within all the major perspectives. During the 1950s, psychoanalysts behaved as though they were the first to discover countertransference. All, of course, subordinated their explorations of it to the whole range of metapsychologies then known, from the most conservative of classical positions to the most radical of contemporary ones. Regardless of their widely divergent views about exploring countertransference in theory and practice, however, react to it they now found they must.

How did this major shift in clinical direction come about? By the 1950s, psychoanalysts knew they had arrived at a therapeutic point of no return. They now began to accept as ineluctable reality the experience of countertransference within the actual field of inquiry. What they and their patients decided to do about it, of course, still remained a matter of personal judgment and individual decision. But they could no longer ignore it by simply appealing to Freud's arbitrary convention to suppress it. It was no longer as easy to fall back on the power of his authority because many had already disengaged themselves, to greater or lesser degrees, from the aegis of his conceptual and clinical approach on other equally significant issues. Most important for the topic under discussion, I propose, are the two major breakthroughs that took their therapeutic inquiry far beyond his. One empirical, the other interpretive, both were initiated in the early 1920s and complete by around 1940.

First, at the empirical level, some psychoanalysts developed the new psychoanalysis of resistance, variously termed by Reich as character armor, by Anna Freud and Hartmann as defense mechanism, by Sullivan and Thompson as security operation. And, second, at the interpretive level, they introduced the new principle of adaptation, as Hartmann termed it, or consensual validation, as Sullivan termed it, by means of participant observation. These new developments transformed the structure of psychoanalytic inquiry in profound ways. And they deeply altered the clinical picture, I emphasize for this volume, precisely because they brought psychoanalysts more directly into the coparticipant therapeutic inquiry with their patients in innovative ways, and with unexpected results. The most powerful and enduring result, of course, was the new treatment of countertransference.

Consider the high points of this major shift, consolidated during the 1930s. A decade earlier, Ferenczi and Rank's original and pioneering experiments made the actual experience of psychoanalyst and patient in the here and now part of the actual psychoanalytic inquiry (Ferenczi and Rank, 1923). They took the first step that led to the new study of countertransference. In their effort to consider the actual experience patients underwent in their analysis, they were, to my knowledge, the first to recommend exploring the present experience within the analytic hour—without, however, discounting the ongoing interpretable effects of the oedipal past—and the first, also, to introduce the notion of experience itself into clinical discussion. No one had, on the record, suggested to practicing psychoanalysts that the dynamic range of actual clinical inquiry involved this aspect of their direct relatedness with patients from the beginning. In my view, from this seminal idea evolved the direct relatedness with patients that later formed the basis for the experiential field of therapy.

While Ferenczi and Rank obviously did not realize the full impact of their discovery, they initiated a long-range movement in creative psychoanalytic research. Reich, after conducting a landmark seminar on character analysis at the Vienna Psychoanalytic Institute in 1927, published this new approach some six years later (Reich, 1933). This was soon followed by Anna Freud's classic on the ego's mechanisms of defense (A. Freud, 1936). Three years later, Hartmann's innovative study of the ego's autonomous functions and their role in adaptation was published (Hartmann, 1939). And in 1940, Sullivan published his unique operationalist study of the interpersonal self made up of reflected appraisals through consensual validation (Sullivan, 1940). Among others, both in the United States and abroad, these psychoanalytic writers moved the center of interpretive metapsychology away from the psychic determinism of oedipal history and toward the environment in which both they and their patients sought adaptation from the id-ego perspective, or sought consensual validation from the interpersonal perspective. And they all contributed to the 1930s movement of psychoanalytic research into the environing relational conditions of human experience.

How then did this new treatment of resistance contribute to the sudden rise of conceptual and clinical interest in countertransference? In a general sense, I think, it meant that patients were not as readily seen as the clear crystal pools into which psychoanalysts could gaze to find reflected the interpretive metapsychologies they found useful in understanding themselves. New discoveries in ego psychology, object relations, and interpersonal relations during that decade tended to show how a fugitive psychoanalytic narcissism had forced patients to locate the meaning of their psychic pain and suffering on the singular grid of their psychoanalyst's instinctual-libidinal metapsychology. This new clinical inquiry into the analysis of resistance directly changed the approach at the level of interpretation. Namely, it moved from the absolutism of a single universal perspective to a pluralism of perspectives based on direct experience. The field of therapy could now hold more than one metapsychology. No longer were psychoanalysts—nor, for that matter, patients—as easily ostracized from the experience of clinical psychoanalytic inquiry on the strength of their individual differences at the interpretive and speculative level. Now that psychic resistance could be explored and brought to conscious awareness, it became possible for both psychoanalyst and patient to hold metapsychological differences in conscious awareness as well, yet continue their therapeutic inquiry without prejudice or prejudgment.

III

I will now explore the change at the interpretive level. Recall the functions of character armor, defense mechanism, or security operation, all forms of the reactive sector of the total personality most generally termed resistance. In some respects, these functions always critically capture the unconscious psychology of the psychoanalyst against whom they are patterned to defend and protect the resistive patient. In so far as the resistances are rooted beyond awareness and function as unconscious patterns, they are, of course, always fair material for psychoanalytic inquiry. But the point is individual patients bring some particular resistance into play, conscious or unconscious, no matter how close to, or wide of, the mark, only because it proves in some sense adaptive or consensual to their particular others—in this case their psychoanalysts. Otherwise, that particular response does not function as resistance, but as something else.

What does this actually mean for the psychoanalysis of resistance in ego psychology, object or interpersonal relations, or in any other interpretive context? First, if the psychoanalysis of resistance at all succeeds, patients become aware of its origins and its functions both within the psyche and within the environment. Since patients set the pattern of their resistance in specific response to particular psychoanalysts, they may, if only on the strength of that increased awareness, also come to realize something new about the defensive psychology of their particular psychoanalysts being uniquely resisted then and there. In systematic terms, patients are particularly alert and responsive to those special aspects of countertransference, counterresistance, and counteranxiety brought into sharper focus by special aspects of their own resistance, or their own transference and anxiety.

There is still another serendipitous result, unanticipated yet greatly influential on later psychoanalytic research, especially in countertransference, that follows from the new ego, interpersonal, object-relational metapsychologies. Under the earlier libido perspective, psychoanalysts saw no need for their patients to have an ego or self-system to speak of. By the 1930s, however, they were observing and carefully studying it in systematic detail, thereby fully acknowledging its presence, function, and development. As a result, patients could come to possess a demonstrably enlarged scope of awareness of both self and other, be more clear both inside and outside the therapeutic field, and cooperate in reconstructing the ego or self-system. Nothing was more natural than for patients to turn the strength of this new awareness and reconstruction toward the psychology of their immediately environing others —especially their psychoanalysts—and describe the perceived aspects of countertransference against which they thought they had gone into resistance. From that clinical experience it is but a short step to coordinating within the overall structure of psychoanalytic knowledge, on principle, the probable observation of the personal psychology of psychoanalysts, including their countertransference, as it directly emerges with their patients, now capable of knowing themselves better in transference, resistance, and anxiety, through the reconstructed ego or self-system.

Clinical psychoanalysis had thus arrived at a condition of inquiry it had never before faced, let alone worked with. From that point on, it was only a hardened intellectual rigidity, opaqueness, and self-deception—in sum, deep countertransference—that permitted ego, interpersonal, object-relation psychoanalysts to avoid such psychoanalytic inquiry on a priori grounds. They could not, in the final analysis, proscribe its happening with them. They could, rather, decide whether and how to participate in their own unique ways with their patients, observing it directly. Their patients, with their newly found clarity of self-awareness, now had the freedom to exercise their gifts of increased capacity and curiosity. This freedom to experience has been precisely the goal to which any two coparticipants committed themselves from the beginning. Yet psychoanalysts had hardly expected that their patients, by becoming more aware of themselves, would also become more intimately aware of them. The wide acceptance of this newly formulated principle of adaptation or consensual validation deeply transformed the clinical conditions of traditional psychoanalytic inquiry. Patients quite naturally began going beneath the outward manifestations of their psychoanalysts's clinical presence then, and they continue, therapeutic conditions permitting, to do even more of that now.

Those ego-interpersonal psychoanalysts who strictly followed the classical principle of neutrality, and refused even to listen to intuitions expressed about countertransference, counterresistance, and counteranxiety, forced patients to check them out elsewhere, thus cutting off the possibility of extending the therapeutic inquiry into a more genuinely cooperative endeavor. But those willing to listen to their patients began to hear things their predecessors had never heard before. On the first level, they directly experienced the countertransference of their defensive operations that they had already discovered in their own personal analyses and in interpersonal consensus with their peers. Long before their patients had noticed them, these patterns were available to their conscious awareness as probable countertransference.

On a second level were other observations which proved more difficult to deal with. When patients observed some unconscious or dissociated aspect of their psychoanalysts's psychology not yet fully interpersonal, psychoanalysts were not as readily able to fall back on the adaptive or consensual understanding of how their patients were perceiving them. This countertransference as yet unavailable to their conscious reach, they therefore tended to counterresist. Because they could not as quickly bring it to conscious awareness, they usually remained silent and/or claimed it for further personal analysis, effectively removing it from that phase of the clinical psychoanalytic inquiry. At some points, of course, such observations of countertransference emerged as a matter of course, inevitable and unavoidable under the theory of unconscious psychic experience. Most likely, patients took the silence to suggest the probability of their psychoanalysts's agreement without self-knowledge.

Psychoanalysts may or may not have been able to become aware of what their patients saw. Yet the pursuit of the adaptive or consensual point of view brought this observation, directed outside their own awareness, to a crucial position in the established structure of the inquiry. It remained there, untapped at its source during psychoanalytic inquiry, until the psychological means of relating to it later appeared in the form of the psychic center of the psychoanalytic self. (I discuss this notion further below.)

The historical rationale of this development is now clear. Ego psychology, object relations, and interpersonal relations rebuilt the structure of psychoanalytic inquiry under the adaptive or consensual point of view. Consistently followed, those perspectives brought countertransference into evidence and made it readily available for exploration in all future psychoanalysis. The change may be epitomized as follows: If adaptive or consensual observation moved psychoanalysts into closer relational proximity to their patients, it also moved patients into closer relational proximity to their psychoanalysts. During the adaptive or consensual study of their external relations, they expanded clinical psychoanalytic inquiry into unexpected internal directions. As psychoanalysts and patients began to experience one another as coparticipants in a shared field of inquiry—both, now, capable of participant observation—they found they could do it from both sides of the field. And they became both participant observers and observed participants with one another.

All the major publications on these features of countertransference appeared during the productive decade from the early fifties to the beginning of the sixties. By then, the new clinical standpoint of observing and interpreting countertransference was firmly established. After that, however, the research lost its forward momentum and started to limit itself to the increasing refinement of observation and interpretation. It was, I believe, caught up in unacknowledged yet pressing and unremitting counteranxiety, which proved even more difficult than countertransference for psychoanalysts to get at. They could move counteranxiety around by reconstructing the ego or self-system, but could not yet lay bare its generative roots by psychological means. It remained, therefore, unpsychoanalyzable. In the absence of new major efforts at the empirical level of psychoanalytic inquiry, the research in this area ground to a full halt. Trapped in the dead end of impenetrable anxiety and counteranxiety, the work became overly duplicative and unregenerative.

This situation changed with the formulation of the psychology of the self, which occurred during the 1970s. I explicitly refer to the psychic center of the psychoanalytic self, a center of personal and interpersonal experience, a psychic point of origin and function, a unique source of immediate and reflective activity. It provides patients and psychoanalysts with the psychic agency of the anxieties and the counteranxieties they each generate during their coparticipant inquiry, and, in that measure, are directly responsible for, and, of course, the psychic agency of their transferences and resistances and countertransferences and counterresistances.

But even before their formulation of the psychic center of the psychoanalytic self, something new and irreversible had already happened. By the 1960s, countertransference was widely considered a fully established part of the experiential field of therapy. Psychoanalysts and patients could directly study its manifestations during clinical psychoanalytic inquiry in accordance with the capacities, interests, and perspectives of any two particular coparticipants. Later, after formulating the psychic center in the 1970s, they could explore transference and countertransference together without the interpretive support of coinciding views on metapsychology, and without empirical stoppage at the disruptive emergence of anxiety and counteranxiety. Whatever the shared limitations now in force between a particular psychoanalyst and patient, they were, essentially, matters of private preference or personal decision, and they put an individual stamp on the structure of every psychoanalytic inquiry.

All the papers included in this collection, though they were written from differing points of emphasis across the spectrum of possible perspectives, had a common source of inspiration: to enlarge the defined range of psychoanalytic inquiry for the two coparticipants in the experiential field of therapy. The papers also share a common outcome: to bring clinical psychoanalysis to a level of empirical development from which there was no turning back to the study of transference without reference to countertransference, of resistance without reference to counterresistance, of anxiety without reference to counteranxiety, or any variation among them.

IV

I would like to summarize the change in psychoanalytic direction from the absolutism of interpretive metapsychology to the direct inquiry into psychic experience. As the ego, object-relational, interpersonal points of view matured during the 1940s, they were read quite literally as programmatic guidelines for psychoanalytic therapy. Yet when taken to their logical conclusion, these guidelines caused some rather surprising clinical events to occur. For they applied not only to the social and cultural experience of psychoanalysts and patients outside the field of therapy but, with radical procedural effect, to their psychic experience inside it as well. Most important for the working definitions of transference and countertransference, I am suggesting, that psychoanalysts and patients were both seeking adaptation to one another by the means of participant observation. Hence, the new study of the psychoanalyst's personality in general, and of countertransference, counterresistance, and counteranxiety in particular, the unexpected by-product of the adaptive or consensual point of view, was nonetheless inevitable.

The crucial point about this study of the experiential field of therapy as a whole, in the 1970s, is countertransference as the focus of research from which flow the many sorts of issues which continue to dominate contemporary psychoanalytic discussion: first, bringing together those perspectives from the 1930s into a unified movement of thought within a coordinated structure of inquiry; second, distinguishing the various metapsychologies from the empirical and systematic psychology of psychoanalysis; third defining the psychoanalytic experience as undergone within a field of therapy created by any two particular coparticipants; fourth, discovering their complex meeting in transference and countertransference within that field; and fifth, introducing the psychology of the self as both subject and object, especially, in my view, the psychic center of the psychoanalytic self, for the analysis of anxiety and counteranxiety. Only the adaptive view of psychoanalyst and patient interpersonally relating from both sides of the experiential field of therapy could have brought the study of countertransference so readily to the fore, from which these major current issues derived in due course.

The critical transformation of psychoanalysis from 1910 to the 1980s, I am proposing, traces back through the pioneering research, in the early 1920s, of the actual experience patients lived through in relation to their psychoanalysts. For the first time, psychoanalysts thereby gained new insight into the ongoing experience of transference *in vivo*. Yet as these psychoanalysts turned their attention to clinical reality and studied the actual experience of their patients, they laid the groundwork for the psychoanalytic study of resistance. Then, as they turned their attention to the personal psychology of the psychoanalyst against whom the resistance was offered under the adaptive or consensual point of view, from the 1940s onward, they laid the groundwork for the study of countertransference arising in the experiential field of therapy. But, as they focused attention on the procedural intricacies of direct inquiry into transference and countertransference interlocking at their origins, from the 1960s onward, they encountered the pressures of unpsychoanalyzable anxiety and counteranxiety.

It is mainly clinical anxiety and counteranxiety, I propose, that led to the study of the psychic center of the psychoanalytic self. This psychoanalytic self was not limited to the self-object psychology singularly designed for the traditional interpretation of transference, but rather included the self-subject as its psychic center of dynamic origin—generating, moving, and directing itself quite regularly to arise during the psychoanalysis of either resistance to the study of transference, or counterresistance to the study of countertransference, in the experiential field of therapy.

I would like to conclude with a sketch of these major developments across fifty years, beginning with the experience and exploration of resistance in the 1920s and culminating in the psychic center of the psychoanalytic self in the 1970s. This dialectic moved from focus on the patient and the study of resistance, to a focus on the psychoanalyst being resisted and the study of countertransference and counterresistance, and, finally, to focus on the patient in anxiety, and the psychoanalyst in counteranxiety, for the study of the psychic center of the psychoanalytic self as the inner point from which the transference, resistance, anxiety, and the countertransference, counterresistance, and counteranxiety ultimately took their active origin. This is where some practicing psychoanalysts find themselves today, working with the psychic sources of the self that intitiate, generate, or move themselves into the experiential field of therapy of their own accord. It seems as though they sought an answer to such questions as : Whose transference or countertransference is it? Or whose resistance or counterresistance, anxiety or counteranxiety? Who makes it move? Who responds with it? Who repeats it? Who changes with it? Who, in short, makes it conscious?

What is this psychic center of the psychoanalytic self but the sense of psychic reality, the awareness of self-moving experience, of coming into being, the direct perception of "something there" within, deeper and more profound than anything identifiable by the special and particular bodily senses by which external realities are ordinarily revealed. It is a sense of active striving toward self-fulfillment, latent and manifest throughout the full range of one's capacities and curiosities. William James (1890) once termed it "the self of selves." It means that psychoanalysts and patients, in their unique ways, each face the deeply private sources of their respective distortions of transference and countertransference on their own, no matter who first makes the observation with the other in the experiential field of therapy. It means that no one transforms one's respective distortions of transference and countertransference in the final analysis but oneself.

REFERENCES

Ferenczi, S. and Rank, O. (1923). *The Development of Psychoanalysis,* New York: Dover Publications, 1956.

Freud, A. (1936). *The Ego and the Mechanisms of Defense.* New York: International Universities Press, 1946.

Hartmann, H. (1939). *Ego Psychology and the Problem of Adaptation.* New York: International Universities Press, 1958.

James, W. (1890). *Principles of Psychology.* 2 volumes. New York: Dover Publications, 1950.

Reich, W. (1933). *Character Analysis.* New York: Orgone Institute Press, 1945.

Sullivan, H. (1940). *Conceptions of Modern Psychiatry.* Washington, D.C.: W. A. White Psychiatric Foundation, 1947.

1. The Future Prospects of Psychoanalytic Therapy

Sigmund Freud

Since the objects for which we are assembled here today are mainly practical, I shall choose a practical theme for my introductory address and appeal to your interest in medical, not in scientific, matters. I can imagine what your opinion about the success of our therapy probably is, and I assume that most of you have already passed through the two stages that all beginners go through, that of enthusiasm at the unexpected increase in our therapeutic achievements, and that of depression at the magnitude of the difficulties which stand in the way of our efforts. Whichever of these stages in development, however, each of you may happen to be going through at the moment, my intention today is to show you that we have by no means come to the end of our resources for combating the neuroses, and that we may expect a substantial improvement in our therapeutic prospects before very long.

This improvement will come, I think, from three sources:

1. From internal progress.
2. From increased prestige.
3. From the general effect of our work.

1. Under 'internal progress' I understand advances *(a)* in our analytic knowledge, *(b)* in our technique.

(a) Advances in our knowledge. We are, of course, still a long way from knowing all that is required for an understanding of the unconscious minds of our patients. Now it is clear that every advance in our knowledge means an increase in the power of our therapy. As long as we understood nothing, we accomplished nothing; the more we understand the more we shall achieve. At its beginning psychoanalytic treatment was inexorable and exhaustive.

An address delivered before the Second International Psycho-analytical Congress at Nuremberg in 1910. First published in *Zentralblatt*, Bd. I., 1910; reprinted in *Sammlung*, Dritte Folge. [Translated by Joan Rivière.]

The patient had to say everything himself, and the physician's part consisted of urging him on incessantly. Today things have a more friendly air. The treatment is made up of two parts, out of what the physician infers and tells the patient, and out of the patient's work of assimilation, of 'working through', what he hears. The mechanism of our curative method is indeed quite easy to understand; we give the patient the conscious idea of what he may expect to find *(bewusste Erwartungsvorstellung)*, and the similarity of this with the repressed unconscious one leads him to come upon the latter himself. This is the intellectual help that makes it easier for him to overcome the resistances between conscious and unconscious. Incidentally, I may remark that it is not the only mechanism made use of by the analytic method; you all know that far more powerful one that lies in the use of the 'transference'. I intend soon to undertake an exposition of these various factors, which are so important for an understanding of the cure, in a practice of psycho-analysis. And, further, in speaking to you I need not rebut the objection that the way in which we practise the method today obscures its testimony to the correctness of our hypotheses; you will not forget that this evidence is to be found elsewhere, and that a therapeutic procedure cannot be performed in the same way as a theoretical investigation.

Now let me refer briefly to various fields in which we both have much to learn that is new and do actually make new discoveries daily. First of all, there is the matter of symbolism in dreams and in the unconscious—a fiercely contested subject, as you know! It is no small credit to our colleague, W. Stekel, that, indifferent to all the objections of our opponents, he has undertaken a study of dream symbols. In this there is indeed much still to learn; my *Traumdeutung*, which was written in 1899, awaits important amplification from researches into symbolism.

I will say a few words about one of the symbols that has lately been recognized. Not long ago it came to my knowledge that a psychologist whose views are not too distant from ours had remarked to one of us that we undoubtedly overestimated the hidden sexual significance of dreams; his most frequent dream was of going upstairs, and there could certainly be nothing sexual about that. Our attention being thus drawn to it, we began to study the incidence of stairs, steps, and ladders in dreams, and soon could establish the fact that stairs and such things are certainly a symbol of coitus. The underlying element which the two things have in common is not difficult to discover; one climbs an acclivity in rhythmic movements, accompanied by increasing breathlessness, and in a few rapid leaps can be down below again. Thus the rhythm of coitus reappears in climbing steps. We will not forget to adduce the usages of speech in this connection. It shows us that 'mounting' is used quite simply as a symbol for the sexual act. In German one says 'the man is a *Steiger, nachsteigen'*. In French the steps of a stair are called *'marches';* *'un vieux marcheur', ein alter Steiger* both mean an old profligate. The dream material from which these newly recognized symbols are derived will in due time be put before you by the committee we are about to form for collecting and studying symbols. An account of another interesting symbol, of the idea of 'rescue' and its changes in significance, will appear in the second volume of our *Jahrbuch*. However, I must break off here or I shall not reach my other points.

Every one of you will know from his own experience the total change in one's attitude to a new case when once one has thoroughly mastered the structure of some typical cases of illness. Assuming now that we had narrowly defined the regular elements in the composition of the various forms of neurosis, just as we have already succeeded in doing for hysterical symptom-formation, how much more assured we should be in our prognoses! Just as an obstetrician knows by examining the placenta whether it has been completely expelled or whether noxious fragments of it still remain, so we should be able, independently of the success of the cure and the patient's present condition, to say whether the work has been completely carried to an end or whether we have to expect relapses and fresh onsets of illness.

(b) I will hasten on to the innovations in the field of technique, where indeed nearly everything still awaits definitive settlement, and much is only now beginning to come clear. There are now two aims in psycho-analytic technique: to save the physician effort and to open up for the patient the freest access to his unconscious. You know that our technique has been transformed in important respects. At the time of the cathartic treatment we set ourselves the aim of elucidating the symptoms, then we turned away from the symptoms to discovering the 'complexes', to use Jung's indispensable word; now, however, our work is aimed directly at finding out and overcoming the 'resistances', and we can with justification rely on the complexes' coming to light as soon as the resistances have been recognized and removed. Some of you have since shown a desire to formulate and classify these resistances. Now I beg you to examine your material and see whether you can confirm the following statement: In male patients the most important resistances to the treatment seem to be derived from the father complex and to express themselves in fear of the father, and in defiance and incredulity towards him.

Other innovations in technique relate to the physician himself. We have begun to consider the 'counter-transference', which arises in the physician as a result of the patient's influence on his unconscious feelings, and have nearly come to the point of requiring the physician to recognize and overcome this counter-transference in himself. Now that a larger number of people have come to practise psycho-analysis and mutually exchange their experiences, we have noticed that every analyst's achievement is limited by what his own complexes and resistances permit, and consequently we require that he should begin his practice with a self-analysis and should extend and deepen this constantly while making his observations on his patients. Anyone who cannot succeed in this self-analysis may without more ado regard himself as unable to treat neurotics by analysis.

We are also now coming to the opinion that the analytic technique must undergo certain modifications according to the nature of the disease and the dominating instinctual trends in the patient. Our therapy was, in fact, first designed for conversion hysteria; in anxiety hysteria (phobias) we must alter our procedure to some extent. The fact is that these patients cannot bring out the material necessary for resolving the phobia so long as they feel protected by retaining their phobic condition. One cannot, of course, induce them to give up their protective measures and work under the influence of anxiety from the beginning of the treatment. One must therefore help them by interpreting their unconscious to them until they can make up their minds to do without the protection of their phobia and expose themselves to a new comparatively moderate degree of anxiety. Only when they have done so does the material necessary for achieving solution of the phobia become accessible. Other modifications of technique that seem to me not yet ready for discussion will be required in the treatment of obsessional neurosis. In this connection very important questions arise that are not yet elucidated: how far the instincts involved in the conflict in the patient are to be allowed some gratification during the treatment, and what difference it them makes whether these impulses are active (sadistic) or passive (masochistic) in nature.

I hope you have received the impression that, when all that can at present be merely glimpsed is known and when we have established all the improvements in technique to which deeper experience with our patients must lead us, then our medical practice will reach a degree of precision and certainty of success which is not to be had in all medical specialities.

2. I said that we had much to expect from the increase in prestige that must accrue to us as time goes on. I need hardly say much to you about the

importance of authority. Only very few civilized persons are capable of existing without reliance on others or are even capable of coming to an independent opinion. You cannot exaggerate the intensity of man's inner irresolution and craving for authority. The extraordinary increase in the neuroses since the power of religion has waned may give you some indication of it. The impoverishment of the ego due to the tremendous effort in repression demanded of every individual by culture may be one of the principal causes of this state of things.

Hitherto the weight of authority with its enormous 'suggestive' force has been against us. All our therapeutic successes have been achieved in spite of this suggestion; it is surprising that any success was to be had at all in the circumstances. I will not let myself go to the extent of describing to you the agreeable things that happened during the time when I alone represented psycho-analysis. I know that when I assured my patients that I knew how to relieve them permanently of their sufferings they looked round my modest abode, thought of my want of fame and honours, and regarded me like a man who possesses an infallible system in a gambling place, of whom people say that if he could do what he professed he would look very different. Nor was it really at all pleasant to operate on people's minds while colleagues whose duty it was to assist took a pleasure in spitting into the field of operation, and while at the first signs of blood or restlessness in him the patient's relatives threatened one. An operation may surely cause reactions; in surgery we became used to that long ago. Nobody believed in me, in fact, just as even today very few believe in us; under such conditions many an attempt was bound to fail. To estimate the increase in our therapeutic capacities that will ensue when general recognition is accorded us, you should think of the different positions of gynecologists in Turkey and in the West. All that a woman's physician may do there is to feel the pulse of an arm which is stretched out to him through a hole in the wall. And his curative results are in proportion to the inaccessibility of their object; our opponents in the West wish to restrict our access over our patients' minds to something very similar. But now that the force of public opinion drives sick women to the gynecologist, he has become their helper and saviour. Now do not say that, even if the weight of public opinion comes to our aid and so much increases our successes, that will in no way prove the validity of our hypotheses. Suggestion is supposed to be able to do anything, and our successes would then be results of suggestion and not of psycho-analysis. Public opinion is at present suggesting hydropathic cures, diet cures, and electricity cures for nervous persons, but that does not enable these measures to remove the neuroses. It will be seen whether psycho-analytic treatment can accomplish more than they.

But now, to be sure, I must damp the ardour of your expectations. The community will not hasten to grant authority to us. It is bound to offer resistance to us, for we adopt a critical attitude towards it; we accuse it of playing a great part itself in causing the neuroses. Just as we make any single person our enemy by discovering what is repressed in him, so the community cannot respond with sympathy to a relentless exposure of its injurious effects and deficiencies; because we destroy illusions we are accused of endangering ideals. It seems, therefore, that the state of things from which I expect such great advantages for our therapeutic results will never arrive. And yet the situation is not so hopeless as one might think at the present time. Powerful though the feelings and the self-interest of men may be, yet intellect is a power too. It has not, perhaps, the power that makes itself felt immediately, but one that is all the more certain in the end. The most mordant verities are heard at last, after the interests they injure and the emotions they rouse have exhausted their frenzy. It has always been so, and the unwelcome truths which we psychoanalysts have to tell the world will undergo the same fate. Only it will not come very quickly; we must be able to wait.

3. Finally, I have to explain to you what I mean by the 'general effect' of our work, and how I come to set my hopes on it. This consists in a very remarkable therapeutic constellation that could perhaps not be repeated anywhere else and that will appear strange to you too at first, until you recognize in it something you have long been familiar with. You know, of course, that the psychoneuroses are substitutive gratifications of instincts the existence of which one is forced to deny to oneself and others. Their capacity to exist depends on this distortion and disguise. When the riddle they hold is solved and the solution accepted by the sufferers these diseases will no longer be able to exist. There is hardly anything quite like it in medicine; in fairy tales you hear of evil spirits whose power is broken when you can tell them their name, which they have kept secret.

Now in place of a single sick person put the whole community of persons liable to neuroses, persons ill and persons well; in place of the acceptance of the solution in the first put a general recognition in the second; and a little reflection will show you that this substitution cannot alter the result at all. The success the therapy has with individuals must appear in the many too. Diseased people cannot let their various neuroses become known—their apprehensive over-anxiousness, which is to conceal their hatred, their agoraphobia, which betrays disappointed ambition, their obsessive actions, which represent self-reproaches for evil intentions and precautions against them—when all their relatives and every stranger from whom they wish to conceal their thoughts and feelings know the general meaning of these symptoms, and when they know themselves that the manifestations of their disease produce nothing that others cannot instantly understand. The effect, however, will not be merely that they will conceal their symptoms—a design, by the way, that would be impossible to execute; for this concealment will destroy the purpose of the illness. Disclosure of the secret will have attacked, at its most sensitive point, the 'etiological equation' from which the neuroses descend, will have made the 'advantage through illness' illusory, and consequently in the end nothing can come of the changed situation brought about by the indiscretions of physicians but an end of producing these illnesses.

If this hope seems utopian to you, you may remember that certain neurotic phenomena have already been dispelled by this means, although only in quite isolated instances. Think how common hallucinations of the Virgin Mary were in peasant girls in former times. So long as such a phenomenon brought a flock of believers and resulted perhaps in a chapel being built on the sacred spot, the visionary state of these maidens was inaccessible to influence. Today even the priesthood has changed its attitude to such things; it allows police and medical men to visit the seer, and since then the Virgin appears very seldom. Or allow me to study the same processes that I have been describing as taking place in the future in an analogous situation that is on a smaller scale and consequently more easily appreciated. Suppose that a number of ladies and gentlemen in good society planned a picnic at an inn in the forest one day. The ladies made up their minds that if one of them wanted to relieve a natural need she would say aloud that she was going to pick flowers; but a wicked fellow heard of this secret and printed on the programme, which was sent round to the whole party—'If the ladies wish to retire they are requested to say that they are going to pick flowers'. Of course after this no lady would think of availing herself of this flowery pretext, and other freshly devised formulas of the same kind would be seriously compromised by it. What would be the result? The ladies would own up to their natural needs without shame and none of the men would take exception to it. Let us return to the serious aspect of our problem. A number of people who find life's conflicts too difficult to solve have taken flight into neurosis and in this way won an unmistakable, although in the end too costly, advantage through illness. What would these people have to do if their flight into illness were barred by the indiscreet revelations of psycho-analysis? They would have to be honest, own up to the instincts that are at work in them, face the conflict, fight for what they want or go without, and the tolerance from the community that is bound to ensue as a result of psycho-analytical knowledge would help them in their task.

Let us remember, however, that it is not for us to advance upon life as fanatical hygienists or therapeutists. We must admit that this ideal prevention of all neurotic illness would not be advantageous to every individual. A good number of those who now take flight into illness would not support the conflict under the conditions we have assumed, but would rapidly succumb or would commit some outrage which would be worse than if they themselves fell ill of a neurosis. The neuroses have in fact their biological function as defensive measures and their social justification; the 'advantage through illness' that they provide is not always a purely subjective one. Is there one of you who has not at some time caught a glimpse behind the scenes in the causation of a neurosis and had to allow that it was the least of the evils possible in the circumstances? And should one really require such sacrifices in order to exterminate the neuroses, while the world is all the same full of other inextinguishable miseries?

Should we therefore abandon our efforts to explain the hidden meaning of neurotic manifestations, regarding it as dangerous to the individual and harmful to the interests of society; should we give up drawing the practical conclusion from a piece of scientific insight? No; I think that nevertheless our duty lies in the other direction. The 'advantage through illness' provided by the neuroses is indeed on the whole and in the end detrimental to the individual as well as to society. The distress that our work of revelation may cause will affect but a few. The change to a more honest and honourable attitude in the world in general will not be bought too dearly by these sacrifices. But above all, all the energies that are today consumed in the production of neurotic symptoms, to serve the purposes of a world of phantasy out of touch with reality, will, even if they cannot at once be put to uses in life, help to strengthen the outcry for those changes in our civilization from which alone we can hope for better things for our descendants.

I will let you go, therefore, with the assurance that you do your duty in more than one sense by treating your patients psycho-analytically. You are not merely working in the service of science, by using the only and irreplaceable opportunity for discovering the secrets of the neuroses; you are not only giving your patients the most efficacious remedy for their sufferings available at the present time; but you are contributing your share to that enlightenment of the many from which we expect to gain the authority of the community in general and thus to achieve the most far-reaching prophylaxis against neurotic disorders.

2. The Development of Psychoanalysis: A Historical Critical Retrospect

Sandor Ferenczi and Otto Rank

Now that we have in a brief outline described what we mean by the psycho-analytic method, we are able to look back and to recognize that a series of mistakes in the technique correspond to remaining stationary at certain stages of development in analytic perception. It is only natural that such inhibitions in development not only were possible and occurred in all the phases of the analytic progress, but also that they still exist, or repeat themselves to-day.

We wish not only to show in individual points how this is to be interpreted, and thus to throw a side light on the historic development of psycho-analysis, but also principally to help to avoid such faulty developments in the future. What now follows is actually the presentation of a series of incorrect methods, that is of such as no longer correspond to an up-to-date conception of the psycho-analytic technique.

In view of the general clinical, phenomenalistic point of view in medicine, it is not to be wondered at that in the medical practice of psycho-analysis a kind of descriptive analysis, actually a contradiction in terms, was reached. Such an analysis, as a rule, limited itself to listening, or to an expansive description of the symptoms, or the perverse wishes of the patient, without any essential therapeutic effect resulting from this mere "talking out," because the dynamic factor of experience was neglected.

A similarly misunderstood kind of analysis consisted in the collecting of associations, as if these were in themselves the essential thing, and not merely rising bubbles of consciousness showing us where, or perhaps at what depth under the surface, the active affects were concealed, and particularly what motives drove the patient in a given case to use the ways of association that he seemed to prefer.

Less harmless was the fanaticism for interpreting, which resulted in over-looking, in a cut and dried translation according to the dictionary, the fact that the technique of interpretation is but one of the means of help in understanding the unconscious mental condition of the patient, and not the aim, or certainly not the chief aim, of the analysis. This translation of the associations of the patient is of the same value as in the realm of language from which the comparison is taken. The unavoidable preliminary work to the understanding of the whole text, is the looking up of unknown words, but it is not an aim in itself. This "translation" must be followed by the "interpretation," so as to give a comprehensible connection. Viewed from this angle, the frequent disputes over the correctness of an interpretation, i.e., translation, disappear. Questions from analysts whether this or that "interpretation"—in our sense of the word *translation* is meant—be correct or the query what this or that, perhaps in a dream, "means," show an incomplete understanding of the whole analytic situation and an overestimation, such as we have just pointed out, of isolated details. These can mean sometimes one thing, sometimes another. The same symbol in the same patient can have, or take on, a different meaning under the pressure or the loosening of a resistance. In an analysis fine details, apparent incidentals such as voice, gesture, expression, are so important. So much depends upon the successful interpolation, upon the comprehensible relationship, upon the meaning that the expressions of the patient acquire by his own unconscious commentary with the help of our interpretation. Thus the technique of translation forgot in the interest of the "correct" translation of details, that the whole, that is the analytic situation of the patient as such, also has a meaning, and indeed the chief meaning. Only from an understanding of the whole can the correct interpretation of the translated parts follow; this is then free and certain, whereas the fanaticism of translation leads to mere routine work and is therapeutically fruitless.

Another faulty method was holding fast to the already overcome phase of the analysis of the symptoms. It is well known that there was an early period of psycho-analysis in which, by proceeding from the separate symptoms, and by suggestive pressure those memories were called forth, which, working in the unconscious, produced the symptoms. On account of the later development in the psychoanalytic technique this method has long been given up. It is, indeed, not even a question of getting the symptoms to disappear, which every suggestive method can easily accomplish, but rather preventing their return, which means making the ego of the patient more capable of resistance. For this purpose an analysis of the whole personality is necessary. The analyst should, according to Freud's direction, always proceed from what is at the time the mental surface and must not pursue the associative connections with the symptoms. Evidently it was too tempting and easy to obtain information about the neurotic, or perverse behavior of the patient by directly asking him and thus let him directly remember the history of the development of his abnormality.[1] Only a series of converging experiences can place us in the position of understanding the many "interpretations" which one symptom can have in a particular case. Direct questions merely succeeded in turning the attention of the patient towards this factor at the wrong time, thus establishing his resistances at this point, for the patient was able to misuse this, in itself, not entirely unjustified direction of his attention. Thus it could happen that the "analysis" was unduly protracted, but the original infantile story, without the reconstruction of which no treatment can be called a real analysis, was never reached.

We must deal, somewhat more in detail, with one phase of analysis that can be called the "analysis of complexes" and that preserves an important stage of the amalgation with academic psychology. The word *complex* was first used by Jung as the simplification of a complicated psychological fact, to designate certain tendencies, characteristic for the person in question, or a related group of affect-colored conceptions. This interpretation of the word, which was constantly becoming more comprehensive, and had thus come to have almost no meaning, was then limited by Freud who described the unconscious repressed parts of those group conceptions with the name *complex*. As the more subtle, labile, fluctuating processes of cathexis in the psyche became accessible to research, the acceptance of such inflexible, separate mental components became more and more superfluous. They were too coherent, they could only be excited and displaced in toto, they were much too "complex," as more exact analysis showed, to be treated as elements which could not be further reduced. Indeed in the newer works of Freud, this conception merely figures as the survival of a period of psychoanalysis, for which we have actually no more use, especially since the creation of our meta-psychology.

The most consistent thing would have been to do away entirely with this now useless rudiment of an earlier time, and to give up the terminology, which had become dear to most analysts, in favor of a better understanding. Instead of doing this, the whole of mental life was often regarded as a mosaic of such complexes, and the analysis then carried out with the object of "analyzing out" one complex after the other, or the attempt was made of treating the whole personality as a sum total of father-mother-, brother-, and sister-complexes. It was naturally easy to collect material for these, since every one has, of course, all the complexes, that is, every one must, in the course of his development, somehow get on with the persons and objects that surround him. The connected recounting of complexes, or the attributes of these, may have its place in descriptive psychology, but not in the practical analysis of the neurotic, nor does it even belong in the psycho-analytic study of literary or ethno-psychological products, where it must undoubtedly lead to a monotony in no way justified by the many-sidedness of the material, and scarcely tempered by giving preference, first to one and then to the other complex.

Although such a flattening out may have to be put up with at times, as unavoidable in a scientific presentation, one should not therefore transfer such a cramped interest into the technique. The analysis of complexes easily misleads the patient into being pleasing to his analyst, by bringing him "complex material" as long as he likes, without giving up any of his really unconscious secrets. Thus there came to be histories of illnesses in which the patients recounted memories, evidently fabricating them, in a way that never happens in unprejudiced analyses, and can only be looked upon as the product of such a "breeding of complexes." Such results should naturally not be used subjectively either to show the correctness of one's own method of interpreting, or as theoretic conclusions, nor yet as leading to any sort of evidence.[2]

It happened particularly frequently that the associations of the patient were directed to the sexual factor at the wrong time, or that they remained stuck at this point if—as so often happens—he came to the analysis with the expectation that he must constantly talk exclusively of his actual or infantile sexual life. Aside from the fact that this is not so exclusively the case as our opponents think, permitting such an indulgence in the sexual often gives the patient the opportunity to paralyze the therapeutic effect of the privation he must undergo.

An understanding of the many-sided and important mental contents that underlie the collective name *castration complex* was also not exactly furthered by bringing the theory of the complexes into the dynamics of the analysis. On the contrary, we are of the opinion that the premature theoretic condensation of the facts under the conception of the complex interfered with the insight into deeper layers of mental life. We believe that the full appreciation of that which the analytic practitioner has accustomed himself to finish off with the label *castration complex* is still lacking, so that this attempt at an explanation should not lightly be regarded as the ultimate explanation of such varied mental phenomena and processes of the patient. We can, from the dynamic standpoint, which is the only justifiable one in practice, often recognize in the forms of expression of the castration complex, as they manifest themselves in the course of the analysis, only one of the kinds of resistance that the patient erects against his deeper libidinal wishes. In the early stages of some analyses the castration anxiety can often be uncovered as an expression of the dread, transferred onto the analyst, as a protection against further analysis.

As we have already intimated, technical difficulties arose also from the analyst's having too much knowledge. Thus the importance of the theory of sexual development constructed by Freud, misled some analysts to apply in a mistaken and over-dogmatic fashion in the therapy of the neuroses, certain systems of organization and autoeroticisms, which first gave us an understanding of normal sexual development. In thus searching for the constructive elements of the theory of sex, in some cases, the actual analytic task was neglected. These analyses might be compared to psychochemical "element analyses." Here again one could see that the theoretical importance did not always correspond to the value in the practical analysis. The technique need not methodically lay bare all the, as it were, prescribed historic phases of the development of the libido, still less should the uncovering of all theoretically established details and gradations be used as a principle of healing in the neuroses. It is also practically superfluous to demonstrate all the original elements of a highly complicated "connection," while missing the intellectual thread, which combines the few fundamental elements into new and varying phenomena. The same thing holds for the erotogenic zones as for the complexes, for example the urethral or the anal erotic, and for the stages of organization the oral, anal-sadistic and other pregenital phases; there can be no human development without all of these, but one must not in the analysis attribute to them the importance, for the history of the illness, of which the resistance under the pressure of the analytic situation gives the illusion.

On closer observation a certain inner connection between "element analyses" and "complex analyses" could be recognized, insofar as the latter, in their attempts to plumb the psychic depths, struck upon the granite of the complexes and thus the work was spread out over the surface instead of going to the bottom. Such analyses then usually tried to make up for the lack of depth in the dynamics of the libido by an excursion into the theory of sex, and united rigid attributes of complexes with equally schematically treated principles of the theory of sex, whereas they missed just the play of forces that takes place between the two.

Such an attitude naturally led to a theoretic over-estimation of the factor of quantity, to ascribing everything to a stronger organ—eroticism, a point of view that resembled that of the pre-analytical school of neurologists—who blinded themselves to any insight into actual play of forces of the pathological causes by the catch words *inheritance, degeneration,* and *disposition.*

Since the theory of the instincts and also the sciences of biology and physiology have been called upon partly as a help in understanding mental phenomena, in particular since the so-called *pathoneurosen,* that is the neuroses on the organic level, the organ-neuroses, and even organic illnesses are treated psycho-analytically, disputes about border-line cases have taken place between psycho-analysis and physiology. The stereotyped translation of physiological processes into the language of psycho-analysis is incorrect. Insofar as one attempts to approach organic processes analytically the rules of psycho-analysis must be strictly adhered to here also. One must try to forget, so to speak, one's organic, medical and physiological knowledge and to bear in mind only the mental personality and its reactions.

It was also confusing when simple clinical facts were at once combined with speculations about becoming, being, and duration and such deliberations treated like established rules in practical analysis, whereas Freud himself constantly emphasizes the hypothetical character of his last synthetic works. Often enough such a wandering into speculation seems to have been a dodging of uncomfortable technical difficulties. We know how a desire to condense everything prematurely under a speculative principle can wreak vengeance from the point of view of technique (The Jungian theory).[3]

It was also a mistake, while neglecting the individual, in the explanation of the symptoms, to make cultural and phylogenetic analogies at once, no matter how fruitful the latter might be in themselves. On the other hand, the overestimate of the actual factors led to an anagogic prospective interpretation, which was useless so far as the pathologic fixations were concerned. The adherents of the "anagogic," as well as some of those of the "genetic" school, in their interest in the future and in the past, neglected the present condition of the patient. And yet almost all of the past, and everything that the unconscious attempts, insofar as it is not directly conscious or remembered (and this occurs extremely seldom), expresses itself in actual reactions in relation to the analyst or to the analysis, in other words in the transference to the analytic situation.

The requirements of the Breuer-Freud catharsis that the affects, displaced upon symptoms, should be led back directly to the pathologic memory traces, and at the same time brought to a discharge and bound again proved to be unrealizable, that is, it succeeds only in the case of incompletely repressed, mostly preconscious memory material as in the case of certain derivatives of the actual unconscious. This itself, the uncovering of which is the chief task of the analysis, since it was never "experienced" can never be "remembered," one must let it be produced on the ground of certain indications. The mere communication, something like "reconstruction," is in itself not suited to call forth affect reactions; such information glides off from the patients without any effect. They can only convince themselves of the reality of the unconscious when they have experienced—mostly indeed only after they have frequently experienced—something analogous to it in the actual analytic situation, that is, in the present. Our new insight into the topography of mental life and the functions of the separate depth levels gives us the explanation for this state of affairs. The unconscious repressed material has no approach to motility, nor to those motor innervations in the sum total of which the affect discharge consists; the past and the repressed must find their representative factors in the present and the conscious (preconscious) in order that they may be affectively experienced and develop further. In contrast to the stormy abreaction one could designate the unwinding bit by bit of the affects in analysis as a fractional catharsis.

We believe, moreover, in general that affects in order to work convincingly must first be revived, that is made actually present and that what has not affected us directly and actually must remain mentally ineffective.

The analyst must always take into account that almost every expression of his patient springs from several periods, but he must give his chief attention to the present reaction. Only from this point of view can he succeed in uncovering the roots of the actual reaction in the past, which means changing the attempts of the patient to repeat into remembering. In this process he need pay little attention to the future. One may quietly leave this care to the person himself who has been sufficiently enlightened about his past and present mental strivings. The historic, cultural and phylogenetic analogies also need, for the most part, not be discussed in the analysis. The patient need hardly ever, and the analyst extremely seldom, occupy himself with this early period.

At this place we must consider certain misunderstandings about the enlightenment of people who are being analyzed. There was a phase, in the development of psycho-analysis, in which the goal of the analytic treatment consisted in filling the gaps in the memory of the patient with knowledge. Later one recognized that the neurotic ignorance proceeded from the resistance, that is from not wishing to know, and that it was this resistance that had to be constantly uncovered and made harmless. If one proceeds thus the amnesic gaps in the chain of memories fill themselves in, for the most part automatically, for the other part with the help of sparse interpretations and explanations. The patient therefore learns nothing more and nothing other than what he needs, and in the quantity requisite to allay the predominating disturbances. It was a fatal mistake to believe that no one was completely analyzed who had not also been theoretically familiarized with all the separate details of his own abnormality. Naturally it is not easy to set a boundary line up to which the instruction of the patient should be carried. Interruption of the correct analysis by formal courses of instruction may satisfy both the analyst and the patient, but cannot effect any change in the libido-attitude of the sick person. A further result of such instruction was that, without noticing it, one pushed the patient into withdrawing himself from the analytical work by means of identifying himself with the analyst. The fact that the desire to learn and to teach creates an unfavorable mental attitude for the analysis is well known but should receive much more serious attention.[4]

At times one heard from analysts the complaint that this or that analysis failed on account of "too great resistances" or a too "violent transference." The possibility in principle of such extreme cases is admitted; we do find ourselves at times confronted with quantitative factors, which we must in no way practically underestimate, since they play an important part in the final outcome of the analysis, as well as in its causes. But the factor of quantity, so important in itself, can be used as a screen for incomplete insight into the play of forces that finally decide the kind of application and the distribution of those very quantities. Because Freud once uttered the sentence, "Everything which impedes the analytic work is resistance," one should not, every time the analysis comes to a standstill, simply say, "this is a resistance." This resulted, particularly in patients with an easily aroused sense of guilt, in creating an analytic atmosphere in which they, so to speak, were fearful of making the *faux pas* of having a resistance, and the analyst found himself in a helpless situation. One evidently forgot another utterance of Freud's, namely, that in the analysis we must be prepared to meet the same forces, which formerly caused the repression as "resistances," as soon as one sets to work to release these repressions.

Another analytical situation that one was also in the habit of labelling incorrectly as "resistance" is the negative transference, which, from its very nature, cannot express itself otherwise than as "resistance" and the analysis of which is the most important task of the therapeutic activity. One need, of course, not be afraid of the negative reactions of the patient for they constitute, with iron necessity, a part of every analysis. Also the strong positive transference, particularly when it expresses itself in the beginning of the cure, is only a symptom of resistance that requires to be unmasked. In other cases, and particularly in the later stages of an analysis, it is an actual vehicle for bringing to light desires that have remained unconscious.

In this connection an important rule of psycho-analytic technique must be mentioned in regard to the personal relation between the analyst and the patient. The theoretic requirement of avoiding all personal contact outside of the analysis mostly led to an unnatural elimination of all human factors in the analysis, and thus again to a theorizing of the analytic experience.

From this point of view some practitioners all too readily failed to attribute that importance to a change in the person of the analyst, which results from the interpretation of the analysis as a mental process, the unity of which is determined by the person of the analyst. A change of analysts may be unavoidable for outer reasons in rare, exceptional cases, but we believe that technical difficulties—in homosexuals, for example—are not simply to be avoided by the choice of an analyst of the opposite sex. For in every correct analysis the analyst plays all possible roles for the unconscious of the patient; it only depends upon him always to recognize this at the proper time and under certain circumstances to make use of it consciously. Particularly important is the role of the two parental images—father and mother—in which the analyst actually constantly alternates (transference and resistance).

It is not an accident that technical mistakes occurred so frequently just in the expression of transference and resistance. One was easily inclined to let oneself be surprised at these elementary experiences in the analysis and strangely enough forgot just here the theory that had been incorrectly pushed into the foreground in the wrong place. This may also be due to subjective factors in the analyst. The narcissism of the analyst seems suited to create a particularly fruitful source of mistakes; among others the development of a kind of narcissistic counter-transference that provokes the person being analyzed into pushing into the foreground certain things that flatter the analyst and, on the other hand, into suppressing remarks and associations of an unpleasant nature in relation to him. Both are technically incorrect: the first because it can lead to an apparent improvement of the patient that is only intended to bribe the analyst and in this way to win a libidinal counter-interest from him; the second because it keeps the analyst from the necessity of noticing the delicate indications of criticism, which mostly only venture forth hesitatingly, and helping the patient to express them plainly or to abreact them. The anxiety and the sense of guilt of the patient can never be overcome without this self-criticism, requiring indeed a certain overcoming of himself on the part of the analyst; and yet these two emotional factors are the most essential for bringing about and maintaining the repression.

Another form under which technical inaccessibility hid itself was an incidental remark of Freud's to the effect that the narcissism of the patient could set limits to the degree to which he could be influenced by the analysis. If the analysis did not progress well, one consoled oneself with the thought that the patient was "too narcissistic." And since narcissism forms a connecting link between ego and libidinal strivings in all normal, as well as abnormal, mental processes, it is not difficult to find proofs in his behavior and thoughts for the narcissism of the patient. Particularly one should not handle the narcissistically determined "castration" or "masculinity" complexes as if they set the limits for analytic solution.[5]

When the analysis struck upon a resistance of the patient one often overlooked to what extent a pseudo-narcissistic tendency was brought into the question. The analyses of people who bring a certain theoretic knowledge with them into their analyses are particularly calculated to convince one that a great deal of what one was theoretically inclined to ascribe to narcissism, is actually secondary, pseudo-narcissistic and can by continued analysis be completely solved in the parental relationship. Naturally it is necessary in doing this to take up analytically the ego-development of the patient, as indeed it is in general necessary in the analysis of the resistances to consider the up-to-now much-too-neglected analysis of the ego, for which Freud has recently given valuable hints.

The newness of a technical point of view introduced by Ferenczi under the name of *activity* resulted in some analysts', in order to avoid technical difficulties, overwhelming the patient with commands and prohibitions, which one might characterize as a kind of "wild activity." This, however, must be looked upon as a reaction to the other extreme, to holding too fast to an over-rigid "passivity" in the matter of technique. The latter is certainly sufficiently justified by the theoretic attitude of the analyst who must at the same time be an investigator. In practice, however, this easily leads to sparing the patient the pain of necessary intervention, and to allowing him too much initiative in his associations as well as in the interpretation of his ideas.[6]

The moderate, but, when necessary, energetic activity in the analysis consists in the analyst's taking on, and, to a certain extent, really carrying out those roles that the unconscious of the patient and his tendency to flight prescribe. By doing this the tendency to the repetition of earlier traumatic experiences is given an impetus, naturally with the goal of finally overcoming this tendency by revealing its content. When this repetition takes place spontaneously it is superfluous to provoke it and the analyst can simply call forth the transformation of the resistance into remembering (or plausible reconstruction).

These last purely technical remarks lead back to the often-mentioned subject of the reciprocal effect of theory and practice.

NOTES

1. This rejection of the principle of the "analysis of symptoms" naturally does not preclude at times asking the patient the reason for the particular obtrusiveness of some symptomatic expression (for example the so-called temporary symptoms).
2. Stekel, who attributed the same neurotic symptom first to sexuality, then to crime, and finally to religion, may be taken as an extreme example of the subjectivity of such a passion for complexes. He may in this way, since he asserted everything, possibly have been right in some one of his single utterances.
3. It is well known that Jung went so far as to neglect the mnemonic importance of the infantile experiences brought to light in the analysis and of the personalities playing an important part in them in favor of an analysis on the "subjective-level." It shows a high degree of flight from reality to be willing to acknowledge the existence and force of only the idealized, or much too impersonal conception, of the obscure derivations of the original memories of objects and of people.
4. This holds also for persons who come to be analyzed only for the sake of learning (the so-called "didactic analyses"). In such cases it occurs only too easily that the resistances get displaced onto the intellectual field (science) and so remain unexplained.
5. We know that Adler, who evidently did not succeed in the analysis of the libido, remained stuck at this point.
6. Patients with a strong "masochistic" attitude are particularly fond of making use of an "over-passive technique' on the part of the analysts by themselves undertaking interpretations on the "subjective level" by doing which they satisfy their tendency to torment themselves, at the same time opposing the deeper interpretation with a skeptical resistance. In the same way, one can, moreover, get any "anagogic" interpretation of dreams that one likes by letting somewhat instructed patients interpret the dream elements, without getting behind the dynamics of the resistance overcompensated by morality.

3. The Transference Phenomenon in Psychoanalytic Therapy

Janet MacKenzie Rioch

The significance of the transference phenomenon impressed Freud so profoundly that he continued through the years to develop his ideas about it. His classical observations on the patient Dora formed the basis for his first formulations of this concept. He said, "What are transferences? They are the new editions or facsimiles of the tendencies and phantasies which are aroused and made conscious during the progress of the analysis; but they have this peculiarity, which is characteristic for their species, that they replace some earlier person by the person of the physician. To put it another way: a whole series of psychological experiences are revived, not as belonging to the past, but as applying to the person of the physician at the present moment." [1]

According to Freud's view, the process of psychoanalytic cure depends mainly upon the patient's ability to remember that which is forgotten and repressed, and thus to gain conviction that the analytical conclusions arrived at are correct. However, "the unconscious feelings strive to avoid the recognition which the cure demands"; [2] they seek instead, emotional discharge, regardless of the reality of the situation.

Freud believed that these unconscious feelings, which the patient strives to hide, are made up of that part of the libidinal impulse that has turned away from conciousness and reality, due to the frustration of a desired gratification. Because the attraction of reality has weakened, the libidinal energy is still maintained in a state of regression attached to the original infantile sexual objects, although the reasons for the recoil from reality have disappeared. [3]

Freud stated that in the analytic treatment, the analyst pursued this part of the libido to its hiding place, "aiming always at unearthing it, making it accessible to consciousness and at last serviceable to reality." [4] The patient tries to achieve an emotional discharge of this libidinal energy under the pressure of the compulsion to repeat experiences over and over again rather than to become conscious of their origin. He uses the method of transferring to the person of the physician past psychological experiences and reacting to this, at times, with all the power of hallucination.[5] The patient vehemently insists that his impression of the analyst is true for the immediate present, in this way avoiding the recognition of his own unconscious impulses.

Thus, Freud regarded the transference-manifestations as a major problem of the resistance. However, Freud said, "It must not be forgotten that they (the transference-manifestations) and they only, render the invaluable service of making the patient's buried and forgotten love-emotions actual and manifest."[6]

Freud regarded the transference-manifestations as having two general aspects—positive and negative. The negative, he at first regarded as having no value in psychoanalytic cure and only something to be "raised"[7] into consciousness to avoid interference with the progress of the analysis. He later[8] accorded it a place of importance in the therapeutic experience. The positive transference he considered to be ultimately sexual in origin, since Freud said, "To begin with, we knew none but sexual objects."[9] However, he divided the positive transference into two components—one, the repressed erotic component, which was used in the service of resistance; the other, the friendly and affectionate component, which, although originally sexual, was the "unobjectionable" aspect of the positive transference, and was that which "brings about the successful result in psychoanalysis, as in all other remedial methods."[10] Freud referred here to the element of suggestion in psychoanalytic therapy, about which I wish to speak in detail a little later on.

At the moment, I should like to state that, although not agreeing with the view of Freud that human behavior depends ultimately on the biological sexual drives, I believe that it would be a mistake to deny the value and importance of his formulations regarding transference phenomena. As I shall indicate shortly, I differ on certain points with Freud, but I do not differ with the forumlation that early impressions acquired during childhood are revived in the analytical situation, and are felt as immediate and real—that they form potentially the greatest obstacles to analysis if unnoticed, and, as Freud put it, the greatest ally of the analysis when understood. I agree that the main work of the analysis consists in analyzing the transference phenomena, although I differ somewhat as to how this results in cure. It is my conviction that the transference is a strictly interpersonal experience. Freud gave the impression that under the stress of the repetition-compulsion the patient was bound to repeat the identical pattern, regardless of the other person. I believe that the personality of the analyst tends to determine the character of the transference illusions, and especially to determine whether the attempt at analysis will result in cure. Horney[11] has shown that there is no valid reason for assuming that the tendency to repeat past experiences again and again has an instinctual basis. The particular character structure of the person requires that he integrate with any given situation according to the necessities of his character structure.

In discussing my own views regarding the transference and its use in therapy, it is necessary to begin at the beginning and to point out in a very schematic way how a person acquires his particular orientation to himself and the world—which one might call his character structure, and the implications of this in psychoanalytic therapy.

The infant is born without a frame of reference, as far as interpersonal experience goes. He is already acquainted with the feeling of bodily movement—with sucking and swallowing—but, among other things, he has had no knowledge of the existence of another *person* in relationship to himself. Although I do not wish to draw any particular conclusions from this analogy, I want to mention a simple phenomenon, described by Sherif,[12] connected with the problem of the frame of reference. If you have a completely dark room, with no possibility of any light being seen, and you then turn on a small pinpoint of light, which is kept stationary, this light will soon appear to be moving about. I am sure a good many of you have noticed this phenomenon when gazing at a singe star. The light seems to move, and it does so, apparently because there is no reference point in relation to which one can establish it at a fixed place in space. It just wanders around. If, however, one can at the same time see some other fixed object in the room, the light immediately becomes stationary. A reference point has been stablished, and there is no longer any uncertainty, any vague wandering of the spot of light. It is fixed. The pinpoint of light wandering in the dark room is symbolic of the original attitude of the person to himself, undetermined, unstructured, with no reference points.

The newborn infant probably perceives everything in a vague and uncertain way, including himself. Gradually, reference points are established; a connection begins to occur between hunger and breast, between a relief of bladder tension and a wet diaper, between playing with his genitals and a smack on the hand. The physical boundaries and potentialities of the self are explored. One can observe the baby investigating the extent, shape, and potentialities of his own body. He finds that he can scream and mother will come, or will not come, that he can hold his breath and everyone will get excited, that he can smile and coo and people will be enchanted, or just the opposite. The nature of the emotional reference points that he determines depends upon the environment. By that still unknown quality called "empathy," he discovers the reference points that help to determine his emotional attitude toward himself. If his mother does not want him, is disgusted with him, treats him with utter disregard, he comes to look upon himself as a thing-to-be-disregarded. With the profound human drive to make this rational, he gradually builds up a system of "reasons why." Underneath all these "reasons" is a basic sense of worthlessness, undetermined and undefined, related directly to the original reference frame. Another child discovers that the state of being regarded is dependent upon specific factors—all is well as long as one does not act spontaneously, as long as one is not a separate person, as long as one is good, as the state of being good is continuously defined by the parents. Under these conditions, and these only, this child can feel a sense of self-regard.

Other people are encountered with the original reference frame in mind. The child tends to carry over into later situations the patterns he first learned to know. The rigidity with which these original patterns are retained depends upon the nature of the child's experience. If this has been of a traumatic character so that spontaneity has been blocked and further emotional development has been inhibited, the original orientation will tend to persist. Discrepancies may be rationalized or repressed. Thus, the original impression of the hostile mother may be retained, while the contact with the new person is rationalized to fit the original reference frame. The new person encountered acts differently, but probably that is just a pose. She is just being nice because she does not know me. If she really knew me, she would act differently. Or, the original impressions are so out of line with the present actuality, that they remain unconscious, but make themselves apparent in inappropriate behavior or attitudes, which remain outside the awareness of the person concerned.

The incongruity of the behavior pattern, or of the attitude, may be a source of astonishment to the other person involved. Sullivan[13] provides insight into the process by the elucidation of what he calls the "parataxic distortions." He points out that in the development of the personality, certain integrative patterns are organized in response to the important persons in the child's past. There is a "self-in-relation-to-A" pattern, or "self-in-relation-to-B" pattern. These patterns of response become familiar and useful. The person learns to get along as a "self-in-relation-to-A" or -B, -C, and -D, depending on the number of important people to whom he had to adjust in the course of his early development. For example, a young girl, who had a severely dominating mother and a weak, kindly father, learned a pattern of adjustment to her mother which could be briefly described as submissive, mildly rebellious in a secret way, but mostly lacking in spontaneity. Toward the father she developed a loving, but contemptuous attitude. When she encountered other people, regardless of sex, she oriented herself to them partly as the real people they were, and partly as she had learned to respond to her mother and father in her past. She thus was feeling toward the real person involved as if she were dealing with two people at once. However, since it is very necessary for people to behave as rational persons she suppressed the knowledge that some of her reactions were inappropriate to the immediate situation, and wove an intricate mesh of rationalizations, which permitted her to believe that the person with whom she was dealing really was someone either to be feared and submitted to, as her mother, or to be contemptuous of, as her father. The more nearly the real person fitted the original picture of the mother and father, the easier it was for her to maintain that the original "self-in-relation-to-A or -B" was the real and valid expression of herself.

It happened, however, that this girl had had a kindly nurse who was not a weak person, although occupying an inferior position in the household. During the many hours when she was with this nurse, she was able to experience a great deal of unreserved warmth, and of freedom for self-realization. No demands for emotional conformity were made on her in this relationship. Her own capacities for love and spontaneous activity were able to flourish. Unfortunately, the contact with this nurse was all too brief. But there remained, despite the necessity for the rigid development of the patterns towards the mother and father, a deeply repressed, but still vital experience of self, which most closely approximated the fullest realization of her potentialities. This, which one might call her *real self,* although "snowed under" and handicapped by all the distortions incurred by her relationship to the parents, was finally able to emerge and become again active in analysis. In the course of this treatment, she learned how much her reactions to people were "transference" reactions, or as Sullivan would say, "parataxic distortions."

I have deliberately tried to schematize this illustration. For instance, when I speak of the early frame of reference and then just mention the parents, I do not overlook all the other possible reference frames. Also, one has to realize that one pattern connects with another—the whole making a tangled mass that only years of analysis can unscramble. I also have not taken the time to outline the compensatory drives that the neurotic person has to develop in order to handle his life situation. Each compensatory manœuver causes some change in his frame of reference, since the development of a defensive trait in his personality sets off a new set of relationships to those around him. The little child who grows more and more negativistic, because of injuries and frustrations, evokes more and more hostility in his environment. However, and this is important, the basic reactions of hostility on the part of the parents, which originally induced his negativism, are still there. Thus, the pattern does not change much in character—it just gets worse in the same direction. Those persons whose later life experience perpetuate the original frames of reference, are more severely injured. A young child, who has a hostile mother, may then have a hostile teacher. If, by good luck, he got a kind teacher and if his own attitude were not already badly warped, so that he did not induce hostility in this kind teacher, he would be introduced into a startlingly new and pleasant frame of reference, and his personaltity might not suffer too greatly, especially if a kindly aunt or uncle happened to be around. I am sure that if the details of the life histories of healthy people were studied, it would be found that they had had some very satisfactory experiences early enough to establish in them a feeling of validity as persons. The profoundly sick people have been so early injured, in such a rigid and limited frame of reference, that they are not able to make use of kindliness, decency, or regard when it does come their way. They meet the world as if it were potentially menacing. They have already developed defensive traits entirely appropriate to their original experience, and then carry them out in completely inappropriate situations, rationalizing the discrepancies, but never daring to believe that people are different from the ones they early learned to distrust and hate. By reason of bitter early experience, they learn never to let their guards down, never to permit intimacy, lest at that moment the death blow would be dealt to their already partly destroyed sense of self-regard. Despairing of real joy in living, they develop secondary neurotic goals which give a pseudo-satisfaction. The secondary gains at first glance might seem to be what the person was really striving for—revenge, power and exclusive possession. Actually, these are but the expressions of the deep injuries sustained by the person. They can not be fundamentally cured until those interpersonal relationships that caused the original injury are brought back to consciousness in the analytical situation. Step by step, each phase of the long period of emotional development is exposed, by no means chronologically;

the interconnecting, overlapping reference frames are made conscious; those points at which a distortion of reality, or a repression of part of the self *had* to occur, are uncovered. The reality gradually becomes "undistorted," the self refound in the personal relationship between the analyst and the patient. This personal relationship with the analyst is the situation in which the transference distortions can be analyzed.

In Freud's view, the transference was either positive or negative, and was related in a rather isolated way to a particular person in the past. In my view, the transference is the experiencing in the analytic situation the entire pattern of the original reference frames, which included at every moment the relationship of the patient to himself, to the important persons, and to others, as he experienced them at that time, in the light of his interrelationships with the important people.

The therapeutic aim in this process is not to uncover childhood memories that will then lend themselves to analytic interpretation. Here, I think, is an important difference to Freud's view. Fromm[14] has pointed this out in a recent lecture. Psychoanalytic cure is not the amassing of data, either from childhood, or from the study of the present situation. Nor does cure result from a repetition of the original injurious experience in the analytic relationship. What is curative in the process is that in tending to reconstruct with the analyst that atmosphere which obtained in childhood, the patient acutally achieves something new. He discovers that part of himself which had to be repressed at the time of the original experience. He can only do this in an interpersonal relationship with the analyst, which is suitable to such a rediscovery. To illustrate this point: if a patient had a hostile parent towards whom he was required to show deference, he has to repress certain of his own spontaneous feelings. In the analytic situation, he tends to carry over his original frame of reference and again tends to feel himself to be in a similar situation. If the analyst's personality also contains elements of a need for deference, that need will unconsciously be imparted to the patient, who will, therefore, still repress his spontaneity as he did before. True enough, he may act or try to act as if analyzed, since by definition, that is what the analyst is attempting to accomplish. But he will *never* have found his repressed self, because the analytic relationship contains for him elements actually identical with his original situation. Only if the analyst provides a genuinely *new* frame of reference—that is, if he is truly non-hostile, and truly not in need of deference—can this patient discover, and it is a real *discovery*, the repressed elements of his own personality. Thus, the transference phenomenon is used so that the patient will completely reexperience the original frames of reference, and himself within those frames, in a truly different relationship with the analyst, to the end that he can discover the invalidity of his conclusions about himself and others.

I do not mean by this to deny the correctness of Freud's view of transference also acting as a resistance. As a matter of fact, the tendency of the patient to reestablish the original reference frame is precisely because he is afraid to experience the other person in a direct and unreserved way. He has organized his whole system of getting along in the world, bad as that system might be, on the basis of the original distortions of his personality and his subsequent vicissitudes. His capacity for spontaneous feeling and acting has gone into hiding. Now it has to be sought. If some such phrase as the "capacity for self-realization" is substituted in place of Freud's concept of the repressed libidinal impulse, much the same conclusions can be reached about the way in which the transference-manifestations appear in the analysis as resistance. It is just in the safest situation, where the spontaneous feeling might come out of hiding, that the patient develops intense feelings, sometimes of a hallucinatory character, that relate to the most dreaded experiences of the past. It is at this point that the nature and the use by the patient of the transference distortions have to be understood and correctly interpreted, by the analyst. It is also here that the personality of the analyst modifies the transference reaction. A patient cannot feel close to a detached or hostile analyst and will therefore never display the full intensity of his transference illusions. The complexity of this process, whereby the transference can be used as the therapeutic instrument and, at the same time, as a resistance may be illustrated by the following example: a patient had developed intense feelings of attachment to a father surrogate in his everyday life. The transference feelings towards this man were of great value in elucidating his original problems with his real father. As the patient became more and more aware of his own personal validity, he found this masochistic attachment to be weakening. This occasioned acute feelings of anxiety, since his sense of independence was not yet fully established. At that point, he developed very disturbing feelings regarding the analyst, believing that she was untrustworthy and hostile, although prior to this, he had succeeded in establishing a realistically positive relationship to her. The feelings of untrustworthiness precisely reproduced an ancient pattern with his mother. He experienced them at this particular point in the analysis in order to retain and to justify his attachment to the father figure, the weakening of which attachment had threatened him so profoundly. The entire pattern was elucidated when it was seen that he was reexperiencing an ancient triangle, in which he was continuously driven to a submissive attachment to a dominating father, due to the utter untrustworthiness of his weak mother. If the transference character of this sudden feeling of untrustworthiness of the analyst had not been clarified, he would have turned again submissively to his father surrogate, which would have further postponed his development of independence. Nevertheless, the development of this transference to the analyst brought to light a new insight.

I wish to make one remark about Freud's view of the so-called narcissistic neuroses. Freud felt that personality disorders called schizophrenia or paranoia could not be analyzed because the patient was unable to develop a transference to the analyst. It is my view that the real difficulty in treating such disorders is that the relationship is essentially nothing but transference illusions. Such persons hallucinate the original frame of reference to the exclusion of reality. Nowhere in the realm of psychoanalysis can one find more complete proof of the effect of early experience on the person than in attemtping to treat these patients. Frieda Fromm Reichmann[15] has shown in her work with schizophrenics the necessity to realize the intensity of the transference reactions, which have become almost completely real to the patient. And yet, if one knows the correct interpretations, by actually feeling the patient's needs, one can over years of time do the identical thing that is accomplished more quickly and less dramatically with patients suffering a less severe disturbance of their interpersonal relationships.

Another point I wish to discuss for a moment is the following: Freud took the position that all subsequent experience in normal life is merely a repetition of the original one.[16] Thus love is experienced for someone today *in terms of* the love felt for someone in the past. I do not believe this to be exactly true. The child who has not had to repress certain aspects of his personality enters into a new situation dynamically, not just as a repetition of what he felt, say, with his mother, but as an active continuation of it. I believe that there are constitutional differences with respect to the total capacity for emotional experience, just as there are with respect to the total capacity for intellectual experiences. Given this constitutional substratum, the child engages in personal relationships not passively as a lump of clay waiting to be molded, but most dynamically, bringing into play all his emotional potentialities. He may possibly find someone later whose capacity for response is deeper than his mother's. If *he* is capable of the greater depth, he experiences an expansion of himself. Many later in life have met a "great" person and have felt a sense of newness in the relationship which is described to others as "wonderful" and which is regarded with a certain amount of awe. This is not a "transference" experience, but represents a dynamic extension of the self to a new horizon.

In considering the process of psychoanalytic cure, Freud very seriously discussed the relationship of analysis to suggestion therapy and hypnosis. He believed, as I previously mentioned, that part of the positive transference could be made use of in the analysis to bring about the successful result. He said, "In so far we readily admit that the results of psychoanalysis rest upon a basis of suggestion; only by suggestion we must be understood to mean that which we, with Ferenczi, find that it consists of influence on a person through and by means of the transference-manifestations of which he is capable. The eventual independence of the patient is our ultimate object when we use suggestion to bring him to carry out a mental operation that will necessarily result in a lasting improvement in his mental condition." [17] Freud elsewhere indicated very clearly that in hypnosis, the relationship of the patient to the hypnotist was not worked through, whereas in analysis the transference to the analyst was resolved by bringing it entirely into consciousness. He also said that the patient was protected from the unwitting suggestive influence of the analyst by the awakening of his own unconscious resistances. [18]

I should like to discuss hypnosis a little more in detail and to make a few remarks about its correlation with the transference phenomenon in psychoanalytic therapy.

According to White, [19] the subject under hypnosis is a person striving to act like a hypnotized person as that state is continuously defined by the hypnotist. He also said that the state of being hypnotized was an "altered state of consciousness." However, as Maslow [20] pointed out, it is not an abnormal state. In everyday life transient manifestations of all the phenomena that occur in hypnosis can be seen. Such examples are cited as the trancelike state a person experiences when completely occupied with an absorbing book. Among the phenomena of the hypnotic state are the amnesia for the trance; the development of certain anesthesias, such as insensitivity to pain; deafness to sounds other than the hypnotist's voice; greater ability to recall forgotten events; loss of capacity to initiate activities spontaneously; and a much greater suggestibility. This heightened suggestibility in the trance state is the most important phenomenon of hypnosis. Changes in behavior and feeling can be induced, such as painful or pleasant experiences, headaches, nausea, or feelings of well-being. Post-hypnotic behavior can be influenced by suggestion, this being one of the most important aspects of experimental hypnosis for the clarifying of psychopathological problems.

The hypnotic state is induced by a combination of methods which may include relaxation, visual concentration, and verbal suggestion. The methods vary with the personality of the experimenter and the subject.

Maslow has pointed out the interpersonal character of hypnosis, which accounts for some of the different conclusions by different experimenters. Roughly, the types of experimenters may be divided into three groups—the dominant type, the friendly or brotherly type, and the cold, detached, scientific type. According to the inner needs of the subject, he will be able to be hypnotized more readily by one type or the other. The brotherly hypnotist cannot, for instance, hypnotize a subject whose inner need is to be dominated.

Freud[21] believed that the relationship of the subject to the hypnotist was that of an emotional, erotic attachment. He commented on the "uncanny" character of hypnosis and said that "the hypnotist awakens in the subject a portion of his archaic inheritance which had also made him compliant to his parents." What is thus awakened is the concept of "the dreaded primal father," "towards whom only a passive-masochistic attitude is possible, towards whom one's will has to be surrendered."

Ferenczi[22] considered the hypnotic state to be one in which the patient transferred onto the hypnotist his early infantile erotic attachment to the parents with the same tendency to blind belief and to uncritical obedience as obtained then. He called attention to the paternal or frightening type of hypnosis and the maternal or gentle, stroking type. In both instances the situation tends to favour the "conscious and unconscious imaginary return to childhood."

The only point of disagreement with these views that I have is that one does not need to postulate an *erotic* attachment to the hypnotist or a "transference" of infantile sexual wishes. The sole necessity is a willingness to surrender oneself. The child whose parent wishes to control him, by one way or another, is forced to do this, in order to be loved, or at least to be taken care of. The patient transfers this willingness to surrender to the hypnotist.[23] He will also transfer it to the analyst or to the leader of a group. In any one of these situations the authoritative person, be he hypnotist, analyst, or leader, promises by reason of great power or knowledge the assurance of safety, cure, or happiness, as the case may be. The patient, or the isolated person, regresses emotionally to a state of helplessness and lack of initiative similar to the child who has been dominated.

If it is asked how in the first place the child is brought into a state of submissiveness, it may be discovered that the original situation of the child had certain aspects that already resembled a hypnotic situation. This depends upon the parents. If they are destructive or authoritarian they can achieve long-lasting results. The child is continuously subjected to being told *how* and *what* he is. Day in and day out, in the limited frame of reference of his home, he is subjected to the repetition, over and over again: "You are a naughty boy." "You are a bad girl." "You are just a nuisance." "You are always giving me trouble." "You are dumb," "you are stupid," "you are a little fool." "You always make mistakes." "You can never do anything right"; or, "That's right; I love you when you are a good boy." "That's the kind of boy I like." "Now you are a nice boy." "Smile sweetly." "Pay attention to mother." "Mother loves a good boy who does what she tells him." "Mother knows best, mother always knows best." "If you would listen to mother, you would get along all right. Just listen to her." "Don't pay attention to those naughty children. Just listen to your mother."

Over and over again, with exhortations to pay attention, to listen, to be good, the child is brought under the spell. "When you get older, never forget what I told you. Always remember what mother says, then you will never get into trouble." These are like post-hypnotic suggestions. "You will never come to a good end. You will always be in trouble." "If you are not good, you will always be unhappy." "If you don't do what I say, you will regret it." "If you do not live up to the right things (again, "right" as continuously defined by the mother) you will be sorry."

It has been called to my attention that the Papago Indians deliberately make use of a certain method of suggestion to influence the child favorably. When the child is falling asleep at night the grandfather sits by him and repeats over and over—"You will be a fast runner. You will be a good hunter."[24]

Hypnotic experiments, according to Hull,[25] indicate that children, on the whole, are more susceptible than adults. Certainly, for many reasons, including that of learning the uses and misuses of language, there is a marked rise of verbal suggestibility up to five years, with a sharp dropping off at around the eighth year. Ferenczi referred to the subsequent effects of threats or orders given in childhood as "having much in common with the post-hypnotic command-automatisms." He pointed out how the neurotic patient followed out, without being able to explain the motive, a command repressed long ago, just as in hypnosis a post-hypnotic suggestion was carried out for which amnesia had been produced.

It is not my intention in this paper to try to explain the altered state of consciousness that is seen in the hypnotized subject. I have had no personal experience with hypnosis. The reason I refer to hypnosis in discussing the transference is in order to further an understanding of the analytic relationship. The child may be regarded as being in a state of "chronic hypnosis," as I have described, with all sorts of post-hypnotic suggestions thrown in during this period. This entire pattern—this entire early frame of reference —may be "transferred" to the analyst. When this has happened the patient is in a highly suggestible state. Due to a number of intrinsic and extrinsic factors, the analyst is now in the position of a sort of "chronic hypnotist." First, by reason of his position of a doctor he has a certain prestige. Second, the patient *comes* to him, even if expressedly unwillingly; still if there were not something in the patient that was cooperative he would not come at all, or at least he would not stay. The office is relatively quiet, external stimuli relatively reduced. The frame of reference is limited. Many analysts maintain an anonymity about themselves. The attention is focussed on the interpersonal relationship. In this relatively undefined and unstructured field the patient is able to discover his "transference" feelings, since he has few reference points in the analytic situation to go by. This is greatly enhanced by having the patients assume a physical position in the room whereby he does not see the analyst. Thus the ordinary reference points of facial expression and gesture are lacking. True enough, he can look around or get up and walk about. But for considerable periods of time he lies down—itself a symbolically submissive position. He does what is called "free association." This is again giving up—willingly, to be sure—the conscious control of his thoughts. I want to stress the willingness and cooperativeness of all these acts. That is precisely the necessary condition for hypnosis. The lack of immediate reference points permits the eruption into consciousness of the old patterns of feeling. The original frame of reference becomes more and more clearly outlined and felt. The power the parent originally had to cast the spell is transferred to the analytic situation. Now it is the analyst who is in the position to do the same thing—placed there partly by the nature of the external situation, partly by the patient who comes to be freed from his suffering.

There is no such thing as an impersonal analyst, nor is the idea of the analyst's acting as a mirror anything more than the "neatest trick of the week." Whether intentionally or not, whether conscious of it or not, the analyst does express, day in and day out, subtle or overt evidences of his own personality in relationship to the patient.

The analyst may express explicitly his wish not to be coercive, but if he has an unconscious wish to control the patient, it is impossible for him correctly to analyze and to resolve the transference distortions. The patient is thus not able to become free from his original difficulties and for lack of something better, adopts the analyst as a new and less dangerous authority. Then the situation occurs in which it is not "my mother says" or "my father says," but now "my analyst says." The so-called chronic patients who need lifelong support may benefit by such a relationship. I am of the opinion, however, that frequently the long-continued unconscious attachment—by which I do *not* mean genuine affection or regard—is maintained because of a failure on the analyst's part to recognize and resolve the sense of being under a sort of hypnotic spell that originated in childhood.

To develop an adequate therapeutic interpersonal relationship, the analyst must be devoid of those personal traits that tend unconsciously to perpetuate the originally destructive or authoritative situation. In addition to this, he must be able, by reason of his training, to be aware of every evidence of the transference phenomena; and lastly, he must understand the significance of the hypnotic-like situation which analysis helps to reproduce. If, with the best of intentions, he unwittingly makes use of the enormous power with which he is endowed by the patient, he may certainly achieve something that looks like change. His suggestions, exhortations, and pronouncements, based on the patient's revelation of himself, may certainly make an impression. The analyst may say, "You must not do this just because I say so." That is in itself a sort of post-hypnotic command. The patient then strives to be "an analyzed person acting on his own account"—because he was told to do so. He is still not really acting on his own.

It is my firm conviction that analysis is terminable. A person can continue to grow and expand all his life. The process of analysis, however, as an interpersonal experience, has a definite end. That end is achieved when the patient has rediscovered his own self as an actively and independently functioning entity.

NOTES

1. Freud, Sigmund, *Collected Papers;* London, Hogarth, 1933 3: 139.
2. Reference note 1; 2: 321.

3. Reference note 1; 2: 316.
4. Ibid.
5. Reference note 1; 2: 321.
6. Reference note 1; p. 322.
7. Reference note 1; p. 319.
8. Freud, Sigmund, *Gesammelte Werke;* London, Imago, 1940 12: 223.
9. Reference note 1; p. 319.
10. Ibid.
11. Horney, Karen, *New Ways in Psychoanalysis;* New York, Norton, 1939 (313 pp.).
12. Sherif, Muzafer A. F., *The Psychology of Social Norms;* New York, Harper, 1936 (xii and 210 pp.).
13. Sullivan, Harry Stack, Conceptions of Modern Psychiatry. *Psychiatry* (1940) 3: 1–117.
14. Fromm, Erich, Lectures on *Ideas and Ideologies* presented at the New School for Social Research, New York City, 1943.
15. Fromm-Reichmann, Frieda, Transference Problems in Schizophrenics. *Psychoanalytic Quart.* (1939) 8: 412–426.
16. Reference note 1; p. 387.
17. Reference note 1; p. 319.
18. Reference note 8; p. 226.
19. White, Robert W., A Preface to the Theory of Hypnotism. *J. Abnormal and Social Psychol.* (1941) 36: 477–505.
20. Maslow, A. H., and Mittelmann, Bela, *Principles of Abnormal Psychology;* New York, Harper, 1941 (x and 638 pp.).
21. Freud, Sigmund, *Group Psychology and the Analysis of the Ego;* London, The International Psycho-Analytical Press, 1922 (134 pp.).
22. Ferenczi, Sandor, *Sex in Psycho-Analysis;* Boston, Badger, 1916 (338 pp.)—in particular, Introjection and Transference.
23. I am indebted to Erich Fromm for suggestions in the following discussion.
24. Underhill, Ruth, *Social Organization of the Papago Indians* [Columbia University Contributions to Anthropology: Vol. 30]; New York, Columbia University Press, 1939 (ix and 280 pp.).
25. Hull, Clark L., *Hypnosis and Suggestibility;* New York, Appleton-Century, 1933 (xii and 416 pp.).

4. The Surprised Psychoanalyst

Theodor Reik

If wishes were horses and beggars could ride, we psychologists would always be able to recognize the what, the how, and the why of what goes on in other people's minds. However, we learned long ago to renounce this wish and to be content with what we can discover by trial and error and hard work. The funny thing is that there are times when it seems as if our wishes were indeed horses and we poor beggars could ride. It is when we realize in a flash the secret thoughts of others and understand their hidden motives.

There are enviable people who boast that they have telepathic gifts and there are thoughtreaders who give performances of their mysterious ability. There are, however, situations in which every one of us seems to have these gifts of thoughtreading. Strange that we do not make a fuss about this and that nobody discusses the matter at greater length.

We do not report to the world that on our last walk with a friend he expressed exactly what we had thought ourselves just a minute before, or that we were able to say precisely what on this or that occasion our wife was thinking. If we feel any satisfaction about it at all, we do not boast about it, and it occurs to us rarely to connect it with extrasensory perception. It seems that we are content to register such occasions, and, were we asked about them, we would perhaps answer that such thoughtreading is a natural result of our intimate knowledge and understanding of the other's personality. Yes, we would even deny that the phenomenon deserves the name of *thoughtreading*. But why? Whether we know a person or not is not the essential question, it seems to me. If it were, our astonishment at the gifts of a professional thoughtreader would really concern the fact that he can read the thoughts of unknown men and women while we common mortals can do the same magical thing only with a few, very well-known persons. It would be only a difference in degree.

The existence of the phenomenon itself cannot be doubted. Why do we not make any attempt to find a psychological explanation for it and why do we take it for granted? We need not observe the shadow of an obelisk in order to recognize how high the sun stands in the sky. A post on the road tells us the same story. For practical purposes it might be even more important to read the thoughts of persons who are near to us rather than those of strangers upon whom we chance and whom we shall never see again. It might be more interesting to know the thoughts of your sweetheart, your friend, your sister, than those of an unknown lady or gentleman you have met at a cocktail party. If we could always read these thoughts, if we could predict them—it would have consequences that no fantasy, not even that of a thoughtreader, would be able to foresee.

These and similar reflections could preface an inquiry into the unconscious communication between the analyst and the analyzed person. Not only are thoughts read here, but unconscious thoughts at that; and not only thoughts, but emotions, impulses, and drives as well. Psychoanalysts make their observations and put their trust in God and Freud. They are confident that they will understand what takes place in the patient when they only apply what they have learned in books, in courses, and in seminars. As if you could learn experiences! There are courses in music appreciation and much can be learned about composers and compositions, but what is best in music cannot be "learned." Some analysts teach their students that they have to "identify" themselves with the patients, as if that were a process dependent upon one's will, like raising one's arm. *Identification* is an anemic and theoretical name for what really takes place. To that no name can be given.

An old American novel is prefaced by the sentence, "Whatever is incredible in this story is true."[1] Similarly an analyst reporting his experiences with puzzling communications could tell incredible cases that are true. They would, however, lose their incredibility were we to trace them back to what happens in the minds of the analyst and the patient. This is the difficult task we have never attempted. If we could approach the problem from both sides, if we could grasp the psychological material and the mechanisms in a pincer movement, we would understand so much better what happens, whereas now we only know that it happens.

Every analyst has had the experience of having the patient speak words that the analyst has thought a few brief seconds ago. Sometimes the patient introduces his remarks in this way: "You will perhaps think now that . . ." But he only projects what he himself thought. It has happened to every analyst that the patient who may have energetically rejected an analytic interpretation unconsciously, confirms it in the next sentence that he speaks. These are very simple cases that are not surprising and their psychological explanation is not difficult to reach.

It is also easy to understand that the analyst sometimes grasps something the patient did not know because he did not want to remember it. In these cases the analyst's memory is not handicapped by the repression that handicaps the patient. But even here the process is not purely intellectual, is not mechanical understanding like that of a mathematical problem. This, however, would be inconceivable were not the unconscious of the psychoanalyst cooperating with his intelligence.

A man remembered that after the death of his mother he lived with an aunt and his cousins. Among the many memories he could reproduce from those years was one that appeared puzzling to him. He was not, as far as he could remember, especially squeamish as a boy of ten. He remembered clearly, however, that he had refused to eat from a plate on which the food of other members of the family had been served or to touch a fork his cousins had used. He even remembered that more than once he had quarreled with his benevolent aunt, who reproached him for his behavior. He could not understand such fastidiousness now.

What happened in me, the analyst, that made me say: "I think that must be traced back to the precautions your mother took during the years of her disease"?

Here is nothing mysterious. In the beginning of his analysis the patient had given me a sketch of his life. His mother had died of tuberculosis after many years of suffering. Only a few memories of his mother, none of them significant, were preserved. It seemed as if all that mattered in his life happened after her death. The only thing that appeared important to him was that his mother never kissed him or his sister. When now, many weeks later, he told me about his fastidious behavior in the home of his aunt, the idea occurred to me spontaneously that the boy was simply following a caution he had acquired earlier in his life. The presentation of his earlier boyhood years and the memory he had told me before, that his mother never kissed him, were suddenly there. I suddenly understood why the boy had refused to eat from used plates and why his mother never kissed him. It was not that he was fastidious, but he had been warned by his mother herself, who knew that she had tuberculosis. He remembered, after my interpretation, that his mother had plates and knives and forks of her own that no other member of the family used. Most memories of the disease of his mother as well as of his own boyhood years had been repressed and had made some traits of his behavior incomprehensible to him.

One afternoon another patient complained of a heavy feeling on his chest. "It is," he said, "as if a stone were laid on me." Unconscious memory and emotional understanding of the patient enabled me to remind him that his family planned to erect a tombstone on his father's grave the next day. I realized this suddenly—but why? The patient was talking about other remote subjects in this session—but he unconsciously thought of his father whose death did not consciously grieve him.

I am in the fortunate position of being able to report two cases that will illuminate the psychology of such unconscious communication, with Freud himself as the psychoanalyst. The first concerns me. I had an emotional conflict that caused me considerable disturbance in my middle forties and I asked Freud for help. Almost twenty-five years after my own psychoanalysis, and after many years of practicing analysis, I found myself for a few weeks as a patient on the couch of the best analyst. Those were unforgettable weeks. The penetrating sagacity, the human understanding, the wisdom, and the kindness of the great man were never clearer to me than in those short weeks. The old man seemed to know all that was in me, my weaknesses and shortcomings as well as my strengths—all that was hidden to others and to myself. From a height of observation, with a psychological discernment never met in any other human being he showed me a picture of myself whose traits, strange and familiar at the same time, I would never have recognized as my own. And how true were these traits! I knew it then and learned to know it even better later on.

Toward the end of these too-short weeks I found myself reconciled with myself and ready to accept myself. Strangely encouraged, I had occasion once again to admire his fine unconscious understanding. In the last session I clinked the coins in my pocket while giving myself up to free associations. I casually remarked that playing with money showed my anal-erotic tenden-ceis. Freud answered seriously: "That is, of course, nonsense. You think of your brothers and you are glad that you are now able to send them money." I tried to trace my thoughts back. I had not thought of my brothers con-sciously just then, but the thought had crossed my mind a few minutes before, a fleeting thought that I could now, because I was earning more than my two older brothers, give them a certain amount monthly. I had let the association pass by unexpressed but had instead listened to the metallic sound of the coin with which I had played at the beginning of the analytic session. I had often before spoken of my two brothers, who used to slip bills into my pocket when I was a student. Instead of the by-passed thought I had half-jokingly mentioned a psychoanalytic theory—but this theory had a connec-tion with the unspoken association. Another psychoanalyst, a representative of an older-brother figure, had published a paper the other day concerning anal eroticism. In clinking the coins I had unconsciously demonstrated: I am now rich; I am richer than my brothers. Freud swept aside my theoretical remark contemptuously, as it deserved, and penetrated to the essential thought, which concerned my feelings of superiority to my older brothers.

My other report antedates this revealing incident by twenty years. It, too, concerns Freud. At that time I was twenty-six years old, an inexperienced analyst and much worried about the numerous problems my first patients presented to me. I had a British patient who had come to a standstill in his associations. He asserted that nothing occurred to him, that he had no thoughts. When he spoke it was obvious that it was only to pass the time of the session. In this emergency I asked Freud what I should do. He told me smilingly: "Ask him to think of something that is remotest from his thoughts, something he would never think of." I followed his advice. At first the patient was silent. It was obvious that he was making an attempt to think of something very remote. He then said: "The swamps of Wutipe." That was certainly geographically remote. It nevertheless gave me the clue Freud had expected. Some months ago the father of the patient had died. It was in these swamps that, as a missionary in China, he had contracted the disease that led to his death. I was able to remind the patient of what he had told me about that long ago, and he broke into sobs. At the end of the session he said, "I don't know what the hell I cried about."

I have thought of Freud's advice often enough since, the last time a few weeks ago. During his psychoanalytic session, a patient said that nothing occurred to him. Silence. After ten minutes: "It is a blank, a complete blank . . . like a curtain in a theater." Then without asking him, I could tell the patient what he had thought. He had read in the newspaper that day that the play of a young writer who, as he knew, had been a patient of mine, would be produced in a short time. He himself had written a play some years ago, which had been performed on Broadway and had not been a success. The concealed thought concerned the play of this other patient and his own intense jealousy of the young writer who had won success and fame before him.

All this is less convincing than instances in which the analyst walks to the hidden spot with the directness and the certainty of a somnambulist, apparently led by nothing but blind instinct. It seems there is no clue to the train of thought, nothing in the preceding life story of the patient that could serve as a hint or be used as an allusion to the thing that emerges suddenly from the analyst's memory. A case sometimes contains material consciously and willfully kept back by the patient. In some of them there is no way for the facts to come to the knowledge of the analyst. I have notes on two such cases.

The first concerned an experience in Holland in 1935. I was treating a young German woman who had been a member of the Socialist party. Despite the fact that she came of an old gentile family, she had had to flee Hitler's Third Reich. In Holland she had come to psychoanalysis because serious disturbances interfered with her work. Among them was the memory of a love affair that had lasted for several years and had ended before she left Germany. The man had been a prominent physician. He was married and he had promised to divorce his wife and marry my patient. When Hitler came, he did not have the moral courage to sacrifice his career. He had broken off the relationship with her and returned to his wife. It was obvious that my patient had suffered more from this disappointment than from the other blows of destiny and that she still loved the man to whom she had been devoted for so long and who was lost to her.

We had been discussing the problem for a few months and she still had not overcome her grief. At a certain point the analysis reached a deadlock. One session at this time took the following course. After a few sentences about the uneventful day, the patient fell into a long silence. She assured me that nothing was in her thoughts. Silence from me. After many minutes she complained about a toothache. She told me that she had been to the dentist yesterday. He had given her an injection and then had pulled a wisdom tooth. The spot was hurting again. New and longer silence. She pointed to my bookcase in the corner and said, "There's a book standing on its head."

Without the slightest hesitation and in a reproachful voice I said, "But why did you not tell me that you had had an abortion?" I had said it without an inkling of what I would say and why I would say it. It felt as if, not I, but something in me had said that. The patient jumped up and looked at me as if I were a ghost. Nobody knew or could know that her lover, the physician, had performed an abortion on her. The operation, especially dangerous because of the advanced state of her pregnancy, was, of course, kept very secret because abortion in the case of gentiles was punishable by death in Germany. To protect the man she still loved, she had decided to tell me all except this secret.

When I look back on the psychological situation, I can, of course, realize what brought me to my surprising statement. I must have felt for some time that the patient was keeping something secret when she spoke of the physician. Then came the session with the long pauses. I can follow the subterranean thread between her few associations now. Toothache, the injection by the dentist, the pulling of the wisdom tooth, the book that stands on its head. If I had followed this train of associations logically, I might perhaps — perhaps — have come to the same conclusion. Here was a displacement from below to above, from the genital region to the mouth . . . an operation . . . pain . . . the position of the book and the embryo on its head. I did not, however, use my logical powers and I can only warn my students against using them in such situations. Logical operation subjects the analyst to errors and mistakes he would not make if he trusted his psychological rather than his logical gifts. An understanding of the process and the insertion of the logical links in the chain can and sometimes should be attempted afterward but not during the process.

When I look back on the session, what was it that happened in me? At first there was silence in me as in the patient; then suspense, a waiting for something to come; her words echoed in me; a new suspense; a new resounding of her words, and then all blank and dark for a second, out of which came the knowledge, nay, the certainty, that she had had an abortion, that she thought with grief of the baby for which she had longed and which she had to give up. I did not give a damn about logic and what I had learned in the books. I did not think of any psychoanalytic theory. I just said what had spoken in me despite and against all logic, and I was correct.

The second instance, though less impressive, proves that the analytic technique, if only applied with inner sincerity, operates with the precision of a scalpel used in surgery. An Englishman, who had become a professor of mathematics at an unusually early age, was sent to me by Freud for psychoanalysis. He complained about different nervous symptoms but mostly because his work was never as complete as he had foreseen. The problems he told me about were, of course, far beyond my poor understanding of mathematics. What became obvious, however, was that he often approached the most difficult problems with a courage and boldness that won him the admiration of other professors of mathematics. He had published a series of articles on certain problems that, until then completely unsolved, he brought close to solution. But he could not go beyond this point to a complete solution. He failed and felt frustrated whenever this point was reached in his thinking. It was as if all his intellectual powers left him suddenly, as if all that had been so ingeniously prepared and built up faded and evaporated. It came to nothing, as if a bad demon had suddenly wiped it away.

He had described the process several times with all its specific mathematical traits. I had gained no insight. His life story showed nothing conspicuous. He was, it seemed, happily married and had a child. What then impelled me after a few months to tell him that I was convinced that he had a premature emission in sexual intercourse? I suddenly felt the impulse to tell him—it was certainly at the "psychological moment." The patient, shy in this respect as so many British young men were twenty years ago, had not spoken of his sexual life and nothing in his report led me to surmise such a sexual peculiarity. Nothing but his vivid and repeated description of what happened when he dealt with a mathematical problem. I could tell him what I unconsciously guessed. He approached his wife with strong desire and he was bold and energetic in the first phases of the sexual act but suddenly he had to let go without pleasure, without reaching the climax of sensations and the release had rather the character of weakening than of resolving the tension. He had never discussed his present sex life with anybody.

He looked at me with amazement. The sudden revelation was rewarded. It opened the door to the center of his problem. Back at the university he could write to me that he had overcome his difficulties in both fields and that he was happy and grateful to psychoanalysis upon which he looked as upon magic. There was, however, nothing magical in my conclusion. I had unconsciously transferred what he had told me about his mathematical difficulties to the sexual sphere. But note: while I verbalized it, I was not conscious of any logical operations of the kind.

Let me add one little instance. It is representative of hundreds of others attesting to the secret communication that takes place between the psychoanalyst and his patient. A man told me a dream in which the following part appeared. *I am with my father on board ship. My father shows me a cabin near that of the captain. I aks my father: "Does mother know that you are leaving?" He begins to cry and says, "I have forgotten to tell her," and we decide to telephone before the ship leaves the harbor. We move and we come to Lands End.*

There were no associations to the dream. He did not know where the name Lands End came from nor any ship on which he had gone with his father. Nothing occurred to him about the dream. Why did I ask him then and there whether he knew the play *Outward Bound*? "Do I know it?" he answered astonished. "I saw it in the theater and then as a movie and I just thought of it. That is strange." The play, which I had seen many years ago in Vienna, shows a ship on which the passengers are all dead without knowing it. The captain is God.

What did I know of the patient that would have led to this idea? Nothing beyond the fact that his father had died two years before and that now, stirred up by going over his life in psychoanalysis, his old relations with his father had won increasing significance for him. In the preceding session I had quoted a sentence Freud once wrote—most of his students overlook it—that the death of his father is the most important event in a man's life. The dream regressed to another experience that had subterranean connections with the subject, the play *Outward Bound,* which shows the transition from death to life in the form of a ship voyage. The patient was, as I realized without saying it, under the ban of a superstitious fear that he would soon die, as his father had. A great part of the dream, whose interpretation here would lead us too far, is only to be understood when one turns certain sentences around. They have to be read like Chinese and Hebrew writing. Thus it is not his father but himself who would cry if he had to leave without saying farewell to his mother, and so on. It is remarkable that the play occurred to him as well as to me. It had never been mentioned between us before. Something in the atmosphere of the dream, the ship, Lands End, the mood of leave-taking that pervades it, the strange mixture of everyday language and something extraordinary—all that and perhaps more must have made me think of a half-forgotten play seen many years ago on another continent.

I know that many analysts add theoretical considerations to their interpretations. They explain minutely and conscientiously how they arrived at their results. I do not consider such a technique false, but wasteful and unsatisfactory. Wasteful because it means an unnecessary intellectual effort on the part of the psychoanalyst. He has to expend energy and time needed for other things. Suppose I consult a physician and he makes a diagnosis of my disease after careful examination. Perhaps he tells me that I have bronchitis. He does not go into a long discussion of the reasons and considerations that led him to this conclusion. I consider the technique unsatisfactory also because the psychoanalyst will be able to name only a few of the reasons that led him to a certain interpretation. Many others, such as previous impressions, little signs, intonations, gestures, and so on, remain unconscious, but they were operating and contributed to the interpretation.

And of what use would such theoretical discussions and explanations be? To convince the patient? But he will not be convinced by logical and theoretical arguments if he is reluctant to accept them. And if he is ready to trust the analyst, he does not need them. Yes, we sometimes realize that a patient *does not believe* that an analytic interpretation is true. *He knows it.*

That may sound paradoxical but experience proves that it is possible. My recommendation to the student is thus to present his impression or interpretation in the form of a statement without adding his reasons or adding them only in exceptional cases. (Training another analyst, for instance, is such a case.) I need not emphasize that precautions have to be taken before interpretations of this kind are uttered.

Here are a few cases that at a given moment were beyond the comprehension of the analyst. The conscious understanding of the psychological foundations of an interpretation here did not precede the grasping of their concealed meaning. It followed the penetration. Of course, these are exceptions, comparable to sudden advances of a military force that makes use of a favorable situation on the spur of the moment. Such improvised movements take place side by side with the long-prepared, tactical procedures. It will be obvious from the reports of the cases that the conjecture of concealed meanings and motives takes its point of departure from an actual symptom or a combination of traits. After grasping the hidden meaning the psychoanalyst is often able to use this insight for the psychological evaluation of the patient's personality. What he guesses sometimes affords the possibility of looking into a shaft of the unconscious that was not perceived before. Understanding the single symptom helps bring to light aspects of the patient's character.

In some cases where the psychoanalysis has progressed a good deal, the process is reversed. The analyst has won a good insight into the personality of the patient. Many sessions have given him opportunity to study his character, to observe his peculiar traits, to understand the forces that govern his neurosis. When a new symptom is discovered, a fear has come out of hiding, a compulsive activity or an obsession idea has emerged, the analyst can use his psychological understanding of the whole person to guess more quickly and adequately the unconscious meaning of the symptom or to find the motives and mechanisms behind its production.

I had been analyzing a young American artist for a few months in Vienna when he told me of a phobia he had not mentioned before. Our sessions up to this point had been occupied with his life story and the compulsion against which he desperately fought. He had grown up in a very puritanical milieu. His parents had been very religious people and the child was strictly educated. On Sundays every activity except praying was forbidden. A spirit of gloominess and sinfulness had cast a shadow over his boyhood. In his late teens he had freed himself from the religious beliefs and practices of his parents, whose house he had left. He had come to Vienna because he wanted to get rid of a terrible compulsion that tempted him to play sexually with six- or seven-year-old girls. He had in fact yielded to this temptation several times and was later on crushed by guilt-feelings and fears.[2] After several months we arrived at a reconstruction of the events and motives that had led the patient to his perversion. When he was six or seven years old, he shared his room with a governess who had often taken the little boy into her bed and used him sexually. What he now tried to do to little girls had at first been done to him when he was a small boy. It was a case of turning a passive experience, which the child could not master psychically, into an active one. This reconstruction of the seduction story was, of course, the result of hard and patient analytic work comparable to the solution of a jigsaw puzzle and obtained with the help of all the means that the analytic technique has at its disposal.

In a pause in the work centering around his obsession, he told me about a phobia that had frightened him for many years and which he was again experiencing on his walks in the streets of Vienna. He became panicky when he saw smoke, from chimneys for instance, or sparks. It was not difficult to guess that forgotten impressions from his childhood played the main role in the genesis of this phobia. Ideas of hell-fire and the punishments of the damned emerged suddenly in my thoughts—I understood immediately the origin of his fears.

In the recognition of the motives of his compulsion (and other symptoms not discussed here) before he brought up the phobia, I had followed the usual path of analytic penetration, putting together into the picture all elements that had emerged. The insight into his other symptoms, into his doubts and fears, had made me familiar with his particular personality. When he gave me all the details of the fire-and-smoke phobia, I could already use this knowledge. I recalled the description of his religious background. I was aware of the contrast between his official freethinking and old convictions that lingered in his unconscious. The solution of his compulsion took many weeks; the guessing of the meaning of the smoke-phobia, only a few minutes. The contrast of the two procedures can best be compared to the following situation.

Some boys study with their botany teacher the leaves, flowers, and fruits of an apple tree. When they recognize such a tree in a garden later on, they assume that it will bear apples, not nuts or plums, because they remember the special leaves and flowers of an apple tree.

At this point I want to introduce a new term for the reaction of the analyst to the communications, words, gestures, pauses, and so forth, of the analyzed person. I call the sum of this reaction, which includes all kinds of impressions, *response*. The analytic response is thus the emotional and intellectual reply to the speech, behavior, and appearance of the patient, and includes awareness of the inner voices of the analyst. Every interpretation, all that the analyst says, the form of his explanation and exposition, are all preceded, and to a great extent determined, by this response. The response is, so to speak, the inside experience of that which the analyst perceives, feels, senses, regarding the patient. It is clear from the preceding chapters that the main part of that response is in its nature unconscious or, to put it otherwise, that only a small part of it becomes conscious. The response is thus the dark soil in which our understanding of psychical processes is rooted. Out of these roots, which are hidden deep in the earth, emerges our intellectual, logical grasp of the problems. Out of these concealed roots grows the tree of psychoanalytic knowledge.

The student is warned not to trust to the false teachers who instruct him that he should approach the material offered by the patient from the start with the instrument of conscious knowledge and theoretical learning. *This form of approach is false, leads the analyst astray, and gets the analysis nowhere fast.* Rather than trust to what he theoretically knows, the analyst should trust to what he feels, to what his senses tell him, the known senses and the unknown ones. Mistrust conscious and theoretical knowledge as a receiving station for the language of the unconscious. It will be difficult, I know, to make the analysts unlearn what they have so long applied and to undo the damage that instruction in their training has done. *It is better not to understand than to misunderstand.* To follow one's misconstructions and misapprehensions with great logic is much more dangerous than to admit to oneself that one has not yet understood and is ready to wait until one begins to comprehend. It is better to wait for the dawn than to strike out in the wrong direction in the dark.

The response of the analyst is the emotional answer to the communications of the patient. It is that which takes place in the analyst's mind from the first vague impressions until he sees the unconscious processes of the other person with full clarity. ("The other person" is, of course, oneself in the case of self-observation and self-analysis.) *Response at the moment in which we reach the deepest insights into the unconscious has the nature of surprise.* Such surprise-response will, of course, never emerge when the analyst approaches unconscious material theoretically. He will then see only what he expects to see and neglect, distort, or overlook what does not fit his scheme. The new things he meets will not become objects for new study because they will be labeled quickly and put on theoretical file. For these analysts psychoanalysis will always be a "science," a drawer full of formulas and terms, and never an experience.

In that case, how can it become an experience for the patient? Only he who has once been caught by surprise and has experienced and mastered that sudden emotion can catch another by surprise. I have already warned the student not to follow those false teachers who recommend the use of "intelligence" in the approach to the unconscious. What emerges from the depths can only be caught with something originating in the depths. I am teaching my students to do the sensible thing, but the sensible thing is not always that which our intelligence demands. The analyst who absorbs the noises and voices of the day too keenly will never hear the secret fountains that speak loud only in the night.

The analyst, as he is often trained in psychoanalytic institutes, is an interpreting automaton, a robot of understanding, an independent analytic intellect who has become a person without ever becoming a personality. He confuses the calmness and control of the observer with lack of sensitivity, objectivity in judgment with absence of sensation and feeling. When he sits behind the patient, he tries to be everything else but himself. But only he who is entirely himself, only he who has the sharpest ear for what his own thoughts whisper to him, will be a good psychoanalyst.

I am of the opinion, not shared by many New York analysts, that the personality of the psychoanalyst is the most important tool he has to work with. My stand here is in sharp contrast to that of those teachers who train their students to forget themselves when they try to understand unconscious phenomena. I admonish my pupils to be acutely alert to their own responses. The most important advice on the technique of psychoanalysis is nowhere to be found in the textbooks. The teacher who has discussed technique and technicalities should at the end remind his student: *"This above all: to thine own self be true."*

NOTES

1. *The Circuit Rider,* by Edward Eggleston.
2. As is known from the biographies of Dostoyevsky, it was this same temptation that beset this writer. It is likely he gave in to it at least once.

5. Countertransference and Anxiety

Mabel Blake Cohen

Transference has been defined by Freud[1] as the "re-impressions and repro-
ductions of the emotions and phantasies . . . characterized by the replace-
ment of a former person by the physician." This definition does not make
explicit the concept that such attitudes must be irrational—that is, not appropriately held in relation to the person who is the analyst—though this is
generally accepted. Countertransference can be roughly defined as the converse of transference: the repetition of previously acquired attitudes toward
the patient, such attitudes being irrational in the given situation. Much time
and attention has been given to the study of the transference attitudes of the
patient in analysis, but until recent years comparatively very little to the study
of countertransference, which had been assumed to be absent, except in
situations where the analyst was incompletely analyzed. This assumption has
gradually given way to the recognition that countertransference attitudes are
present in all analytical situations, perhaps roughly proportionate to the
degree of success of the therapist's analysis, but nonetheless present in all.[2]

In the belief that the study of the countertransference can provide useful
material to the analysis, just as does the study of the transference, this paper
represents an attempt to continue the analysis and dynamic understanding of
the phenomenon.

The analytic situation can be looked upon as an interaction between two
people, therapist and patient. Using a mathematical analogy, we have an
equation that contains two variables, patient and therapist. Each main variable is itself a complex term composed of many factors, known and unknown. But of the two variables, that representing the therapist is known to
a much greater degree than that representing the patient. In solving the
equation, if the therapist variable can become known, the equation can be
solved and the value of the patient variable determined. Many of the therapist's attitudes and reactions to the patient are utilized on a nonverbal experiential level, of course, as the result of training. The more experienced and

capable the therapist, the more use he makes of such material. Yet the lack of concrete description and study of this aspect of treatment tends to keep it obscure, to hamper its use in training, and to prevent further development of theory and technique pertaining to it. Far too often the young therapist enters into his first treatment experiences with the concept that he should not have "countertransference feelings" toward the patient, that entertaining such feelings is evidence that he is incompletely analyzed or technically incompetent. This leads to an attempt to suppress such attitudes where they are conscious and to a tendency to discourage a widening of awareness to include those which are less easily available because more anxiety-connected. The contrary point of view, that of welcoming as wide an awareness as possible of all one's responses to a patient, with the hope of understanding the sources of whatever anxiety or other complex feelings and impulses the patient may inspire in one, is far more conducive to the development of the needed skills as well as the needed objectivity and friendliness in the analyst.

But the point of greatest importance is that when the treatment is in a phase of difficulty, the analyst may often obtain valuable clues as to the nature of the obstacles in the way of the patient's favorable development by careful observation of the responses elicited in himself at such times. One may assume that such responses elicited in the therapist by the patient's behavior are similar to (though not necessarily identical with) those elicited from some important person in the patient's previous life. Of course, one also assumes that the responses elicited in the therapist are similar to (though not necessarily identical with) his responses to some person of importance in his own life. And therefore, by recognizing some particular constellation of feelings in his response to the patient, understanding their roots and meaning in his own life, the therapist may extrapolate from his own experience to make a guess as to what the patient's experience has been in the past and is currently in the therapeutic relationship. These data, being available to both participants, may be used to document and make more convincing an interpretation of the problem of the patient.

AN OPERATIONAL DEFINITION

Some discussion of a working definition of the term countertransference is necessary, since it is by no means agreed upon by analysts that it can be correctly considered the converse of transference. D. W. Winnicott, for instance, has recently written about the importance of attitudes of hate from analyst to patient, particularly in dealing with psychotic and antisocial patients. He speaks mainly of "objective countertransference," meaning "the analyst's love and hate in reaction to the actual personality and behavior of the patient based on objective observation."[3] However, he also mentions countertransference feelings that are under repression in the analyst and need more analysis. His concept of "objective countertransference" will not be included under the term countertransference if the latter is used as the converse of transference. Frieda Fromm-Reichmann[4] has separated the responses of the psychoanalyst to the patient into those of a private and those of a professional person and recognizes the possibility of countertransference distortions occurring in both aspects. Franz Alexander[5] has used the term to mean all of the attitudes of the doctor toward the patient, while Sandor Ferenczi[6] has used it to cover the positive, affectionate, loving, or sexual attitudes of the doctor toward the patient. Michael Balint, looking at a somewhat different aspect, calls attention to the fact that every human relation is libidinous, not only the patient's relation to his analyst, but also the analyst's relation to the patient. He says that no human being can in the long run tolerate any relation that brings only frustration and that it is as true for the one as for the other. "The question is, therefore, . . . how much and what kind of satisfaction is needed by the patient on the one hand and by the analyst on the other, to keep the tension in the psycho-analytical situation at or near the optimal level."[7]

In developing his theory of interpersonal relations, Harry Stack Sullivan has defined the psychotherapeutic effort of the analyst as being carried on by the method of participant observation. He says, "The expertness of the psychiatrist refers to his skill in participant observation of the unfortunate patterns of his own and the patient's living, in contrast to merely participating in such unfortunate patterns with the patient."[8] In the use of the term *unfortunate patterns* Sullivan includes the concept of countertransference, or in his words "parataxic distortions."

In several important recent papers, Leo Berman, Paula Heimann, Annie Reich, Margaret Little, and Maxwell Gitelson have made a beginning in the attempt to clarify the concept and to formulate some dynamic principles regarding the phenomena included in this category. Berman[9] is mainly concerned with defining the optimal attitude of the analyst to the patient, an attitude that he characterizes as "dedicated." This description is based on the assumption that the analyst's emotional responses to the patient will be quantitatively less than those of the average person and of shorter duration, as the result of being quickly worked through by self-analysis. This, then, would represent an ideal goal of minimal and easily handled countertransference responses.

Heimann[10] takes a step forward when she states that the analyst's emotional responses to his patient within the analytic situation represent one of the most important tools for his work, and that the analyst's countertransference is an instrument of research into the patient's unconscious. This important formulation is, in my opinion, the basis upon which the study of the analyst's part of the interaction with the patient should be built. Previously, the statement has frequently been made that the analyst's unconscious understands the patient's unconscious. However, it is presumed that much hitherto-unconscious material becomes available to awareness after a successful analysis, so that the understanding should theoretically not be only on an unconscious level but should be formulable in words.

Reich[11] has classified a number of countertransference attitudes of the analyst's. She separates them into two main types: those where the analyst acts out some unconscious need with the patient, and those where the analyst defends against some unconscious need. On the whole, countertransference responses are reflections of permanent neurotic difficulties of the analyst, in which the patient is often not a real object but rather is used as a tool by means of which some need of the analyst is gratified. In some instances, there may be sudden, acute countertransference responses that do not necessarily arise from neurotic character difficulties of the analyst. However, Reich points out that the interest in becoming an analyst is itself partially determined by unconscious motivation, such as curiosity about other people's secrets, which is evidence that countertransference attitudes are a necessary prerequisite for analysts. The contrast between the healthy and neurotic analyst is that in the one the curiosity is desexualized and sublimated in character, while in the other it remains a method of acting out unconscious fantasies.

Margaret Little continues the search for an adequate definition of countertransference, concluding that it should be used primarily to refer to "repressed elements, hitherto unanalysed, in the analyst himself that attach to the patient in the same way as the patient 'transfers' to the analyst affects, etc., belonging to his parents or to the objects of his childhood: i.e. the analyst regards the patient (temporarily and varyingly) as he regarded his own parents." However, in addition, Little thinks that other aspects of the analyst's attitudes toward the patient, such as some specific attitude or mechanism with which he meets the patient's transference, or some of his conscious attitudes, should be considered countertransference responses. She confirms Heimann's statement that the use of countertransference may become an extremely valuable tool in psychoanalysis, comparing it in importance to the advances made when transference interpretations began to be used therapeutically. She sees transference and countertransference as inseparable phenomena; both should become increasingly clear to both doctor and patient as the analysis progresses. To that end, she advocates judicious use of countertransference interpretations by the analyst. "Both are essential to psycho-analysis, and counter-transference is no more to be feared or avoided than is transference; in fact it *cannot* be avoided, it can only be looked out for, controlled to some extent, and perhaps used."[12]

Gitelson,[13] in a comprehensive paper, continues to clarify the phenomena under scrutiny. He goes back to the original definition of countertransference used by Freud—the analyst's reaction to the patient's transference—and separates this set of responses from another set which he refers to as the transference attitudes of the analyst. These transference attitudes, which are the result of "surviving neurotic transference potential" in the analyst, involve "total" reactions to the patient—that is, over-all feelings about and toward the patient—while the countertransference attitudes are "partial" reactions to the patient—that is, emergency defense reactions elicited when the analysis touches upon unresolved problems in the analyst.

This classification, while valid enough, does not seem to forward investigation to any great extent. For example, Gitelson feels in general that the existence of "total" or transference attitudes toward a patient is a contraindication for that analyst to work with that patient, whereas the partial responses are more amenable to working through via the processes of self-analysis. I am extremely skeptical whether it is possible for one to avoid "total" reactions to a patient—that is, general feelings of liking for, dislike of, and responsiveness toward the patient, and so on, are present from the time of the first interview. These do vary in intensity; when extreme, they may indicate that a nontherapeutic relationship would result should the two persons attempt working together. On the other hand, their presence in awareness may permit the successful scrutiny and resolution of whatever problem is involved, whereas their presence outside of awareness would render this impossible. In other words, it is not so much a question whether "total" responses are present or not, but rather a question as to their amenability to recognition and resolution. For this reason, some other type of classification would, in my opinion, be more useful for investigative purposes.

This comment by no means disputes the validity of Gitelson's criticism of the rationalization of much countertransference acting-out under the heading of "corrective emotional experience." He emphasizes that motherly or fatherly attitudes in the analyst are often character defenses unrecognized as such by him. Although the analyst, according to Gitelson, cannot deny his personality nor its operation in the analytic situation as a significant factor, this does not mean that his personality is the chief instrument of the therapy. He also reports the observation that when the analyst appears as himself in the patient's dreams, it is often the herald of the development of an unmanageably intense transference neurosis, the unmanageability being the difficulties of the analyst's situation. Similarly, when the patient appears as himself in the analyst's dreams, it is often a signal of unconscious countertransference processes going on.

In summary, then, we see that the recent studies on countertransference have included in their concepts attitudes of the therapist that are both conscious and unconscious; attitudes that are responses both to real and to fantasied attributes of the patient; attitudes that are stimulated by unconscious needs of the analyst and attitudes that are stimulated by sudden outbursts of affect on the part of the patient; attitudes that arise from responding to the patient as though he were some previously important person in the analyst's life; and attitudes that do not use the patient as a real object but rather as a tool for the gratification of some unconscious need. This group of responses covers a tremendously wide territory, yet it does not include, of course, all of the analyst's repsonses to the patient. On what common ground are the above attitudes singled out to be called countertransference?

It seems to this writer that the common factor in the above responses is the presence of anxiety in the therapist—whether recognized in awareness or defended against and kept out of awareness. The contrast between the dedicated attitude described as the ideal attitude of the analyst—or the analyst as an expert in problems of living, as Sullivan puts it—and the so-called countertransference responses, is the presence of anxiety, arising from the variety of different sources in the whole field of patient-therapist interrelationship.

If countertransference attitudes and behavior were to be thought of as determined by the presence of anxiety in the therapist, we might have an operational definition that would be more useful than the more descriptive one based on identifying patterns in the analyst that were derived from important past relationships. The definition would, of course, have to include situations both of felt discomfort and also those where the anxiety was out of awareness and replaced by a defensive operation. Such a viewpoint of countertransference would be useful in that it would include all situations where the analyst was unable to be useful to the patient because of difficulties with his own responses.

The definition might be precisely stated as follows: *When, in the patient-analyst relationship, anxiety is aroused in the analyst with the effect that communication between the two is interfered with by some alteration in the analyst's behavior (verbal or otherwise), then countertransference is present.*

The question might be asked, if countertransference were defined in this way, would the definition hold good for transference responses also? It would seem that on a very generalized level this might be so, but on the level of practical therapeutic understanding such a statement would not be enlightening. While it could safely be said of every patient that the appearance of his anxiety or defensive behavior in the treatment situation was due to an impairment of communication with the analyst that in turn was due to his attributing to the analyst some critical or otherwise disturbing attitude that in its turn was originally derived from his experience with his parents—still this would leave out of consideration the fact that the patient's whole life pattern and his relation to all of the important authority figures in it would show a similar stereotyped defensive response. So that, certainly in the early stages of treatment and to a lesser extent in later stages, the anxiety responses of the patient are for the most part generalized and stereotyped rather than particularized with special reference to his relationship with the analyst.

This, however, is not true of the analyst. Having been analyzed himself, most of such anxiety-laden responses as he has experienced with others have entered awareness and many of them have been worked through and abandoned in favor of more mature and integrated responses. What remain, then, are not such stereotyped or universal responses. To illustrate, all patients do not automatically represent sibling rivals, while it is possible that a particular, unusually competitive patient may still represent a younger sibling to an analyst who had some difficulties in his own life with being the elder child.

To speak of the same thing from another point of view, the analyst is not working on his problems in the analysis; he is working on the patient's. Therefore, while the patient brings his anxiety responses to the analysis as his primary concern, the fact that the analyst's problems are not under scrutiny permits him a greater degree of detachment and objectivity. This is, to be sure, only a relative truth, since the analyst at times and under certain circumstances is certainly bringing his problems into the relationship, and at times, at least in some analyses, the attention of both the patient and the analyst are directed to the analyst's problems. However, it is on the whole valid to describe the analytic situation as one designed to focus attention on the anxieties of the patient and to leave in the background the anxieties of the therapist, so that when these do appear they are of particular significance in terms of the relationship itself.

CLASSIFICATION OF COUNTERTRANSFERENCE RESPONSES

Using the above definition, we can attempt to classify the situations in analysis when anxiety-tinged processes are operating in the analyst. The classification suggested below is not a clear-cut separation of such situations, since the groups shade off into one another. Nor are any of the responses to be thought of as entirely free of neurotic attitudes on the part of the therapist. Even in the most extreme examples of situational stress (where ordinarily the analyst's response is thought of as being an objective response to the stress rather than a neurotic response), personal, characterological factors will color his response, as will also the nature of his relationship with the patient. Take, for instance, the situation where the analyst comes to his office in a state of acute tension as the result of a quarrel with his wife. With one patient he may remain preoccupied with his personal troubles throughout the hour, while with another he may be able shortly to bring his attention to the analytic situation. Something in each patient's personality and method of production, and in the analyst's response to each, has affected the analyst's behavior.

Anxiety-arousing situations in the patient-analyst interaction have been classified as follows: (1) situational factors—that is, reality factors such as intercurrent events in the analyst's life; and also, social factors such as need for success and recognition as a competent therapist; (2) unresolved neurotic problems of the therapist; (3) communication of the patient's anxiety to the therapist.

Situational Factors

This group of responses is, of course, very much influenced by the character make-up of the doctor. How much need for conformity to convention he retains will influence his response to the patient who shouts loudly during an analytic hour. But the response will also be affected by the degree to which his office is soundproof, whether there is another patient in the waiting room, whether a colleague in an adjoining office can overhear, and so on. So that, even leaving out the private characterological aspect of the situation for the therapist, there remains a sizable set of reality needs which, if threatened, will lead to unanalytic behavior on his part.

The greatest number of these have to do with the physician's role in our culture. There is a high value attached to the role of successful physician. This is not, of course, confined to the vague group of people known as the public; it is also actively present in the professional colleagues. There is a reality need for recognition of his competence by his colleagues, which has a dollars and cents value as well as an emotional one. While it is true that his reputation will not be made or broken by one success or failure, it does not follow that a suicide or psychotic breakdown in a patient does not represent a reality threat to him. Consequently, he cannot be expected to handle such threatening crises with complete equanimity. In addition to such a reality need to be known as competent by his colleagues and the public, there is a potent and valid need on the doctor's part for creative accomplishment. This appears in the therapeutic situation as an expectation of and a need to see favorable change in the patient. It is entirely impossible for a therapist to participate in a treatment situation where the goal is improvement or cure without suffering frustration, disappointment, and at times anxiety when his efforts result in no apparent progress. Such situations are at times handled by therapists with the attitude, "Let him stew in his own juice until he sees that he will have to change," or by the belief that he, the doctor, must be making an error that he does not understand and should redouble his efforts. Frequently, the resolution of such a difficulty can be achieved by the realization on the part of the therapist that his reality fear of failure is keeping him from recognizing an important aspect of the patient's neurosis having to do with laying the responsibility for his welfare on another's shoulders. The reality fear of failure cannot be ignored but rather has to be put up with, so to speak, since an attempt on the part of the therapist to remove it by "making" the patient get well is bound to increase the chances of failure.

Further difficulties are introduced by the traditional cultural definition of the healer's role—that is, according to the Hippocratic oath. The physician-healer is expected to play a fatherly or even god-like role with his patient, in which he both sees through him—knows mysteriously what is wrong with his insides—and also takes responsibility for him. This magic-healer role has heavy reinforcement from many of the personal motivations of the analyst for becoming a physician and a psychotherapist. These range from needs to know other people's secrets, as mentioned by Reich, to needs to cure oneself vicariously by curing others, needs for magical power to cover up one's own feelings of weakness and inadequacy, needs to do better than one's own analyst. Unfortunately, some aspects of psychoanalytical training tend to reinforce the interpretation of the therapist as a magically powerful person. The admonition, for instance, to become a "mature character," while excellent advice, still carries with it a connotation of perfect adjustment and perhaps brings pressure to bear on the trainee not to recognize his immaturities or deficiencies. Even such precepts as to be a "mirror" or a "surgeon" or "dedicated" emphasize the analyst's moral power in relation to the patient and, still worse, institutionalize it as good technique. Since the patient, too, enters the analytic situation with an inevitable belief in the analyst's power, it is regrettably easy for both persons to participate in a mutually gratifying relationship that satisfies the patient's dependency and the doctor's need for power.

The main situations in the patient-doctor relationship that undermine the therapeutic role and therefore may result in anxiety in the therapist can be listed as follows: (1) when the doctor is helpless to affect the patient's neurosis; (2) when the doctor is treated consistently as an object of fear, hatred, criticism, or contempt; (3) when the patient calls on the doctor for advice or reassurance as evidence of his professional competence or interest in the patient; (4) when the patient attempts to establish a relationship of romantic love with the doctor; (5) when the patient calls on the doctor for other intimacy.

To illustrate, I would like to use an example in which the doctor's social role of taking responsibility for a sick person came into conflict with the patient's therapeutic needs.

A young woman in analysis following a schizophrenic episode, had periodically during several years of treatment become acutely disturbed as the result of recurring conflicts in her relationship with her mother. Her lifelong pattern, developed as early as five years of age, had been to get into trouble in such a way that she was actually injured and persecuted by others. The analyst was forced to play an active role in the patient's affairs at such critical times in order to prevent realistic catastrophes. One method of preventing self-injury was to make himself available to the patient by telephone whenever her tension was such that she felt unable to carry on. He also used advice giving about how to handle specific situations to prevent her being kicked out of college and discharged from a job. At the beginning of treatment, this activity was, or seemed to be, necessary to prevent the patient's complete failure and hospitalization. However, though she improved and more and more of her psychotic character was modified by treatment, the recurrent crises persisted with undiminished intensity and it still seemed that the therapist must use the same means to prevent the same catastrophes. Eventually, the therapist decided, though with severe misgivings about the danger of psychosis and with considerable feeling that he was refusing to take a responsibility that he had agreed to in becoming the patient's doctor in the first place, to withdraw the supportive telephone conversations and the active advice giving in times of crisis. The patient throve, promptly took over the management of the cirses herself, and eventually went on to finish her analysis with satisfactory result.

In this example there is probably some neurotic involvement on the part of the therapist in that he was unable to discern the point at which his patient became capable of handling her own affairs and continued to think of a neurotic transference attitude as still being an ego deficiency of psychotic severity. However, the severity of the patient's illness and the correspondingly great degree of real responsibility assumed by the doctor by virtue of his taking the case acted as a second, more realistic, pressure in preventing him from recognizing the time when she was ready for more mature behavior.

Unresolved Neurotic Problems of the Therapist

This is a subject on which it is very difficult to generalize since such problems will be different in every therapist. To be sure, there are large general categories into which most therapists can be classified, and hence there are certain over-all attitudes that may be held in common, as for instance the category of the obsessional therapist who still retains remnants of a compulsive need to be in control, or the masochistically overcompensated therapist who compulsively makes reparation to the patient, as described by Little.

One may scrutinize all analysts, from the top of the ladder to the bottom, and, as is obvious, will find characteristic types of patients chosen and characteristic courses of analytic treatment in each case. Gitelson seems to undervalue this factor when he says that the analyst "cannot deny his personality nor its operation in the analytic situation as a significant factor. . . . This is far from saying, however, that his personality is the chief instrument of the therapy that we call psycho-analysis. There is a great difference between the selection and playing of a role and the awareness of the fact that one has found one's self cast for a part. It is of primary importance for the analyst to conduct himself so that the analytic process proceeds on the basis of what the patient brings to it.''[14]

It is not the selection and playing of a role that creates the countertransference problem of the average, relatively healthy analyst, but the fact that one habitually and incessantly plays a role that is determined by one's character structure, so that one is at times handicapped from seeing and dealing with the role in which one is cast by the patient.

A relatively simple example of transference-countertransference distortion in a treatment situation will be used to illustrate some of the problems. It was chosen largely because of its short duration and simplicity.

A patient arrives for his hour five minutes late. He reacts with feelings of guilt and the expectation of being criticized. On arrival, he notices a certain stiffness in the facial expression of the physician, which is a hangover from a telephone conversation the physician was having just before the patient's arrival. The patient, instead of inquiring whether the doctor is offended by his tardiness, immediately plunges into an explanation of why it happened. The physician (who is certainly not very alert at the moment) wonders why the patient is responding in such a guilty manner to such a small offense, but (being a person who likes to be thought of as kindly and who is therefore inclined to become anxious when treated as a tyrant) does not inquire but merely waits in silence for the patient to ''get down to business.'' The lack of response convinces the patient that the physician is unmollified by his explanation. He thinks (but does not say) that he had better produce some pretty good free associations this hour to make up for his lateness. The hour goes on. The patient notices that he is dismissed two minutes early. (Up to this time, the analyst is unaware that the patient is so upset, and the part played by his facial expression in the sequence of events has also escaped his notice.)

On the way home the patient begins to think that the early stopping was a retaliation on the doctor's part for his lateness and resolves to come early next time. He comes five minutes early for his next appointment and the doctor is detained by his previous patient so that he is not ready to start until five minutes after the scheduled time. The patient now believes that the doctor's lateness—which is for the same amount of time as his own—is deliberate, to continue punishing him for his tardiness the previous hour. A very tangled emotional situation is the result. The patient has, he thinks, clear proof that the doctor is malicious toward him. The doctor has a patient who is blocking, anxious, and resentful, without the ghost of a notion why. Finally, at this point when the patient's blocking and anxiety have become acute, the analyst makes an inquiry and then hears the patient's account of what happened.

It is apparent that, in order to deal with the distortions introduced by the patient, the doctor needs to be aware of the following things: (1) that he has an unamiable expression on his face when the patient arrives five minutes late for the first hour, and (2) that he is annoyed (made anxious) by the patient's imputation of malice to him. If he were aware of (1), he would, perhaps, be in a position to interrupt the fearful apologies of the patient with a question as to why the patient thinks he is angry. If he were unaware of (1) or did not think it wise to interrupt, still if he were aware of his anxiety reaction (2), he would be in a position to recognize that his annoyance at being apologized to was leading to a somewhat sulky silence on his part. Once this were within awareness, the annoyance could be expected to lift and the therapeutic needs of the situation could then be handled on their own merits.

Communication of the Patient's Anxiety to the Therapist

This is a most interesting and somewhat mysterious phenomenon that is exhibited on occasion—and perhaps more frequently than we realize—by both analysts and patients. It seems to have some relationship to the process described as empathy. It is a well-known fact that certain types of persons are literally barometers for the tension level of other persons with whom they are in contact. Apparently cues are picked up from small shifts in muscular tension as well as changes in voice tone. Tonal changes are more widely recognized to provide such cues, as evidenced by the common expression, "It wasn't what he said but the way he said it." But there are numbers of instances where the posture of a patient while walking into the consulting room gave the cue to the analyst that anxiety was present, even though there was no gross abnormality but merely a slight stiffness or jerkiness to be observed. A somewhat similar observation can be made in supervised analyses, where the supervisee communicates to the supervisor that he is in an anxiety-arousing situation with the patient, not by the material he relates, but by some appearance of increased tension in his manner of reporting.

It is a moot point whether anxiety responses of therapists in situations where the anxiety is "caught" from the patient can be considered to be entirely free of personal conflict on the part of the analyst. It would seem probable that habitual alertness to the tension level of others, however desirable a trait in the analyst, must have had its origins in tension-laden atmospheres of the past, and hence must have specific personal meaning to the analyst.

The contagious aspects of the patient's anxiety have been most often mentioned in connection with the treatment of psychotics. In dealing with a patient whose defenses are those of violent counteraggression, most analysts experience both fear and anxiety. The fear is on a relatively rational basis— the danger of actually suffering physical hurt. The anxiety derives from (1) retaliatory impulses toward the attacker, (2) wounded self-esteem that one's helpful intent is so misinterpreted by the patient, and (3) a sort of primitive envy of or identification with the uncontrolled venting of violent feelings. It has been found by experience in attempting to treat such patients that the therapist can function at a more effective level if he is encouraged to be aware of and handle consciously his irrational responses to the patient's violence.

A milder variant of this response can frequently be found in office practice. It can be noted that when affect of more than usual intensity enters the treatment situation the analyst tends to interrupt the patient. This interruption may take any one of a variety of forms, such as a relevant question, an interpretative remark, a reassuring remark, a change of subject. Whatever its content, it has the effect of diluting the intensity of feeling being expressed and/or shifting the trend of the associations. This, of course, is technically desirable in some instances, but when it occurs automatically, without aware-ness and therefore without consideration of whether it is desirable or not, its occurrence must be attributed to uneasiness in the analyst. Ruesch and Prestwood[15] have made an extended study of the phenomenon of commu-nication of patients' anxiety to the therapist, in which they demonstrated that the communication is much more positively correlated with the tonal and expressive qualities of speech than with the verbal content. Such factors as rate of speech, frequency of use of personal pronouns, frequency of expres-sions of feeling, and so on, showed significant variations in the anxious patient as contrasted with either the relaxed or the angry patient. In this study, the subjective responses of a number of psychiatrists while listening to sections of recorded interviews varied significantly according to the emo-tional tone of the material. A relaxed interview elicited a relaxed response in the listening psychiatrists; the anxious interviews were responded to with a variety of subjective feelings, from being ill-at-ease to being disturbed or angry.

These uncomfortable responses, coupled with numerous types of avoid-ance behavior on the part of the analyst, such as those mentioned above, appear to occur much more frequently than has been hitherto realized. It is difficult to detect them except by an "ear witness," since the therapist himself will usually be unable to report them subsequent to an hour. They were noticed to occur frequently in a study of intensive psychotherapy by experienced analysts that was carried out by means of recorded interviews.[16]

In this particular type of anxious response on the part of the analyst, the chances seem particularly good that careful self-observation will give the therapist more information about what is going on with the patient. This would be even more useful if further classification of these responses were made and the study of recorded interviews included in the training of analysts.

A young man with a severe character neurosis entered treatment and lost no time in convincing his therapist of the urgency of his need for it. However, his attitude was also that of a person who was about to depart. He gave the doctor to understand that he was highly skeptical of the value of treatment, that the concept of free association seemed like nonsense to him, and that his interest in keeping his appointments was of the slightest. His analyst found himself involved in trying to show the patient, by his work, what was the use and meaning of psychoanalysis. He felt on trial, and as though he would have to be careful not to make the patient too anxious lest he abandon his effort to help himself and discontinue treatment. The analyst also found himself offering the patient reassurance, against his better judgment. This pattern of the doctor's being on tenterhooks and the patient's being always on the point of withdrawal first made the analyst uncomfortable and discouraged, and then eventually came to his conscious notice. Thereupon, he was able to observe that the patient was in fact intensely attached to treatment and had no remote intention of withdrawing. However, the threat of withdrawal had been since childhood the patient's chief means of eliciting sympathy, concern, and attention from the significant adults in his life. This defense had worked equally well with the analyst until the analyst noticed his apprehension and insecurity with the patient. Following this, the defensive withdrawal proved to be analyzable.

In a similar way, it seems that the patient applies great pressure to the analyst in a variety of nonverbal ways to behave like the significant adults in the patient's earlier life. It is not merely a matter of the patient's seeing the analyst as like his father, but of his actually manipulating the relationship in such a way as to elicit the same kind of behavior from the analyst. Conscious use of one's observations of how one fits in with the patient's needs can therefore be a fruitful source of information about the patient's patterns of interaction.

METHODS OF HANDLING COUNTERTRANSFERENCE RESPONSES

Provided one accepts the hypothesis that even successfully analyzed therapists are still continually involved in countertransference attitudes toward their patients, the question arises: What can be done with such reactions in the therapeutic situation? Experience indicates that the less intense anxiety responses, where the discomfort is within awareness, can be quickly handled by an experienced and not too neurotic analyst. These are probably chiefly the situational or reality stimuli to anxiety. But where awareness is interfered with by the occurrence of a wide variety of defensive operations, is there anything to be done? Is the analyst capable of identifying such anxiety-laden attitudes in himself and proceeding to work them out? Certainly there are such extreme situations that the analyst unaided cannot handle them and must seek discussion with a colleague or further analytic help for himself. However, there is a wide intermediate ground where alertness to clues or signals that all is not well may be sufficient to start the analyst on a process of self-resolution of the difficulty.

The following is a tentative and necessarily incomplete list of situations that may provide a clue to the analyst that he is involved anxiously or defensively with the patient. It includes signals that I have found useful in my own work and in supervision, but it probably could be added to by others according to their particular experience.

(1) The analyst has an unreasoning dislike for the patient.
(2) The analyst cannot identify with the patient, who seems unreal or mechanical. When the patient reports that he is upset, the analyst feels no emotional response.
(3) The analyst becomes overemotional in regard to the patient's troubles.
(4) The analyst likes the patient excessively, feels that he is his best patient.
(5) The analyst dreads the hours with a particular patient or is uncomfortable during them.
(6) The analyst is preoccupied with the patient to an unusual degree in intervals between hours and may find himself fantasying questions or remarks to be made to the patient.
(7) The analyst finds it difficult to pay attention to the patient. He goes to sleep during hours, becomes very drowsy, or is preoccupied with personal affairs.
(8) The analyst is habitually late with a particular patient or shows other disturbance in the time arrangement, such as always running over the end of the hour.
(9) The analyst gets into arguments with the patient.
(10) The analyst becomes defensive with the patient or exhibits unusual vulnerability to the patient's criticism.

(11) The patient seems to misunderstand the analyst's interpretations consistently or never agrees with them. This is, of course, quite often correctly interpreted as resistance on the part of the patient, but it may also be the result of a countertransference distortion on the part of the analyst such that his interpretations actually are wrong.

(12) The analyst tries to elicit affect from the patient—for instance, by provocative or dramatic statements.

(13) The analyst is overconcerned about the confidentiality of his work with the patient.[17]

(14) The analyst is angrily sympathetic with the patient regarding his mistreatment by some authority figure.[18]

(15) The analyst feels impelled to do something active.[19]

(16) The analyst appears in the patient's dreams as himself, or the patient appears in the analyst's dreams.[20]

In discussing this list, I would like to recapitulate briefly some of the points mentioned earlier in the paper. It becomes apparent that in order to broaden the scope of psychoanalytic therapy, to expedite and make more efficient the analytic process, and to increase our knowledge of the dynamics of interaction, ways and means of studying the transference-countertransference aspects of treatment need to be developed. It is my opinion that this can best be accomplished by setting up the hypothesis that countertransference phenomena are present in every analysis. This is in agreement with the position of Heimann and Little. These phenomena are probably frequently either ignored or repressed, partly because of a lack of knowledge of what to do with them, partly because analysts are accustomed to deal with them in various nonverbal ways, and partly because they are sufficiently provocative of anxiety in the therapist to produce one or another kind of defense reaction. However, since the successfully analyzed psychotherapist has tools at his command for recognizing and resolving defensive behavior via the development of greater insight, the necessity for suppressing or repressing countertransference responses is not urgent. Where the analyst deliberately searches for recognition and understanding of his own difficulties in the interrelationship, his first observation is likely to be that he has an attitude similar to one of those mentioned in the above list. With this as a signal, he may then, by further noticing in the analytic situation what particular aspects of the patient's behavior stimulate such responses in him, eventually find a way of bringing such behavior out into the open for scrutiny, communication, and eventual resolution. For instance, sleepiness in the analyst is very frequently an unconscious expression of resentment at the emotional barrenness of the patient's communication, perhaps springing from a feeling of helplessness on the part of the analyst. When the analyst recognizes that he is sleepy as a retaliation for his patient's uncommunicativeness, and that he is making this response because, up to now, he has been unable to find a more effective way of handling it, the precipitating factor—the uncommunicativeness—can be investigated as a problem.

In addition to this use of his responses as a clue to the meaning of the behavior of the patient, the analyst is also constantly in need of using his observations of himself as a means of further resolution of his own difficulties. For instance, an analyst who had doubts of his intellectual ability habitually overvalued and competed with his more intelligent patients. This would become particularly accentuated when he was trying to treat patients who themselves used intellectual achievement as protection against fears of being overpowered. Thus the analyst, as the result of his overestimation of such a patient's capacity, would fail to make ordinary garden-variety interpretations, believing that these must be obvious to such a bright person. Instead, he would exert himself to point out the subtler manifestations of the patient's neurosis, with the result that there would be much interesting talk but little change in the patients.

This type of error can go unnoticed while the analyst learns eventually that he is unable to treat successfully certain types of patients. However, it can also be slowly and gradually rectified as the result of further experience. In such a case, the analyst is learning on a nonverbal level. However, if some such signal as finding himself fantasying questions or remarks to put to the patient in the next hour is noted by the analyst, he then has the means of expediting and bringing into full awareness the self-scrutiny that can lead to resolution.

It will be noted that the focus of attention of these remarks is on the analyst's own self-scrutiny, both of his responses to the patient's behavior and of his defensive attitudes and actions. Much has been said by others (Heimann, Little, and Gitelson) regarding the pros and cons of introducing discussion of countertransference material into the analytic situation itself. That, however, is a question that, in my opinion, it is not possible to answer in the present state of our knowledge. Rather, it is my intent here to discuss the possible ways and means of improving the analyst's awareness of his own participation in the patient-analyst interaction and of improving his ability to formulate this to himself (or to an observer) clearly. It would seem more feasible to devise techniques for utilizing such material in the therapeutic situation after the area has been more precisely explored and studied—or, rather, concurrently with further study and exploration.

One further point might be added regarding the contrast between the subjective experience of the analyst when anxiety is not present and when it is. When anxiety is not present, he may experience a feeling of being at ease, of accomplishing something, of grasping what the patient is trying to communicate. Certainly in periods when progress is being made, something of the same feeling is shared by the patient, even though he may at the same time be working through troubled areas. Perhaps the loss of the feeling that communication is going on is the most commonly used signal that starts the analyst on a search for what is going wrong.

CONCLUSIONS

The study of countertransference responses provides a rich field for the further investigation of the doctor-patient relationship in psychoanalysis and intensive psychotherapy. This is made more feasible by the possibility of using recordings of interviews both as research tools and as training adjuncts. As the therapist increases his awareness of the nature of his participation with the patient—both on the basis of his own emotional needs and on the basis of the roles cast for him by the patient—his therapeutic management of the interaction can become more precise and the range of neurotic problems that he is able to tackle can be expected to increase.

NOTES

1. See Freud's definition [taken from *Bruchstück* (Fragment), as translated by Ernest Jones] in Leland E. Hinsie and Jacob Shatzky, *Psychiatric Dictionary;* New York, Oxford Univ. Press, 1940.
2. Margaret Little, "Countertransference and the Patient's Response to It," *Internat. J. Psychoanal.* (1951) 32: 32–40.
3. D. W. Winnicott, "Hate in the Counter-transference," *Internat. J. Psychoanal.* (1949) 30: 69–74; p. 70.
4. Frieda Fromm-Reichmann, *Principles of Intensive Psychotherapy;* Chicago, Univ. of Chicago Press, 1950.
5. Franz Alexander, *Fundamentals of Psychoanlaysis;* New York, Norton, 1948.
6. Sandor Ferenczi, *Further Contributions to the Theory and Technique of Psycho-analysis;* London, Hogarth Press, 1950.
7. Michael Balint, "Changing Therapeutic Aims and Techniques in Psycho-analysis," *Internat. J. Psychoanal.* (1950) 31: 117–124; p. 122.
8. Harry Stack Sullivan, "The Theory of Anxiety and the Nature of Psychotherapy," *Psychiatry* (1949) 12: 3–12; p. 12.

 9. Leo Berman, "Countertransference and Attitudes of the Analyst in the Therapeutic Process," *Psychiatry* (1949) 12: 159–166.
10. Paula Heimann, "On Counter-transference," *Internat. J. Psychoanal.* (1950) 31: 81–84.
11. Annie Reich, "On Counter-transference," *Internat. J. Psychoanal.* (1951) 32: 25–31.
12. Reference note 2; p. 40.
13. Maxwell Gitelson, "The Emotional Position of the Analyst in the Psycho-analytic Situation," *Internat. J. Psychoanal.* (1952) 33: 1–10.
14. Ibid; p. 7.
15. Jurgen Ruesch and A. Rodney Prestwood, "Anxiety," *Arch. Neurol. and Psychiat.* (1949) 62: 1–24.
16. Alexander Halperin, Edward M. Ohaneson, Otto A. Will, Mabel B. Cohen, and Robert A. Cohen, "A Personality Study of Successful Naval Officers," unpublished report to the Office of Naval Research.
17. Fromm-Reichmann, personal communication.
18. Ibid.
19. Reference note 13.
20. Ibid.

6. Human Reactions of Analysts to Patients

Ralph M. Crowley

Analysts have all been patients. When they finish their analyses and stop being patients, they cannot stop being human. If they could, they would not do their patients any good. Yet analysts' emotional reactions to patients are often termed counter-transference with connotations of something disparaging and to be avoided. I believe that the human emotional reactions of analysts to their patients not only cannot be avoided, but can be used to facilitate analytic understanding and progress. They also deserve attention as phenomena worthy of study. Such study and research can cast further light on the nature of the psychoanalytic process.[1]

I use counter-transference to mean those reactions of an analyst to a patient that are inappropriate and irrational. I agree with Mabel Cohen that for counter-transference to be present, anxiety must be aroused in the analyst.[2] As she points out, this definition of counter-transference has the advantage of including all situations where an analyst is unable to be useful to a patient because of difficulties with his own responses.

This way of distinguishing counter-tranference from the totality of an analyst's reactions has its precedent in distinguishing a patient's transference reactions from the totality of his reactions to his analyst. Clara Thompson has pointed out in her paper on transference that not all the reactions a patient has to his analyst are abnormal, inappropriate, irrational, or transferred from somewhere in his past.[3] Some of these reactions are quite germane to the actual analytic situation and to the actual behaviour or character of the analyst. In other words, the reactions are products of rational judgment and rational attitudes and emotions and correspond to the reality of the person of the analyst. Thompson distinguishes these attitudes and reactions from transference. The latter term she reserves for irrational attitudes.

Based on a paper read as part of a symposium on counter-transference held by the William Alanson White Association, New York, December 6, 1950.

Similarly, an analyst may have rational and reality-based feelings and attitudes toward his patient, which I do not include in my use of the term counter-transference.[4] Some authors use that term to include these appropriate, unexaggerated non-defensive, and non-anxious reactions of an analyst to patients.[5] These responses, however, are neither counter, that is, provoked only by the patient, nor are they transference reactions in the sense of being unanalyzed and irrational. They are much neglected. Their significance is belittled and their usefulness to therapy is not realized.[6] Although in practice it is difficult to separate them from counter-transference reactions, I think there is a scientific advantage in so doing. There is also a practical advantage in that such a distinction emphasizes the existence of rational reactions especially when irrational reactions are mixed with them. Since the literature is liberal with illustrations of the irrational counter-transference responses of analysts, I shall not add more here.[7] I shall, however, illustrate the other types, namely, mixed counter-transference–appropriate reactions and the more or less totally appropriate reactions.

Analysts, like others, do have emotional reactions that are almost entirely rational and appropriate. For example, during a session in which a patient is telling a story about himself and his wife, the analyst notices he, himself, is irritated and impatient. He next asks himself why, and he discovers he would like to know the significance the story has for the patient. This leads the analyst to observe the patient's story was wordy, circumstantial, and unduly prolonged. This is something that is normally productive of annoyance in most people, and is an example of a reaction appropriate to the stimulus. As we shall see later, it can be easily utilized to advance therapy.

The following example illustrates a partially appropriate and partially counter-transference reaction. An analyst finds that he has not been listening to the patient and, in fact, feels quite angry, and is thinking, "what a stupid story" or "how can anyone be so boring?" Being an analyst, he realizes that he is not understanding something, and remembers that he often listened to long-winded tales from his father with mounting rage and inability to extricate himself. He sees this is something he has frequently done with this patient, feeling angry, withdrawing, and saying nothing, and that his reaction to him has become in many respects like that he had toward his father and that he has to anyone who tells circumstantial tales. Irrational elements are plain here—the transference from the father to the patient, the character defenses of submitting and becoming enraged and blaming and belittling the other person. It is these elements that make for the analyst's exaggerated anger. Nevertheless, there was also a real provocation. The patient was being long-winded and pointless, and this fact should not be overlooked to the detriment of therapy and to unwarranted loss of self-esteem on the part of the analyst.

To return to the rational reactions of analysts, I wish briefly to illustrate a number of these. An analyst feels sorry for a patient, and discovers from examining his feeling that the way the patient operates with many people is to make them sorry for her as a helpless victim of circumstances. An analyst feels afraid of a certain patient, and a Rorschach shows active homocidal tendencies. An analyst notices sexual phantasies about a patient, who, it turns out, was behaving in coyly seductive ways and having sexual phantasies herself, without mentioning them. Another analyst wonders why he especially liked a certain patient and discovers this patient is the only one in his practice who is really moving in his analysis while all the others are sitting passively waiting for him to get them out of it. Is the analyst's liking for this patient irrational?

An analyst becomes amazed at continued dramatic demands, and discovers that the patient is expressing his impatience at not being able to get over a lifelong problem in a few weeks. It is not counter-transference when an analyst feels astonished at a tale of unrealistic self-damaging aggressive behaviour toward a superior, nor when he is surprised at hearing from a sociologist, who is studying racial relations, of feeling rage against a Negro who held on to the same subway strap with him on a crowded subway. The patient who feels at home with anger will certainly find ways of provoking his analyst to anger.

Several remarks can be made about these rational emotional reactions. First they not only include simple likes and dislikes, and feeling well disposed or angry, but also a great many reactions such as amusement, astonishment, disgust, dismay, pity, fear, tenderness—in fact, all the wonderful possibilities in the varied gamut of human feelings. While I have mentioned mainly emotions and attitudes, appropriate reactions include as well, ideas, opinions, judgments, and phantasies about patients.

Second, many of these reactions have to do with a patient's motives. Theodor Reik states in *Listening with the Third Ear*, that "the nature of an individual's unconscious motives is revealed by the effect of his actions and behaviour on others."[8] I think it is also true that what a person is like generally, not only his unconscious motivations, is revealed by his effect on others. This would then be especially true of his effect on an analyst who is a person trained to observe himself and others. It follows, then that from noticing at any given moment our own reactions with patients, we, as analysts, can learn much about what our patients are really like and what they are doing with us in the analysis.

This brings me to the question of the utilization of rational emotional reactions in psycho-analytic therapy. Since studying this topic I have begun to notice how seldom we and our supervisees seem to use our own emotional reactions in therapy. We are perhaps not aware of them sufficiently, or we may belittle them, or we may not be admitting their existence due to what has been called a paranoid reaction toward one's own counter-transference.

Let me return to one of the examples of appropriate emotional reactions, namely, the irritation in response to the circumstantially told tale. This irritation is valuable in therapy in helping make the analyst aware of what the patient is doing at the moment, namely, being circumstantial. Not only this, the therapist may become aware that this is something the patient does often, that it is a manifestation of his character structure. It can inspire him to go further and wonder 'why' this pointless storytelling—perhaps even ask the patient about it. In this way his attention and that of the patient is called to the fact that the patient does not know why he tells pointless stories and, further, attempts to evade knowing. He does not wish to take responsibility for the meaning of what he says, but leaves all this up to the analyst. With the help of other material, still further exploration of the various facets of the patient's character structure is made possible. In fact, I believe analysis cannot be done successfully in any other way than by use of the analyst's own personal reactions to the material—otherwise his comments and interpretations are bound to be mediocre.

Similarly, any counter-transference feeling can be so used, including those exaggeratedly irrational and defensive reactions. In these, it is tremendously important for the analyst to burrow through the exaggerated parts of his reactions to the healthy rational substratum, and not to be distracted from doing this by the conventional evaluation of his personal reactions as valueless, useless, harmful, or as a reflection on the completeness of his analysis. For example, the irrational anger at aimlessness must not be dismissed as foolish and inappropriate. The anger may be inappropriate in great part. This must be recognized, and then the anger must be used to detect what the patient did to provoke it and exactly why, as one would in a reaction that was entirely rational and appropriate.

So far I have discussed utilizing emotional reactions to one's patient only in terms of revealing something about the patient or his part in the emotional climate of the analysis. Another possibility is that of revealing to the patient something about the analyst and his part in the analysis at the moment. Heimann states that the analyst's feelings should not be communicated to the patient on the basis that they would constitute a burden to him.[9] This, however, is not always the case. Often the patient is aware, at least dimly, of his analyst's feelings, whether communicated or not, and it is helpful for the patient to know that the analyst knows these feelings, too. Such revelation may be a help in reassuring the patient as to his power of testing reality, leading to the reassuring feeling, "I am not entirely crazy." It can help make real the fact that complete rationality is a phantastic goal and that an analyst is human, not superhuman.[10]

Another type of appropriate feeling for patients that is not directly provoked by what patients are or what they do or by how they are currently motivated toward the analyst (although it is not unrelated to these) is the interest in people which analysts bring to their work, if it has not been too trained out of them. Healthy analysts are naturally interested in people. Discussion arose in a small group as to what makes for a person's choosing the discipline of analysis rather than, for example, dentistry. There was much learned discussion and then one of the group asked, "Is my conception too naive? I always thought people went into dentistry because they were interested in teeth, and that they went into analysis because they were interested in people." And 'people' include analysts' patients.

This interest in patients is not unrelated to what the analyst can perceive of the actual character of his patient. For example, an analyst who sees his patient as basically aggressive and destructive, and, at times, with good reason, cannot be interested in helping that patient. If he sees in this aggression a fearful, trapped child who, when he has a chance to be uninvolved, is really a warm person, the analyst's interest is aroused. Now that we have established that analysts do have an interest in helping their patients, would it not be natural that, in some instances, analysts will not only discuss helpfully patients' problems, but also take appropriate action when necessary? Yet taking action is often belittled as an evidence of counter-transference just as a patient's action in giving his analyst a gift is belittled as transference when it often expresses, at least in part, an appropriate sentiment of regard for the analyst's helpfulness.

This helpfulness may be simply that of the analysis itself or may also include extra-analytic help. There are indications for an analyst's helping a patient extra-analytically. It is not irrational counter-transference that makes an analyst call his patient's attention to behaviour destructive to himself, and even forbid it. An extremely anxiety-ridden patient who had been involved in a homo-sexual incident, could not, himself, deal with a blackmailer to whom the patient, between two analytic hours, had given $800. Although the analyst ascertained it was personally safe for the patient to go to the district attorney's office, the patient was too afraid to go. The analyst refused to continue analysis unless either the patient or he went to the district attorney. The patient finally allowed the analyst to go, the blackmailing was nipped in the bud, and the analysis began, for the first time, to take shape. The patient's tremendous anxieties lessened to the extent that he became able to take some charge of his own life.

There are other less dramatic ways in which one may wish to help patients; for example to have an hour in the home during illness, to carry a patient through an unemployed period without fee, to demand that the patient consult a doctor about his health, to bring a doctor to a physically ill patient or to suggest that he stay home from an analytic hour when he has a cold. There are countless other examples that any analyst may recall from his own experience.

I wish now to mention another situation—that of the analysis of a patient who has been a friend prior to analysis. While for good reason one may not have any social relations with certain patients, it is not irrational counter-transference if, in appropriate situations, one has a social relationship with a patient and gives concrete evidence of one's attitudes toward him such as what one likes or does not like about him, what interests one shares with him and which ones are not shared. This real relationship some patients cannot stand, but in many instances it can serve as an immense help both in reducing the analyst to his proper proportions in the eyes of the patient and in increasing his stature when the patient harbours irrational belittling and negative attitudes toward his analyst.

It has been pointed out that transference is the chief means available for making the patient conscious of his unconscious trends. I should like to point out that study of the analyst's feelings and attitudes toward his patient is a much-neglected means of achieving the same purpose. I find it valuable to ask a patient to become aware of my attitudes and feelings about him. I ask him this: "Now what do you think I really think of you?" or "How do you think I regard you?" This calls the patient's attention to hitherto-unnoticed aspects of his personality that are affecting other people, including his analyst. It may also call attention to unnoticed tendencies in the analyst that are affecting the patient.

Emotional reactions of analyst to patients are shown to be ever present and as little to be avoided as are transference reactions of patients to analysts. Their study promises to shed much light on such questions as the nature of analytic cure, and how an analysis ends, if it does.[11] Their precise utilization in practice leaves much room for clinical and technical exploration. Both types of study should lead to a more rational and scientific attitude on the part of analysts and their students to their counter-transference phenomena, and eventually, to the disappearance of a paranoid attitude of avoidance and condemnation.

NOTES

1. Mabel Blake Cohen: "Counter-Transference and Anxiety," *Psychiatry*, XV, 1952, p. 231. This paper is a beginning toward such research in that it advances the theory that counter-transference reactions are characterized by anxiety on the part of the analyst.
2. *Loc. cit.*, Mabel Blake Cohen.
3. Clara Thompson: "Transference as a Therapeutic Instrument," *Psychiatry*, VIII, 1945, p. 273.
4. There is wide variation among psycho-analysts in their definition and use of the term counter-transference. *Loc cit.*, Mabel Blake Cohen; Leo Berman: "Counter-Transference and Attitudes of the Analyst in the Therapeutic Process," *Psychiatry*, XII, 1949, p. 159; Maxwell Gitelson: "The Emotional Position of the Analyst in the Psycho-analytic Situation," *Int. J. Psa*, XXXIII, 1952, p. 1; Edith Weigert: "Contribution to the Problem of Terminating Psycho-analysis," *Psa. Quart.*, XXI, 1952.
5. P. Heimann: "On Counter-Transference," *Int. J. Psa.*, XXXI, 1950, p. 80. Here the term counter-transference is used "to cover all the feelings that the analyst experiences toward his patient," p. 81.
6. The following recent papers are exceptions to this statement and stress the unavoidability and usefulness of the analysts' emotional reactions: Izette deForest: "The Significance of Counter-Transference in Psycho-analytic Therapy," *Psa. Rev.*, XXXVIII, 1951, p. 158; *loc. cit.*, P. Heimann; Margaret Little: "Counter-Transference and the Patient's Response to It," *Int. J. Psa.*, XXXII, 1951, p. 32; *loc. cit.*, Maxwell Gitelson; *loc. cit.*, Edith Weigert.
7. Annie Reich: "On Counter-Transference," *Int. J. Psa.* XXXII, 1951; *loc. cit.*, Maxwell Gitelson; *loc. cit.*, Margaret Little.
8. Theodor Reik: *Listening with the Third Ear*, Farrar, Straus & Co., New York, 1949, p. 487.
9. *Loc cit.*, P. Heimann, p. 83.
10. For a more detailed discussion of indications for such revelations and the dangers involved: *loc. cit.*, Mabel Blake Cohen; *loc. cit.*, Izette deForest; *loc. cit.*, Maxwell Gitelson; *loc. cit.*, Margaret Little; *loc. cit.*, Edith Weigert.
11. *Loc. cit.*, Edith Weigert. Weigert makes just such use of study of counter-transference phenomena to throw light on problems of terminating analyses.

7. Transference and Countertransference: A Historical Survey

Douglass W. Orr

COUNTERTRANSFERENCE: DEFINITIONS

Although the concept of transference, from the point of view of definition, offers some semblance of evolutionary progression to something commanding wide agreement among psychoanalysts, the same cannot be said of countertransference. Definitions of countertransference have varied almost from the first discussions of it, and there remains today widespread disagreement as to what the term comprises. The following can claim to be little more than a catalogue of points of view.

Freud (1910) introduces the term in "The Future Prospects of Psycho-Analytic Therapy":

> . . . We have begun to consider the "counter-transference," which arises in the physician as a result of the patient's influence on his unconcious feelings, and have nearly come to the point of requiring the physician to recognize and overcome this countertransference in himself. . . . Anyone who cannot succeed in this self-analysis may without more ado regard himself as unable to treat neurotics by analysis [19].

In "Observations on Transference-Love," Freud (1915) says of a patient's tendency to fall in love with successive physicians:

> To the physician it represents an invaluable explanation and a useful warning against any tendency to counter-transference which may be lurking in his own mind. He must recognize that the patient's falling in love is induced by the analytic situation and is not to be ascribed to the charms of his person. . . . And it is always well to be reminded of this [25, p. 379].

Freud continues, in this paper, to warn against any attempt to influence the transference by partial gratification and then goes on to develop his well-

---

The first section of this article, which deals with the concept of transference, has been deleted here. The reference for the complete article is: Orr, D. Transference and countertransference: A historical survey. *J. Amer. Psychoanal. Assoc.*, 2: 621–670, 1954.

known dictum that the treatment must be carried through in a "state of abstinence."

On June 3, 1923, at a meeting of the American Psychoanalytic Association, Adolph Stern read one of the first papers—if not the first—dealing extensively with the subject of countertransference which he defines as "the transference that the analyst makes to the patient" (53, p. 167). He continues:

Theoretically, the counter-transference on the part of the analyst has the same origin as the transferences on the part of the patient; namely, in the repressed, infantile material of the analyst. By the same law, it may manifest itself in any form that the transference does. Practically, however, owing to the previous training that the analyst has undergone, his theoretical knowledge and his actual clinical experience reduce considerably the field of activity of the countertransference in comparison with the protean forms which the transference takes in patients [53, pp. 168f.)]

Stern also differentiates libidinous from ego components in the countertransferences and illustrates various unanalyzed problems in analysts that may give rise to countertransference difficulties.

Ferenczi and Rank, from whom Stern may well have drawn some of his ideas, add to the definition of countertransference:

The narcissism of the analyst seems suited to create a particularly fruitful source of mistakes; among others the development of a kind of narcissistic countertransference which provokes the person being analyzed into pushing into the foreground certain things which flatter the analyst and, on the other hand, into suppressing remarks and associations of an unpleasant nature in relation to him [14, pp. 41f.].

It will be noted in the references already cited that there is an explicit or implied difference in the concept of countertransference as simply a reaction to the patient's transference as distinguished from the analyst's own transference to the patient for whatever reasons and arising from his own unresolved neurotic difficulties. This distinction becomes a persistent theme in later contributions.

E. Glover (1927) devotes considerable space to the subject of countertransference in his published "Lectures on Technique in Psycho-Analysis" (36, pp. 504–520). He distinguishes positive and negative countertransference as well as countertransference and counterresistance. Both are defined for the most part in terms of reactions to patients' transference reactions, particularly in the transference neurosis, but other determinants in the psychology of the analyst are referred to. Glover's discussion adds little to the definition of countertransference, but presents a wealth of technical information.

Healy, Bronner, and Bowers (1930) seem to tread warily:

> What is spoken of as "counter-transference" must also be reckoned with in connection with the analytic situation. By this is meant impulses on the part of the analyst to respond to the patient's affectional trends. Schilder thinks that there is operative here an important psychological law regulating human relations and that the patient's feelings will of necessity call for complementary ones on the part of the analyst . . .[37, p. 444].

Reich (1933) does not define countertransference, but he does discuss countertransference problems, and assumes that they arise from the personal difficulties of the analyst (48, pp. 136–140).

Fenichel (1936) notes that little has been written about the important and practical subject of countertransference. Nor does he undertake to define the term. An implied definition is found, however, in the following:

> The analyst like the patient can strive for direct satisfactions from the analytic relationship as well as make use of the patient for some piece of "acting out" determined by the analyst's past. Experience shows that the libidinal strivings of the analyst are much less dangerous than his narcissistic needs and defenses against anxieties. Little is said about this subject probably because nothing can act as a protection against such misuse of analysis except the effectivenss of the analyst's own analysis and his honesty with himself [11, p. 73].

English and Pearson (1937) give a diffuse definition of countertransference, but one that is followed by others in the literature: "It is impossible for the physician not to have some attitude toward the patient, and this is called *countertransference*" (10). In other words, *everything* that the analyst feels toward his patient is countertransference.

In her book, *New Ways in Psychoanalysis,* Karen Horney (1939) dealt with the concept of countertransference much as she does with that of transference. She deplores a one-sided preoccupation with infantile conflicts and the compulsive repetition of these in adult life. She says:

> The principle that the analyst's emotional reactions should be understood as a "countertransference" may be objected to on the same grounds as the concept of transference. According to this principle, when an analyst reacts with inner irritation to a patient's tendency to defeat his efforts, he may be identifying the patient with his own father, and thus repeating an infantile situation in which he felt defeated by the father. If, however, the analyst's emotional reactions are understood in the light of his own character structure as it is affected by the patient's actual behavior, it will be seen that

his irritation may have arisen because he has, for example, the fantastic notion that he must be able to cure every case and hence feels it a personal humiliation if he does not succeed . . . [40, p. 166].

Horney appears, here, to define countertransference in terms of the analyst's narcissistic or other neurotic reactions to the "actual behavior" of the patient or to such characterological constellations as neurotic ambition or masochistic dependency. In this she was certainly anticipated by Ferenczi, Stern, E. Glover, and W. Reich, but they did not find it necessary to minimize the importance of unresolved infantile conflicts.

The Balints (1939) examine a hallowed precept: "If and when the analyst has influenced the transference situation by any means other than his interpretations, he has made a grave mistake." They point out that the analyst, in fact, impresses himself upon the patient in countless ways—the nature and arrangement of his office, the hardness or softness of his couch, his way of covering or not covering the pillow, the frequency, timing, affective emphasis, and even diction of his interpretations and, indeed, his whole way of working, some of which in itself is likely to be a carry-over from the transference to his own training analyst—and it is the sum total of these and other, subtle or not so subtle, influences, coloring, if not markedly affecting, the patient's transference, that the Balints call countertransference. They add:

Looked at from this point of view the analytical situation is the result of an interplay between the patient's transferences and the analyst's counter-transference, complicated by the reactions released in each by the other's transference on to him. If this is so—and it really is so—are we to conclude that there is no such thing as the "sterile" method of analyzing? That the opinion quoted at the beginning of this paper is based on an ideal never attained in practice? Formerly belief in the absolute validity of the mirror-like attitude was so firm that contesting it was liable to be regarded as a sign of desertion. And now—not only in the present paper—the very possibility of such an attitude is challenged. . . .

The second opinion would lead one to expect that the different analytic atmospheres created by the analyst's personality would exercise a decisive influence upon the actual transference situation and consequently upon the therapeutic results as well. Curiously enough, this does not seem to be so. Our patients, with very few exceptions, are able to adapt themselves to most of these individual atmospheres and to proceed with their own transference, almost undisturbed by the analyst's countertransference. This implies that all of these techniques are good enough to enable patients to build up a transference which is favourable to analytic work. . . . We have not forgotten, of course, that our technique has first to comply with the objective demands of our work and naturally cannot be only an outlet for the emotions of the analyst. . . . The objective task demands that a patient analysed in any of the many individual ways shall learn to know his own unconscious mind and not that of his analyst. The subjective task demands that analysing shall not be too heavy an emotional burden, that the individual variety of technique shall procure sufficient emotional outlet for the analyst . . . [5, pp. 228–229].

Sharpe (1947) uses the term *countertransference* to include both conscious and unconscious reactions of analyst to patient:

"Counter-transference" is often spoken of as if it implied a love-attitude. The counter-transference that is likely to cause trouble is the unconscious one on the analyst's side, whether it be an infantile negative or positive one or both in alternation. The unconscious transference is the infantile one and when unconscious will blind the analyst to the various aspects of the patient's transference. . . . We deceive ourselves if we think we have no countertransference. It is its nature that matters. We can hardly hope to carry on an analysis unless our own counter-transference is healthy, and that healthiness depends upon the nature of satisfactions we obtain from the work, the deep unconscious satisfactions that lie behind the reality ones of earning a living, and the hope of effecting cures [50, p. 4].

Another set of distinctions is suggested by Winnicott (1949):

One could classify counter-transference phenomena thus:
(1) Abnormality in counter-transference feelings, and set relationships and identifications that are under repression in the analyst. The comment on this is that the analyst needs more analysis. . . .
(2) The identifications and tendencies belonging to an analyst's personal experiences and personal development which provide the positive setting for his analytic work and makes his work different in quality from that of any other analyst.
(3) From these two I distinguish the truly objective counter-transference, or if that be difficult, the analyst's love and hate in reaction to the actual personality and behavior of the patient, based on objective observation [55, pp. 69f.].

Winnicott thus subsumes conscious and unconscious, normal and neurotic reactions on the analyst's part under the concept of countertransference.

Berman (1949) distinguishes countertransference from attitudes in the therapeutic process:

In this paper, "countertransference" means the analyst's reactions to the patient as though the patient were an important figure in the analyst's past life. By "attitudes" I mean the emotional reactions of the analyst as a person during the treatment hour, including his reasonable and appropriate emotional responses and his characteristic defenses. It is assumed that the totality of the analyst's emotional reactions, as in all interpersonal relationships, represents a blending, to a varying degree, of appropriate, defensive, and transference responses to the patient, but that the appropriate ones largely predominate [7, p. 159].

Heimann (1950) objects to such distinctions:

For the purpose of this paper I am using the term "counter-transference" to cover all the feelings which the analyst experiences towards his patient.
It may be argued that this use of the term is not correct, and that counter-transference simply means transference on the part of the analyst. However, I would suggest that the prefix "counter" implies additional factors [38, p. 81].

Fromm-Reichmann (1950) summarizes a trend that was given impetus by Harry Stack Sullivan and is seen to some extent also in contributions of Karen Horney, Clara Thompson, and "the Chicago school":

Recently the significant vicissitudes of the psychiatrist's relationship to his patients has been brought increasingly into the focus of therapeutic attention. This holds true for its transferred and for its factual aspects. . . . H. S. Sullivan has introduced the term "parataxis" instead of "transference" and "countertransference." Parataxic interpersonal experiences are distortions in people's present interpersonal relationships. They are conditioned by carryovers of a person's previous interpersonal experiences prevalently from infancy and childhood but not always or necessarily from entanglements with his parents [32, pp. 5–6].

Having mentioned "the Chicago school," I should add, as a matter of interest, that the term *countertransference* does not appear in the well-known book by Alexander and French (1946). The principle of flexibility advocated by these authors may include control or manipulation of the transference as well as other technical maneuvers designed to effect a "corrective emotional experience." The deliberate assumption of certain attitudes or roles by the therapist might, according to some definitions, be considered "countertransference"—and might actually be *caused by* countertransference (the unconscious variety) in some instances—but these possibilities are not discussed in the work cited (4).

Annie Reich (1951) excludes the analyst's conscious reactions from her definition of countertransference:

Counter-transference thus comprises the effects of the analyst's own unconscious needs and conflicts on his understanding or technique. In such cases the patient represents for the analyst an object of the past on to whom past feelings and wishes are projected, just as it happens in the patient's transference situation with the analyst. The provoking factor for such an occurrence may be something in the patient's personality or material or something in the analytic situation as such. This is counter-transference in the proper sense. . . . [The concept of countertransference may also be understood in a much wider sense to include] all expressions of the analyst's using the analysis for acting-out purposes. We speak of acting out whenever the activity of analysing has an unconscious meaning for the analyst. Then his response to the patient, frequently his whole handling of the analytic situation, will be motivated by hidden unconscious tendencies. Though the patients in these cases are frequently not real objects to whom something is transferred but only the tools by means of which some needs of the analyst, such as to allay anxiety or to master guilt feelings, are gratified, we have used the term counter-transference. This seemed to us advisable because this type of behavior is so frequently mixed up and fused with the effects of counter-transference proper that it becomes too schematic to keep the two groups apart [47, p. 26].

A. Reich points out further that the phenomena of countertransference proper occur suddenly, under specific circumstances and with certain patients. She therefore calls this "acute countertransference." The other type, representing the expression of a habitual need of the analyst and therefore an aspect of his character, she calls "chronic countertransference." The former, again, is "countertransference proper"; the latter, an "acting-out type of countertrans-ference."

According to Little (1951), the term countertransference is used to mean "any or all of the following":

(a) The analyst's unconscious attitude to the patient.
(b) Repressed elements, hitherto unanalyzed, in the analyst himself which attach to the patient in the same way as the patient "transfers" to the analyst affects, etc., belonging to his parents or to the objects of his childhood: i.e., the analyst regards the patient (temporarily and varyingly) as he regarded his own parents.
(c) Some specific attitude or mechanism with which the analyst needs the patient's transference.
(d) The whole of the analyst's attitudes and behaviour towards his patient. This includes all the others and any conscious attitudes as well [41, p. 32].

Little discusses principally the second of the above:

Repressed counter-transference is a product of the unconscious part of the analyst's ego, that part which is nearest and most closely belonging to the id and least in contact with reality. It follows from this that the repetition compulsion is readily brought to bear on it; but other ego activities besides repression play a part in its development, of which the synthetic or integrative activity is most important. As I see it, counter-transference is one of those compromise formations in the making of which the ego shows such surprising skill; it is in this respect essentially of the same order as a neurotic symptom, a perversion or a sublimation. In it libidinal gratification is partly forbidden and partly accepted; an element of aggression is woven in with both the gratification and the prohibition, and the distribution of the aggression determines the relative proportions of each. Since counter-transference, like transfer-ence, is concerned with another person, the mechanisms of projection and introjection are of special importance [41, p. 33].

Yet another point of view is expressed by Gitelson (1952) who differentiates (1) reactions to the patient as a whole from (2) reactions to partial aspects of the patient. The former are defined as transferences, the latter countertransferences:

It is my impression that total reactions to a patient are *transferences* of the analyst to his patients and are revivals of ancient transference potentials. These may be manifested in the over-all attitude towards patients as a class or may exacerbate in the "whole response" to particular patients. These attitudes may be positively or negatively toned. They are likely to manifest themselves very early in the contact with a patient and determine the tendency of the analyst towards the whole case. . . . Finally, they undermine the possibility of the inner reconstruction that analysis can provide. . . .

In contrast to transference, the counter-transferences of the analyst appear later and occur in the context of an established analytic situation. They comprise the analyst's reactions to (1) the patient's transference, (2) the material that the patient brings in, and (3) the reactions of the patient to the analyst as a person. . . . [When it happens that the analysis touches on unresolved problems in the analyst,] then we can expect the same type of *emergency response* as we see in patients when they unexpectedly encounter something new in themselves. . . . I think that this means that the analyst remains liable to need to resort to *emergency defense reactions* and that such reactions are at the center of the analytic phenomenon which we call "counter-transference" [34, pp. 4–6].

Having reviewed most of the pertinent literature, Mabel Cohen (1952) says:

In summary, then, we see that the recent studies on counter-transference have included in their concepts attitudes of the therapist which are both conscious and unconscious; attitudes which are responses both to the real and to the fantasied attributes of the patient; attitudes which are stimulated by unconscious needs of the analyst and attitudes which are stimulated by sudden outbursts of affect on the part of the patient; attitudes which arise from responding to the patient as though he were some previously important person in the analyst's life; and attitudes which do not use the patient as a real object but rather as a tool for the gratification of some unconscious need. This group of responses covers a tremendously wide territory, yet it does not include, of course, all of the analyst's responses to the patient. . . . [8, pp. 232f.].

Cohen asks on what common ground are the above attitudes singled out to be called countertransference? She answers: "It seems to this writer that the common factor in the above responses is the presence of anxiety in the therapist—whether recognized in awareness or defended against and kept out of awareness" (8, p. 235). She then continues by proposing an operational definition as follows:

When, in the patient-analyst relationship, anxiety is aroused in the analyst with the effect that communication between the two is interfered with by some alteration in the analyst's behavior (verbal or otherwise), then countertransference is present [8, p. 235].

Anxiety-arousing situations, evoking countertransferences thus defined, may be classified as follows:

(1) Situational factors—that is, reality factors such as intercurrent events in the analyst's life; and also, social factors such as need for success and recognition as a competent therapist. (2) Unresolved neurotic problems of the therapist. (3) Communication of the patient's anxiety to the therapist [8, p. 236].

The most recent contribution to be considered here is that of Fliess (1953) who further delineates the concept of countertransference by distinguishing it from counteridentification. He holds to a traditional view of the former, as follows:

If consistency of designation is required to identify a concept unambiguously, the term "countertransference" must, by virtue of its definition be reserved for the equivalent, in the analyst, of what is termed "transference" in the patient. It is then immediately obvious that countertransference is not, as in transference, an occurrence desirable and prerequisite to the treatment, but undesirable and a hindrance. . . . [15, p. 268].

Fliess points out that countertransference, if its regressive nature is to be understood, will be expected to be in part counteridentification; "it is the clinical coexistence of the two that necessitates their discussion under one title, and that allows one to anticipate . . . a defective identification behind the defective object relation" (15, p. 279). As for the nature of counteridentification:

The analyst's faulty involvement with his patients is that found in *folie à deux: the identification is mutual, a response of the analyst to the patient's identifying with him, and repetitive in both patient and analyst of an early "constituent" identification.* This term, designed to denote those identifications which the ego does not merely contain but of which it consists, is employed here in order to show that a counter-identification, regressive as it is, interferes with the nonregressive identification, which, as "empathy," represents a particular phase of the analyst's work [15, pp. 279f.].

COUNTERTRANSFERENCE: TECHNICAL HANDLING

Discussion of the technical handling of countertransference inevitably varies with differences in definition of the concept itself. Is countertransference simply the analyst's response to the *patient's transference,* and does this mean his conscious response, his unconscious response or both? Or does it mean the *analyst's transference reactions* to the patient, whether to his transference, to other attributes of the patient or to the patient as a whole? Or does countertransference include all attitudes and feelings of the analyst toward the patient whatever they are and whatever may give rise to them? Does it also include attitudes consciously assumed or roles deliberately planned and enacted in order to effect a corrective emotional experience? Does it, indeed, as the Balints suggest, comprise everything the analyst brings to the analytic situation—his office, his technique, and all that he was, is, and ever hopes to be?

Freud (1910) recognizes the patient's influence on the analyst's *unconscious* feelings, and strongly advises the analyst to recognize and overcome these feelings by extending and deepening his own self-analysis (19). Later, however, Freud (1915) makes passing reference to the fully conscious feelings. Following a discussion of the choices open to the analyst in dealing with the transference love of his patients, Freud concludes: "In my opinion, therefore, it is not permissible to disavow the indifference one has developed by keeping the counter-transference in check" (25, p. 383). And, in a sort of primer of "don't's" for beginners in psychoanalysis, Cole (1922) says:

Don't fail to note signs of a counter transference. These will be found in the analyst's dreams and should be dealt with immediately. A counter transference means the need for further analysis for the analyst. "The analyst can proceed in the analysis only so far as he is analyzed himself" (Freud) [9, p. 44].

Whether he considers it countertransference or not, Freud (1923) notes the importance of the analyst's personality in the therapeutic situation. Speaking of the difficulties of analyzing an unconscious sense of guilt, Freud says:

. . . Perhaps it may depend, too, on whether the personality of the analyst allows of the patient's putting him in the place of his ego-ideal, and this involves a temptation for the analyst to play the part of prophet, saviour, and redeemer to the patient. Since the rules of analysis are diametrically opposed to the physician's making use of his personality in any such manner, it must be honestly confessed that here we have another limitation to the effectiveness of analysis; after all, analysis does not set out to abolish the possibility of morbid reactions, but to give the patient's ego *freedom* to choose one way or the other [29, p. 72].

This remarkable passage would appear to state the central issue in much current controversy as to the essential nature of psychoanalysis, especially as to technique!

Stern (1923) takes the traditional view that countertransference interferes with the analytic process:

In the foregoing only the most commonly met with situations likely to give rise to a counter-transference have been considered. True, in some respects the difficulty in the situation may be ascribed to faulty technique. But it was pointed out that the cause of the faulty technique lies frequently in the fact that the analyst, owing to his own resistances, has reacted to the unconsciously determined activities of the patient as if they were consciously determined, and taking place in the present; especially in the fact that the analyst misinterpreted the phenomena of the transference [53, p. 174].

Clearly, the moral is more analysis for the analyst.

As noted above, E. Glover's lectures (1927) contain a wealth of technical suggestions. He points out that even the well-analyzed analyst is by no means invulnerable to the impact of the patient's material, particularly in the transference neurosis; "hence, even if we make the greatest allowance for a hypothetical state of being thoroughly analyzed,' it is evident that at least some analytical 'toilet' is a part of the analyst's necessary routine . . . " (36, p. 507). Glover suggests that the danger signals of countertransference have much in common with the general indications of resistance in any analytic situation, but with distinctive features related to the specialized nature of the analyst's activities. After discussing various technical pitfalls, especially those related to the analyst's narcissistic or sadistic tendencies, Glover adds:

. . . *what distinguishes analytic technique proper from the gratification of uncon-scious attitudes is its adaptation to the unconscious requirements of the patient. Indications for self-inspection are: that we act always in a stereotyped way or that we cannot immediately justify our interventions or silences on good analytical grounds. We cannot go far wrong if we always know not only why we intervene or are silent, but also what effect we hope to produce by so doing. A third indication is that we cannot explain to ourselves satisfactorily why a patient is still in difficulty.* These considerations allow us ample latitude to alter our procedure in difficult or exceptional cases, the criterion being that we are fully aware of the significance of our change in technique and the effects it may produce [36, pp. 513f.].

It is of especial interest that Glover distinguishes and discusses countertransference phenomena and technical difficulties in terms of different stages of ego and libido development, and that he illustrates the insidious as well as the more blatant problems, all of which, as he says, call for eternal vigilance and "that constant attitude of individual watchfulness which we have described as the 'analyst's toilet' " (36, p. 520).

W. Reich (1933) likewise assumes that countertransference difficulties arise from the personal problems of the analyst, and he mentions particularly those related to the analyst's repressed aggression, his inability to tolerate the patient's sexuality, his tendency to experience the patient's transference narcissistically and his inability to control sadism expressed in the famous "analytic silence" (48, p. 137). He adds, however:

. . . it is a mistake to interpret the general analytic rule that one has to approach the patient as a blank screen onto which he projects his transferences in such a manner that one assumes, always and in every case, an unalive, mummy-like attitude. Under such circumstances, few patients can "thaw out," and this leads to artificial, un-analytic measures. It should be clear that one approaches an aggressive patient unlike a masochistic one, a hyperactive hysteric unlike a depressive one, that one changes one's attitude to one and the same patient according to the situation, that, in brief, one does not behave neurotically oneself, even though one may have to deal with some neurotic difficulties in oneself.

One cannot give up one's own individuality, a fact which one will consider in the choice of patients. But one should be able to expect that this individuality is not a disturbing factor and that the training analysis should establish the necessary minimum in plasticity of character [48, p. 139].

Fenichel (1936) agrees with Reich's last point, noting that the fear of the countertransference may lead an analyst to the suppression of all human freedom in his own reactions to patients. Patients sometimes have the impression, he adds, "that an analyst is a special creation and is not permitted to be human! Just the opposite impression should prevail. The patient should always be able to rely upon the humanness of the analyst. The analyst is no more permitted to isolate analysis from life than is a patient who misuses lying on an analytic couch for the same purpose of isolation" (11, p. 74).

English and Pearson (1937) express in popular terms the prevailing view of the mid-1930's:

. . . The good psychotherapist . . . is able and willing to conceal any feelings he may have beyond desire to help the patient. Overt pity, sympathy, criticism, intolerance, affection, etc., are best kept out of the attitude of the psychotherapist. His role is to skillfully and tactfully mirror the patient's emotions and conflicts in such a way that the patient will see their origin and the futility of their endless repetition. The good psychotherapist must necessarily keep out of the therapeutic relationship any personal prejudices he may have upon arbitrary social questions such as divorce, contraception, religious belief. His attitude may be inquiring but impartial . . . [10, p. 303].

In a discussion of the contraindication for psychoanalytic treatment, Fenichel (1945) mentions contraindications to anaylsis with a particular analyst and points out that difficulties in treatment may be due to the analyst. Any analyst, he says, may be more effective with some types of patients than with others, but:

. . . this difference should never reach a degree at which work with certain personalities becomes entirely impossible. An analyst has to have the width of empathy to work with any type. If the reality in this respect differs too much from the ideal state of affairs, the mistake may be the analyst's; it may be rooted either directly in a negative countertransference or in a disappointment because a certain type of patient does not fulfill some expectation that the analyst unduly and unconsciously connects with his work; in such cases the analyst himself should be analyzed more thoroughly [12, p. 580].

In his book, *Technique of Psychoanalytic Therapy,* Lorand (1946) mentions various countertransference feelings, and then adds: "All such feelings can disturb the treatment unless the analyst is able to refrain from displaying them. Lack of such control is always due to unresolved problems within the unconscious of the analyst" (42, p. 209). He cites Freud's admonitions to this effect and Ferenczi's teaching that one of the most important functions of the analyst is his ability to handle the countertransference. Lorand uses ample clinical material to illustrate two points: (1) that the analyst must be constantly aware of his countertransference, be his feelings friendly or antagonistic, and (2) that the analysis is especially endangered by *unrecognized* countertransference attitudes (43).

Although Winnicott's article (1949) deals particularly with the treatment of psychotics, the author apparently holds that the same principles may apply in the analysis of others as well. Two passages will illustrate Winnicott's point of view:

I suggest that if an analyst is to analyse psychotics or anti-socials he must be able to be so thoroughly aware of his counter-transference that he can sort out and study his *objective* reactions to the patient. These will include hate. Counter-transference phenomena will at all times be the important things in the analysis [55, p. 70].
. . . I believe an analysis is incomplete if even towards the end it has not been possible for the analyst to tell the patient what he, the analyst, did unbeknown for the patient whilst he was ill, in the early stages. Until the interpretation is made the patient is kept to some extent in the position of the infant, one who cannot understand what he owes to his mother [55, p. 74].

During the past ten years the psychoanalytic literature on the subject of countertransference—variously defined—has dealt with several principal themes; some old, some new: (1) the analyst as "mirror" vs. the analyst as "human being"; (2) the question of whether the analyst stays out of the analysis as much as is humanly possible, except for the work of interpretation, in order to facilitate development of the transference neurosis or whether he intervenes more actively in order to attenuate the transference, to manipulate it or to assume attitudes or play roles designed to provide the patient with a more healthy interpersonal experience than he has known before; and finally (3) when inevitable countertransference feelings or situations develop, whether or not to communicate these to the patient, together with a partial or complete analysis of them in order to mitigate or undo their effects. The technical material of the papers yet to be considered is in some instances so detailed that only the general points of view can be indicated.

Berman (1949) detects a paradox in the writings of Freud and other analysts, and suggests: "The answer could simply be that the analyst is always both the cool detached surgeon-like operator on the patient's psychic tissues, and the warm, human, friendly, helpful physician. I think that such an answer is essentially correct" (7, pp. 160f.). But the matter is not easily disposed of. The problem is:

. . . how to integrate into the body of psychoanalytic knowledge, theory and technique, the awareness, clinically, that the analytic situation is, in a sense, a personal one for the analyst, and most if not all patients either dimly sense this fact or have occasion to observe it quite directly. It seems to be disturbing to realize and face fully how cathected, and sometimes highly cathected, the patient and his analysis may be for the analyst [7, pp. 160f.].

Berman then describes the *dedication* that characterizes the attitude of the effective analyst toward his patients, "in the sense of the dedication of the good leader and fond parent that makes an analyst's attitudes of kindly acceptance, patience and so on, genuine and effective" (7, p. 161). Berman believes that much of therapeutic value comes from the patient's testing of the analyst, provided that the analyst handles himself well:

In brief, I think it is in the patient's experience of the *process* through which the analyst under stress achieves realistic and well-integrated functioning that an important therapeutic factor is to be found. The sound functioning the analyst has found prior to his work with a given patient may not ring very true to this patient until he has, to refer again to the military analogy, exposed the analyst to a fresh baptism of fire [7, pp. 162f.]. [Finally] In regard to the technical question of how open and truthful the analyst should be about his various feelings toward the patient in order to provide the emotional experience the patient requires, it seems that the verbal expression of such feelings is needed only infrequently and to a limited extent [7, p. 165]. [In dealing with certain defenses, however,] . . . it may be necessary for the analyst to express himself verbally as to his feelings toward the patient [7, p. 165].

Paula Heimann (1950) summarizes her position as follows:

In my view Freud's demand that the analyst must "recognize and master" his counter-transference does not lead to the conclusion that the counter-transference is a disturbing factor and that the analyst must become unfeeling and detached, but that he must use his emotional response as a key to the patient's unconscious. This will protect him from entering as a co-actor on the scene which the patient re-enacts in the analytic relationship and from exploiting it for his own needs. At the same time he will find ample stimulus for taking himself to task again and again and for continuing the analysis of his own problems. This, however, is his private affair, and I do not consider it right for the analyst to communicate his feelings to his patient. In my view such honesty is more in the nature of a confession and a burden to the patient. In any case it leads away from the analysis. The emotions roused in the analyst will be of value to his patient, if used as one more source of insight into the patient's unconscious conflicts and defenses; and when these are interpreted and worked through, the enduring changes in the patient's ego include the strengthening of his reality sense so that he sees his analyst as a human being, not a god or a demon, and the "human" relationship in the analytic situation follows without the analyst's having recourse to extra-analytic means [38, pp. 83–84].

Fromm-Reichmann (1950) also stresses the importance of the therapist's self-awareness:

. . . Every psychiatrist now knows that there must be a fluctuating interplay between doctor and patient. This inevitably follows from the interpersonal character of the psychotherapeutic process. The psychiatrist who is trained in the observation and inner realization of his reactions to patient's manifestations can frequently utilize these reactions as a helpful instrument in understanding otherwise hidden implications in patient's communications. Thus the therapist's share in the reciprocal transference reactions of doctor and patient in the wider sense of the term may furnish an important guide in conducting the psychotherapeutic process [32, pp. 5–6].

Few analysts are as forthright as Little (1951) in advocating interpretation of the countertransference to the patient. This is important, she believes, to correct the impact of mistaken or mistimed interpretations (caused by countertransference) and in order to permit the patient to express his anger. She says:

Not only should the mistake be admitted (and the patient is entitled not only to express his own anger but also to some expression of regret from the analyst for its occurrence, quite as much as for the occurrence of a mistake in the amount of his account or the time of his appointment), but its origin in the unconscious counter-transference may be explained, unless there is some definite contra-indication for so doing, in which case it should be postponed until a suitable time comes, as it surely will. Such explanation may be essential for the further progress of the analysis, and it will have only beneficial results. . . . Only harm can come from the withholding of such an interpretation.

Le. me make it clear that I do not mean that I think counter-transference interpretations should be unloaded injudiciously or without consideration on the heads of hapless patients, any more than transference interpretations are given without thought today. I mean that they should neither be positively avoided nor perhaps restricted to feelings which are justified or objective. . . . (And of course they *cannot* be given unless something of the counter-transference has become conscious.) The subjectivity of the feelings needs to be shown to the patient, though their actual origin need not be gone into (there should not be "confessions"); it should be enough to point out one's own need to analyze them; but above all the important thing is that they should be recognized by both analyst and patient [41, p. 37].

Gitelson (1950) completed his paper before he read the one by Little (41), but in a postscript he expresses his essential agreement with her. He says:

Counter-transferences thus constitute an accidental casting of the analyst in an intrusive part in the psycho-analytic drama. Through the analysis of the counter-transference the analyst can reintegrate his position as an analyst and regain a position from which he can use the interfering factor for the purpose of analysing the patient's exploitation of it. In some instances this may mean a degree of self-revelation (by which I do not mean confession). But in a going analysis it may be found possible. In such a situation one can reveal as much of oneself as is needed to foster and support the patient's discovery of the reality of the actual interpersonal situation as contrasted with the transference–counter-transference situation [34, p. 7].

In volume I of *The Annual Survey of Psychoanalysis* (33), M. Balint and Tarachow epitomize two articles, apparently unrelated, that approach the problem of countertransference, albeit from different directions. The first is Oberndorf's "Unsatisfactory Results of Psychoanalytic Therapy" in which the author advocates discussion with colleagues in unsatisfactory cases and expresses the conviction that faulty countertransference reactions will be uncovered in many such situations. It is his impression that analyst and patient seduce each other into interminable analysis such that everything is analyzed but nothing changes. Too great preoccupation with the past may result in neglect of current disturbing realities and—one should add—of the transference, a point that Ferenczi and Rank (14, p. 37) made thirty years ago.

The second article is Grotjahn's "About the 'Third Ear' in Psychoanalysis," a critical review of Reik's *Listening With the Third Ear*. Of this, Balint and Tarachow observe: "Reik's approach to the countertransference problem is an autobiographic one. To him the analyst's willingness to trust his own passively arrived at perceptions of the patient's unconscious, constitutes the core of sound analytic technique'' (33, p. 239). Balint and Tarachow believe that these two articles represent a trend:

On the whole, one gets the impression that psychoanalytic technique is entering a new phase, rather reluctantly, to be sure. The preceding phase was chiefly concerned with the analysis of the transference, i.e., the patient's contribution; the new one, if we are right, will aim at the countertransference, the analyst's contribution [33, p. 240].

Mabel Cohen (1952) stresses the virtue of constant self-awareness on the part of the analyst, but she is conservative in the matter of interpretation of the countertransference. She states her position as follows:

It will be noted that the focus of attention of these remarks is on the analyst's own self-scrutiny, both of his responses to the patient's behavior and of his defensive attitudes and actions. Much has been said by others (Heimann, Little, Gitelson) regarding the pros and cons of introducing discussion of countertransference material into the analytic situation itself. That, however, is a question which, in my opinion, it is not possible to answer in the present state of our knowledge. . . . It would seem more feasible to devise techniques for utilizing such material in the therapeutic situation after the area has been more precisely explored and studied—or, rather, concurrently with further study and exploration [8, p. 242].

As noted above, Fliess (1953) defines countertransference as the equivalent, in the analyst, of the patient's transference. He adds:

The technique to abolish it becomes evident if the aforementioned definition is kept in mind. Transference, we have been taught by Freud, must be analyzed when it has become, or is about to become, a resistance; countertransference, always resistance, must always be analyzed. . . . If the analyst has, as he should, become aware of a countertransference phenomenon before the patient has done so, he will perform all or most of this self-analysis outside of the analytic hour. If the analyst has produced a symptom of countertransference, of which the patient, without recognizing it as such, is naturally aware, part of the self-analysis may have to be communicated to the patient [15, pp. 268–269].

SUMMARY

It is difficult to summarize an article that is itself a summary. I have attempted to review historically the psychoanalytic concepts of transference and countertransference from two points of view: (1) definition and meaning as psychological phenomena, particularly as encountered in psychoanalytic therapy; and (2) technical handling during the process of psychoanalytic treatment. I did not undertake to discuss other aspects of psychoanalytic technique or to deal with the related and tremendously important subject of theory of neurosis. It would appear, however, that further clarification of the concepts of transference and countertransference as well as of other issues of psychoanalytic technique must await a better integration of ego psychology, and particularly more definitive knowledge of early ego development, into psychoanalytic psychology and theory of neurosis. There is almost universal agreement on the crucial importance of transference and countertransference in clinical psychoanalysis, but far from unanimous agreement on how these concepts are to be understood and still less on how the phenomena themselves are to be dealt with in psychoanalytic treatment.

BIBLIOGRAPHY

1. Alexander, F. (1924–1925) *Psychoanalysis of the Total Personality*. New York: Coolidge Foundation Pub., 1946, pp. 168–169.
2. Alexander, F. (1924) A metapsychological description of the process of cure. *Internat. J. Psychoanal., 6*:13–34, 1925.
3. Alexander, F. Psychoanalysis revised. *Psychoanal. Quart., 9*:1–36, 1940.
4. Alexander, F., and French, T. *Psychoanalytic Therapy*. New York: Ronald Press Co., 1946, pp. 41–54, 71–95.
5. Balint, A., and Balint, M. On transference and counter-transference. *Internat. J. Psychoanal., 20*:223–230, 1939.
6. Balint, M. Changing therapeutical aims and techniques in psychoanalysis. *Internat. J. Psychoanal., 31*:117–124, 1950.
7. Berman, L. Countertransferences and attitudes of the analyst in the therapeutic process. *Psychiatry, 12*:159–166, 1949.
8. Cohen, M. B. Countertransference and anxiety, *Psychiatry, 15*:231–243, 1952.
9. Cole, E. M. A few "don'ts" for beginners in the technique of psycho-analysis. *Internat. J. Psychoanal., 3*:43–44, 1922.
10. English, O. S., and Pearson, H. J. *Common Neuroses of Children and Adults*. New York: W. W. Norton, 1937, p. 303.
11. Fenichel, O. (1940) *Problems of Psychoanalytic Technique*. Albany, N.Y.: Psychoanalytic Quarterly, Inc., 1941, pp. 27f., 71–75.
12. Fenichel, O. *The Pychoanalytic Theory of Neurosis*. New York: W. W. Norton, 1945.
13. Ferenczi, S. (1909) Introjection and transference. *Sex in Psychoanalysis*. Boston: Gorham Press, 1916.
14. Ferenczi, S., and Rank, O. (1923) *The Development of Psychoanalysis*. New York and Washington: Nervous & Mental Disease Publishing Co., 1925.
15. Fliess, R. Countertransference and counteridentification. *J. Amer. Psychoanal. Assoc. 1*:268–284, 1953.
16. Freud, A. (1936) *The Ego and the Mechanisms of Defense*. New York: International Universities Press, 1948, pp. 18–25.
17. Freud, S. (1905) Fragment of an analysis of a case of hysteria. *Collected Papers, 3*:139. London: Hogarth Press, 1946.
18. Freud, S. (1909) Notes upon a case of obsessional neurosis. *Collected Papers, 3*:331, 337 and 345. London: Hogarth Press, 1946.

19. Freud, S. (1910) The future prospects of psycho-analytic therapy. *Collected Papers, 2:*289. London: Hogarth Press, 1946.

20. Freud, S. (1910) Observations on "wild" psycho-analysis. *Collected Papers, 2:*302. London: Hogarth Press, 1946.

21. Freud, S. (1911) Psycho-analytic notes upon an autobiographical account of a case of paranoia (dementia paranoides). *Collected Papers, 3:*431–434 (fn) and 435. London: Hogarth Press, 1946.

22. Freud, S. (1912) The dynamics of the transference. *Collected Papers, 2:*314–322. London: Hogarth Press, 1946.

23. Freud, S. (1913) Further recommendations in the technique of psycho-analysis. *Collected Papers, 2:*344, 354, 359, 360, and 364. London: Hogarth Press, 1946.

24. Freud, S. (1914) Further recommendations in the technique of psycho-analysis. *Collected Papers, 2:*370 and 374. London: Hogarth Press, 1946.

25. Freud, S. (1915) Further recommendations in the technique of psycho-analysis. *Collected Papers, 2:*377, 381, and 386. London: Hogarth Press, 1946.

26. Freud, S. (1915–1917) *A General Introduction to Psychoanalysis.* New York: Liveright, 1935, pp. 374–389.

27. Freud, S. (1919) Turnings in the ways of psycho-analytic therapy. *Collected Papers, 2:*396–399. London: Hogarth Press, 1946.

28. Freud, S. (1922) *Beyond the Pleasure Principle.* New York: Liveright, 1950, p. 19.

29. Freud, S. (1923) *The Ego and the Id.* London: Hogarth Press, 1950, p. 72.

30. Freud, S. (1925) *An Autobiographical Study.* London: Hogarth Press, 1948, pp. 75–77.

31. Freud, S. (1938) *An Outline of Psychoanalysis.* New York: W. W. Norton, 1949, pp. 67–70, 77.

32. Fromm-Reichmann, F. *Principles of Intensive Psychotherapy.* Chicago: University of Chicago Press, 1950.

33. Frosch, J., et al. (Eds.) *The Annual Survey of Psychoanalysis.* New York: International Universities Press, 1950.

34. Gitelson, M. The emotional position of the analyst in the psycho-analytic situation. *Internat. J. Psychoanal., 33:*1–10, 1952.

35. Glover, E. 'Active therapy' and psychoanalysis. *Internat. J. Psychoanal., 5:*269–311, 1924.

36. Glover, E. Lectures on technique in psycho-analysis. *Internat. J. Psychoanal., 8:*311–338 and 486–520, 1927, and *9:*7–46 and 181–218, 1928.

37. Healy, W., Bronner, A. F., and Bowers, A. M. *The Structure and Meaning of Psychoanalysis.* New York: Alfred A. Knopf, 1931, pp. 436–438.

38. Heimann, P. On counter-transference. *Internat. J. Psychoanal., 31:*81–84, 1950.

39. Hendrick, I. *Facts and Theories of Psychoanalysis.* New York: Alfred A. Knopf, 1939, pp. 194–195 (fn).

40. Horney, K. *New Ways in Psychoanalysis.* New York: W. W. Norton, 1939, pp. 156–158, 169.

41. Little, M. Counter-transference and the patient's response to it. *Internat. J. Psychoanal., 32:*32–40, 1951.

42. Lorand, S. Comments on the correlation of theory and technique. *Psychoanal. Quart., 17:*32–50, 1948.

43. Lorand, S. *Technique of Psychoanalytic Therapy.* New York: International Universities Press, 1946, pp. 209–222.

44. Macalpine, I. The development of the transference. *Psychoanal. Quart. 19:*501–519, 1950.

45. Nunberg, H. Transference and reality. *Internat. J. Psychoanal., 32:*1–9, 1951.

46. Payne, S. M. Notes on developments in the theory and practice of psychoanalytic technique. *Internat. J. Psychoanal., 27:*12–18, 1946.
47. Reich, A. On counter-transference. *Internat. J. Psychoanal., 32:*25–31, 1951.
48. Reich, W. (1933) *Character-Analysis.* New York: Orgone Institute Press, 1945, pp. 4f., 119–140.
49. Rioch, J. The transference phenomenon in psychoanalytic therapy. *Psychiatry, 6:*147–156, 1943.
50. Sharpe, E. F. The psycho-analyst. *Internat. J. Psychoanal., 28:*1–6, 1947.
51. Silverberg, W. V. The concept of transference. *Psychoanal. Quart., 17:*309–310, 1948.
52. Sterba, R. The fate of the ego in analytic therapy. *Internat. J. Psychoanal., 15:*117–126, 1934.
53. Stern, A. On the counter-transference in psychoanalysis. *Psychoanal. Rev., 11:*166–174, 1924.
54. Strachey, J. The nature of the therapeutic action of psychoanalysis. *Internat. J. Psychoanal., 15:*130–137, 1934.
55. Winnicott, D. W. Hate in the counter-transference. *Internat. J. Psychoanal., 30:*69–74, 1949.

8. Exploring the Therapeutic Use of Countertransference Data

Edward S. Tauber

This paper is designed to illustrate the fact that countertransference phenomena may under certain circumstances afford an opportunity to evoke new material about the patient, the analyst, or the relationship, and that they may be used therapeutically to increase mutual spontaneity. The author believes that there is a real need for developing a scientific method to utilize constructively the negative components introduced by the therapist in the treatment situation and to determine which of these components are worthy of mutual exploration. According to classical psychoanalytic theory, countertransference reactions represent unanalyzed portions of the therapist's personality that either transparently or unwittingly interfere with the treatment situation. These reactions may be due to blind spots, private needs, irrelevant attitudes, biases, or moral prejudices; and they call for a change to a more productive orientation, necessitating their analysis. This is the basis in psychoanlytic theory for recognizing that any person engaged in intensive psychotherapeutic work with others needs a training analysis—a recognition that represents one of the most valuable discoveries in psychoanalysis.

It seems to me, however, that this emphasis on the negative value of countertransference reactions, important as it is, has tended to preclude the possibility of using these very reactions for achieving therapeutic goals. That is, the analyst may be so concerned with avoiding countertransference reactions that he does not take time to examine the content of the reaction fully. In this way, for instance, he may deliberately try to forget a dream he has had about a patient; or he may fail to mention to a supervisor some fleeting thought he has had about the patient. In other words, there is a taboo on anything that vaguely resembles countertransference reactions, and only the

This paper was originally given before a postgraduate seminar at the Medical School of the University of Mexico on November 30, 1952.

grossest type are explored even in supervision. Eventually the gross counter-transference phenomena tend to diminish; the more subtle ones remain, but are probably handled by selective inattention. This taboo has the harmful effect of inhibiting the analyst from recognizing the creative spontaneous insights that may occur to him in a dream, or in making use of a marginal thought or a slip of the tongue.

It is my impression that the analyst takes in more about the patient than he realizes; that there may be special reasons for the analyst's inability to bring some of his unconscious grasp of the patient into his own conscious aware-ness; and that by discussing some of the countertransference fragments, both the analyst and the patient may find out that the analyst has a richer under-standing of the patient that can be put to good use in the exploratory process of analysis.

The very nature of the analytic setting is such that the analyst plays a relatively passive role and maintains an incognito. Many patients seem to respond to this setting by presenting an incognito of their own. Such a patient may give the analyst no clues even for suspecting that his behavior in therapy really represents only a small part of his total functioning and way of living. As a result, both the analyst's taboo on countertransference attitudes and the patient's subtle incognito limit the amount of potentially useful information available for analytic progress. Thus the analytic procedure seems to require a constant infusion of new materials, fresh appraisals, and a challenging reconsideration of issues in the light of provocative data. Otherwise the analysis can become stagnant, and the so-called standardization of the proce-dure and the established scientific postulates can themselves become targets of the patient's resistance. This, of course, does not imply that the counter-transference reactions should be construed as license for acting out with the patient, but only that mutual exploration of their significance can open up more areas of development in the therapeutic situation.

With this as a hypothesis, I have discussed openly with several patients for mutual clarification, dream material of mine that involved them, and also some fleeting fragments of an intrusive nature. I shall illustrate this by three different instances.

ILLUSTRATION 1

Over a period of several weeks, the analyst has two successive dreams about patient A. In presenting his first dream, the analyst pointed out that he thought it might throw some light on his attitude toward the patient and he asked the patient for his impression of the dream:

The patient and the analyst are sitting at a small table in a sidewalk café, perhaps in Paris. The patient is saying very little, but has a very troubled expression on his face. He appears worried. The analyst says to him, "Why not try to tell me what is the matter?"

The patient seemed to respond to this dream in a very meager fashion. Except for a polite nod, he indicated no particular interest in giving his impressions and seemed to have something else he wished to talk about. Thus an analysis of the dream was not pursued. The analyst's second dream about the patient occurred several weeks later and was reported to the patient:

The patient and the analyst are sitting at a table in an expensive bar, having a drink. They are talking casually, but the content of the conversation is not recalled. Suddenly as they are about to leave the bar, two men not previously noticed jump on the patient. The situation develops swiftly, and the analyst cannot tell if the patient is really being attacked, or if these are just old college chums who are taking the patient by surprise, and roughhousing with him. The dream ends as the analyst quickly goes to the patient to ask him if this is serious and if he needs help, or if they are all joking.

At first the patient made no comments about the dream, except to say that it expressed the analyst's belief that the patient was withholding data and at the same time seemed in need of help. The analyst asked the patient, "Do you think that I believe that you are in need of help?" The patient responded in equivocal fashion, indicating that perhaps he thought the analyst had this feeling about him.

But later in the hour, the patient showed by his manner that the dream had something to say to him that was worth considering. His associations implied that the patient-doctor relationship had always been satisfactory and that he felt it was essential to keep it that way, that his experience in life had led him to believe that it was best to let sleeping dogs lie, that one can never work out a satisfactory solution by getting too deeply involved or by making one's ultimate position known. He then went on to make the important suggestion that both dreams had a hoax-like quality: although they manifestly indicated the analyst's concern for him, at the same time he suspected that the analyst was perfectly happy with the friendly, unstressed quality of the relationship; and although the analyst was trying to indicate in a sense that he believed they should go deeper into these issues, he had some private reasons for avoiding the challenge.

The analyst found this latter comment thought-provoking, and he could not answer it with either a flat denial or an affirmation. The analyst seriously asked himself whether he was guilty of wanting to avoid difficulties. The analyst's association to this was to remember information from outside sources about the patient that was not too favorable. He did not feel free under the circumstances to communicate this information to the patient. The analyst then made some comments about the dream in which he indicated that in one sense he believed it implied that he was having some difficulty obtaining the maximum degree of participation from the patient, and that possibly the dream was an indirect method of conveying to the patient the analyst's desire for deeper collaboration.

The analyst's first verbalized association was that the dream was an attempt to provoke the patient to reveal more clearly the transference picture. The analyst acknowledged the possibility that he might have an unconscious fear of knowing something inauspicious about the patient; although he was not aware of the nature of this fear, it might become apparent later. The analyst pointed out that the dream, in its manifest content, contained a rather obvious message, which could be known to both participants. But he reminded the patient that he, the analyst, could easily have some blind spots about the meaning of the dream, and the patient should develop his own ideas about the dream.

The next session was an extremely fruitful one, because it conveyed to both of them—more strikingly than perhaps at any other time—the essence of the patient's real fear of closeness. It had always been difficult for the patient to convey the emotional atmosphere of his home situation; although he had previously made sensible statements about his home situation, they often lacked the affect that is so essential in the analytic setting. In this particular instance, however, the patient's usual nonchalance was lacking, and his distress at an impending social engagement was touchingly revealed. After the patient had expressed this distress, the analyst was able to tell the patient about a previous occasion when he had sensed the patient's deep fear of his closeness to his mother. They both then realized that the issue had been hit upon—namely, that the analyst had been afraid to push this particular point for fear of a panic reaction in the patient. In other words, the dreams seemed to have revealed a pleasant but timid coaxing of the patient, as if the analyst were saying, *One can still go about this matter of his problems, even while having a drink*. Stated in other terms, the dreams were expressions of the analyst's ambivalence, in that he both urged the patient to greater activity, and had some reservations himself about the safety of it.

ILLUSTRATION 2

The analyst had the following dream about patient B, a young married woman who had been in analysis for a few months:

The dream takes place on an island in the Mediterranean. The patient and the analyst are walking together, and there is no conversation. It seems to be dusk. The atmosphere has a romantic quality. The analyst is trying to understand something, although nothing has been said. That is all there is to the dream.

When the analyst reported the dream to the patient, she made no comment. Prior to the analytic session, the analyst decided to report the dream to the patient although he had not considered the dream carefully. When she failed to say anything about it, the analyst noted on the spur of the moment that the patient did not seem to feel that the romantic components of her marriage were satisfactory, although there had been no mention of it in their work together. He admitted that there was no significant information to justify this association, but it had come to him anyway, and he wondered whether it had any validity. Subsequently the patient went into the subject of her marriage, revealing that the analyst's association had a rather pertinent bearing on her problem. The analyst wondered why this would have to come up in a dream. The patient seemed to have no thoughts on the matter. It occurred to the analyst, however, that he had been deliberately avoiding the subject of the patient's marriage since she had had so much distress in the analysis and had seemed to have a need to believe that her marriage at least was sound. The dream came to his assistance, however, and prevented his employing some further useless philanthropic attitude toward the patient, which could only have delayed the handling of a problem of importance to her. It turned out that her relationship with her husband was not as happy as she wished to believe.

ILLUSTRATION 3

This illustration has to do with a fleeting thought that came to the analyst's mind during an analytic session. The analyst revealed this thought to the patient, saying at the same time that ordinarily he would not have done so, because it seemed to be out of order and to have nothing to do with the mutual inquiry. The analyst asked the patient for his reaction to this thought, and stated that he would also contribute his own associations. Here is the setting in which the thought occurred:

The patient was describing some details of his marriage. Having had occasional temporary episodes of sexual impotence prior to marriage, he was remarking that he hoped that under the stress of his present marital problem he would not again have the same disturbance. He added that because he anticipated that his wife would react adversely, such a disturbance would be extremely frightening to him. The analyst had this sudden, unaccounted-for thought, which he revealed to the patient: "Send your wife here to me. I can explain the situation to her in such a way that she won't be disturbed."

The patient quickly reacted to this remark. He said that it revealed to him that the analyst really had a lack of confidence in him and did not believe that if he became impotent, he would be able to work out the problem with his wife. While the patient was talking, the analyst had the fleeting thought that what he, the analyst, had said seemed to be an expression of ambition, as if he were trying to prove to the patient that he had the power to straighten out the matter—a kind of credit-taking fantasy. The analyst communicated this to the patient; the patient reacted by looking pale and angry, and by insisting that it proved that the analyst was merely trying to deny admitting his deeper feeling of the patient's inadequacy by accusing himself of ambition.

The patient was silent at the beginning of the next day's session. The analyst urged the patient to say what was on his mind, but the patient was still uncommunicative and seemed slightly uneasy and uncomfortable. Prior to this session, the analyst had had some thoughts about his remarks of the session before, and he now proceeded to communicate them to the patient:

The analyst explained that he suspected that his behavior of the day before represented an unconscious mimicking of the patient's mother or identification with her, and that it was motivated in order to recapture with the patient a relationship the patient had with his mother that had never come out strongly in the analysis. In other words, the analyst believed that this unconscious device was aimed at forcing the patient to reveal a sensitive area that could have remained concealed under the ordinary conditions of analysis.

The patient reacted to this latter comment by blushing and saying, with some anger, "You are trying to get off the hook." By this the patient meant that the analyst had originally indicated a lack of confidence in the patient, and had first attempted to deny this by explaining his comment as an expression of his own ambition. Then, when that was not satisfactory, the analyst tried a new tactic—namely, to explain his behavior as an unconscious therapeutic maneuver. But the patient did not believe that the analyst's associations explained away his lack of confidence in the patient.

At the next session the patient was quite eager to relate a dream that he had had the night before:

There is a huge ballroom filled with couples dancing. A doctor, whom the patient has known for many years and has regarded as an ally of his from early childhood, is dancing with his wife. The dance steps are elaborate, consisting of the partners' stepping away from each other and coming together again. Suddenly the patient's mother, standing alone on the sidelines, gets into the doctor's arms before his wife can complete the steps necessary to bring her into his arms. Apparently the doctor showed no objection to the swift change in partners, and willingly continued to dance with the patient's mother. The patient, who observed all this, said nothing, but was disappointed in the doctor's behavior.

The patient's associations were that the doctor and the analyst were the same person, and that the analyst had betrayed him. The patient felt that this dream was his way of expressing what he believed the analyst had meant about their relationship at the time the analyst had commented on the patient's anticipated potency problem. The analyst's interpretation of the patient's dream was in line with the patient's comments. In effect, the dream indicated that the patient felt that the analyst had turned away from him after having had a satisfactory relationship with him, and had now become an ally of his mother. It indicated that the patient did feel disappointed in the analyst's earlier remarks on the grounds that the analyst had later suspected —namely, that the analyst had unconsciously simulated the patient's mother. In other words, the analyst believed that his remarks represented an unconscious attempt to stimulate or provoke emotional data in an area that was important but still insufficiently explored. The matter was left with the patient, however, who was urged to attempt to clarify in the analytic work the important critical problem of whether or not the analyst's attitude was genuinely hostile. These analytic hours had emphasized for the patient the necessity to be concerned with the real and assumed attitudes of the analyst, and also that he could not and should not be satisfied with an uncritical acceptance of the analyst's appraisal of his own attitudes.

It seemed to the analyst that two important points were brought out clearly through this incident. First, the patient was obliged to move away from a somewhat artificially arrived at conception of the analyst's attitude toward him; and he was forced to consider the analyst as a human being with whom he was working rather than a special category of person who fitted his defensive needs. Second, the analyst's experiment of expressing a private thought—which was out of order at first glance—provoked material reflecting quite genuinely the patient's convincing doubt about his mother's alleged faith in him, a point that he had previously indicated with relatively unimpressive affect.

Sometimes it is useful to enter into the parataxis with the patient in order to recapture more vividly the quality of the memory, or to simulate in some way the significant parent or other figure in order to illuminate the history of the current distortion. The romantic dream reported in Illustration 2 is also an example of the analyst's unconsciously entering the parataxic field of the patient. That is, the therapist responds to the patient's irrational needs in an inappropriate fashion—namely, with his own irrational reveries or dreams. Yet the question must be raised as to whether the therapist does not enter the parataxic areas of the patient's life much more often than he realizes, if he dares to recognize this. The distinction as to when this unconscious operation is of value or not has to be explored further. One point that seems indisputable is that once the intrusion is made, the therapist must be able to assume responsibility for his actions and thoughts with honesty and without defensiveness. Furthermore, it is my opinion that the therapist probably avoids burdening the patient as long as the solution of his own problems of living is in good measure meaningful.

In this paper, I have tried to identify more clearly certain issues inherent in the procedure of utilizing countertransference data in the treatment setting. From my observations, I would say that countertransference reactions are more likely to occur during fallow or lengthy resistant periods. They function at such times to provoke contact with the patient, to break into the resistance by surprise. The surprise is not a random jiggling of the controls to see what will happen, but occurs in a setting of deep concentration, in which the analyst is trying to reach the patient. The surprise is an expression of spontaneity, and as such can have constructive and unconstructive implications. The analyst must be free to follow through and participate in the truest sense of the word—there is no time at that point for sophistical defensive operations. The special responsibility of the therapist at such a time is to recognize that he may be making irrational demands on the patient and that he must be able to handle this. It is not the patient's job to support him if his spontaneity creates tensions. Thus the utilization of countertransference reactions in the treatment setting is not license to carry on wildcat, irresponsible experimentation. If the therapist feels he is playing with fire, he should not deal with countertransference reactions with his patient; in other words, the optimal conditions for such exploration are not at hand.

If one wishes to appraise the possibly injurious effects of exploring countertransference reactions in the therapeutic situation, the only injury that I believe requires serious consideration is that which could be imposed on the patient by the therapist's own attitudes. If the therapist is serious, responsible, competent and resourceful, it seems highly improbable that the patient will react with panic or a depression, or that he will suddenly leave treatment. It is, moreover, significant that in my own experience the examination of countertransference reactions has not led to further bogging down and resistance. The more usual result has been the re-establishment of varying degrees of contact, further activity, and more hopefulness.

9. The Role of the Analyst's Personality in Therapy

Clara Thompson

From the earliest years of psychoanalytic therapy, the fact that the analyst, as a factor in the analytic situation, has to be taken into consideration, has not been overlooked. In an attempt to maintain a scientific setting, Freud sought to make the personal equation of the analyst as inconspicuous as possible. To this end, it was recommended that there should be no social contact between patient and therapist, that the patient should know as few facts as possible about the analyst's life, and that the analyst should sit behind the couch so that any changes in his facial expression would be unobserved. In this way, it was hoped that an objective neutral atmosphere would be created, in which the patient, without distraction, could present his own life problems and project upon the analyst any role needed.

From the beginning, Freud realized that complete anonymity could not be attained. For example, the sex of the analyst would be apparent, his approximate age could not be concealed, and whether he had a cold or not might be evident. The patient might learn something about him from others also, etc. These facts were thought to be regrettable defects in the sensitive instrument, the analyst, that was to be used to study the patient.

After a time, it became apparent that other problems might arise, that in spite of all precautions some problem of the analyst might lead to his emotional involvement in the situation. For example, an attractive female patient might succeed in stirring him erotically, especially if his own love life was unsatisfactory, or a hostile patient might succeed in finding a vulnerable spot and rouse the analyst's defensiveness or anger. In short, any weakness in the therapist might accidentally be exploited to the detriment of successful treatment. Freud pointed out that when these situations happened, something comparable to the acting out of the patient took place on the part of the analyst, and so he called them countertransference phenomena. Eventually, i.e. by 1920, the solution for such problems was sought in the analysis of the analyst. In this way, it was hoped that the analyst's objectivity would be improved. However, most of the so called "training" analyses, at first, were very brief, usually not more than six months at most. Consequently what happened in many cases was that the analyst became more expert at concealing his problems—that is, a better defense was formed as a result of intellectual insight, with a resulting increased rigidity of the analyst's personality. He became afraid to show warmth or spontaneous interest in the patient, not knowing where natural interest ended and his personal problems began. Ferenczi was the first to point out in the 1920s that the personal analysis of an analyst should, if anything, be longer and deeper than that of a patient, instead of the reverse. As time went on, this idea was taken over, so that today one of the most important aspects of training is a long and thorough personal analysis.

However, the goal, although not specifically so stated, in most institutes has been to make the analyst a clean sheet of paper, so to speak, so that the student often gets the feeling that after his analysis is completed, he ought to have no further problems. This also has had its unfortunate results. Perfection is an impossible and probably always a neurotic goal. The fear of having any shortcomings is increased, and since it is an impossible goal, there are always defects to be concealed. So defenses against imperfections are still erected with resulting rigidities of personality.

Ferenczi had a solution for this, and that was for the doctor to admit his mistakes to the patient. This suggestion did not meet with acceptance by most analysts. Freud, himself, thought it was dangerous in that it would tend to destroy the authority of the therapist. Nevertheless, since the early 1930s, a few analysts have worked along lines similar to Ferenczi's with good results, e.g. Sullivan, Fromm-Reichmann and myself—to name those whom I know most about, and, in the past ten years, there has been a movement in the direction of greater participation of the therapist in the analytic situation with a resulting greater frankness about his own role. This must include, at times, admission of mistakes, oversights due to personal problems, irritability, etc.

Today, countertransference studies frequently appear in the literature, and it is even possible that the tendency to stress the significance of the analyst's emotional reactions in the treatment has swung the emphasis too far in the opposite direction. We may be overvaluing the importance of this contribution to the analytic picture.

However, the present stress on the role of the analyst's personality has opened new fields for observation. In the first place, the analyst need no longer feel defensive about being natural and spontaneous. This, in turn, makes it possible for the patient to react more genuinely. Nevertheless, it stresses the fact that the analytic situation is much more complicated than we earlier assumed. Thus, we can no longer simply suggest to the patient that whatever hostility he shows, *clearly* is displaced from his father or mother. We have to consider our own possible contribution to it. Thus, if he says, "I think you did not like what I said about you last time," the thoughtful analyst must carefully determine what his actual reaction was. In other words, did the patient correctly observe a resentment reaction. Such honesty is important in helping the patient in his appraisal of reality. At the same time, as I implied earlier, it is possible in trying this new approach to lean over backwards in taking the blame, thus overlooking other factors.

However, setting aside criticisms of overenthusiastic use of the analyst's emotional reactions in understanding the patient, I wish to consider what new data about the patient is made available by awareness of emotional participation, and what it can teach us of the analyst's role in "cure."

In the first place, we must recognize that the analyst's blind spots are always a hazard. However, the hazard is greater when there is a stake in denying them. Not only is the patient needlessly confused by this, but, possibly even more important, denial aids the analyst in repressing his own possibility of insight. A frank discussion with the patient, encouraging him to tell all that he has observed or thinks he has observed may actually increase the analyst's insight into himself to the benefit of both. It is important to remember that unresolved difficulties always exist, that the understanding of oneself is never complete and that one can profitably seek, throughout a lifetime, for greater self knowledge. Such an attitude is an excellent safeguard against smug satisfaction and the Jehovah complex, which can keep us from a genuine sympathy and understanding of others.

Even when an irrational or countertransference attitude in the analyst has been demonstrated, new insight about the patient can be gained as a result of the experience if it is faced realistically.

Excessive acting out in the analytic situation would point to a blind spot in the analyst. What seems to happen in this situation is that the analyst happens to be similar in a personality difficulty to an authority figure of the patient's, so both fall into a familiar pattern of reacting to each other without either one's being well aware of what is going on. Thus, for example, a female patient with a loud, complaining voice harangued the analyst for many months before he was aware that nothing of importance in the therapy was happening. When the situation was examined, he recalled that this particular type of voice was characteristic of his mother, and that he had early developed an imperviousness to her tirades, and did not hear what his mother was saying. He had, all unwittingly, been treating the patient in the same way. Awareness of this not only benefited him, but told him something about the patient, which was helpful to her. In general, excessive acting out should always lead to the analyst's exploring his own contribution to the situation. Although, of course, we know that some patients tend to act out more than others—in their own right.

An analyst reported that he found it difficult to stay awake during hours with a certain patient. The patient talked in a flat, mumbling voice. There seemed to be no fluctuations indicating emotional content. The analyst found it almost impossible to listen. The problem was taken up in terms of "the patient is telling you something by this very attitude." The analyst thought about it—"he acts as if he thought I wouldn't be interested in him—but I actually act as if I weren't. I was interested in the beginning—what happened?!" Then it occurred to him that on several occasions he had been aware of a slight feeling of anxiety over a dream reported by the patient, but the patient's monotonous voice had made it easy for him to overlook this. In one, the patient was in a small boat on a stormy sea. No help was around and the boat was sinking. In another, the patient was swimming far away from shore and could not get back. He was finally washed ashore dead. The analyst then saw that the patient had made him anxious, that he had a very genuine fear of the patient's committing suicide, that he had been dealing with this anxiety by not listening, sticking his head in the sand, so to speak. The feeling was "if I don't notice this, it won't happen." This is not the end of this story. This analyst was not usually threatened by suicidal possibilities. He had dealt with many other difficult situations adequately. He presently realized that the particular circumstances of this patient's life touched closely on a tragic situation in his own family. In other words, this patient, by his problem, threatened this analyst with an awareness of his anxiety about his own problem. Since his own difficulties were so deeply involved, the analyst wisely decided to transfer the patient to another analyst.

In another case, a young analyst was having difficulties with a dramatic acting-out type of hysterical woman. She reported that she was much worse since beginning treatment. Her husband became very alarmed and began calling the analyst, and corroborated her statement that she was much worse and was threatening suicide. The analyst had been treating all this as evidence of her hostility, pointing out her desire for revenge, etc. Whatever he said seemed to make matters worse. He was urged to think how he felt towards this woman, not diagnostically, but personally. He realized he had felt a kind of hostile challenge in her from the beginning. She had stirred some hostile, slightly sadistic trend in him, and he had had the feeling he wouldn't let her put anything over on him. Because of this, he had been seeing only the hostility in her behavior. It was suggested that he try to think of how frightened she must be, and how, because of his attitude, she must feel she had no support from him. Maybe her behavior was a screaming cry for help. The analyst saw this and was able to change his attitude with unusually gratifying results. The patient soon stopped threatening and began to face her problems. It seemed clear that she felt at last that he wanted to help her. By seeing her as a little frightened child, and not his hysterical mother, he had lost his own fear of her, and with it his defensive hostility.

Not only do many crises in analysis arise from the unconscious emotional involvement of the analyst, but also many stalemates may be resolved by the analyst's study of his own reactions. The case of the patient with the loud scolding voice is one example. Another example is the following: A young analyst had a woman patient who acted out with great violence during the hour. She sometimes gave the analyst a push as she left the session. On one occasion she kicked him. At another time, she grabbed his hair. He remained impervious. To the best of his knowledge, he was behaving as an analyst should. In other words, he believed he was not supposed to get involved in the patient's emotional scenes. Undoubtedly, he was correct as long as her explosions were completely genuine. But nothing else was happening, and the frequency of the violent behavior was increasing. The supervisor got the impression that the patient was enjoying her little game, and suggested this to the young analyst. He was asked how he felt when he got his hair pulled and was kicked. He admitted it made him angry, but he thought he ought not to show it. He was advised to tell the patient he thought it unnecessary, that he didn't like it, and he thought it didn't help her. He did so at the next opportunity. The behavior stopped immediately. He found she had been reacting to his imperviousness—"I've got to make you feel something," she said. This analysis has since gone to a successful conclusion with a real personality change in the patient.[1]

Thus far, I have discussed the analyst's personality in respect to the way his problems create blind spots and difficulties. Some of the problems stem from unanalyzed bits of the analyst's personality. Most of those quoted were of more superficial origin—in one case, a current problem in the analyst's life, and in two of the cases the difficulty was largely due to the analyst's inexperience. But all demonstrated the resistance-producing quality—that is, they blocked progress.

I want to turn now to a consideration of the analyst's total personality as a *positive* instrument. Here the emphasis will not be on the pathological aspects of his character, but on the kind of person he is, and its impact on the patient. Hanna Colm in the November 1955 issue of *Psychiatry* has presented the possibilities developing in considering the analytic situation in terms of a mutual human relation. She develops it in terms of the field theory. The analyst brings to the situation his whole past, that is—all of his ways of relating, and his field gradually begins to interact with the patient's field. At first, the analyst encounters the fringe areas of the patient, i.e. his defenses, but eventually the center area of both is reached. Her assumption is that the center area of the patient can be reached only by a center reaction of the analyst. By his awareness of his own spontaneous reactions, he becomes aware of the needs and motives of the patient. The patient, on his part, experiences acceptance and can, therefore, relate with his center (or core) reaction. The total personality of the analyst affects the total personality of the patient. Some of the attitudes may, at times, be countertransference or parataxis, to use Sullivan's term. In other words, they are based on irrational attitudes in the analyst developed in other circumstances, but, because he has had a long analysis, most of the personality is not irrational, and yet one analyst must of necessity differ from another.

Many types of people become analysts. Some are detached people, some have a slightly obsessional aura, some are highly imaginative, some impractical ivory tower types, others are very practical and down to earth, etc. Some are men, some are women and there are all variations of age from about thirty on. Also, especially in the United States, they vary greatly in their cultural backgrounds. There are Southerners, mid-Westerners, people from big Eastern cities, Europeans, first and second generation descendants of Europeans, and so on. When these are put into the mill of psychoanalytic training, it would be absurd to expect a uniform product. In fact, it would be disastrous if analysis *could* produce a uniform product, because it would mean that some of the essence of the personality had been destroyed.

In my early years as an analyst, I was taught the idea that any well-trained analyst could do a good job on an analyzable patient. It is possible that some success can always be achieved, but I now believe that one analyst can sometimes take a particular patient further than another because his temperament and life experiences fit him to understand this type of patient especially well. I think patients may unconsciously react to this when they choose an analyst. As I said before, the analyst comes to his patient bringing his whole past, his whole life experience. This includes special interests and values. It can be hoped that prejudices and unconstructive values are at a minimum, but there are possibilities of wide variations nevertheless.

Many years ago, I wrote a paper on the choice of an analyst (*Psychiatry*, 1938). As we know, many patients who consult us do not return after the first interview. A great many of these do not go to anyone else either, at least for some time: but others soon find another analyst. The question is *why*. It seemed to me that when given a choice, patients have preferences based sometimes on irrational and sometimes on rational needs. I pointed out at that time that one factor in this was a need to find someone who was similar to an early authority figure with whom one could continue present defensive attitudes undisturbed and that when this happened, there was difficulty because the analyst's personality was not sufficiently different from the earlier authority figure to make the transference elements clear. Therefore, they often went unnoticed, and an acting out of the old pattern continued without insight. Thus, a somewhat authoritarian analyst might fit the picture of an authoritarian father, and the patient might continue to play a submissive role without awareness of it on either his part or the analyst's, because the analyst on his part needed some submissiveness in a patient. However, I have since thought that most patients are not so self-destructive as to seek an analytic situation where the worst aspects of early authority figures predominate.

Perhaps they often seek repetitions of types from early life of people who can be trusted. For example, one patient had had bad experiences with mother figures, not only with the real mother, but with a woman later in college, who extracted a confession from her and then later used it against her in a seriously devastating way. This woman was unable to confide in a woman until after a long analysis with a man. She made one attempt to talk to a woman analyst at first, but immediately reacted with great panic. Obviously the initial analysis could best be done by a man. Her father had not been destructive, and she could show her feelings to men. She had, incidentally, developed a way of seeming to confide in women. She would tell the most intimate facts, but it was all as if she were talking of someone else. Her real feelings were locked away somewhere. I am not maintaining that she could not have been analyzed by a woman if no other analyst were available, but it would have taken longer, and the initial disturbance would have been more violent requiring an unusual degree of self understanding on the part of the analyst.

This points up the fact that in addition to the search for an analyst with whom early situations can be factually repeated, there is also a search for someone who can be trusted, someone who understands and to whom one can communicate undefensively. There are certainly difficulties in analyzing a person of another culture. An analyst of sixty may be less capable of contact with an adolescent than, say, an analyst of thirty, and so on.

Analysts who live in cities where there are many psychoanalysts are fortunate in that they can choose their patients in terms of their own aptitudes as therapists. Often, the analyst today consciously does this, but many also do it unconsciously by somehow discouraging the patient from staying with him. When we consider that the personality of the analyst is the instrument by which the patient is to be aided in self knowledge, this initial weeding out is probably a good thing.

However, the analyst must make every effort to understand why this person especially interests him, for he could be influenced by countertransference motives. That is, his choice might be based on some parataxic need of his own such as when the patient's social or professional position would make the patient a "feather in his cap" by adding to his own prestige. Or, if he has not mastered his own vanity needs, he may succumb to a patient who shows great admiration for him. These would be unconstructive bases of choice and would probably lead to unfortunate results unless the analyst gained insight during the treatment.

It is essential that the choice be made on the basis of understanding and respect for the patient. By this, I do not mean that the analyst has to like what the patient is doing, but the analyst has to feel that a genuine urge towards health is motivating the patient and that in his relation to the analyst at least, honesty will predominate or, at least, be earnestly striven for.

I once had a patient who was a great liar. For this reason he was an entertaining conversationalist, but in the analytic situation it often created confusion. I presently began to wonder why I had accepted him for treatment, since I considered honesty so essential. After hesitating unnecessarily long, I finally told him I found it impossible to trust his statements and that I felt this was seriously affecting our relationship. He was justly angry that I had waited so long in bringing up the subject. ''Of course you don't like it and you shouldn't. But how can I trust you if you keep this feeling to yourself?'' We then worked on the dynamics of his lying. It had originally developed as an attempt to play the clown in order to get some attention—for he was a neglected child. It came out chiefly in situations in which he felt inadequate. It proved to be not a basic dishonesty, but an attempt at socialization, and it disappeared under treatment. My insistence on the importance of honesty had blinded me to the fact that in this instance the dishonesty was analyzable.

We must relate to the patient with more than our intellects. We feel things that sometimes do not reach the level of verbal awareness. For example, why do I frequently yawn with a certain patient, why do I feel restless with another, and vaguely annoyed at times with a third? Is it simply the time of day or my state of weariness, or is there some more serious failure of communication? In the case of the yawning, I discovered in one case that it was especially frequent when a strong parasitic clinging tendency was predominant during the hour. We both found that this was a useful clue that the hour seemed to be getting nowhere, and that it actually was more effective in altering her attitude than a direct statement would have been. Undoubtedly, yawning can mean different things in different situations.

A persistent attitude of good will and genuine concern for his welfare will eventually reach through the patient's distrust and despair. But—it must be genuine! A merely technically correct behavior is usually detected by the patient, if not consciously, then unconsciously. In short, an analyst must really like his fellow man in order to help him.

I once had a very hostile patient who had a diabolical ability to make his attacks effective by finding the most vulnerable spots in others. During a long and stormy analysis, in which he successfully laid bare all my weaknesses, I never became angry with him because I was sure that, basically, our relationship was sound, and that he trusted me as much as he was capable of trusting anyone, and that he had a genuine desire to understand himself.

Finally, I wish to bring up another aspect of the analyst's personality that has its impact upon the patient, and that is the role of the analyst's values in treatment. Herbert S. Spohn, Ph.D. has made an interesting survey of the influence of social values upon the clinical judgments of psychotherapists. He made a study of sixty-five therapists, twenty-nine of whom professed a Fruedian orientation of varying degrees of orthodoxy, and twenty-six who professed a Sullivanian orientation. He does not mention the orientation of the other ten in the brief abstract I have seen. I believe the full report is not yet published. The area tested was the therapist's criteria for mental health. His findings, in brief, were that in the Sullivanian or Frommian orientation group, there was a significantly greater tendency to reject the current entrepreneur values as the goal of therapy than was the case with the Freudian-oriented therapists. He speculated that while the greater explicit criticism of contemporary values of the first school played a role, he felt of greater interest was the fact that theoretical therapy orientations and personal social values are associated. That is—within limits—a therapist may choose his school of orientation according to his personal social values, and that his personal social values influence his goal for patients. I am sure the study does not intend to state that the therapist actively indoctrinates his own patients with his views, although that also has been known to happen, but it must influence, to some extent, the issues on which he places emphasis. In this way, his views are conveyed to the patient. Thus, it is not unimportant what a therapist thinks about many things, e.g. marriage, divorce, success, religion, politics—to mention a few obvious issues. His views are usually not stated, but their influence is implicit in his approach. For example, let us take the issue of divorce. If a therapist has a strong conviction that marriage should be maintained at all costs if possible, he will tend to ignore, consciously or unconsciously, or fail to encourage exploration of facts and feelings that would lead the patient to favor divorce.

Recently a young man patient of mine became very annoyed with me because I failed to show any interest in the relative prestige merits of cars. Since I do not own a car, myself, one could dismiss my attitude by saying I just don't happen to be interested in cars. My first reaction to his remark was just that, but as I continued to think about it, I realized that I was also reacting to the man's need for showy success. It was not one of my values, and I was indirectly conveying this idea to him by my lack of interest in his ambition to own a Cadillac.

Analysts who long for status and prestige invariably have trouble analyzing patients who have status and prestige needs. It is unnecessary to labor the point further, I think.

In conclusion, I would like to raise the question: Is there a type of personality in a therapist that will produce optimum results in patients? Psychoanalytic institutes have been trying for several years to determine this. Certain things are obvious. Freud's first requirement was that an analyst must be a man of ethical integrity. He also needs to be relatively free of blind spots, and able to keep a flexible and open mind about himself. That is, he must be a person who can sensitively interact with others and continue to learn about himself in that situation. He must have a genuine respect for others. A great variety of personality types can fulfill these requirements and the great variety is desirable because of the differing needs of different patients.

When it comes to a consideration of the relative merits of an analyst's values, there may be more divergence of opinion as to what type is best. I personally believe the patients' interests are best served by analysts who are not conformists—and certainly not blind conformists—but are always ready to seek new values in the interest of what is good for man. This, of course, puts me in the Sullivanian group. But the Sullivanian orientation did not make me a seeker after truth, no matter where it leads. It only gave me a greater opportunity to develop this aspect of myself. I found the school whose thinking and values approximated what I was seeking for myself.

Patients are not in such a fortunate position. They have less opportunity to know in advance the values of their prospective therapists. It has been established in hypnosis that it is difficult to get a hypnotized subject to do something contrary to his own wishes and values. Perhaps some failures in analysis are due to our attempts, wittingly or unwittingly, to force patients into a mold that they cannot accept. In this respect, an analyst's values are not unimportant for the outcome of the analysis.

NOTE

1. Some of the examples quoted have been worked out with the aid of a third person (supervisor), who could observe the total picture in a more detached way than the participants. It is my opinion that this is the most important function of a supervisor, especially after the basic principles of technique have become comfortable working tools. In fact, I think that small group discussion of problems about patients can be profitably used by analysts all of their lives. During the past few years, I have participated in a small seminar of graduates in which the emphasis is entirely on countertransference problems. It is a kind of miracle club, in which the participants swear the patient must have been listening in, because he reacts so often as predicted to the insight gained by the analyst. Should we not all subject this delicate, sensitive instrument—our own personality—to frequent overhauling! I do not mean necessarily extensive analysis, but checking on the spots where things are not going smoothly, especially with our patients. We do this as a matter of course with our cars, radios, microscopes—why not with the most delicate instrument of all—ourselves!

10. Countertransference

Lucia E. Tower

I. THEORETICAL CONSIDERATIONS

References to countertransference appeared very early in psychoanalytic literature. Originally, they paid mostly lip service to its existence, with unelaborated statements that, of course, analysts could have transference reactions to their patients. Little else was said, other than to imply that these were dubious reactions and should be controlled, and for analysts to discuss their countertransference reactions in public would be somewhat indecently self-revealing. About ten years ago, a moderate number of articles began to appear. The general overtone of these articles has been of a rather embarrassed sort, as though these were major imperfections in our therapeutic procedures, and of course certain countertransference phenomena are considered reprehensible in the extreme.

The literature on countertransference has recently been excellently reviewed by Douglass Orr (18). I shall make only cursory comments about this literature because my main purpose is to present some ideas of my own and some detailed case material. Despite wide agreement among analysts about transference, there has been wide disagreement about countertransference. Freud's first reference to it in 1910 was rather forbidding: "We have begun to consider the 'counter-transference' . . . arising as a result of the patient's influence on his [the physician's] unconscious feelings, and have nearly come to the point of requiring the physician to recognize and overcome this counter-transference in himself" (9, p. 289).

It is striking that a natural and inevitable phenomenon, so rich in potential for understanding, should have sustained so forbidding a tone toward its existence for forty-five years. I refer to the fact that no analyst has ever been presumed to have been so perfectly analyzed that he no longer has an unconscious, or is without susceptibility to the stirring up of instinctual impulses and defenses against them. The very phraseology of our training practices belies the mask of the "perfect analyst." We state that the student's personal analysis should "serve as a first-hand experience with the unconscious"; it should gain him "working freedom from his own disturbing emotional patterns";[1] and it should enable him to continue his self-analysis on his own. At no time is it expected that he will have been perfectly analyzed. In addition, our recommendations for periodic reanalysis of analysts presuppose a large unconscious reservoir of sources for the development of new neurotic responses to emotional pressures from analytic patients upon the analyst's unconscious.

Conflicting conceptions of countertransference have covered a wide range. There were early ideas that it was the analyst's conscious emotional reaction to the patient's transference; attitudes that it covered every conscious or unconscious reaction about the patient, normal or neurotic; mechanistic constructions of the interpersonal relation between patient and analyst into some schematized oedipal picture (20); characterological disposition and personal eccentricities of the analyst were included; reactions to the patient as a whole have been considered transferences, and to partial aspects of the patient, countertransferences; anxiety in the analyst has been taken to be the common denominator to all countertransference reactions and every anxiety-producing response in the analyst considered countertransference (7); and finally, only sexual impulses toward patients have been regarded as countertransference. Major differences center around "seeing the analyst as a mirror—versus the analyst as a human being" (18). Countertransferences are considered as being simply transferences—and nothing else—versus their not being transferences and being almost anything else.

Other differences center around questions of whether or not to discuss countertransferences with patients;[2] whether countertransferences are always present and therefore reasonably normal; or whether they are always abnormal. "Carry over"[3] is mentioned several times as particularly ominous in its implications. Almost invariably there are explicit prohibitions against any erotic countertransference manifestations. Only once, I believe, is it suggested that unless there are periods or occasions of "carry over," the analysis will not be successful, and only once, I believe, is it suggested that there may be under normal, and perhaps even useful, circumstances something approaching a countertransference neurosis. Mostly the latter are strenuously criticized.

The forbidding nature of writings on the subject is indicated by the following typical quotes (slightly edited):

Our countertransference must be healthy [23].

It is assumed that the appropriate responses predominate [6].

At least some analytical toilet is a part of the analyst's necessary routine [12].

Countertransference is the same as transference—it is then immediately obvious that countertransference is undesirable and a hindrance [8].

The [countertransference mistake] should be admitted, to allow the patient to express his anger, and he is entitled to some expression of regret from the analyst [16].

It is not safe to let even subtle manifestations of the countertransference creep inadvertently into the inter-personal climate. The analyst must recognize and control these reactions [1].

All of these—and similar attitudes—presuppose an ability in the analyst consciously to *control* his own unconscious. Such a supposition is in violation of the basic premise of our science—namely, that human beings are possessed of an unconscious that is *not* subject to conscious control, but that is (fortunately) subject to investigation through the medium of the transference (and presumably also the countertransference) neurosis.

Common evidences of countertransference are given as:

anxiety in the treatment situation;
disturbing feelings toward patients;
stereotype in feelings or behavior toward patients;
love and hate responses toward patients;
erotic preoccupations, especially ideas of falling in love with a patient;
carry over of affects from the analytic hour;
dreams about patients and acting-out episodes.

The very recent literature on this subject includes a number of perceptive articles, rich with descriptive material and clinical examples, and with a much less forbidding tone.

I would employ the term *countertransference only* for those phenomena which are transferences of the analyst to his patient. It is my belief that there are inevitably, naturally, and often desirably, many countertransference developments in every analysis (some evanescent—some sustained), that are a counterpart of the transference phenomena. Interactions (or transactions) between the transferences of the patient and the countertransference of the analyst, going on at unconscious levels, may be—or perhaps always are—of vital significance for the outcome of the treatment. The intellectual verbalizations, consisting of the communications of the patient, and the interpretive activity of the analyst are the media through which deep underground channels of communication develop between patient and doctor. Interpretations as such do not cure, nor will any analyst ever be remembered primarily for his interpretative brilliance by any patient with whom he has been successful. This is not, however, to depreciate the importance of interpretation in the analytic procedure. Obviously, only through the patient's verbal communications, and the painstaking, dispassionate, interpretative efforts of the analyst is it possible, little by little, so to peel away defenses that those deep insights and communications can be obtained that we know to be the essence of the curative effect of the analytic process.

Transferences and countertransferences are unconscious phenomena, based on the repetition compulsion, are derived from significant experiences, largely of one's own childhood, and are directed toward significant persons in the past emotional life of the individual. Habitual characterological attitudes should not be included as countertransference phenomena, since these will find expression in almost any situation, and nearly always in virtually the same form. They lack the specificity to a given situation of the countertransference phenomena. The fact that instinct derivatives have been permitted to become ego-syntonic through being incorporated into the character structure makes such attitudes essentially conscious or preconscious in character, in contrast to the transference phenomena, which derive from deep unconscious conflicts, in a given situation at a given time, and in response to a given individual, in which are mobilized old, affectively significant experiences in relation to earlier important figures. Indoctrination of patients, for example, is probably not usually a countertransference phenomenon, but an impulse derivative. Many other things incorrectly discussed as "countertransferences" are simply defects in the analyst's perceptions or experience.

There are many difficulties in presenting countertransference problems for discussion. There is a scarcity of good clinical material, which derives substantially from the defensive systems of analysts toward the problem in general. The same resistances toward awareness of countertransference are seen among analysts in higher degree and in more insidious form than they are in patients in their resistances to transference insights. This is for good reason. The practicing analyst is under constant assault and has a precarious position to maintain. He has little motivation to change himself, and if he does develop such motivation, it is usually for personal reasons. The patient comes to the analyst for the purpose of being changed, and he values the procedure only if he feels changes are under way. The analyst, however, becomes anxious when he becomes aware of changes effected by emotional pressures from his patients, and there is no one except himself to push him into facing them.

Aside from the resistances of analysts to countertransference explorations and the time not yet having been ripe, there are simple practical reasons for the scarcity of our information on the subject. During the treatment hour, an analyst habitually forces down fantasy about himself. It does take time to analyze anyone, including oneself, and a busy analyst, spending most of his day with patients, naturally pushes aside much potentially illuminating material about himself that comes into his own mind from time to time. Another factor is that many countertransference phenomena when catapulted into consciousness create a sort of emergency. Countertransference acting-out episodes, for example, confront the analyst with a situation of surprise necessitating rapid action and good judgment. He must concentrate on keeping the analytic situation in hand, and often the surprise and shock blot out memory of the processes leading up to the incident, probably due to repression out of the discomfort he experiences.

The decision long ago that analysts themselves should be analyzed before they practice analysis was a tremendous departure from any previous form of medical training. The idea of making a doctor into a patient before he can practice as a doctor is itself traumatic. After all one goes through to become an analyst, to have to become aware of the pervasiveness of countertransference phenomena is a threat and a letdown. The importance of analyzing the prospective analyst was recognized early. Carried into action, it was a major factor, probably, in the rapid advancement of our science. For many years, however, this was as far as it could go. In a sense, the preparatory or personal analysis of the future analyst offered some of the protection that the dream offers our patients. They often regard the dream as a foreign body, over which they have no control, remote in time, and something for which they need not have any feeling of guilt. Similarly, the preliminary personal analysis is often regarded by the practicing analyst, remote in time, forced on him, and related to former problems, as having no connection with present operations, about which there may thus be a bolstering of defenses and rationalizations. The analysis (or observations) of the functioning analyst may be a most important future "royal road" toward understanding the treatment process. Analysts doing supervision are in a position to understand and to make such observations.

Group resistances to exploration of the unconscious of the analyst in the treatment situation follow well-known patterns. There is an unexpressed fear of studying the functioning analyst, as though to report any of his responses were to be permissive about reactions of dubious character. In almost every paper written on countertransference, some tribute has been paid to this group rigidity, in the form of moralizing and pious prohibition, despite intelligent and sympathetic discussion of countertransference problems. Virtually every writer on the subject of countertransference, for example, states unequivocally that no form of erotic reaction to a patient is to be tolerated. This would indicate that temptations in this area are great, and perhaps ubiquitous. This is the one subject about which almost every author is very certain to state his position. Other "countertransference"[4] manifestations are not routinely condemned. Therefore, I assume that erotic responses to some extent trouble nearly every analyst. This is an interesting phenomenon and one that calls for investigation. In my experience, virtually all physicians, when they gain enough confidence in their analysts, report erotic feelings and impulses toward their patients, but usually do so with a good deal of fear and conflict. The following story is typical:

A candidate, who had had a partial therapeutic analysis prior to beginning his training, was talking about a very attractive woman patient whose treatment was winding up successfully. The patient had presented a prolonged and irritating resistance of silence. The candidate said: "This was the patient, perhaps, of all my patients, toward whom I have had the most sexual countertransference. I would sit and have sexual fantasies about her during those periods of silence. I used to think that if I ever went into a training analysis, I would never tell about this, because of what Dr. X [the previous analyst] said. When I had told him about it, he had seemed angry and had said [in effect], 'But how *can* you be interested in such a sick patient—and besides, you have no right to have any such fantasies toward any patient.' I am puzzled because I think I have gotten a lot of insight from my fantasies. I really never thought that I would be able to tell you about this, and I'm damned if I know how I was able to. I wish I knew what you had done to make me feel that it was alright to tell you. . . . Now I remember: once I had been talking about being 'attracted' to a certain patient. I was being quite guarded and wasn't admitting that the attraction was sexual, only that I was attracted, and you said, 'But how do you know that your feelings toward her may not be really helpful to her?'[5] It was this that made it possible for me to talk about my sexual fantasies. . . . *Now* I'm beginning to wonder: did your remark really include acceptance of sexual fantasies (i.e., feelings) or did it just refer to being attracted?"

This man was an excellent therapist and there was no acting-out behavior. Nevertheless, this man had an artificial fear of erotic and countertransference responses that was related to what he perceived to be the prohibitive attitude of the group to which he aspired to belong. Essentially he did not have within himself a feeling that there was anything wrong with his having these responses.

In our selection of candidates for training, we are disposed to pay close attention to the libidinal resources of the applicant, on the theory that large amounts of available libido are necessary to tolerate the heavy task of a number of intensive analyses. At the same time, we deride almost every detectable libidinal investment made by an analyst in a patient. There is much that is obscure about our understanding of the vicissitudes and functions of the analyst's libido in the treatment relationship. I believe this is a large and important topic in itself. It is not enough to talk just about dedication, empathy and rapport, important as these are. I have brought the analyst's libidinal responses into this discussion because they evoke so much countercathexis among analysts; I feel that this countercathexis belongs to the category of rigidity defenses of the analytic group. Suffice it to say that various forms of erotic fantasy and erotic countertransference phenomena of a fantasy and of an affective character are in my experience ubiquitous and presumably normal. Among the conspicuous characteristics of these phenomena are the facts that they are aim-inhibited in the sense of being virtually without impulse toward action, and are in most instances in high degree separated in point of time from erotic transferences of the patient.

Fantasies and feelings toward patients are profuse in all of us, and are now fairly generally accepted especially where they overlap reality-based considerations. Almost all the rational and irrational feelings that we can have toward people in our daily lives, we may at times feel toward our patients. Feelings, however, that seem excessive or inappropriate to what the patient appears to be, or to what he is saying, and especially if they are associated with anxiety, undoubtedly have countertransference significance. Dreams about patients are, of course, usually significant and should always be explored for specific countertransference meaning.

I have for a very long time speculated that in many—perhaps every—intensive analytic treatment there develops something in the nature of countertransference structures (perhaps even a "neurosis") that are essential and inevitable counterparts of the transference neurosis. These countertransference structures may be large or small in their quantitative aspects, but in the total picture they may be of considerable significance for the outcome of the treatment. I believe they function somewhat in the manner of a catalytic agent in the treatment process. Their understanding by the analyst may be as important to the final working through of the transference neurosis as is the analyst's intellectual understanding of the transference neurosis itself, perhaps because they are, so to speak, *the vehicle for the analyst's emotional understanding of the transference neurosis.* Both transference neurosis and countertransference structure seem intimately bound together in a living process and both must be taken continually into account in the work that is psychoanalysis. In fact, I doubt that there is any interpersonal relationship between any two people, and for any purpose whatever, that does not involve, in greater or lesser degree, something in the nature of this living psychological process—interaction at an unconscious and transference level.

We cannot assume that we more than scratch the surface in the preparatory analyses of future analysts in regard to their understanding of themselves and their transference potentials in future analytic work. In addition I am inclined to believe that there are levels of transference that transcend any capacity we now have to gain access to them. There are perhaps even levels of transference to which we will never have access, at any rate by psychological means, because they lie at the borderline between that which is biological and that which is hereditary in us. The phenomenon of falling in love—so little comprehended dynamically—may lie at this borderline.

It is one thing, however, to be able, from experience and training, to formulate consciously the possible occurrence of given countertransference problems. It is another thing to be able to fulfill the cautions with which one charges oneself with 100 per cent efficiency as one goes deeper and deeper into an analytic treatment, week after week, month after month, and year after year, becoming more and more identified with, interested in, and deeply aware of a patient and his problems. If nothing else, too much attention to possible unfavorable countertransference reactions could lead an analyst to some kind of a fixed defense by virtue of which very significant material could be overlooked. Every analyst of experience knows that as he gets deeper and deeper into an analysis, he somehow or other loses a certain perspective on the total situation.

I would conjecture that the development of countertransference neurotic structures in an analyst over a long period of time might be something like Einstein's theory of relativity. This theory has to do with the fact that light is supposed to travel in a straight line from one point to another, and actually does so in our own little world and with our own short distances of measurement. However, when light travels the gigantic distances known to us in terms of millions of light years, other factors previously not understood or even conceived of enter into the picture; and Einstein proved that over these vast reaches of time and space, there is a drift from the straight line in the beam of light. So, too, the hypothetically perfectly trained and perfectly analyzed analyst should be able to pursue an utterly straight course of avoiding all those countertransference pitfalls which his personal analysis should have taught him to anticipate and to avoid. And, undoubtedly, by and large, he is increasingly able to do so and over considerable periods of time. Ultimately, however, it would appear that even under the most ideal circumstances there are bound to be certain drifts, so to speak, from the utterly straight direction of the analyst's performance and understanding of a case, and it is these very slow almost imperceptible drifts which develop in him in unconscious response to hidden pressures and motivations from his patient, which I think constitute the essence of the development of a countertransference structure in and of itself. It is irrelevant to this thesis that these may be most minor excrescences on a very large total structure—the treatment situation. I simply do not believe that any two people, regardless of circumstance, may closet themselves in a room, day after day, month after month, and year after year, without something happening to each of them in respect to the other. Perhaps the development of a major change in the one, which is, after all, the purpose of the therapy, would be impossible without at least some minor change in the other, and it is probably relatively unimportant whether that minor change in the other is a rational one. It is probably far more important that the minor change in the other, namely, the therapist, be that which is specifically important and necessary to the one for whom we hope to achieve the major change. These changes in the therapist would be compounded in my view from the ego-adaptive responses and the unconscious countertransferences of the analyst, interacting upon each other in such a way as to expand his ego-integrative powers specifically to cope with the particular patient's transference resistances. It is in the nature of the transference resistances as they are built up by the patient that they should ferret out and hurl themselves against the weakest spots in the therapist's armamentarium.

Focusing in this manner on one small aspect of a long and involved treatment procedure may inadvertently create an impression that I do not at all wish to create—namely, an illusion that the matter under study is felt to be quantitatively of major importance or qualitatively very different from the bulk of our experience. It is the defensiveness of the analytic group about countertransference phenomena that makes it necessary to caution against such misinterpretation.

I do not like the term *countertransference neurosis* and would not employ it. It has, however, crept into our literature, and it has some reason for existence through analogy with the term *transference neurosis*. However, this latter is perhaps also a misnomer, in view of what actually occurs in an analysis. In general, the transference phenomena are experienced in multiple and varying forms throughout any analytic experience, and by both patient and therapist. A discrete, well-structured, easily describable transference neurosis as such probably seldom occurs, and by the same token even less frequently does a discrete countertransference neurosis develop. The term *neurosis* is very loosely used in our literature. It is employed as an epithet (with the specificity of the word *rheumatism*) or a well-defined psychiatric diagnosis, or as a catch-all for any and all of the immaturities, eccentricities, and emotional conflicts of those people who come to us for assistance. It is easy for us to say that their transferences to us comprise another neurosis to be given the test-tube treatment, but it is another matter entirely to concede that our own transferences to them are similar in kind, though—one hopes —microscopic in quantity by comparison.

I reserve for further and future thought understanding of the nature and meaning of countertransference affect, or lack of it, in psychoanalysis. Increasing personal and group maturity should make its contemplation scientifically a little more tolerable. To some extent this has already begun to occur, but it is still most gingerly approached. A paper presented to The Chicago Psychoanalytic Society four years ago by Adelaide Johnson touched tangentially on this problem and evoked the most massive anxiety and countercathexis in the audience I have observed in many years of psychoanalytic meetings. This reaction seemed all out of proportion to the valid objections that could be raised against the argument of the paper.

If one accepts the premise that countertransferences should be understood as transferences of the analyst, and that they are normal and ubiquitous, countertransference affects have a theoretical *raison d'être* in the universally accepted dictum that true insight is achieved in analysis of transferences only with accompanying and appropriate releases of affect. The fact that the analytic group, despite its vaunted preliminary personal analyses as a means of removing "blind spots," should still defend itself strenuously against applying to its own operations the same dynamic interpretations that it systematically applies to its patients' operations is further testimony to the interminability of the analytic process and the strengths of the repressive forces of the ego.

II. CLINICAL MATERIAL

I have selected for discussion countertransference elements from the analyses of four of my own patients, as I have been able to perceive these. In three cases, countertransference affects of fair intensity played a role at times. Two cases were reasonably successful analyses, one perhaps should have been more successful. I believe my fear of countertransference involvements in this case limited the results. One relatively unsuccessful case was marked by little countertransference affect, an inability to clarify in my own mind my countertransference involvement, if any, and little deep emotional communication between myself and the patient. I wish to emphasize that I believe in general an external observer could not have detected anything out of the ordinary in any one of these analyses.

I have chosen material that I feel demonstrates rather simply some of the points under discussion in part I. In addition, I have chosen material that I can be reasonably comfortable about presenting. None of these cases were really painful failures. Also, I have selected material from long, fairly "classically" conducted analyses for reasons that should be obvious. All of the patients seemed to be both analyzable and to require thorough analysis. I do not believe the experiences I had with these patients are particularly unusual in comparison with many other cases of my own and cases I have supervised with other analysts, except for somewhat striking and above or below average countertransference.

I will begin with an example of a specific countertransference reaction with acting out. Many years ago a patient, referred after a near-psychotic reaction, to an "analysis" with an untrained person was utterly enraged at the referral, because of the frustration of her claims upon the previous therapist. Week after week, and month after month, she raged at me in a vituperative manner, despite my having the greatest of patience with her. I endured a quantity of abuse from her, such as I have never taken from any other patient. At times, I would get irritated with the abuse, but mostly I rather liked the patient, was genuinely interested in helping her and was somewhat surprised at my ability to control my irritation with her. I eventually came to understand that what was for the most part a desirable therapeutic attitude, offered a certain countertransference complication. The following episode brought this problem to my attention.

One beautiful spring day I walked out of my office, twenty minutes before this patient's hour, with my appointment book lying open on my desk. I had a delicious luncheon, alone, which I enjoyed more than usual, and strolled back to the office, in time for my next appointment, only to be informed that my patient had been there and had left extremely angry. It was obvious that I had forgotten her appointment, unconsciously and purposely, and it suddenly came over me that I was absolutely fed up with her abuse to the point of nonendurance. At this point, I began to be angry at my patient, and between this time and the next time she came in, I was in a substantial rage against her. Part of this rage I related to guilt, and part to some anxiety about how I would handle the next treatment interview, which I expected would surpass all previous abuse, and I was now aware of the fact that I was no longer going to be able to tolerate this abuse. I fantasied (which of course was a hope) that my patient would terminate her treatment with me. At her next appointment, she glared at me and said, in an accusatory manner, "Where were *you* yesterday?" I said only, "I'm sorry, I forgot." She started to attack me, saying she knew I had been there shortly before, and went on with her customary vituperation. I made no comment, for the most part feeling it was better that I say nothing. This went on for five or ten minutes and abruptly she stopped. There was a dead silence and all of a sudden she started to laugh, saying, "Well, you know, Dr. Tower, really I can't say that I blame you." This was absolutely the first break in this obstinate resistance. Following this episode, the patient was much more cooperative and after one or two short recurrences of the abusiveness, probably to test me, the defense disappeared entirely, and she shortly went into analysis at deep transference levels. At first glance, this seems so unimportant an episode that it hardly warrants description. One would say I was irritated with the patient and missed her hour because of aggression, which of course was true. But the real countertransference problem was not that. Actually, my acting-out behavior was reality-based and brought a resolution to the countertransference problem, which was that I had been patient with her too long. This tendency in myself I could trace in detail from certain influences upon me in my earliest childhood. I had gotten into difficulties from this tendency from time to time during my development. I understood this in part, and yet it was not sufficiently resolved in my personality. This prolonged abusive resistance need not have lasted so long, had I been freer to be more aggressive in the face of it. The manner in which I repressed my aggression and allowed it to accumulate to a point where I was forced to act it out, was not an entirely desirable therapeutic procedure. Thus, a theoretically good therapeutic attitude, namely, that of infinite patience and effort to understand a very troubled patient, was actually in this situation a negative countertransference structure, virtually a short-lived countertransference neurosis, which undoubtedly wasted quite a bit of the patient's time, and but for my sudden resolution of it through acting out might well have gone on for a considerably longer time. I gave this little episode a good deal of thought in subsequent years, and eventually came to understand more of its true significance.

However, it is only recently that I might have questioned whether this countertransference reaction, which had such clear negative implications at certain levels in this treatment, might perhaps at other levels have had equally positive implications. This particular disposition of mine might well have facilitated this patient's eventual ability to deal fully and affectively with her most highly defended problem—the passive homoerotic aspect of the transference—for it had been an acute paranoid type reaction that brought her into treatment with me.

In the following material I attempt to trace countertransference developments in two analyses that lend themselves to many comparisons.

This is material from the cases of two men, both successful business men of fairly similar backgrounds, near my own age, both liked me as a person, and I liked both of them as people. Both were intelligent, married, and had children; both had long analyses. One analysis was successful in a working through at the very deepest transference levels, of an intense transference neurosis, resulting in great symptomatic improvement, much maturation, and increased success. In the second, there was no real working through of a transference neurosis, the analysis was unsatisfactory to me, and I felt insecure about the patient's future. There was symptomatic improvement, and the patient was not too dissatisfied, but I eventually counseled him to seek analysis with someone else, which he did after a considerable resistance.

I was initially more favorably inclined toward the second patient, who seemed highly motivated for treatment, more adequate, and whose psychosexual development seemed more normal. The first and more successful patient, on the other hand, was initially ambivalent, derisively hostile, and created early doubts in me about taking him for treatment.

Both parental marriages had been stable, the fathers being somewhat passive but reasonably successful. Both mothers seemed compulsive, and both patients seemed to have suffered deep developmental defects in relation to the mother, the first, and successful patient, perhaps less so. The course and content of his analysis suggested mainly regression from oedipal conflict, while this as a dominant feature was by no means as demonstrable in the second case.

Both patients presented severe problems of inhibition of masculine assertiveness with passive homosexual reaction formations. Both had deep, unconscious problems of an oral sadistic, murderous disposition toward a female sibling; both had developed fairly serious neurotic symptomatology in late adolescence, and in both there were schizoid features. Both reacted against homosexual problems by early flight into marriages with aggressive, controlling, narcissistic women. Both wives were attractive, compulsive, disturbed, and so highly defended that neither would consent to treatment, despite the fact that both marriages were stormy. The husbands were devoted, and struggled to keep the marriages going. The wives resented their husbands' treatment and attempted to sabotage it. I had occasion to become acquainted with both wives, although this was not sought by me. I did not experience troublesome negative feelings about either of them, despite their anxiety-ridden efforts to undercut the husbands' treatment.

With both men, I was quite aware of the contributions that they themselves made to the difficulties with their wives, namely, that both were too submissive, too hostile, in a sense too devoted, and both wives were frustrated for lack of sufficient uninhibited masculine assertiveness from their husbands. In both instances, this was extensively interpreted and worked over, but without much change in the picture.

Obviously, this was a problem that could not be satisfactorily worked through without thorough analysis of its deep sources in the conflict that each had toward the female sibling, and behind that, the murderous rage toward the mother, as an oral sadistic regression from oedipal conflict. I went through phases of (countertransference?) protectiveness, in both cases; that with the first man was toward the marriage and the wife; with the second it was toward the man himself. Both patients confronted me, in transference material, with suggestions that I was being too protective and as I became conscious of this, I believe I was reasonably able to correct this.

In the first case, the protectiveness was directed toward avoiding secondary disturbance in the wife. She had at one time been thought by a psychiatrist to be psychotic, and I wished, realistically, not to provoke a blowup in her with all of the disruptive effects upon a family that such an episode can have. The protectiveness in the second case was directed toward the patient himself, and on a similar basis. This patient himself had once been thought to be psychotic. There was a Rorschach examination of this patient which, in brief, showed the case to be a deeply set neurosis; analytic treatment was indicated though it could be expected to be very difficult. It was a very productive record, with no schizophrenic material. While energy and drive appeared extremely high, the personality organization was such as to lead to expectation of a boiling over of affects into the world at large. Imagination was limited and there were reduced avenues of escape into an inner life.

The symptomatology which brought these patients to treatment was similar: diffuse anxiety with some depression, a strong awareness of massive inhibition, and a certain amount of confusion, particularly regarding sexual roles. Both, thus, would be classed as anxiety neurosis. The more normal psychosexual development of the second case, and my initial more favorable feeling toward him, would suggest theoretically that if my own libidinal organization approached the so-called normal and if I were to develop countertransference deviations, these would be more likely to be manifested toward the second patient, rather than the first, who when he came into treatment presented some not too attractive psychosexual problems. In fact, exactly the reverse proved to be the case.

Both patients presented irritating difficulties in communication: mumbling, halting speech, circumstantiality, repetitiveness, minutiae. There were times in both analyses when I became quite irritated with the communication problem. Only late in the treatment of both, as the infantile neuroses unfolded, did I begin to perceive some of the differences between what appeared to be fairly similar speech difficulties. The communication problem in the first case was a highly structured resistance, with the concealed purpose of destroying my power as an analyst and getting revenge upon me for my attentions to any and all other siblings and all males. The speech blocks in this case concealed biting, sardonic, destructive, object-oriented impulses, and disappeared with the working through in the transference of the deep oral sadistic problem. The communication problems of the second patient appeared to be an extension of the hidden anaclitic character of his ego, were essentially clinging in character and designed to acquire an object rather than to destroy a frustrating one, and were never in any substantial way relieved. Despite my long and conscientious effort to help this man, I do not think that I succeeded in any way commensurate with the amount of time and energy expended by both of us upon the attempt.

At this point, one might say that it has long been known that cases that we classify as transference neuroses, as the first patient would seem to be, are far more accessible to analytic procedures than the narcissistic neuroses, as was apparently the diagnosis of the second patient. Why should one have to bring in considerations of countertransference as a factor in the ultimate success of these treatments? This is all very true and, at the same time, too simple. It was, indeed, a very long time before I could differentiate sharply between these two cases, as I have just done, and it is also after the fact, so to speak. For a long time the first patient appeared to be most narcissistic. Certain delinquencies in this man and his much more severe psychosexual problems pointed this up. Additionally, I am not trying to prove that counter-transference neurotic phenomena are the sole, or even major, factors involved in therapeutic progress. My purpose is to attempt to demonstrate their existence in a far more pervasive and perhaps significant manner than is generally conceded; to offer some evidence that they may be of crucial importance under certain circumstances, and to make some small contribution toward tracing their origins, development, and resolution in the course of an analytic treatment.

This brings me to crucial turning points in the analyses of these two men. So far, I have discussed the emotional and practical situations with which I was confronted, and the background material that seems pertinent to a framework in which I might or might not develop some relatively organized countertransference response. Both men presented me with a specific problem, calculated potentially to stir up some countertransference responses of a reasonably normal character, in any female analyst who might be somewhat off guard. I refer to the fact that both these rather nice men were dependently attached to wives who defensively resented and made efforts to undermine the analyses, who were possessive of their husbands, and depreciating of them in a refined kind of way. Both men had much aggression against their wives, of which both were afraid, and had varying forms of overcompensatory behavior in regard to this. Both were therefore bound, sooner or later, to make efforts to play the analyst off against their wives, and both were bound, eventually, to attempt to exploit the analyses in the heterosexual transference, for whatever gratification they might be able to seduce from the analyst. Both were, of course, inevitably bound to succeed or fail, to some extent in terms of the deeper aspects of the resolution of the Oedipus conflict in the analyst's own personality. Of all of this I was, of course, theoretically aware from very early in the treatment of both men, and was consistently and reasonably well on guard to watch my own reactions, especially toward the large amount of complaining material brought against the wives. I was equally on guard against letting myself become irritated with the respective wives for their subversive behavior in regard to their husbands' treatment.

The turning point in the first case developed as follows: Toward the end of the second year of this analysis, despite much intellectual knowledge of his difficulties, when there seemed virtually no improvement in the marital situation, the communications block, or in his dependency defense, the patient's wife developed a severe psychosomatic illness. I took careful note of this fact at the time, speculating to myself that this illness might bind her anxiety, which seemed so prepsychotic. I wondered if this might not be an out for her, in that she could now abandon her controlling, attacking behavior and lean on her husband more, without too much ego anxiety. I thought this might benefit the marital relation. What I took note of consciously, however, must have remained detached from what already was developing unconsciously in me as the nucleus of a small countertransference reaction toward the total situation. I believe this man's developing transference neurosis was slowly and inexorably pushing me in the direction of actually being to him, in some small measure, the overconcerned and overidentified mother figure (which he felt his wife was not) who, regardless of the merits of the situation, would see things much more in terms of his evaluation of them, and would identify with his hostilities, rather than being the completely dispassionate observer. I believe that, despite my cautions, I had been imperceptibly pushed by his transference pressures into regarding his wife as more of a problem than she had initially appeared to be. At any rate, I failed to observe that she had actually slowly become somewhat less of a problem, for, despite the patient's chronic, exasperating resistance, he *was* dealing with his domestic situation with more firmness and gentleness. Whether this was concealed from me by the patient, or I, for my own unconscious reasons, was blind to it, is beside the point. Very probably both were true. By this time the ego satisfactions of an improved functioning outside of the treatment were disrupted by strong, unconscious, frustrated libidinal drives in the transference neurosis. These were to make the most of the possession of a truly interested, maternally perceived person out of those transference needs as well as out of whatever unconscious potential I had to offer in the direction of fulfilling them.

This man's mother had, in reality, twice in his life deserted him emotionally at very crucial periods. There was a remoteness between mother and son that I never did fathom but that inclined me to consider whether this was not a quite detached mother. Some of the later phases of the analysis of his transference neurosis bore this out, and revealed why it was perhaps of crucial importance for this particular patient that he literally be able to seduce me, to some small extent, into a countertransference deviation toward the side of his hostile dependent defenses against his wife, before he would be able to trust me with his deepest transference neurotic needs of me. These, I believe, are some of the factors that led to my intellectual speculations about the meaning of the wife's psychosomatic illness, remaining detached from the slowly developing countertransference blindness about the wife.

This all came to a head about a year later. I had been getting both uneasy and frustrated with the monotonous masochistic and depressive character of this patient's resistance. I suddenly had a dream that so startled me that it blotted out all recollection of what led up to it. The dream was very simply that I was visiting in this patient's home. Only his wife was there, she seemed glad to have me, and was being most hospitable and gracious. The general tone of the visit was much like that of an afternoon chat of friendly wives, whose husbands were, perhaps, friends or colleagues. The dream vaguely disturbed me.

As I started to think about it, I realized that I had known for some time, but had not taken note of the fact, that the wife was no longer interfering in her husband's treatment. This was due to his better adjustment, to a developing confidence that I was no true threat to her, and a decreasing direct envy of her husband's relationship to me. I also remembered, at this point, that almost a year previously I had speculated about the meaning of the wife's psychosomatic illness and had then largely forgotten it. In other words, I realized that I had unconsciously developed a somewhat fixed attitude of being too afraid of her psychotic potential, and had ignored her improvement. The dream pointed up to me that I had been derelict in identifying with her in the marital situation; that in effect she really did want me to come into her home and would welcome my having a better perspective upon her. The dream said that the wife was much more positively oriented toward me than I had given her credit for during the past year, and that it was time that I look in on the domestic scene from her point of view.

After I had given all of this very careful thought and felt fairly sure of my ground, I went into action. First, I picked up the analysis of the subtle acting out on his part against his wife within the domestic situation, a point that had been neglected for some time. I became very direct in discussing the aggression against his wife through the mechanism of his masochism and his dependent hostility, which we both now understood much better than in the earlier analysis of these problems. Following this, I discussed again and more actively his attempts to play off his wife and myself against each other, and how he had exaggerated and prolonged the bad marital situation for purposes of transference gratification. All of this had been previously extensively worked over, but with insufficient effect. It is, of course, obvious that in my own unconscious some resurgent oedipal conflict in the form of an overdetermined competition with and fear of another woman in a triangular situation lay behind my countertransference response.

Following this active repairing of the holes in the analysis, so to speak, the patient shortly took over the analysis very assertively. From a complaining, low-voltage approach for nearly the three years, he began moving with the greatest directness. He began subjecting me to intense emotional pressures; he himself carried the analysis back into a comprehensive review of his entire development, with new insights into crucial life experiences, and with minute attention to reconstructing the infantile situation. There were new recoveries of early memories, especially of primal scene material and of a peculiarly unexpressed remoteness between the parents.

Following extensive reworking over of the oedipal material—without, however, enough reliving of castration anxiety to make me feel secure about a working through—the patient switched to the deepest oral material. This had been displaced from the sister born when he was about two, to the sister born during the height of the oedipal period. With the opening up of this material the first intense, undefended affect of the entire analysis made its appearance. There was a long period characterized by profound depressive feelings and naked rage, feelings largely confined to the analytic hours. With this outpouring of affect, the patient's block in communication disappeared permanently. Dream and fantasy material in this phase included almost every form of sadistic attack or indignity conceivable. This was, of course, phallic sadism couched in oral language. During this period the relationship between us was very tense. The quantity of the patient's affect alone would have constituted a severe burden upon any one attempting to deal with it. In addition, he subjected me to the most persistent, minute, and discomforting scrutiny, as though tearing me apart—cell by cell. My every move, my every word, was watched so closely that it literally felt to me that if I made even one slight false move, all would be lost. The threat, however, was not to myself. The affect created in me was more of the following order: if I were to fail to meet this test, he would fall apart, and would never again trust another human being. On several occasions I experienced dreams that directly anticipated oncoming material, as though from my own unconscious came forewarning of what was to come,[6] and fortified me to deal with the massive quantity of his affect when it hit.

During this period, every hour was exhausting and often the feelings engendered in me during the hour would carry over. On several occasions, I began to be worried about the extent of this carry over. All my disposition to become morbid about this was dispelled rather suddenly and amusingly. I was to go off one afternoon for a vacation, having seen the patient that morning. This had, in itself, stepped up both the sadistic and depressive feelings with which he burdened me. I went off feeling at a very low ebb and on the verge of anger with the whole business. The depression and irritation in me lasted for several hours and then suddenly disappeared completely. Nothing extraneous happened to dispel it, nor did I make any conscious effort to do so. I doubt that I even thought of this patient, except in the most casual way throughout the entire vacation. The fact that this could happen so spontaneously led me to the reassuring conclusion that my disturbing feelings did not of themselves mean that I was getting involved in any quantitatively excessive countertransference problem that might prove to have unfavorable implications, either for him or for myself. It seemed to me only that what had been going on was that my unconscious had somehow finally become sufficiently attuned to his unconscious, that I was able to tolerate the affect connected with his feelings of utter despair, because of affects and attitudes in myself over which I had no conscious control, but which *were* appropriate to his needs, in order to work this problem through. As I have thought it over since, to understand what had been going on in myself in response to this patient, it seems compounded of two factors. On the one hand there developed in me, on a transient basis, an amount of masochism sufficient to absorb the sadism that he was now unloading, and that had terrified him throughout his entire life. The other ingredient of my affective response was, I believe, a joining with him and a supporting of him, through identification, in a true unconscious grief reaction. This, I believe, was similar to the "sadness" of affect in the therapist, of which Adelaide Johnson (15) and Michael Balint (3) have written. As he unloaded his sadism, free from fear of loss of control, and of any fear of retaliation, I believe that his man's ego was finally and permanently freed of the binding of this sadism into his superego. The depressive affect had become wholly free of self-depreciation and guilt and had taken on the quality of a true mourning for a lost love object.

Following this, the patient returned to the oedipal situation, and with intense affect. The repressed competition with the father was brought out in the transference in a quite usual way, with fantasies about men in the analyst's life, competition with father surrogates, and real fear derived from competitive impulses toward these men as erotic transference impulses arose toward the analyst. With this final working through of the oedipal material, the patient went on to termination. The improvement and personality changes in this patient have now been sustained for some time, and I have the impression that the wife's difficulties are largely intrinsic only, and are not being contributed to by her husband.

Interestingly, it was only with the development and resolution of my countertransference response to the marital situation, and the breaking through of the patient's resistance against communication, with the outpouring of long stored-up affect, that I began to have feelings of very much liking this man as a person. I do not mean that I had previously disliked him. Precisely here, I believe, lies evidence that in this case the countertransference response had a beneficial effect. I am inclined to think that it was only after this man's unconscious perceived that he had *actually* forced me into a countertransference response that he became sufficiently confident of his powers to influence me, and of my willingness, at least in small part, to be influenced or subjugated by him. It was only then that he could finally allow me to penetrate his masochistic defense, and give me access to the deep unconscious sadism so long bound into his superego, for it now became both possible and necessary to turn that sadism upon me. This massive sadism, deriving presumably from an infantile depression, had been re-experienced in the oedipal situation, causing strong regressive admixtures of oral sadism into the phallic sadism of the oedipal conflict. I do not believe that without the experience, perceived by his unconscious, of actually having been able in some small way to bend me affectively to his needs, this man would have succeeded in going into these deepest sources of his neurosis. That he was able so to bend me to his will, simultaneously repaired the wound in his masculine ego, and eliminated his *infantile* fear of *my* sadism in the mother transference. It would seem that he had finally achieved an inner confidence that his controls were *in fact* adequate, and that I *in fact* trusted them.[7]

Interestingly, his unconscious also perceived that I had changed in my feeling about him. During this period, he made a number of comments about my affection for him, which bore no references to sexual love. They were simple statements of fact. I do not think he ever gave conscious thought to whether I had changed. He never asked for any confirmation, never indicated that he felt not liked previously; these were simple and casual statements of a perception of something, which from his point of view was timeless, incontrovertible, and unambivalent. His unconscious *had* correctly perceived something that had actually developed in me. In fact, I think it is possible that any final successful working through of a deep and thorough analysis involves some development of this sort. That there are many more or less successful analyses that are in fact nevertheless partial analyses is well known to all of us. Many, clearly, never should be other than partial. I doubt that there is any thorough working through of a deep transference neurosis, in the strictest sense, that does not involve some form of emotional upheaval in which *both* patient and analyst are involved. In other words, there is both a transference neurosis and a corresponding countertransference "neurosis" (no matter how small and temporary) that are both analyzed in the treatment situation, with eventual feelings of a substantially new orientation on the part of both persons toward each other.

I do not know whether the crucial episode that seemed to me to be a turning point in the second case was a sudden perception on my part of the reality that this man was unanalyzable by me, and the real countertransference difficulty was my illusion that I could treat this man. The resistance described earlier had become chronic. Slowly, there *were* gains that in all honesty I would have to look upon as psychotherapeutic largely. Slowly, I became aware of a subtle smeary overtone in his attitudes toward his wife, and also toward me in the analysis. It lay, however, so nebulously concealed behind the manifest oral-sadistic and oral-dependent material that somehow I was never able to bring it out into the open where it could be dealt with. Even now I wonder if it was not really some derivative of the fuzziness in this man's ego boundaries. I found myself slowly and increasingly identified with and sympathetic for his wife, related primarily to my perception of this vaguely smeary attitude toward her. I was aware also, step by step, of changes in her attitudes, how her interference gradually slowed down, how she began to cooperate with him about his analysis, and finally turned to me with despair because there were no significant changes for the good in his attitude toward her. This patient made intense protestations of dependent and erotic need for me in a manner in which such material usually appears. From hindsight, I would say the reason I was not moved by this was that it was not structured and was thus interpretively intangible, and that deep down this man did *not* have a mobilizable strength capable of bending me to *his* will, as did the first patient. I believe that with his deep anaclitic ego organization, his maximum potential would have been to seduce me into bending him toward *my* will. Consequently, I must have always felt that these protestations were overcompensatory, not contained, and not truly transference.

The turning point in this case came when he suddenly and unpredictably developed a schizoid depressed state. I had no warning that this was coming, had little material with which to understand it, and before I could evaluate what was happening, he came for a five o'clock appointment one day, following several days of intense anxiety and obsessive suicidal fantasies. He became severely agitated, the suicidal fantasies suddenly gave way to a violent outburst of murderous feelings, such that I became truly alarmed. I felt he was very close to an ego break and might very well go out the window, or off the fire escape, out of fear of the murderous ideas. The office was deserted, the secretaries having gone home. I announced quickly and calmly that I thought he was far too upset to discuss his problems that evening, would he please go home, take a sedative, try to find distraction and return first thing in the morning when he might feel more calm. The patient followed my request, in a trance-like state, and left. Slowly I was able to pull him out of this acute apparently near-psychotic state. After this episode I never again had confidence in my ability to do anything with this man psychoanalytically, nor did I ever see him again outside of office hours. Eventually I terminated his relationship with me and arranged his treatment with someone else. I felt that perhaps this might be worked through with a male analyst whom he would perceive as a person able to control him. We eventually parted company with mutual good feeling, rather of a surface character. However, out of all this long effort at therapy, I think little in the way of really deep mutual (i.e., nonverbal) communication of feeling ever occurred between us.

If this man was unanalyzable by me—or by a woman—I would conjecture that the reason lay in that the defect in his masculine ego was reparable only by identification and actual incorporation of a masculine ego in a treatment situation with a man, and perhaps only after experiencing an intense passive homoerotic transference. Apparently I could not offer him this, and neither was I able to mobilize any affect in the homoerotic material he did bring. In contrast, the defect in the masculine ego of the first man was apparently actually repaired by a small victory over me in the transference. In other words, there were built-in controls in his ego, which I unconsciously perceived, and this permitted me without undue anxiety to respond in very small but perhaps crucial measure to this man as woman to man, at the same time that my dominant relation to him was that of physician to patient. Built-in controls appeared absent in the second case, and would have to be acquired by identification and incorporation before he could live out affectively his underlying sadism, or move me to trust him as woman.[8]

A number of years ago I analyzed a young man who had essentially the same problems and personality structure as the first of the two cases just discussed, and whose analysis reached virtually the same depth with similar mutual affective intensity. This case was not carried through to a fully successful result, and I believe that it should have been. There were further countertransference complications in this case, in that I could never decide whether this was one of those rare cases in which the analyst should actively foster a divorce. In retrospect, I believe two important factors were operative in me. First, my discomfort with the transference-countertransference affect blocked me in a full working through of this problem. Secondly, I was probably intimidated by the pressures of an older and very aggressive analyst, who was treating the wife and who was openly determined that this marriage be successful. I terminated the case prematurely, with all the usual supposedly mutual understandings and rationalizations between us about indications for terminating. The fact that the patient's unconscious correctly perceived what I had unconsciously done to him, and why, was proved by some rage-motivated, fairly serious acting out he did against me afterward, which I understood immediately but which unfortunately did not come to my attention until far too late for me to do anything about it. Fortunately, the young man later obtained further analysis with someone else.

III. SUMMARY AND CONCLUSIONS

An attempt has been made to clarify present conceptions of psychoanalysts about countertransference and to bring some clinical material to bear upon a thesis that these conceptions need simplification and modification, and that countertransference phenomena are inherently dynamically operative in all treatment procedures.

It is emphasized that countertransference is only one of a number of responses of the analyst of equal or greater importance to the treatment situation. (Empathy, rapport, intuition, intellectual comprehension, and ego-adaptive responses are, of course, other very significant elements.)

The treatment situation between patient and analyst at its deepest and nonverbal levels probably follows the protype of the mother-child symbiosis so sensitively described by Benedek and involves active libidinal exchanges between the two through unconscious nonverbal channels of communication. Thus, broadly speaking, patients do affect their analysts. At these deep levels of interchange the dominant trends of constructive or of destructive use of the treatment situation by the patient are probably derivatives of the earliest relationships to the mother.

In the successful analysis the patient not only brings out in full form his *own* worst impulses, but perhaps, in addition, accomplishes a similar purpose, in minor form, with reference to the analyst, in part as a testing, in part as a becoming deeply aware of the analyst as a human being with limitations. At the same time, he accomplishes, for the purposes of his own ego strengthening, a capacity to handle the analyst's defects constructively, to forgive him for his aggression, his countertransference acting out, and to establish a mature adequately positive libidinal relationship with him, despite these imperfections.

The term *countertransference* should be reserved for transferences of the analyst—in the treatment situation—and nothing else. As such, they are syntheses of the analyst's unconscious ego, and together with the patient's transferences, both are products of the combined unconscious work of patient and analyst. They are multiple and varied in their origins and manifestations, and change from day to day and from patient to patient. They are normal phenomena, taking root in the repetition compulsion. They become "abnormal," or perhaps better described as interfering, excessive, fixed, or unworkable, on the basis of both qualitative and quantitative factors in their synthesis, as well as the manner in which they impinge on the analytic situation.

An effort has been made to explore the concept and the possible functions of a countertransference "neurosis" as such. There is evidence that structured formations may occur more consistently than generally supposed and that they may under certain circumstances perform useful functions. This usefulness may be a more or less temporary phenomenon and derive from the source and the character of the structure itself. On the other hand its uncovering, analysis, and resolution by the analyst may be useful to a deeper emotional understanding by the analyst of the transference neurosis.

I believe that in all instances where anything more than the most superficial relationship develops between patient and therapist, and inevitably, in true deep analytic procedures, there are many countertransference reactions and that something in the nature of a countertransference neurosis develops, which, no matter how small, may be of great significance for the course of the treatment, in the sense of a catalytic agent. By definition, a catalyst is an ordinarily inert substance that in a given milieu is capable of accelerating, or of decelerating, a chemical process. It does not seem too unrealistic to think that there may be similar phenomena at those deep levels of interpersonal relationship which one finds in the psychoanalytic treatment process.

Scientific study of the psychoanalyst's unconscious in the treatment situation should improve our therapeutic efficiency and do much to provide a solid scientific basis upon which to evaluate treatment techniques. Such study would likewise illuminate that which is defensive and acting out upon the therapist's part, and that which is scientifically and demonstrably constructive.

NOTES

1. Report of The Committee on Training Standards, Board on Professional Standards, American Psychoanalytic Association, November 1953.
2. Some suggestions along this line seem to approach the "wild analysis" level.
3. "Carry over": affects persisting in the analyst in response to and following an analytic interview.
4. The quotation marks at this point are used because these responses are by no means all countertransference. Many should be quite simply regarded as psychophysiological.
5. This was said in the sense of: One could at least be open-minded to the idea that the patient's unconscious awareness of the positive nature of the therapist's countertransference was of specific value to this patient.
6. Mostly disguised masochistic response to sadism.
7. I hope that it is entirely clear that nothing of my affective response was *ever* made a manifest element in the treatment.
8. At a conscious level I had for a long time a reverse impression of the element of control in these two patients.

BIBLIOGRAPHY

1. Alexander, F. Some quantitative aspects of psychoanalytic technique. *J. Amer. Psychoanal. Assoc., 2:*692–701, 1954.
2. Balint, A., and Balint, M. On transference and counter-transference. *Internat. J. Psychoanal., 20:*223–230, 1939.
3. Balint, M. Changing therapeutical aims and techniques in psycho-analysis. *Internat. J. Psychoanal., 31:*117–124, 1950.
4. Benedek, T. Adaptation to reality in early infancy. *Psychoanal. Quart. 7:*200–215, 1938.
5. Benedek, T. Countertransference in the training analyst. *Bull. Menninger Clin., 18:*12–16, 1954.
6. Berman, L. Countertransference and attitudes of the analyst in the therapeutic process. *Psychiatry, 12:*159–166, 1949.
7. Cohen, M. B. Countertransference and anxiety. *Psychiatry, 15:*231–243, 1952.
8. Fliess, R. Countertransference and counteridentification. *J. Amer. Psychoanal. Assoc., 1:* 268–284, 1953.

9. Freud, S. (1910) The future prospects of psycho-analytic therapy. *Collected Papers, 2:* 285–296. London: Hogarth Press, 1946.

10. Frosch, J., et al. (Eds.) *Annual Survey of Psychoanalysis, 1:*237–248. New York: International Universities Press, 1950.

11. Gitelson, M. The emotional position of the analyst in the psycho-analytic situation. *Internat. J. Psychoanal., 33:*1–10, 1952.

12. Glover, E. *Technique of Psycho-Analysis.* New York: International Universities Press, 1955.

13. Greenson, R. Panel discussion on "Sublimation." *J. Amer. Psychoanal. Assoc., 3:*525–527, 1954.

14. Heimann, P. On counter-transference. *Internat. J. Psychoanal., 31:*81–84, 1950.

15. Johnson, A. Transference and countertransference in late analysis of the oedipus. (To be published.)

16. Little, M. Counter-transference and the patient's response to it. *Internat. J. Psychoanal., 32:*32–40, 1951.

17. Lorand, S. *Technique of Psychoanalytic Therapy.* New York: International Universities Press, 1946, pp. 209–222.

18. Orr, D. W. Transference and countertransference: A historical survey. *J. Amer. Psychoanal. Assoc., 2:*621–670, 1954.

19. Payne, S. M. Notes on developments in the theory and practice of psycho-analytic technique. *Internat. J. Psychoanal., 27:*12–18, 1946.

20. Racker, H. A contribution to the problem of counter-transference. *Internat. J. Psychoanal., 34:*313–324, 1953.

21. Reich, A. On counter-transference. *Internat. J. Psychoanal., 32:*25–31, 1951.

22. Rioch, J. The transference phenomenon in psychoanalytic therapy. *Psychiatry, 6:*147–156, 1943.

23. Sharpe, E. F. The psycho-analyst. *Internat. J. Psychoanal., 28:*1–6, 1947.

24. Tauber, E. S. Exploring the therapeutic use of countertransference data. *Psychiatry, 17:* 331–336, 1954.

25. Winnicott, D. W. Hate in the counter-transference. *Internat. J. Psychoanal., 10:*69–74, 1949.

26. Round-table discussion: Doctor-patient relationship in therapy. *Am. J. Psychoanal., 15:*3–21, 1955.

11. The Meanings and Uses of Countertransference

Heinrich Racker

I

Freud describes transference as both the greatest danger and the best tool for analytic work. He refers to the work of making the repressed past conscious. Besides these two implied meanings of *transference,* Freud gives it a third meaning: it is in the transference that the analysand may relive the past under better conditions and in this way rectify pathological decisions and destinies. Likewise three meanings of *countertransference* may be differentiated. It too may be the greatest danger and at the same time an important tool for understanding, an assistance to the analyst in his function as interpreter. Moreover, it affects the analyst's behavior; it interferes with his action as object of the patient's re-experience in that new fragment of life that is the analytic situation, in which the patient should meet with greater understanding and objectivity than he found in the reality or fantasy of his childhood.

What have present-day writers to say about the problem of countertransference?[1]

Lorand (16) writes mainly about the dangers of countertransference for analytic work. He also points out the importance of taking countertransference reactions into account, for they may indicate some important subject to be worked through with the patient. He emphasizes the necessity of the analyst's being always aware of his countertransference, and discusses specific problems such as the conscious desire to heal, the relief analysis may afford the analyst from his own problems, and narcissism and the interference of personal motives in clinical purposes. He also emphasizes the fact that these problems of countertransference concern not only the candidate but also the experienced analyst.

Winnicott (24) is specifically concerned with 'objective and justified hatred'

Read at a meeting of the Argentine Psychoanalytic Association in May 1953.

in countertransference, particularly in the treatment of psychotics. He considers how the analyst should manage this emotion: should he, for example, bear his hatred in silence or communicate it to the analysand? Thus Winnicott is concerned with a particular countertransference reaction insofar as it affects the behavior of the analyst, who is the analysand's object in his re-experience of childhood.

Heimann (11) deals with countertransference as a tool for understanding the analysand. The 'basic assumption is that the analyst's unconscious understands that of his patient. This rapport on the deep level comes to the surface in the form of feelings that the analyst notices in response to his patient, in his countertransference.' This emotional response of the analyst is frequently closer to the psychological state of the patient than is the analyst's conscious judgment thereof.

Little (15) discusses countertransference as a disturbance to understanding and interpretation and as it influences the analyst's behavior with decisive effect upon the patient's re-experience of his childhood. She stresses the analyst's tendency to repeat the behavior of the patient's parents and to satisfy certain needs of his own, not those of the analysand. Little emphasizes that one must admit one's countertransference to the analysand and interpret it, and must do so not only in regard to 'objective' countertransference reactions (Winnicott) but also to 'subjective' ones.

Annie Reich (21) is chiefly interested in countertransference as a source of disturbances in analysis. She clarifies the concept of countertransference and differentiates two types: 'countertransference in the proper sense' and 'the analyst's using the analysis for acting-out purposes'. She investigates the cause of these phenomena, and seeks to understand the conditions that lead to good, excellent, or poor results in analytic activity.

Gitelson (10) distinguishes between the analyst's 'reactions to the patient as a whole' (the analyst's 'transferences') and the analyst's 'reactions to partial aspects of the patient' (the analyst's 'countertransferences'). He is concerned also with the problems of intrusion of countertransference into the analytic situation, and states that, in general, when such intrusion occurs the countertransference should be dealt with by analyst and patient working together, thus agreeing with Little.

Weigert (23) favors analysis of countertransference insofar as it intrudes into the analytic situation, and she advises, in advanced stages of treatment, less reserve in the analyst's behavior and more spontaneous display of countertransference.

In the first of my own two papers on countertransference (17), I discussed countertransference as a danger to analytic work. After analyzing the resistances that still seemed to impede investigation of countertransference, I attempted to show without reserve how œdipal and prœcdipal conflicts as well as paranoid, depressive, manic, and other processes persisted in the 'countertransference neurosis' and how they interfered with the analyst's understanding, interpretation, and behavior. My remarks applied to 'direct' and 'indirect' countertransference.[2]

In my second paper (18), I described the use of countertransference experiences for understanding psychological problems, especially transference problems, of the analysand. In my principal points I agreed with Heimann (11), and emphasized the following suggestions: (1) Countertransference reactions of great intensity, even pathological ones, should also serve as tools; (2) Countertransference is the expression of the analyst's identification with the internal objects of the analysand, as well as with his id and ego, and may be used as such; and (3) Countertransference reactions have specific characteristics (specific contents, anxieties, and mechanisms) from which we may draw conclusions about the specific character of the psychological happenings in the patient.

The present paper is intended to amplify my remarks on countertransference as a tool for understanding the mental processes of the patient (including especially his transference reactions)—their content, their mechanisms, and their intensities. Awareness of countertransference helps one to understand what should be interpreted and when. This paper will also consider the influence of countertransference upon the analyst's behavior toward the analysand—behavior that affects decisively the position of the analyst as object of the re-experience of childhood, thus affecting the process of cure.

Let us first consider briefly countertransference in the history of psychoanalysis. We meet with a strange fact and a striking contrast. The discovery by Freud (7) of countertransference and its great importance in therapeutic work gave rise to the institution of didactic analysis which became the basis and center of psychoanalytic training. Yet countertransference received little scientific consideration over the next forty years. Only during the last few years has the situation changed, rather suddenly, and countertransference become a subject examined frequently and with thoroughness. How is one to explain this initial recognition, this neglect, and this recent change? Is there not reason to question the success of didactic analysis in fulfilling its function if this very problem, the discovery of which led to the creation of didactic analysis, has had so little scientific elaboration?

These questions are clearly important, and those who have personally witnessed a great part of the development of psychoanalysis in the last forty years have the best right to answer them.[3] I will suggest but one explanation.

The lack of scientific investigation of countertransference must be due to rejection by analysts of their own countertransferences—a rejection that represents unresolved struggles with their own primitive anxiety and guilt. These struggles are closely connected with those infantile ideals that survive because of deficiencies in the didactic analysis of just those transference problems that latter affect the analyst's countertransference. These deficiencies in the didactic analysis are in turn partly due to countertransference problems insufficiently solved in the didactic analyst, as I shall show later. Thus we are in a vicious circle; but we can see where a breach must be made. We must begin by revision of our feelings about our own countertransference and try to overcome our own infantile ideals more thoroughly, accepting more fully the fact that we are still children and neurotics even when we are adults and analysts. Only in this way—by better overcoming our rejection of countertransference—can we achieve the same result in candidates.

The insufficient dissolution of these idealizations and underlying anxieties and guilt feelings leads to special difficulties when the child becomes an adult and the analysand an analyst, for the analyst unconsciously requires of himself that he be fully identified with these ideals. I think that it is at least partly for this reason that the œdipus complex of the child toward its parents, and of the patient toward his analyst, has been so much more fully considered than that of the parents toward their children and of the analyst toward the analysand. For the same basic reason transference has been dealt with much more than countertransference.

The fact that countertransference conflicts determine the deficiencies in the analysis of transference becomes clear if we recall that transference is the expression of the internal object relations; for understanding of transference will depend on the analyst's capacity to identify himself both with the analysand's impulses and defenses, and with his internal objects, and to be conscious of these identifications. This ability in the analyst will in turn depend upon the degree to which he accepts his countertransference, for his countertransference is likewise based on identification with the patient's id and ego and his internal objects. One might also say that transference is the expression of the patient's relations with the fantasied and real countertransference of the analyst. For just as countertransference is the psychological response to the analysand's real and imaginary transferences, so also is transference the response to the analyst's imaginary and real countertransferences. Analysis of the patient's fantasies about countertransference, which in the widest sense constitute the causes and consequences of the transferences, is an essential part of the analysis of the transferences. Perception of the patient's fantasies regarding countertransference will depend in turn upon the degree to which the analyst himself perceives his countertransference processes—on the continuity and depth of his conscious contact with himself.

To summarize, the repression of countertransference (and other pathological fates that it may meet) necessarily leads to deficiencies in the analysis of transference, which in turn lead to the repression and other mishandling of countertransference as soon as the candidate becomes an analyst. It is a heritage from generation to generation, similar to the heritage of idealizations and denials concerning the imagoes of the parents, which continue working even when the child becomes a father or mother. The child's mythology is prolonged in the mythology of the analytic situation,[4] the analyst himself being partially subject to it and collaborating unconsciously in its maintenance in the candidate.

Before illustrating these statements, let us briefly consider one of those ideals in its specifically psychoanalytic expression: the ideal of the analyst's objectivity. No one, of course, denies the existence of subjective factors in the analyst and of countertransference in itself; but there seems to exist an important difference between what is generally acknowledged in practice and the real state of affairs. The first distortion of truth in 'the myth of the analytic situation' is that analysis is an interaction between a sick person and a healthy one. The truth is that it is an interaction between two personalities, in both of which the ego is under pressure from the id, the superego, and the external world, each personality has its internal and external dependences, anxieties, and pathological defenses; each is also a child with its internal parents; and each of these whole personalities—that of the analysand and that of the analyst—responds to every event of the analytic situation.[5] Besides these similarities between the personalities of analyst and analysand, there also exist differences, and one of these is in 'objectivity'. The analyst's objectivity consists mainly in a certain attitude toward his own subjectivity and countertransference. The neurotic (obsessive) ideal of objectivity leads to repression and blocking of subjectivity and so to the apparent fulfilment of the myth of the 'analyst without anxiety or anger'. The other neurotic extreme is that of 'drowning' in the countertransference. True objectivity is based upon a form of internal division that enables the analyst to make himself (his own countertransference and subjectivity) the object of his continuous observation and analysis. This position also enables him to be relatively 'objective' toward the analysand.

II

The term *countertransference* has been given various meanings. They may be summarized by the statement that for some authors countertransference includes everything that arises in the analyst as psychological response to the analysand, whereas for others not all this should be called countertransference. Some, for example, prefer to reserve the term for what is infantile in the relationship of the analyst with his analysand, while others make different limitations (Annie Reich [21] and Gitelson [10]). Hence efforts to differentiate from each other certain of the complex phenomena of countertransference lead to confusion or to unproductive discussions of terminology. Freud invented the term *countertransference* in evident analogy to transference, which he defined as reimpressions or re-editions of childhood experiences, including greater or lesser modifications of the original experience. Hence one frequently uses the term transference for the totality of the psychological attitude of the analysand toward the analyst. We know, to be sure, that real external qualities of the analytic situation in general and of the analyst in particular have important influence on the relationship of the analysand with the analyst, but we also know that all these present factors are experienced according to the past and the fantasy,—according, that is to say, to a transference predisposition. As determinants of the transference neurosis and, in general, of the psychological situation of the analysand toward the analyst, we have both the transference predisposition and the present real and especially analytic experiences, the transference in its diverse expressions being the resultant of these two factors.

Analogously, in the analyst there are the countertransference predisposition and the present real, and especially analytic, experiences; and the countertransference is the resultant. It is precisely this fusion of present and past, the continuous and intimate connection of reality and fantasy, of external and internal, conscious and unconscious, that demands a concept embracing the totality of the analyst's psychological response, and renders it advisable, at the same time, to keep for this totality of response the accustomed term *countertransference*. Where it is necessary for greater clarity one might speak of 'total countertransference' and then differentiate and separate within it one aspect or another. One of its aspects consists precisely in *what is transferred* in countertransference; this is the part that originates in an earlier time and that is especially the infantile and primitive part within total countertransference. Another of these aspects—closely connected with the previous one—is *what is neurotic* in countertransference; its main characteristics are the unreal anxiety and the pathological defenses. Under certain circumstances one may also speak of a countertransference neurosis (15, 17).

To clarify better the concept of countertransference, one might start from the question of what happens, in general terms, in the analyst in his relationship with the patient. The first answer might be: everything happens that *can* happen in one personality faced with another. But this says so much that it says hardly anything. We take a step forward by bearing in mind that in the analyst there is a tendency that normally predominates in his relationship with the patient: it is the tendency pertaining to his function of being an analyst, that of understanding what is happening in the patient. Together with this tendency there exist toward the patient virtually all the other possible tendencies, fears, and other feelings that one person may have toward another. The intention to understand creates a certain predisposition, a predisposition to identify oneself with the analysand, which is the basis of comprehension. The analyst may achieve this aim by identifying his ego with the patient's ego or, to put it more clearly although with a certain terminological inexactitude, by identifying each part of his personality with the corresponding psychological part in the patient—his id with the patient's id, his ego with the ego, his superego with the superego, accepting these identifications in his consciousness. But this does not always happen, nor is it all that happens. Apart from these identifications, which might be called concordant (or homologous) identifications, there exist also highly important identifications of the analyst's ego with the patient's internal objects, for example, with the superego. Adapting an expression from Helene Deutsch, they might be called complementary identifications.[6] We will consider these two kinds of identification and their destinies later. Here we may add the following notes.

1. The concordant identification is based on introjection and projection, or, in other terms, on the resonance of the exterior in the interior, on recognition of what belongs to another as one's own ('this part of you is I') and on the equation of what is one's own with what belongs to another ('this part of me is you'). The processes inherent in the complementary identifications are the same, but they refer to the patient's objects. The greater the conflicts between the parts of the analyst's personality, the greater are his difficulties in carrying out the concordant identifications in their entirety.

2. The complementary identifications are produced by the fact that the patient treats the analyst as an internal (projected) object, and in consequence the analyst feels treated as such; that is, he identifies himself with this object. The complementary identifications are closely connected with the destiny of the concordant identifications: it seems that to the degree to which the analyst fails in the concordant identifications and rejects them, certain complementary identifications become intensified. It is clear that rejection of a part or tendency in the analyst himself,—his aggressiveness, for instance,—may lead to a rejection of the patient's aggressiveness (whereby this concordant identification fails) and that such a situation leads to a greater complementary identification with the patient's rejecting object, toward which this aggressive impulse is directed.

3. Current usage applies the term 'countertransference' to the complementary identifications only; that is to say, to those psychological processes in the analyst by which, because he feels treated as and partially identifies himself with an internal object of the patient, the patient becomes an internal (projected) object of the analyst. Usually excluded from the concept countertransference are the concordant identifications,—those psychological contents that arise in the analyst by reason of the empathy achieved with the patient and that really reflect and reproduce the latter's psychological contents. Perhaps it would be best to follow this usage, but there are some circumstances that make it unwise to do so. In the first place, some authors include the concordant identifications in the concept of countertransference. One is thus faced with the choice of entering upon a terminological discussion or of accepting the term in this wider sense. I think that for various reasons the wider sense is to be preferred. If one considers that the analyst's concordant identifications (his 'understandings') are a sort of reproduction of his own past processes, especially of his own infancy, and that this reproduction or re-experience is carried out as response to stimuli from the patient, one will be more ready to include the concordant identifications in the concept of countertransference. Moreover, the concordant identifications are closely connected with the complementary ones (and thus with 'countertransference' in the popular sense), and this fact renders advisable a differentiation but not a total separation of the terms. Finally, it should be borne in mind that the disposition to empathy,—that is, to concordant identification,— springs largely from the sublimated positive countertransference, which likewise relates empathy with countertransference in the wider sense. All this suggests, then, the acceptance of countertransference as the totality of the analyst's psychological response to the patient. If we accept this broad

definition of countertransference, the difference between its two aspects mentioned above must still be defined. On the one hand we have the analyst as subject and the patient as object of knowledge, which in a certain sense annuls the 'object relationship', properly speaking; and there arises in its stead the approximate union or identity between the subject's and the object's parts (experiences, impulses, defenses). The aggregate of the processes pertaining to that union might be designated, where necessary, 'concordant countertransference'. On the other hand we have an object relationship very like many others, a real 'transference' in which the analyst 'repeats' previous experiences, the patient representing internal objects of the analyst. The aggregate of these experiences, which also exist always and continually, might be termed *complementary countertransference*.[7]

A brief example may be opportune here. Consider a patient who threatens the analyst with suicide. In such situations there sometimes occurs rejection of the concordant identifications by the analyst and an intensification of his identification with the threatened object. The anxiety that such a threat can cause the analyst may lead to various reactions or defense mechanisms within him—for instance, annoyance with the patient. This—his anxiety and annoyance—would be contents of the 'complementary countertransference'. The perception of his annoyance may, in turn, originate guilt feelings in the analyst and these lead to desires for reparation and to intensification of the 'concordant' identification and 'concordant' countertransference.

Moreover, these two aspects of 'total countertransference' have their analogy in transference. Sublimated positive transference is the main and indispensable motive force for the patient's work; it does not in itself constitute a technical problem. Transference becomes a 'subject', according to Freud's words, mainly when 'it becomes resistance', when, because of resistance, it has become sexual or negative (8, 9). Analogously, sublimated positive countertransference is the main and indispensable motive force in the analyst's work (disposing him to the continued concordant identification), and also countertransference becomes a technical problem or 'subject' mainly when it becomes sexual or negative. And this occurs (to an intense degree) principally as a resistance—in this case, the analyst's—that is to say, as counterresistance.

This leads to the problem of the dynamics of countertransference. We may already discern that the three factors designated by Freud as determinant in the dynamics of transference (the impulse to repeat infantile clichés of experience, the libidinal need, and resistance) are also decisive for the dynamics of countertransference. I shall return to this later.

III

Every transference situation provokes a countertransference situation, which arises out of the analyst's identification of himself with the analysand's (internal) objects (this is the 'complementary countertransference'). These countertransference situations may be repressed or emotionally blocked but probably they cannot be avoided; certainly they should not be avoided if full understanding is to be achieved. These countertransference reactions are governed by the laws of the general and individual unconscious. Among these the law of talion is especially important. Thus, for example, every positive transference situation is answered by a positive countertransference; to every negative transference there responds, in one part of the analyst, a negative countertransference. It is of great importance that the analyst be conscious of this law, for awareness of it is fundamental to avoid 'drowning' in the countertransference. If he is not aware of it he will not be able to avoid entering into the vicious circle of the analysand's neurosis, which will hinder or even prevent the work of therapy.

A simplified example: if the patient's neurosis centers round a conflict with his introjected father, he will project the latter upon the analyst and treat him as his father; the analyst will feel treated as such—he will feel treated badly —and he will react internally, in a part of his personality, in accordance with the treatment he receives. If he fails to be aware of this reaction, his behavior will inevitably be affected by it, and he will renew the situations that, to a greater or lesser degree, helped to establish the analysand's neurosis. Hence it is of the greatest importance that the analyst develop within himself an ego observer of his countertransference reactions, which are, naturally, continuous. Perception of these countertransference reactions will help him to become conscious of the continuous transference situations of the patient and interpret them rather than be unconsciously ruled by these reactions, as not seldom happens. A well-known example is the 'revengeful silence' of the analyst. If the analyst is unaware of these reactions there is danger that the patient will have to repeat, in his transference experience, the vicious circle brought about by the projection and introjection of 'bad objects' (in reality neurotic ones) and the consequent pathological anxieties and defenses; but transference interpretations made possible by the analyst's awareness of his countertransference experience make it possible to open important breaches in this vicious circle.

To return to the previous example: if the analyst is conscious of what the projection of the father-imago upon him provokes in his own countertransference, he can more easily make the patient conscious of this projection and the consequent mechanisms. Interpretation of these mechanisms will show the patient that the present reality is not identical with his inner perceptions (for, if it were, the analyst would not interpret and otherwise act as an analyst); the patient then introjects a reality better than his inner world. This sort of rectification does not take place when the analyst is under the sway of his unconscious countertransference.

Let us consider some applications of these principles. To return to the question of what the analyst does during the session and what happens within him, one might reply, at first thought, that the analyst listens. But this is not completely true: he listens most of the time, or wishes to listen, but is not invariably doing so. Ferenczi (6) refers to this fact and expresses the opinion that the analyst's distractability is of little importance, for the patient at such moments must certainly be in resistance. Ferenczi's remark (which dates from the year 1918) sounds like an echo from the era when the analyst was mainly interested in the repressed *impulses,* because now that we attempt to analyze resistance, the patient's manifestations of resistance are as significant as any other of his productions. At any rate, Ferenczi here refers to a countertransference response and deduces from it the analysand's psychological situation. He says '. . . we have unconsciously reacted to the emptiness and futility of the associations given at this moment with the withdrawal of the conscious charge'. The situation might be described as one of mutual withdrawal. The analyst's withdrawal is a response to the analysand's withdrawal—which, however, is a response to an imagined or real psychological position of the analyst. If we have withdrawn—if we are not listening but are thinking of something else—we may utilize this event in the service of the analysis like any other information we acquire. And the guilt we may feel over such a withdrawal is just as utilizable analytically as any other countertransference reaction. Ferenczi's next words, 'the danger of the doctor's falling asleep . . . need not be regarded as grave because we awake at the first occurrence of any importance for the treatment', are clearly intended to placate this guilt. But better than to allay the analyst's guilt would be to use it to promote the analysis—and indeed so to use the guilt would be the best way of alleviating it. In fact, we encounter here a cardinal problem of the relation between transference and countertransference, and of the therapeutic process in general. For the analyst's withdrawal is only an example of how the unconscious of one person responds to the unconscious of another. This response seems in part to be governed, insofar as we identify ourselves with the unconscious objects of the analysand, by the law of talion; and, insofar as this law unconsciously influences the analyst, there is danger of a vicious circle of reactions between them, for the analysand also responds 'talionically' in his turn, and so on without end.

Looking more closely, we see that the 'talionic response' or 'identification with the aggressor' (the frustrating patient) is a complex process. Such a psychological process in the analyst usually starts with a feeling of displeasure or of some anxiety as a response to this aggression (frustration) and, because of this feeling, the analyst identifies himself with the 'aggressor'. By the term 'aggressor' we must designate not only the patient but also some internal object of the analyst (especially his own superego or an internal persecutor) now projected upon the patient. This identification with the aggressor, or persecutor, causes a feeling of guilt; probably it always does so, although awareness of the guilt may be repressed. For what happens is, on a small scale, a process of melancholia, just as Freud described it: the object has to some degree abandoned us; we identify ourselves with the lost object;[8] and then we accuse the introjected 'bad' object—in other words, we have guilt feelings. This may be sensed in Ferenczi's remark quoted above, in which mechanisms are at work designed to protect the analyst against these guilt feelings: denial of guilt ('the danger is not grave') and a certain accusation against the analysand for the 'emptiness' and 'futility' of his associations. In this way a vicious circle—a kind of paranoid ping-pong—has entered into the analytic situation.[9]

Two situations of frequent occurrence illustrate both the complementary and the concordant identifications and the vicious circle these situations may cause.

1. One transference situation of regular occurrence consists in the patient's seeing in the analyst his own superego. The analyst identifies himself with the id and ego of the patient and with the patient's dependence upon his superego; and he also identifies himself with this same superego—a situation in which the patient places him—and experiences in this way the domination of the superego over the patient's ego. The relation of the ego to the superego is, at bottom, a depressive and paranoid situation; the relation of the superego to the ego is, on the same plane, a manic one insofar as this term may be used to designate the dominating, controlling, and accusing attitude of the superego toward the ego. In this sense we may say, broadly speaking, that to a 'depressive-paranoid' transference in the analysand there corresponds—as regards the complementary identification—a 'manic' countertransference in

the analyst. This, in turn, may entail various fears and guilt feelings, to which I shall refer later.[10]

2. When the patient, in defense against this situation, identifies himself with the superego, he may place the analyst in the situation of the dependent and incriminated ego. The analyst will not only identify himself with this position of the patient; he will also experience the situation with the content the patient gives it: he will feel subjugated and accused, and may react to some degree with anxiety and guilt. To a 'manic' transference situation (of the type called mania for reproaching) there corresponds, then—as regards the complementary identification—a 'depressive-paranoid' countertransference situation.

The analyst will normally experience these situations with only a part of his being, leaving another part free to take note of them in a way suitable for the treatment. Perception of such a countertransference situation by the analyst and his understanding of it as a psychological response to a certain transference situation will enable him the better to grasp the transference at the precise moment when it is active. It is precisely these situations and the analyst's behavior regarding them, and in particular his interpretations of them, that are of decisive importance for the process of therapy, for they are the moments when the vicious circle within which the neurotic habitually moves—by projecting his inner world outside and reintrojecting this same world—is or is not interrupted. Moreover, at these decisive points the vicious circle may be re-enforced by the analyst, if he is unaware of having entered it.

A brief example: an analysand repeats with the analyst his 'neurosis of failure', closing himself up to every interpretation or repressing it at once, reproaching the analyst for the uselessness of the analysis, foreseeing nothing better in the future, continually declaring his complete indifference to everything. The analyst interprets the patient's position toward him, and its origins, in its various aspects. He shows the patient his defense against the danger of becoming too dependent, of being abandoned, or being tricked, or of suffering counteraggression by the analyst, if he abandons his armor and indifference toward the analyst. He interprets to the patient his projection of bad internal objects and his subsequent sado-masochistic behavior in the transference; his need of punishment; his triumph and 'masochistic revenge' against the transferred patients; his defense against the 'depressive position' by means of schizoid, paranoid, and manic defenses (Melanie Klein); and he interprets the patient's rejection of a bond which in the unconscious has a homosexual significance. But it may happen that all these interpretations, in spite of being directed to the central resistance and connected with the transference situation, suffer the same fate for the same reasons: they fall into the 'whirl in a void' *(Leerlauf)* of the 'neurosis of failure'. Now the decisive moments arrive. The analyst, subdued by the patient's resistance, may begin to feel anxious over the possibility of failure and feel angry with the patient. When this occurs in the analyst, the patient feels it coming, for his own 'aggressiveness' and other reactions have provoked it; consequently he fears the analyst's anger. If the analyst, threatened by failure, or to put it more precisely threatened by his own superego or by his own archaic objects which have found an *agent provocateur* in the patient, acts under the influence of these internal objects and of his paranoid and depressive anxieties, the patient again finds himself confronting a reality like that of his real or fantasied childhood experiences and like that of his inner world; and so the vicious circle continues and may even be re-enforced. But if the analyst grasps the importance of this situation, if, through his own anxiety or anger, he comprehends what is happening in the analysand, and if he overcomes, thanks to the new insight, his negative feelings and interprets what has happened in the analysand, being now in this new positive countertransference situation, then he may have made a breach—be it large or small—in the vicious circle.

IV

We have considered thus far the relation of transference and countertransference in the analytic process. Now let us look more closely into the phenomena of countertransference. Countertransference experiences may be divided into two classes. One might be designated 'countertransference thoughts'; the other 'countertransference positions'. The example just cited may serve as illustration of this latter class; the essence of this example lies in the fact that the analyst feels anxiety and is angry with the analysand—that is to say, he is in a certain countertransference 'position'. As an example of the other class we may take the following.

At the start of a session an analysand wishes to pay his fees. He gives the analyst a thousand-peso note and asks for change. The analyst happens to have his money in another room and goes out to fetch it, leaving the thousand pesos upon his desk. During the time between leaving and returning, the fantasy occurs to him that the analysand will take back the money and say that the analyst took it away with him. On his return he finds the thousand pesos where he had left it. When the account has been settled, the analysand lies down and tells the analyst that when he was left alone he had fantasies of keeping the money, of kissing the note goodbye, and so on. The analyst's fantasy was based upon what he already knew of the patient, who in previous sessions had expressed a strong disinclination to pay his fees. The identity of the analyst's fantasy and the patient's fantasy of keeping the money may be explained as springing from a connection between the two unconsciouses, a connection that might be regarded as a 'psychological symbiosis' between the two personalities. To the analysand's wish to take money from him (already expressed on previous occasions), the analyst reacts by identifying himself both with this desire and with the object toward which the desire is directed; hence arises his fantasy of being robbed. For these identifications to come about there must evidently exist a potential identity. One may presume that every possible psychological constellation in the patient also exists in the analyst, and the constellation that corresponds to the patient's is brought into play in the analyst. A symbiosis results, and now in the analyst spontaneously occur thoughts corresponding to the psychological constellation in the patient.

In fantasies of the type just described and in the example of the analyst angry with his patient, we are dealing with identifications with the id, with the ego, and with the objects of the analysand; in both cases, then, it is a matter of countertransference reactions. However, there is an important difference between one situation and the other, and this difference does not seem to lie only in the emotional intensity. Before elucidating this difference, I should like to emphasize that the countertransference reaction that appears in the last example (the fantasy about the thousand pesos) should also be used as a means to further the analysis. It is, moreover, a typical example of those 'spontaneous thoughts' to which Freud and others refer in advising the analyst to keep his attention 'floating' and in stressing the importance of these thoughts for understanding the patient. The countertransference reactions exemplified by the story of the thousand pesos are characterized by the fact that they threaten no danger to the analyst's objective attitude of observer. Here the danger is rather that the analyst will not pay sufficient attention to these thoughts or will fail to use them for understanding and interpretation. The patient's corresponding ideas are not always conscious, nor are they always communicated as they were in the example cited. But from his own countertransference 'thoughts' and feelings the analyst may guess what is repressed or rejected. It is important to recall once more our usage of the term *countertransference*, for many writers, perhaps the majority, mean by it not these thoughts of the analyst but rather that other class of reactions, the 'countertransference positions'. This is one reason why it is useful to differentiate these two kinds of reaction.

The outstanding difference between the two lies in the degree to which the ego is involved in the experience. In one case the reactions are experienced as thoughts, free associations, or fantasies, with no great emotional intensity and frequently as if they were somewhat foreign to the ego. In the other case, the analyst's ego is involved in the countertransference experience, and the experience is felt by him with greater intensity and as true reality, and there is danger of his 'drowning' in this experience. In the former example of the analyst who gets angry because of the analysand's resistances, the analysand is felt as really bad by one part of the analyst ('countertransference position'), although the latter does not express his anger. Now these two kinds of countertransference reactions differ, I believe, because they have different origins. The reaction experienced by the analyst as thought or fantasy arises from the existence of an analogous situation in the analysand—that is, from his readiness in perceiving and communicating his inner situation (as happens in the case of the thousand pesos)—whereas the reaction experienced with great intensity, even as reality, by the analyst arises from acting out by the analysand (as in the case of the 'neurosis of failure'). Undoubtedly there is also in the analyst himself a factor that helps to determine this difference. The analyst has, it seems, two ways of responding. He may respond to some situations by perceiving his reactions, while to others he responds by acting out (alloplastically or autoplastically). Which type of response occurs in the analyst depends partly on his own neurosis, on his inclination to anxiety, on his defense mechanisms, and especially on his tendencies to repeat (act out) instead of making conscious. Here we encounter a factor that determines the dynamics of countertransference. It is the one Freud emphasized as determining the special intensity of transference in analysis, and it is also responsible for the special intensity of countertransference.

Let us consider for a moment the dynamics of countertransference. The great intensity of certain countertransference reactions is to be explained by the existence in the analyst of pathological defenses against the increase of archaic anxieties and unresolved inner conflicts. Transference, I believe, becomes intense not only because it serves as a resistance to remembering, as Freud says, but also because it serves as a defense against a danger within the transference experience itself. In other words, the 'transference resistance' is frequently a repetition of defenses that must be intensified lest a catastrophe be repeated in transference (20). The same is true of countertransference. It is clear that these catastrophes are related to becoming aware of certain aspects of one's own instincts. Take, for instance, the analyst who becomes anxious and inwardly angry over the intense masochism of the analysand within the analytic situation. Such masochism frequently rouses old paranoid and depressive anxieties and guilt feelings in the analyst, who, faced with the aggression directed by the patient against his own ego, and faced with the effects of this aggression, finds himself in his unconscious confronted anew with his early crimes. It is often just these childhood conflicts of the analyst, with their aggression, that led him into this profession in which he tries to repair the objects of the aggression and to overcome or deny his guilt. Because of the patient's strong masochism, this defense, which consists of the analyst's therapeutic action, fails and the analyst is threatened with the return of the catastrophe, the encounter with the destroyed object. In this way the intensity of the 'negative countertransference' (the anger with the patient) usually increases because of the failure of the countertransference defense (the therapeutic action) and the analyst's subsequent increase of anxiety over a catastrophe in the countertransference experience (the destruction of the object).

This example also illustrates another aspect of the dynamics of countertransference. In a previous paper (20), I showed that the 'abolition of rejection'[11] in analysis determines the dynamics of transference and, in particular, the intensity of the transference of the 'rejecting' internal objects (in the first place, of the superego). The 'abolition of rejection' begins with the communication of 'spontaneous' thoughts. The analyst, however, makes no such communication to the analysand, and here we have an important difference between his situation and that of the analysand and between the dynamics of transference and those of countertransference. However, this difference is not so great as might be at first supposed, for two reasons: first, because it is not necessary that the free associations be *expressed* for projections and transferences to take place, and second, because the analyst communicates certain associations of a personal nature even when he does not seem to do so. These communications begin, one might say, with the plate on the front door that says *Psychoanalysis* or *Doctor*. What motive (in terms of the unconscious) would the analyst have for wanting to cure if it were not he that made the patient ill? In this way the patient is already, simply by being a patient, the creditor, the accuser, the 'superego' of the analyst; and the analyst is his debtor.

V

The examples that follow illustrate the various kinds, meanings, and uses of countertransference reaction. First are described situations in which the countertransference is of too little intensity to drag the analyst's ego along with it; next, some situations in which the intense countertransference reaction intensely involves the ego; and finally, some examples in which the repression of countertransference prevents comprehension of the analysand's situation at the critical moment.

1. A woman patient asks the analyst whether it is true that another analyst named N has become separated from his wife and married again. In the associations that follow she refers repeatedly to N's first wife. The idea occurs to the analyst that the patient would also like to know who N's second wife is and that she probably wonders whether the second wife was a patient of N's. The analyst further supposes that his patient (considering her present transference situation) is wondering whether her own analyst might not also separate from his wife and marry her. In accordance with this suspicion but taking care not to suggest anything, the analyst asks whether she is thinking anything about N's second wife. The analysand answers, laughing, 'Yes, I was wondering whether she was not one of his patients'. Analysis of the analyst's psychological situation showed that his 'spontaneous thought' was possible because his identification with the patient in his œdipal desires was not blocked by repression, and also because he himself countertransferred his own positive œdipal impulses, accepted by his conscious, upon the patient.

This example shows how, in the analyst's 'spontaneous thoughts'—which enable him to attain a deeper understanding—there intervenes not only the sublimated positive countertransference that permits his identification with the id and the ego of the patient but also the (apparently absent) 'complementary countertransference'—that is, his identification with the internal objects that the patient transfers and the acceptance in his conscious of his own infantile object relations with the patient.

2. In the following examples the 'spontaneous thoughts', which are manifestly dependent upon the countertransference situation, constitute the guide to understanding.

A woman candidate associates about a scientific meeting at the Psychoanalytic Institute, the first she had attended. While she is associating, it occurs to the analyst that he, unlike most of the other didactic analysts, did not participate in the discussion. He feels somewhat vexed, he thinks that the analysand must have noticed this, and he perceives in himself some fear that she consequently regards him as inferior. He realizes that he would prefer that she not think this and not mention the occurrence; for this very reason, he points out to the analysand that she is rejecting thoughts concerning him in relation to the meeting. The analysand's reaction shows the importance of this interpretation. She exclaims in surprise: 'Of course, I almost forgot to tell you'. She then produces many associations related to transference that she had previously rejected for reasons corresponding to the countertransference rejection of these same ideas by the analyst. The example shows the importance of observation of countertransference as a technical tool; it also shows a relation between a transference resistance and a countertransference resistance.

3. On shaking hands at the beginning of the session the analyst, noticing that the patient is depressed, experiences a slight sense of guilt. The analyst at once thinks of the last session, in which he frustrated the patient. He knows where the depression comes from, even before the patient's associations lead him to the same conclusion. Observation of the countertransference ideas, *before* and *after* the sessions, may also be an important guide for the analyst in understanding the patient's analytic situation. For instance, if a feeling of annoyance before entering the consulting room is a countertransference response to the patient's aggressive or domineering behavior, the annoyance may enable the analyst to understand beforehand the patient's anxiety which, at the most superficial layer, is fear of the analyst's anger provoked by the patient's behavior. Another instance occurs in the analyst who, before entering his consulting room, perceives a feeling of guilt over being late; he realizes that he often keeps this analysand waiting and that it is the analysand's pronounced masochistic submission that especially prompts him to this frustrating behavior. In other words, the analyst responds to the strong repression of aggression in the patient by doing what he pleases and abusing the patient's neurosis. But this very temptation that the analyst feels and yields to in his behavior, and the fleeting guilt feelings he experiences for this reason, can serve as a guide for him to comprehend the analysand's transference situation.

4. The following example from analytic literature likewise shows how the countertransference situation makes it possible to understand the patient's analytic situation in a way decisive for the whole subsequent course of the treatment. It is interesting to remark that the author seems unaware that the fortunate understanding is due to an unconscious grasp of the countertransference situation. I refer to the 'case with manifest inferiority feelings' pub-

lished by Wilhelm Reich (22). After showing how, for a long period, no interpretation achieved any success or any modification of the patient's analytic situation, Reich writes: 'I then interpreted to him his inferiority feelings toward me; at first this was unsuccessful but after I had persistently shown him his conduct for several days, he presented some communications referring to his tremendous envy not of me but of other men, to whom he also felt inferior. And then there emerged in me, like a lightning flash, the idea that his repeated complaints could mean only this: "The analysis has no effect upon me—it is no good, the analyst is inferior and impotent and can achieve nothing with me." The complaints were to be understood partly as triumph and partly as reproaches to the analyst.' If we inquire into the origin of this 'lightning idea' of Reich's, the reply must be, theoretically, that it arose from identification with those impulses in the analysand or from identification with one of his internal objects. The description of the event, however, leaves little room for doubt that the latter, the 'complementary countertransference', was the source of Reich's intuition—that this lightning understanding arose from his own feeling of impotence, defeat, and guilt over the failure of treatment.

5. Now a case in which repression of the countertransference prevented the analyst from understanding the transference situation, while his later becoming conscious of the countertransference was precisely what brought this understanding.

For several days a patient has suffered from intense anxiety and stomachache. The analyst does not understand the situation until she asks the patient when it first began. He answers that it goes back to a moment when he bitterly criticized her for certain behavior, and adds that he has noticed that she has been rather depressed of late. What the patient says hits the nail on the head. The analyst has in truth felt somewhat depressed because of this aggression in the patient. But she has repressed her aggression against the patient that underlay her depression and has repressed awareness that the patient would also think, consciously or unconsciously, of the effect of his criticism. The patient was conscious of this and therefore connected his own anxieties and symptoms with the analyst's depression. In other words, the analyst scotomatized the connection between the patient's anxiety and pain and the aggression (criticism) perpetrated against her. This scotomatization of the transference situation was due to repression of the countertransference, for the aggression that the patient suspected in the analyst, and to which he responded with anxiety and gastric pains (self-aggression in anticipation) existed not only in his fantasy but also in the analyst's actual countertransference feelings.

The danger of the countertransference's being repressed is naturally the greater the more these countertransference reactions are rejected by the ego ideal or the superego. To take, for instance, the case of a patient with an almost complete lack of 'respect' for the analyst, it may happen that the analyst's narcissism is wounded and he acts inwardly with some degree of annoyance. If he represses this annoyance because it ill accords with the demands of his ego ideal, he deprives himself of an important guide in understanding the patient's transference; for the patient seeks to deny the distance between his internal (idealized) objects and his ego by means of his manic mechanisms, trying to compensate his inferiority feelings by behavior 'as between equals' (in reality inverting this situation with the idealized objects by identification with them) and defending himself in this way against conflict situations of the greatest importance. In like manner, sexual excitement in the analyst may point to a hidden seductive behavior and erotomanic fantasies in the analysand as well as to the situations underlying these. Repression of such countertransference reactions may prevent access to the appropriate technique. What is advisable, for instance, when the patient exhibits this sort of hypomanic behavior is not merely analytic 'tolerance' (which may be intensified by guilt feeling over the countertransference reactions), but, as the first step, making the patient conscious of the countertransference reactions of his *own* internal objects, such as the superego. For just as the analyst reacted with annoyance to the almost total 'lack of respect' in the patient, so also do the patient's internal objects; for in the patient's behavior there is aggressiveness against these internal objects which the patient once experienced as superior and as rejecting. In more general terms, I should say that patients with certain hypomanic defenses tend to regard their conduct as 'natural' and 'spontaneous' and the analyst as 'tolerant' and 'understanding', repressing at the same time the rejecting and intolerant objects latently projected upon the analyst. If the analyst does not repress his deeper reactions to the analysand's associations and behavior, they will afford him an excellent guide for showing the patient these same repressed objects of his and the relationship in which he stands toward them.

6. In analysis we must take into account the *total* countertransference as well as the total transference. I refer, in particular, to the importance of paying attention not only to what has existed and is repeated but also to what has never existed (or has existed only as a hope)—that is to say, to the new

and specifically analytic factors in the situations of analysand and analyst. Outstanding among these are the real new characteristics of this object (of analyst or of analysand), the patient-doctor situation (the intention to be cured or to cure, to be restored or to restore), and the situation created by psychoanalytic thought and feelings (as, for instance, the situation created by the fundamental rule, that original permission and invitation, the basic expression of a specific atmosphere of tolerance and freedom).

Let us illustrate briefly what is meant by 'total transference'. During a psychoanalytic session, the associations of a man, under treatment by a woman analyst, concern his relations with women. He tells of the frustrations and rejection he has endured, and his inability to form relationships with women of culture. There appear sadistic and debasing tendencies toward women. It is clear that the patient is transferring his frustrating and rejecting imagoes upon the analyst, and from these has arisen his mistrust of her. The patient is actually expressing both his fear of being rejected by the analyst on account of his sadism (deeper: his fear of destroying her and of her retaliation) and, at bottom, his fear of being frustrated by her—a situation that in the distant past gave rise to this sadism. Such an interpretation would be a faithful reflection of the transference situation properly speaking. But in the total analytic situation there is something more. Evidently the patient needs and is seeking something through the session as such. What is it? What is this specific present factor, what is this prospective aspect, so to speak, of the transference situation? The answer is virtually contained in the interpretation given above: the analysand seeks to connect himself with an object emotionally and libidinally, the previous sessions having awakened his feelings and somewhat disrupted his armor; indirectly he is asking the analyst whether he may indeed place his trust in her, whether he may surrender himself without running the risk of suffering what he has suffered before. The first interpretation refers to the transference only as a repetition of what has once existed; the latter, more complete interpretation refers to what has existed and also to what has never existed and is hoped for anew from the analytic experience.

Now let us study an example that refers to both the total transference and total countertransference situations. The illustration is once again drawn from Wilhelm Reich (22). The analysis has long centered around the analysand's smile, the sole analyzable expression, according to Reich, that remained after cessation of all the communications and actions with which the analysand had begun treatment. Among these actions at the start had been some that

Reich interpreted as provocations (for instance, a gesture aimed at the ana-lyst's head). It is plain that Reich was guided in this interpretation by what he had felt in countertransference. But what Reich perceived in this way was only a part of what had happened within him; for apart from the fright and annoyance (which, even if only to a slight degree, he must have felt), there was a reaction of his ego to these feelings, a wish to control and dominate them, imposed by his 'analytic conscience'. For Reich had given the analy-sand to understand that there is a great deal of freedom and tolerance in the analytic situation and it was this spirit of tolerance that made Reich respond to these 'provocations' with nothing but an interpretation. What the analy-sand aimed at doing was to test whether such tolerance really existed in the analyst. Reich himself later gave him this interpretation, and this interpreta-tion had a far more positive effect than the first. Consideration of the total countertransference situation (the feeling of being provoked *and* the 'analytic conscience' which determined the fate of this feeling) might have been from the first a guide in apprehending the total transference situation, which consisted in aggressiveness, in the original mistrust, *and* in the ray of confi-dence, the new hope that the liberality of the fundamental rule had awakened in him.

7. I have referred above to the fact that the transference, insofar as it is determined by the infantile situations and archaic objects of the patient, provokes in the unconscious of the analyst infantile situations and an intensi-fied vibration of archaic objects of his own. I wish now to present another example that shows how the analyst, not being conscious of such counter-transference responses may make the patient feel exposed once again to an archaic object (the vicious circle) and how, in spite of his having some understanding of what is happening in the patient, the analyst is prevented from giving an adequate interpretation.

During her first analytic session, a woman patient talks about how hot it is and other matters which to the analyst (a woman candidate) seems insignifi-cant. She says to the patient that very likely the patient dares not talk about herself. Although the analysand was indeed talking about herself (even when saying how hot it was), the interpretation was, in essence, correct, for it was directed to the central conflict of the moment. But it was badly formulated, and this was so partly because of the countertransference situation. For the analyst's 'you dare not' was a criticism, and it sprang from the analyst's feeling of being frustrated in a desire; this desire must have been that the patient overcome her resistance. If the analyst had not felt this irritation or if she had been conscious of the neurotic nature of her internal reaction of anxiety and annoyance, she would have sought to understand why the patient 'dared not' and would have told her. In that case the lack of courage that the analyst pointed out to the patient would have proved to be a natural response within a dangerous object relationship.

Pursuing the analyst's line of thought and leaving aside other possible interpretations, we may suppose that she would then have said to the analysand that something the analytic situation (in the relationship between patient and analyst) had caused her fear and made her thoughts turn aside from what meant much to her to what meant little. This interpretation would have differed from the one she gave the patient in two points: first, the interpretation given did not express the object relationship that led to the 'not daring' and, second, it coincided in its formulation with superego judgments, which should be avoided as far as possible.[12] Superego judgment was not avoided in this case because the analyst was identified in countertransference with the analysand's superego without being conscious of the identification; had she been conscious of it, she would have interpreted, for example, the feared aggression from the superego (projected upon the analyst) and would not have carried it out by means of the interpretation. It appears that the 'interpretation of tendencies' without considering the total object relationship is to be traced, among other causes, to repression by the analyst of one aspect of his countertransference, his identification with the analysand's internal objects.

Later in the same session, the patient, feeling that she is being criticized, censures herself for her habit of speaking rather incoherently. She says her mother often remarks upon it, and then she criticizes her mother for not listening, as a rule, to what she says. The analyst understands that these statements relate to the analytic situation and asks her: 'Why do you think I'm not listening to you?' The patient replies that she is sure the analyst is listening to her.

What has happened? The patient's mistrust clashes with the analyst's desire for the patient's confidence; therefore the analyst does not analyze the situation. She cannot say to the patient, 'No, I will listen to you, trust me', but she suggests it with her question. Once again interference by the uncontrolled countertransference (the desire that the patient should have no resistance) converts good understanding into a deficient interpretation. Such happenings are important, especially if they occur often. And they are likely to do so, for such interpretations spring from a certain state of the analyst and this state is partly unconscious. What makes these happenings so important is the fact that the analysand's unconscious is fully aware of the analyst's unconscious desires. Therefore the patient once again faces an object that, as in this case, wishes to force or lure the patient into rejecting his mistrust and that unconsciously seeks to satisfy its own desires or allay its own anxieties rather than to understand and satisfy the therapeutic need of the patient.

All this we infer from the reactions of the patient, who submits to the analyst's suggestion, telling the analyst that she trusts her and so denying an aspect of her internal reality. She submits to the previous criticism of her cowardice and then, apparently, 'overcomes' the resistance, while in reality everything is going on unchanged. It cannot be otherwise, for the analysand is aware of the analyst's neurotic wish and her transference is determined by that awareness. To a certain degree, the analysand finds herself once again, in the actual analytic situation, confronting her internal or external infantile reality and to this same degree will repeat her old defenses and will have no valid reason for really overcoming her resistances, however much the analyst may try to convince her of her tolerance and understanding. This she will achieve only by offering better interpretations in which her neurosis does not so greatly interfere.

8. The following more detailed example demonstrates: (*a*) the talion law in the relationship of analyst and analysand; (*b*) how awareness of the countertransference reaction indicates what is happening in the transference and what at the moment is of the greatest significance; (*c*) what interpretation is most suitable to make a breach in the vicious circle; and (*d*) how the later associations show that this end has been achieved, even if only in part—for the same defenses return and once again the countertransference points out the interpretation the analysand needs.

We will consider the most important occurrences in one session. An analysand who suffers chiefly from an intense emotional inhibition and from a 'disconnection' in all his object relationships begins the session by saying that he feels completely disconnected from the analyst. He speaks with difficulty as if he were overcoming a great resistance, and always in an unchanging tone of voice that seems in no way to reflect his instincts and feelings. Yet the countertransference response to the content of his associations (or, rather, of his narrative, for he exercises a rigid control over his ideas) does change from time to time. At a certain point the analyst feels a slight irritation. This is when the patient, a physician, tells him how, in conversation with another physician, he sharply criticized analysts for their passivity (they give little and cure little), for their high fees, and for their tendency to dominate their patients. The patient's statements and his behavior mean several things. It is clear, in the first place, that these accusations, though couched in general terms and with reference to other analysts, are directed against his own analyst; the patient has become the analyst's super-ego. This situation in the patient represents a defense against his own accusing superego, projected upon the analyst. It is a form of identification with the internal persecutors that leads to inversion of the feared situation. It is, in other words, a transitory 'mania for reproaching' as defense against a paranoid-depressive situation in which the superego persecutes the patient with reproaches and threatens him with abandonment. Together with this identification with the superego, there occurs projection of a part of the 'bad ego', and of the id, upon the analyst. The passivity (the mere receptiveness, the inability to make reparation), the selfish exploitation, and the domination he ascribes to the analyst are 'bad tendencies' of his own for which he fears reproach and abandonment by the analyst. At a lower stratum, this 'bad ego' consists of 'bad objects' with which the patient has identified himself as a defense against their persecution.

We already see that it would be premature to interpret this deeper situation; the patient will first have to face his 'bad ego': he will have to pass in transference through the paranoid-depressive situation in which he feels threatened by the superego-analyst. But even so we are still unsure of the interpretation to be given, for what the patient has said and done has even at the surface still further meanings. The criticism he made to the other physician about analysts has the significance of rebellion, vengeance, and provocation; and, perhaps, of seeking for punishment as well as of finding out how much freedom the analyst allows, and simultaneously of subjugating and controlling this dangerous object, the analyst.

The analyst's countertransference reaction made clear to the analyst which of all these interpretations was most strongly indicated, for the countertransference reaction is the living response to the transference situation at that moment. The analyst feels (in accordance with the law of talion) a little anxious and angry at the aggression he has suffered from the patient, and we may suppose that the patient in his unconscious or conscious fantasy senses this annoyance in the internal object toward which his protesting behavior is directed, and that he reacts to this annoyance with anxiety. The 'disconnection' he spoke of in his first utterance must have been in relation to this anxiety, since it was because of this 'disconnection' that the analysand perceived no danger and felt no anxiety. By the patient's projection of that internal object the analyst is to the patient a tyrant who demands complete submission and forbids any protest. The transgression of this prohibition (the patient's protest expressed to his friend, the physician) must seem to the analyst—in the patient's fantasy—to be unfaithfulness, and must be responded to by the analyst with anger and emotional abandonment; we deduce this from the countertransference experience. In order to reconcile the analyst and to win him back, the patient accepts his anger or punishment and suffers from stomach-ache—this he tells in his associations but without connecting the two experiences. His depression today is to be explained by this guilt feeling and, secondarily, by the object loss resulting from his increased 'disconnection'.

The analyst explains, in his interpretation, the meaning of the 'disconnection'. In reply the patient says that the previous day he recalled his conversation with that physician and that it did indeed cause him anxiety. After a brief pause he adds: 'and just now the thought came to me, well . . . and what am I to do with that?' The analyst perceives that these words once again slightly annoy him. We can understand why. The patient's first reaction to the interpretation (he reacted by recalling his anxiety over his protest) brought the analyst nearer to satisfying his desire to remove the patient's detachment. The patient's recollection of his anxiety was at least one forward step, for he thus admitted a connection that he usually denied or repressed. But his next words frustrated the analyst once again, for they signified: 'that is of no use to me, nothing has changed'. Once again the countertransference reaction pointed out to the analyst the occurrence of a critical moment in the transference, and that here was the opportunity to interpret. At this moment also, in the patient's unconscious fantasy, must have occurred a reaction of anger from the internal object—just as actually happened in the analyst—to which the interpretation must be aimed. The patient's anxiety must have arisen from just this fantasy. His anxiety—and with it his detachment—could be diminished only by replacing that fantasied anger by an understanding of the patient's need to defend himself through that denial ('well . . . what am I to do with that?'). In reality the analyst, besides feeling annoyed, understood that the patient had to protest and rebel, close himself up and 'disconnect' himself once again, deny and prevent any influence, because if the analyst should prove to be useful the patient would fall into intense dependence, just because of this usefulness and because the patient would be indebted to him. The interpretation increased this danger, for the patient felt it to be true. Because of the analyst's tyranny—his dominating, exploiting, sadistic character—this dependence had to be prevented.

The analyst by awareness of his countertransference understood the patient's anxiety and interpreted it to him. The following associations showed that this interpretation had also been accurate.

The patient says shortly afterward that his depression has passed off, and this admission is a sign of progress because the patient is admitting that there is something good about the analyst. The next associations, moreover, permit a more profound analysis of his transference neurosis, for the patient now reveals a deeper stratum. His underlying dependence becomes clear. Hitherto the interpretation has been confined to the guilt feelings and anxiety that accompanied his defenses (rebellion, denial, and others) against this very dependence. The associations refer to the fact that a mutual friend of the patient and of the analyst told him a few days before that the analyst was going away on holiday that night and that this session would therefore be his last. In this way the patient admits the emotional importance the analyst possesses for him, a thing he always used to deny. We understand now also that his protest against analysts had been determined beforehand by the imminent danger of being forsaken by his analyst. When, just before the end of the session, the analyst explains that the information the friend gave him is false, the patient expresses anger with his friend and recalls how the friend has been trying lately to make him jealous of the analyst. Thus does the patient admit his jealousy of the analyst, although he displaces his anger onto the friend who roused his anxiety.

What has happened? And how is it to be explained?

The analyst's expected journey represented, in the unconscious of the patient, abandonment by internal objects necessary to him. This danger was countered by an identification with the aggressor; the threat of aggression (abandonment by the analyst) was countered by aggression (the patient's protest against analysts). His own aggression caused the patient to fear counteraggression or abandonment by the analyst. This anxiety remained unconscious but the analyst was able to deduce it from the counteraggression he perceived in his countertransference. If he had not interpreted the patient's transference situation, or if in his interpretation he had included any criticism of the patient's insistent and continuous rejection of the analyst or of his obstinate denial of any bond with the analyst, the patient would have remained in the vicious circle between his basic fear of abandonment and his defensive identification with the persecutor (with the object that abandons); he would have continued in the vicious circle of his neurosis. But the interpretation, which showed him the analyst's understanding of his conduct and of the underlying anxiety, changed (at least for that moment) the image of the analyst as persecutor. Hence the patient could give up his defensive identification with this image and could admit his dependence (the underlying stratum), his need for the analyst, and his jealousy.

And now once again in this new situation countertransference will show the content and origin of the anxiety that swiftly drives the analysand back to repetition of the defense mechanism he has just abandoned (which may be identification with the persecutor, emotional blocking, or something else). And once again interpretation of this new danger is the only means of breaking the vicious circle. If we consider the nature of the relationship that existed for months before the emotional surrender that occurred in this session, if we consider the paranoid situation that existed in the transference and countertransference (expressed in the patient by his intense characterological resistances and in the analyst by his annoyance)—if we consider all this background to the session just described, we understand that the analyst enjoys, in the patient's surrender, a manic triumph, to be followed of course by depressive and paranoid anxieties, compassion toward the patient, desires for reparation, and other sequelae. It is just these guilt feelings caused in the analyst by his manic feelings that may lead to his failure adequately to interpret the situation. The danger the patient fears is that he will become a helpless victim of the object's (the analyst's) sadism—of that same sadism the analyst senses in his 'manic' satisfaction over dominating and defeating the bad object with which the patient was defensively identified. The perception of this 'manic' countertransference reaction indicates what the present transference situation is and what should be interpreted.

If there were nothing else in the analyst's psychological situation but this manic reaction, the patient would have no alternative but would have to make use of the same old defense mechanisms that essentially constitute his neurosis. In more general terms, we should have to admit that the negative therapeutic reaction is an adequate transference reaction in the patient to an imagined or real negative countertransference in the analyst.[13] But even where such a negative countertransference really exists, it is a part only of the analyst's psychological response. For the law of talion is not the sole determinant of the responses of the unconscious; and, moreover, the conscious also plays a part in the analyst's psychological responses. As to the unconscious, there is of course a tendency to repair, which may even create a disposition to 'return good for evil'. This tendency to repair is in reality a wish to remedy, albeit upon a displaced object, whatever evil one may have thought or done. And as to the conscious, there is, first, the fact that the analyst's own analysis has made his ego stronger that it was before so that the intensities of his anxieties and his further countertransference reactions are usually diminished; second, the analyst has some capacity to observe this countertransference, to 'get out of it', to stand outside and regard it objectively; and third, the analyst's knowledge of psychology also acts within and upon his psychological response. The knowledge, for instance, that behind the negative transference and the resistances lies simply thwarted love, helps the analyst to respond with love to this possibility of loving, to this nucleus in the patient however deeply it is buried beneath hate and fear.

9. The analyst should avoid, as far as possible, making interpretations in terms that coincide with those of the moral superego.[14] This danger is increased by the unconscious identification of the analyst with the patient's internal objects and, in particular, with his superego. In the example just cited, the patient, in conversation with his friend, criticized the conduct of analysts. In so doing he assumed the role of superego toward an internal object that he projected upon the analyst. The analyst identified himself with this projected object and reacted with unconscious anxiety and with annoyance to the accusation. He inwardly reproached the patient for his conduct and there was danger that something of this reproach (in which the analyst in his turn identified himself with the conduct of the patient as superego) might filter into his interpretation, which would then perpetuate the patient's neurotic vicious circle. But the problem is wider than this. Certain psychoanalytic terminology is likely to re-enforce the patient's confusion of the analyst with the superego. For instance *narcissism, passivity,* and *bribery of the superego* are terms we should not use literally or in paraphrase in treatment without careful reflection, just because they increase the danger that the patient will confuse the imago of the analyst with that of his superego. For greater clarity two situations may be differentiated theoretically. In one, only the patient experiences these or like terms as criticism, because of his conflict between ego and superego, and the analyst is free of this critical feeling. In the other, the analyst also regards certain character traits with moral intolerance; he feels censorious, as if he were indeed a superego. Something of this attitude probably always exists, for the analyst identifies himself with the objects that the patient 'mistreats' (by his 'narcissism', or 'passivity', or 'bribery of the superego'). But even if the analyst had totally solved his own struggles against these same tendencies and hence remained free from countertransference conflict with the corresponding tendencies in the patient, it would be preferable to point out to the patient the several conflicts between

his tendencies and his superego, and not run the risk of making it more difficult for the patient to differentiate between the judgment of his own superego and the analyst's comprehension of these same tendencies through the use of a terminology that precisely lends itself to confusing these two positions.

One might object that this confusion between the analyst and the superego neither can nor should be avoided, since it represents an essential part of the analysis of transference (of the externalization of internal situations) and since one cannot attain clarity except through confusion. That is true; this confusion cannot and should not be avoided, but we must remember that the confusion will also have to be resolved and that this will be all the more difficult the more the analyst is really identified in his experience with the analysand's superego and the more these identifications have influenced negatively his interpretations and conduct.

VI

In the examples presented we saw how to certain transference situations there correspond certain countertransference situations, and vice versa. To what transference situation does the analyst usually react with a particular countertransference? Study of this question would enable one, in practice, to deduce the transference situations from the countertransference reactions. Next we might ask, to what imago or conduct of the object—to what imagined or real countertransference situation—does the patient respond with a particular transference? Many aspects of these problems have been amply studied by psychoanalysis, but the specific problem of the relation of transference and countertransference in analysis has received little attention.

The subject is so broad that we can discuss only a few situations and those incompletely, restricting ourselves to certain aspects. We must choose for discussion only the most important countertransference situations, those that most disturb the analyst's task and that clarify important points in the double neurosis, *la névrose à deux*, that arises in the analytic situation—a neurosis usually of very different intensity in the two participants.

1. What is the significance of countertransference anxiety?

Countertransference anxiety may be described in general and simplified terms as being of depressive or paranoid character.[15] In depressive anxiety the inherent danger consists in having destroyed the analysand or made him ill. This anxiety may arise to a greater degree when the analyst faces the danger that the patient may commit suicide, and to a lesser degree when there is deterioration or danger of deterioration in the patient's state of health. But the patient's simple failure to improve and his suffering and depression may also provoke depressive anxieties in the analyst. These anxieties usually increase the desire to heal the patient.

In referring to paranoid anxieties it is important to differentiate between 'direct' and 'indirect' countertransference (17). In direct countertransference the anxieties are caused by danger of an intensification of aggression from the patient himself. In indirect countertransference the anxieties are caused by danger of aggression from third parties onto whom the analyst has made his own chief transferences—for instance, the members of the analytic society, for the future of the analyst's object relationships with the society is in part determined by his professional performance. The feared aggression may take several forms, such as criticism, reproach, hatred, mockery, contempt, or bodily assault. In the unconscious it may be the danger of being killed or castrated or otherwise menaced in an archaic way.

The transference situations of the patient to which the depressive anxieties of the analyst are a response are, above all, those in which the patient, through an increase in frustration[16] (or danger of frustration) and in the aggression that it evokes, turns the aggression against himself. We are dealing, on one plane, with situations in which the patient defends himself against a paranoid fear of retaliation by anticipating this danger, by carrying out himself and against himself part of the aggression feared from the object transferred onto the analyst, and threatening to carry it out still further. In this psychological sense it is really the analyst who attacks and destroys the patient; and the analyst's depressive anxiety corresponds to this psychological reality. In other words, the countertransference depressive anxiety arises, above all, as a response to the patient's 'masochistic defense'—which at the same time represents a revenge ('masochistic revenge')—and as a response to the danger of its continuing. On another plane this turning of the aggression against himself is carried out by the patient because of his own depressive anxieties; he turns it against himself in order to protect himself against re-experiencing the destruction of the objects and to protect these from his own aggression.

The paranoid anxiety in 'direct' countertransference is a reaction to the danger arising from various aggressive attitudes of the patient himself. The analysis of these attitudes shows that they are themselves defenses against, or reactions to, certain aggressive imagoes; and these reactions and defenses are governed by the law of talion or else, analogously to this, by identification with the persecutor. The reproach, contempt, abandonment, bodily assault—all these attitudes of menace or aggression in the patient that give rise to countertransference paranoid anxieties—are responses to (or anticipations of) equivalent attitudes of the transferred object.

The paranoid anxieties in 'indirect' countertransference are of a more complex nature since the danger for the analyst originates in a third party. The patient's transference situations that provoke the aggression of this 'third party' against the analyst may be of various sorts. In most cases, we are dealing with transference situations (masochistic or aggressive) similar to those that provoke the 'direct' countertransference anxieties previously described.

The common denominator of all the various attitudes of patients that provoke anxiety in the analyst is to be found, I believe, in the mechanism of 'identification with the persecutor'; the experience of being liberated from the persecutor and of triumphing over him, implied in this identification, suggests our designating this mechanism as a manic one. This mechanism may also exist where the manifest picture in the patient is quite the opposite, namely in certain depressive states; for the manic conduct may be directed either toward a projected object or toward an introjected object, it may be carried out alloplastically or autoplastically. The 'identification with the persecutor' may even exist in suicide, inasmuch as this is a 'mockery' of the fantasied or real persecutors, by anticipating the intentions of the persecutors and by one's doing to oneself what they wanted to do; this 'mockery' is the manic aspect of suicide. The 'identification with the persecutor' in the patient is, then, a defense against an object felt as sadistic that tends to make the patient the victim of a manic feast; and this defense is carried out either through the introjection of the persecutor in the ego, turning the analyst into the object of the 'manic tendencies', or through the introjection of the persecutor in the superego, taking the ego as the object of its manic trend. Let us illustrate.

An analysand decides to take a pleasure trip to Europe. He experiences this as a victory over the analyst both because he will free himself from the analyst for two months and because he can afford this trip whereas the analyst cannot. He then begins to be anxious lest the analyst seek revenge for the patient's triumph. The patient anticipates this aggression by becoming unwell, developing fever and the first symptoms of influenza. The analyst feels slight anxiety because of this illness and fears, recalling certain previous experiences, a deterioration in the state of health of the patient, who still however continues to come to the sessions. Up to this point, the situation in the transference and countertransference is as follows. The patient is in a manic relation to the analyst, and he has anxieties of preponderantly paranoid type. The analyst senses some irritation over the abandonment and some envy of the patient's great wealth (feelings ascribed by the patient in his paranoid anxieties to the analyst); but at the same time the analyst feels satisfaction at the analysand's real progress, which finds expression in the very fact that the trip is possible and that the patient has decided to make it. The analyst perceives a wish in part of his personality to bind the patient to himself and use the patient for his own needs. In having this wish he resembles the patient's mother, and he is aware that he is in reality identified with the domineering and vindictive object with which the patient identifies him. Hence the patient's illness seems, to the analyst's unconscious, a result of the analyst's own wish, and the analyst therefore experiences depressive (and paranoid) anxieties.

What object imago leads the patient to this manic situation? It is precisely this same imago of a tyrannical and sadistic mother, to whom the patient's frustrations constitute a manic feast. It is against these 'manic tendencies' in the object that the patient defends himself, first by identification (introjection of the persecutor in the ego, which manifests itself in the manic experience in his decision to take a trip) and then by using a masochistic defense to escape vengeance.

In brief, the analyst's depressive (and paranoid) anxiety is his emotional response to the patient's illness; and the patient's illness is itself a masochistic defense against the object's vindictive persecution. This masochistic defense also contains a manic mechanism in that it derides, controls, and dominates the analyst's aggression. In the stratum underlying this we find the patient in a paranoid situation in face of the vindictive persecution by the analyst—a fantasy that coincides with the analyst's secret irritation. Beneath this paranoid situation, and causing it, is an inverse situation: the patient is enjoying a manic triumph (his liberation from the analyst by going on a trip), but the analyst is in a paranoid situation (he is in danger of being defeated and abandoned). And, finally, beneath this we find a situation in which the patient is subjected to an object imago that wants to make of him the victim of its aggressive tendencies, but this time not in order to take revenge for intentions or attitudes in the patient, but merely to satisfy its own sadism—an imago that originates directly from the original sufferings of the subject.

In this way, the analyst was able to deduce from each of his countertransference sensations a certain transference situation; the analyst's fear of deterioration in the patient's health enabled him to perceive the patient's need to satisfy the avenger and to control and restrain him, partially inverting (through the illness) the roles of victimizer and victim, thus alleviating his guilt feeling and causing the analyst to feel some of the guilt. The analyst's irritation over the patient's trip enabled him to see the patient's need to free himself from a dominating and sadistic object, to see the patient's guilt feelings caused by these tendencies, and also to see his fear of the analyst's revenge. By his feeling of triumph the analyst was able to detect the anxiety and depression caused in the patient by his dependence upon this frustrating, yet indispensable, object. And each of these transference situations indicated to the analyst the patient's object imagoes—the fantasied or real countertransference situations that determined the transference situations.

2. What is the meaning of countertransference aggression?

In the preceding pages, we have seen that the analyst may experience, besides countertransference anxiety, annoyance, recollection, desire for vengeance, hatred, and other emotions. What are the origin and meaning of these emotions?

Countertransference aggression usually arises in the face of frustration (or danger of frustration) of desires that may superficially be differentiated into 'direct' and 'indirect.' Both direct and indirect desires are principally wishes to get libido or affection. The patient is the chief object of direct desires in the analyst, who wishes to be accepted and loved by him. The object of the indirect desires of the analyst may be, for example, other analysts from whom he wishes to get recognition or admiration through his successful work with his patients, using the latter as means to this end (17). This aim to get love has, in general terms, two origins: an instinctual origin (the primitive need of union with the object) and an origin of a defensive nature (the need of neutralizing, overcoming, or denying the rejections and other dangers originating from the internal objects, in particular from the superego). The frustrations may be differentiated, descriptively, into those of active type and those of passive type. Among the active frustrations is direct aggression by the patient, his mockery, deceit, and active rejection. To the analyst, active frustration means exposure to a predominantly 'bad' object; the patient may become, for example, the analyst's superego, which says to him 'you are bad'. Examples of frustration of passive type are passive rejection, withdrawal, partial abandonment, and other defenses against the bond with and dependence on the analyst. These signify frustrations of the analyst's need of union with the object.

In summary, we may say that countertransference aggression usually arises when there is frustration of the analyst's desires that spring from Eros, both those arising from his 'original' instinctive and affective drives and those arising from his need of neutralizing or annulling his own Thanatos (or the action of his internal 'bad objects') directed against the ego or against the external world. Owing partly to the analyst's own neurosis (and also to certain characteristics of analysis itself) these desires of Eros sometimes acquire the unconscious aim of bringing the patient to a state of dependence. Hence countertransference aggression may be provoked by the rejection of this dependence by the patient who rejects any bond with the analyst and refuses to surrender to him, showing this refusal by silence, denial, secretiveness, repression, blocking, or mockery.

Next we must establish what it is that induces the patient to behave in this way, to frustrate the analyst, to withdraw from him, to attack him. If we know this we shall know what we have to interpret when countertransference aggression arises in us, being able to deduce from the countertransference the transference situation and its cause. This cause is a fantasied countertransference situation or, more precisely, some actual or feared bad conduct from the projected object. Experience shows that, in somewhat general terms, this bad or threatening conduct of the object is usually an equivalent of the conduct of the patient (to which the analyst has reacted internally with aggression). We also understand why this is so: the patient's conduct springs from that most primitive of reactions, the talion reaction, or from the defense by means of identification with the persecutor or aggressor. In some cases it is quite simple: the analysand withdraws from us, rejects us, abandons us, or derides us when he fears or suffers the same or an equivalent treatment from us. In other cases it is more complex, the immediate identification with the aggressor being replaced by another identification that is less direct. To exemplify: a woman patient, upon learning that the analyst is going on holiday, remains silent a long while; she withdraws, through her silence, as a talion response to the analyst's withdrawal. Deeper analysis shows that the analyst's holiday is, to the patient, equivalent to the primal scene; and this is equivalent to destruction of her as a woman, and her immediate response must be a similar attack against the analyst. This aggressive (castrating) impulse is rejected and the result, her silence, is a compromise between her hostility and its rejection; it is a transformed identification with the persecutor.

To sum up: (*a*) The countertransference reactions of aggression (or of its equivalent) occur in response to transference situations in which the patient frustrates certain desires of the analyst's. These frustrations are equivalent to abandonment or aggression, which the patient carries out or with which he threatens the analyst, and they place the analyst, at first, in a depressive or paranoid situation. The patient's defense is in one aspect equivalent to a manic situation, for he is freeing himself from a persecutor.[17] (*b*) This transference situation is the defense against certain object imagoes. There may be an object that persecutes the subject sadistically, vindictively, or morally, or an object that the patient defends from his own destructiveness by an attack against his own ego (19); in these, the patient attacks—as Freud and Abraham have shown in the analysis of melancholia and suicide—at the same time the internal object and the external object (the analyst). (*c*) The analyst who is placed by the alloplastic or autoplastic attacks of the patient in a paranoid or depressive situation sometimes defends himself against these attacks by using the same identification with the aggressor or persecutor as the patient used. Then the analyst virtually becomes the persecutor, and to this the patient (insofar as he presupposes such a reaction from his internal and projected object) responds with anxiety. This anxiety and its origin is nearest to consciousness, and is therefore the first thing to interpret.

3. Countertransference guilt feelings are an important source of countertransference anxiety; the analyst fears his 'moral conscience'. Thus, for instance, a serious deterioration in the condition of the patient may cause the analyst to suffer reproach by his own superego, and also cause him to fear punishment. When such guilt feelings occur, the superego of the analyst is usually projected upon the patient or upon a third person, the analyst being the guilty ego. The accuser is the one who is attacked, the victim of the analyst. The analyst is the accused; he is charged with being the victimizer. It is therefore the analyst who must suffer anxiety over his object, and dependence upon it.

As in other countertransference situations, the analyst's guilt feeling may have either real causes or fantasied causes, or a mixture of the two. A real cause exists in the analyst who has neurotic negative feelings that exercise some influence over his behavior, leading him, for example, to interpret with aggressiveness or to behave in a submissive, seductive, or unnecessarily frustrating way. But guilt feelings may also arise in the analyst over, for instance, intense submissiveness in the patient even though the analyst had not driven the patient into such conduct by his procedure. Or he may feel guilty when the analysand becomes depressed or ill, although his therapeutic procedure was right and proper according to his own conscience. In such cases, the countertransference guilt feelings are evoked not by what procedure he has actually used but by his awareness of what he might have done in view of his latent disposition. In other words, the analyst identifies himself in fantasy with a bad internal object of the patient's and he feels guilty for what he has provoked in this role—illness, depression, masochism, suffering, failure. The imago of the patient then becomes fused with the analyst's internal objects, which the analyst had, in the past, wanted (and perhaps managed) to frustrate, make suffer, dominate, or destroy. Now he wishes to repair them. When this reparation fails, he reacts as if he had hurt them. The true cause of the guilt feelings is the neurotic, predominantly sado-masochistic tendencies that may reappear in countertransference; the analyst therefore quite rightly entertains certain doubts and uncertainties about his ability to control them completely and to keep them entirely removed from his procedure.

The transference situation to which the analyst is likely to react with guilt feelings is then, in the first place, a masochistic trend in the patient, which may be either of a 'defensive' (secondary) or of a 'basic' (primary) nature. If it is defensive we know it to be a rejection of sadism by means of its 'turning against the ego'; the principal object imago that imposes this masochistic defense is a retaliatory imago. If it is basic ('primary masochism') the object imago is 'simply' sadistic, a reflex of the pains ('frustrations') originally suffered by the patient. The analyst's guilt feelings refer to his own sadistic tendencies. He may feel as if he himself had provoked the patient's masochism. The patient is subjugated by a 'bad' object so that it seems as if the analyst had satisfied his aggressiveness; now the analyst is exposed in his turn to the accusations of his superego. In short, the superficial situation is that the patient is now the superego, and the analyst the ego who must suffer the accusation; the analyst is in a depressive-paranoid situation, whereas the patient is, from one point of view, in a 'manic' situation (showing, for example, 'mania for reproaching'). But on a deeper plane the situation is the reverse: the analyst is in a 'manic' situation (acting as a vindictive, dominating, or 'simply' sadistic imago), and the patient is in a depressive-paranoid situation (19).

4. Besides the anxiety, hatred, and guilt feelings in countertransference, there are a number of other countertransference situations that may also be decisive points in the course of analytic treatment, both because they may

influence the analyst's work and because the analysis of the transference situations that provoke such countertransference situations may represent the central problem of treatment, clarification of which may be indispensable if the analyst is to exert any therapeutic influence upon the patient.

Let us consider briefly only two of these situations. One is the counter-transference boredom or somnolence already mentioned, which of course assumes great importance only when it occurs often. Boredom and somnolence are usually unconscious talion responses in the analyst to a withdrawal or affective abandonment by the patient. This withdrawal has diverse origins and natures; but it has specific characteristics, for not every kind of withdrawal by the patient produces boredom in the analyst. One of these characteristics seems to be that the patient withdraws without going away, he takes his emotional departure from the analyst while yet remaining with him; there is as a rule no danger of the patient's taking flight. This *partial* withdrawal or abandonment expresses itself superficially in intellectualization (emotional blocking), in increased control, sometimes in monotony in the way of speaking, or in similar devices. The analyst has at these times the sensation of being excluded and of being impotent to guide the course of the sessions. It seems that the analysand tries in this way to avoid a latent and dreaded dependence upon the analyst. This dependence is, at the surface, his dependence upon his moral superego, and at a deeper level it is dependence upon other internal objects that are in part persecutors and in part persecuted. These objects must *not* be projected upon the analyst; the latent and internal relations with them must not be made present and externalized. This danger is avoided through various mechanisms, ranging from 'conscious' control and selection of the patient's communications to depersonalization, and from emotional blocking[18] to total repression of any transference relation; it is this rejection of such dangers and the avoidance and mastery of anxiety by means of these mechanisms that lead to the withdrawal to which the analyst may react with boredom or somnolence.

Countertransference anxiety and guilt feelings also frequently cause a tendency to countertransference submissiveness, which is important from two points of view: both for its possible influence upon the analyst's understanding, behavior, and technique, and for what it may teach us about the patient's transference situation. This tendency to submissiveness will lead the analyst to avoid frustrating the patient and will even cause the analyst to pamper him. The analyst's tendency to avoid frustration and tension will express itself in a search for rapid pacification of the transference situations, by prompt 'reduction' of the transference of infantile situations, for example, or by rapid reconstruction of the 'good, 'real' imago of the analyst.[19] The analyst who feels subjugated by the patient feels angry, and the patient, intuitively perceiving this anger, is afraid of his revenge. The transference situation that leads the patient to dominate and subjugate the analyst by a hidden or manifest threat seems analogous to the transference situation that leads the analyst to feel anxious and guilty. The various ways in which the analyst reacts to his anxieties—in one case with an attitude of submission, in another case with inner recrimination—is also related to the transference attitude of the patient. My observations seem to indicate that the greater the disposition to real aggressive *action* in the analysand, the more the analyst tends to submission.

VII

Before closing, let us consider briefly two doubtful points. How much confidence should we place in countertransference as a guide to understanding the patient? And how useful or how harmful is it to communicate to the patient a countertransference reaction? As to the first question, I think it certainly a mistake to find in countertransference reactions an oracle, with blind faith to expect of them the pure truth about the psychological situations of the analysand. It is plain that our unconscious is a very personal 'receiver' and 'transmitter' and we must reckon with frequent distortions of objective reality. But it is also true that our unconscious is nevertheless 'the best we have of its kind'. His own analysis and some analytic experience enables the analyst, as a rule, to be conscious of this personal factor and know his 'personal equation'. According to my experience, the danger of exaggerated faith in the messages of one's own unconscious is, even when they refer to very 'personal' reactions, less than the danger of repressing them and denying them any objective value.

I have sometimes begun a supervisory hour by asking the candidate how he has felt toward the patient that week or what he has experienced during the sessions, and the candidate has answered, for instance, that he was bored, or that he felt anxious because he had the impression that the patient wanted to abandon the analysis. On other occasions I have myself noticed annoyance or anxiety in the candidate relative to the patient. These countertransference responses have at times indicated to me in advance the central problem of the treatment at whatever stage it had reached; and this supposition has usually been verified by detailed analysis of the material presented in the supervisory hour. When these countertransference reactions were very intense they of course referred to unsolved problems in the candidate, and his reactions were distorted echoes of the objective situation. But even without such 'intensity' we must always reckon with certain distortions. One candidate, for instance, reacted for a time with slight annoyance whenever his analysands were much occupied with their childhood. The candidate had the idea that only analysis of transference could further the treatment. In reality he also had a wish that the analysands concern themselves with him. But the candidate was able by analyzing this situation quickly to revive his interest in the childhood situations of the analysands, and he could also see that his annoyance, in spite of its neurotic character, had pointed out to him the rejection of certain transference situations in some analysands.

Whatever the analyst experiences emotionally, his reactions always bear some relation to processes in the patient. Even the must neurotic countertransference ideas arise only in response to certain patients and to certain situations of these patients, and they can, in consequence, indicate something about the patients and their situations. To cite one last example: a candidate, at the beginning of a session (and before the analysand, a woman, had spoken), had the idea that she was about to draw a revolver and shoot at him; he felt an impulse to sit in his chair in a defensive position. He readily recognized the paranoid character of this idea, for the patient was far from likely to behave in such a way. Yet it was soon clear that his reaction was in a certain sense appropriate; the analysand spontaneously remarked that she intended to give him 'a kick in the penis'. On other occasions when the candidate had the same idea, this patient was fantasying that she was the victim of persecution; in this case also the analyst's reaction was, in a way, appropriate, for the patient's fantasy of being persecuted was the consequence and the cause of the patient's sadistic impulses toward the transferred object.

On the other hand, one must critically examine the *deductions* one makes from perception of one's own countertransference. For example, the fact that the analyst feels angry does not simply mean (as is sometimes said) that the patient wishes to make him angry. It may mean rather that the patient has a transference feeling of guilt. What has been said above concerning countertransference aggression is relevant here.

The second question—whether the analyst should or should not 'communicate' or 'interpret' aspects of his countertransference to the analysand—

cannot be considered fully here.[20] Much depends, of course, upon what, when, how, to whom, for what purpose, and in what conditions the analyst speaks about his countertransference. It is probable that the purposes sought by communicating the countertransference might often (but not always) be better attained by other means. The principal other means is analysis of the patient's fantasies about the analyst's countertransference (and of the related transferences) sufficient to show the patient the truth (the reality of the countertransferences of his inner and outer objects); and with this must also be analyzed the doubts, negations, and other defenses against the truth, intuitively perceived, until they have been overcome. But there are also situations in which communication of the countertransference is of value for the subsequent course of the treatment. Without doubt, this aspect of the use of countertransference is of great interest; we need an extensive and detailed study of the inherent problems of communication of countertransference. Much more experience and study of countertransference needs to be recorded.

NOTES

1. I confine myself in what follows to papers published since 1946. I have referred to a previous bibliography in another paper (17).
2. This differentiation accords in essentials with Annie Reich's two types of countertransference. I would add, however, that also when the analyst uses the analysis for his own acting out (what I have termed 'indirect' countertransference), the analysand represents an object to the analyst (a 'subtransferred' object), not merely a 'tool'.
3. Michael Balint (2) considers a similar problem, the scarcity of papers on the system of psychoanalytic training. Investigation of this problem leads him to several interesting remarks on the relationship between didactic analysts and candidates. (See note 5.)
4. Little (15) speaks, for instance, of the 'myth of the impersonal analyst'.
5. It is important to be aware of this 'equality' because there is otherwise great danger that certain remnants of the 'patriarchal order' will contaminate the analytic situation. The dearth of scientific study of countertransference is an expression of a 'social inequality' in the analyst-analysand society and points to the need for 'social reform'; this can come about only through a greater awareness of countertransference. For as long as we repress, for instance, our wish to dominate the analysand neurotically (and we do wish this in one part of our personality), we cannot free him from his neurotic dependence, and as long as we repress our neurotic dependence upon him (and we do in part depend on him), we cannot free him from the need of dominating us neurotically.

    Michael Balint (2) compares the atmosphere of psychoanalytic training with the initiation ceremonies of primitives and emphasizes the existence of superego 'intropressure' (Ferenczi), which no candidate can easily withstand.
6. Helene Deutsch (4) speaks of the 'complementary position' when she refers to the analyst's identifications with the object imagoes.
7. In view of the close connection between these two aspects of countertransference, this

differentiation is somewhat artificial. Its introduction is justifiable only considering the above-mentioned circumstances.

8. It is a partial abandonment and it is a threat of abandonment. The object that threatens to abandon us and the persecutor are basically the same.

9. The process described by Ferenczi has an even deeper meaning. The 'emptiness' and 'futility' of the associations express the empty, futile, dead part of the analysand; they characterize a depressive situation in which the analysand is alone and abandoned by his objects, just as has happened in the analytic situation.

10. Cesio (3) demonstrates in a case report the principal countertransference reactions that arose in the course of the psychoanalytic treatment, pointing out especially the analyst's partial identifications with objects of the patient's superego.

11. By 'abolition of reaction' I mean adherence by the analysand to the fundamental rule that all his thoughts are to be expressed without selection or rejection.

12. If the interpretations coincide with the analysand's superego judgments, the analyst is confused with the superego, sometimes with good reason. Superego judgments must be shown to the analysand but, as far as possible, one should refrain from uttering them.

13. Cf. Little (15, p. 34).

14. Something similar, although not connected with countertransference, is emphasized by Fairbairn (5).

15. See Klein (12, 13). The terms *depressive, paranoid,* and *manic* are here used simply as descriptive terms. Thus, for example, 'paranoid anxieties' involve all the fantasies of being persecuted, independently of the libidinal phase or of the 'position' described by Klein. The following considerations are closely connected with my observations upon psychopathological stratification (19).

16. By the term *frustration* I always refer to the subjective experience and not to the objective facts. This inner experience is determined by a complementary series at one end of which is primary and secondary masochism and at the other end the actual frustrating happenings.

17. This 'mania' may be of 'superego type', as for instance 'mania for reproaching' (identification with the persecuting moral superego), which also occurs in many depressive and masochistic states. It may also be of a 'pre-superego type' (belonging to planes underlying that of moral guilt) as occurs for instance in certain erotomanias, for erotic mockery is identification with the object that castrates by frustrating genitally (19).

18. This emotional blocking and, in particular, the blocking of aggression seems to be the cause of the 'absence of danger' for the analyst (the fact that the analysand does not run away or otherwise jeopardize the analysis), which seems to be one of the conditions for occurrence of countertransference boredom.

19. Wilhelm Reich (22) stressed the frequent tendency in analysts to avoid negative transference. The countertransference situation just described is one of the situations underlying that tendency.

20. Alice Balint (1), Winnicott (24), and others favor communicating to the patient (and further analyzing) certain countertransference situations. Heimann (11) is among those that oppose doing so. Libermann (14) describes how, in the treatment of a psychotic woman, communication of the countertransference played a very important part. The analyst freely associated upon unconscious manifestations of countertransference that the patient pointed out to him.

REFERENCES

1. Balint, Alice: Handhabung der Übertragung auf Grund der Ferenczischen Versuche. *Int. Ztschr. f. Psa.,* XXII, 1936, pp. 47–58.

2. Balint, Michael: On the psychoanalytic training system. *Int. J. Psa.*, XXIX, 1948.
3. Cesio, F.: Psicoanalisis de una melancolia con ataques histero epilépticos. *Rev. de Psicoanálisis*, IX, 1952.
4. Deutsch, Helene: Okkulte Vorgänge während der Psychoanalyse. *Imago*, XII, 1926, pp. 418–433.
5. Fairbairn, W. R. D.: The Repression and the Return of Bad Objects. *Brit. J. Med. Psychology*, XIX, 1943.
6. Ferenczi, Sandor: Missbrauch der Assoziationsfreiheit. In: *Bausteine zur Psychoanalyse, II.* Vienna: Int. Psa. Verlag, 1927, p. 41.
7. Freud, Sigmund: The Future Prospects of Psychoanalytic Therapy (1910). *Coll. Papers*, II. London: Hogarth Press.
8. ——: Further Recommendations in the Technique of Psychoanalysis. On Beginning the Treatment (1913). *Coll. Papers*, II. London: Hogarth Press.
9. ——: The Dynamics of the Transference (1912). *Coll. Papers*, II. London: Hogarth Press.
10. Gitelson, Maxwell: The Emotional Position of the Analyst in the Psychoanalytic Situation. *Int. J. Psa.*, XXXIII, 1952.
11. Heimann, Paula: On Countertransference. *Int. J. Psa.*, XXXI, 1950.
12. Klein, Melanie: A Contribution to the Psychoanalysis of Manic-Depressive States. *Int. J. Psa.*, XVI, 1935.
13. ——: On the Criteria for the Termination of a Psychoanalysis. *Int. J. Psa.*, XXXI, 1950.
14. Libermann, D.: Fragmento del análisis de una psicosis paranoide. *Rev. de Psicoanálisis*, IX, 1952.
15. Little, Margaret: Countertransference and the Patient's Response to It. *Int. J. Psa.*, XXXII, 1951.
16. Lorand, Sandor: *Technique of Psychoanalytic Therapy.* New York: International Universities Press, Inc., 1946.
17. Racker, Heinrich: Contribution to the Problem of Countertransference (1948). *Int. J. Psa.*, XXXIV, 1953, p. 313–324.
18. ——: Observaciones sobre la contratransferencia como instrumento técnico (1951). *Rev. de Psicoanálisis*, IX, 1952, pp. 342–354.
19. ——: Contribution to the Problem of Psychopathological Stratification. *Int. J. Psa.*, XXXVIII, 1957, pp. 223–239.
20. ——: Notes on the Theory of Transference. *Psychoanal. Quart*, XXIII, 1954.
21. Reich, Annie: On Countertransference. *Int. J. Psa.*, XXXII, 1951.
22. Reich, Wilhelm: *Character Analysis* (1933). New York: Orgone Institute Press, 1945.
23. Weigert, Edith: Contribution to the Problem of Terminating Psychoanalyses. *Psychoanal. Quart.*, XXI, 1952.
24. Winnicott, D. W.: Hate in the Countertransference. *Int. J. Psa.*, XXX, 1949.

12. The Schizophrenic's Vulnerability to the Therapist's Unconscious Processes

Harold F. Searles

After several years of doing intensive psychotherapy with schizophrenic patients, I began to realize that schizophrenic experience and behavior consists, surprisingly frequently, in the patient's responding to other persons' unconscious processes. I had long been aware of the tremendous importance of *projection* in these patient's illnesses; but I was slower to see the great— perhaps equally tremendous—part that *introjection* plays, too, in schizophrenia and, hence, in the psychotherapy of schizophrenia. On theoretical grounds one can readily think, concerning any patient whose ego-boundaries are so incomplete as to facilitate massive projection, that by the same token he will be profoundly susceptible, also, to introjection. But in actual clinical work, introjection is a process that is in most instances much more subtle, much less conspicuously displayed, than is projection, and its detection in the arena of the therapeutic relationship tends to call for a higher degree of self-awareness in the therapist than the noticing of the patient's projection generally requires.

The schizophrenic patient's so-frequent delusion of being magically "influenced" by outside forces (radar, electricity, or whatnot) is rooted partially in the fact of his responding to unconscious processes in persons about him —persons who, being unaware of these processes, will not and can not help him to realize that the "influence" comes from a non-magical, interpersonal source.

For two reasons I shall limit this study to an examination of the impact of the *therapist's* unconscious impulses and attitudes upon the schizophrenic patient. First, it is in the setting of the therapeutic relationship that I as a therapist have had my best opportunities to see this mechanism operating. Second, no matter how greatly this mechanism pervades a patient's relationships with all other persons, it must be regarded as having especially crucial significance when it occurs in the therapeutic relationship, both because this relationship is of unparalleled importance in the patient's current experience, and because it is essential that the therapist, and eventually the patient, become as aware as possible of the forces at work in their therapeutic investigation. The potential influence, for good or ill, of the therapist's personality upon the schizophrenic patient is even more awesome than that of the analyst in relation to the neurotic patient; hence it is especially incumbent upon the therapist, here, to be as fully aware as possible of the processes at work in him, and of their impact upon the patient.

I shall not attempt to trace out the presumable countertransference element in these unconscious processes in the therapist; rather, I wish only to show various of the *effects* that they have upon the patient's subjective experience and outward behavior. The data I shall present derive solely from the psychotherapy of schizophrenia; but my experience with non-schizophrenic patients has led me to surmise that the relatively dramatic phenomena to be presented here have analogues, less dramatic and less easily detectable but of much importance nonetheless, in other varieties of psychiatric illness. In short, I surmise that it is in the *therapist's* relationship with a *schizophrenic* patient that he can see most readily certain introjective processes that are actually at work, in some form or other, in *any* relationship involving a patient with any type of neurotic or psychotic illness.

SURVEY OF RELEVANT LITERATURE

In psychoanalytic literature, it is in papers concerning countertransference, of course, that the analyst's unconscious processes have been described, and in actuality this whole vast segment of the literature is relevant to my present subject, a segment that had its historical point of origin in a paper by Freud (8) in 1910, in which he wrote, "We have begun to consider the 'countertransference', which arises in the physician as a result of the patient's influence on his unconscious feelings, and have nearly come to the point of requiring the physician to recognize and overcome this countertransference in himself."

From the subsequent flow of papers concerning countertransference in the analysis of neurotic patients, three recent articles are of greatest relevance here. In 1951, Little (14) noted that "unconsciously we may exploit a patient's illness for our own purposes, both libidinal and aggressive, and he will quickly respond to this."

In 1957, Schroff (16) gave an account of the analysis of a man with a character disorder of which sexual acting out was a prominent feature. He mentioned that, during a period of treatment with an earlier therapist, the man had acted out some of the therapist's unconscious impulses; and Schroff found, in his own work with the patient, that his countertransference problems influenced unfavorably the man's acting out, until late in the eventually successful analysis. This kind of mechanism, incidentally, had been described in a paper in 1952 by Johnson and Szurek (12), in which these authors reported their finding of children's acting out the parents' unconscious antisocial impulses. Barchilon (3), in a paper in 1957 concerning "countertransference cures," reported a number of examples of analytic "cures" that he showed to be based precariously upon not only transference but also countertransference, and he commented that "in more extreme cases, the therapist forces the patient to act out his own unconscious solutions with little relevance to the patient's needs."

Turning now to the literature concerning schizophrenia, we find many papers that have emphasized the schizophrenic's powerful tendency toward incorporation or introjection:[1] a tendency that renders him vulnerable to the kind of phenomena that I shall describe. A few examples of such papers, concerning incorporation or introjection in schizophrenia, are those by Nunberg (15) in 1921, Abraham (1) in 1927, Bychowski (5) in 1930, and Allen (2) in 1935. In 1945, Fenichel (7) commented that "it is possible to demonstrate in persons suffering from delusions of persecution the presence of the pregenital aim of incorporation which was the undifferentiated forerunner of both love and hate. Projection as such is based on a vagueness of the borderline between ego and nonego. Ideas of incorporation also correspond to this vagueness. The incorporated object has become a part of the subject's ego."

Hill (10) in 1955, in his volume, *Psychotherapeutic Intervention in Schizophrenia,* described the parent's unconscious as playing an integral role in the development of schizophrenia in the child. Hill stressed the etiological importance of what one might call the introjection, into the child's superego, of the mother whose own personality-integration is under severe assault from her unconscious affects: "[The patient's] life has been severely restricted, limited, and invaded by the requirements of his parents' conscious and unconscious conflicts and drives. Anything in the unconscious of the parent which would produce anxiety must become a preoccupation of the patient in order to keep down parental anxiety and thereby reduce his own distress."[2]

"One meaning of the futility of the dependence-independence struggle of the schizophrenic . . . is his belief, based upon his observations, that, if he should improve and become well . . . his mother would become psychotic."[3]

Concerning "the mother as a presence in the superego" of the patient: "His superego is to him a very real person within him, who not only advises and threatens or opposes but actually dominates his life with crippling restrictions and interdictions supported by the threat that the superego itself will go crazy."[4]

"There is danger constantly of invasion of primitive superego demands which will disorganize the ego into a psychosis."[5]

Limentani (13), in a paper in 1956 concerning symbiotic identification in schizophrenia, made, in passing, the following reference to a patient's sensitivity to his therapist's unconscious processes: "Richard was so keenly aware of his therapist's mood and reproduced it so closely that the therapist at times gained, from the interviews with the patient, awareness of how he himself felt."

Also in 1956, Bowen (4), in a preliminary report concerning his findings in a research project involving concomitant psychotherapy of schizophrenic patients and their parents, with the latter being housed on the hospital ward with their children, likewise portrayed the schizophrenic's vulnerability to the parent's unconscious affects: "The more we have worked with these family groups at close range, the more we can see the interchangeability of anxiety and symptoms. When we hear a mother express a worry about something that is outside the local setting, and when we get some feel of the intensity of the mother's worry with no expression of the worry in the mother, but at the very same time we see the patient's psychosis increase, it makes us more and more inclined to believe that schizophrenia is a process that exists within the family constellation rather than a problem in the patient alone."

In a paper in 1951 concerning various manifestations of incorporation (which I am here terming *introjection*) in the therapeutic relationship, I described a number of instances in which mutual incorporation was found to be present; one of these examples was from my work with a schizophrenic patient (17). In a paper in 1955 I pointed out that the schizophrenic's fear that he will lose his identity if he comes too close, emotionally, to another person, is a realistic fear insofar as he utilizes the mechanism of unconscious identification with (i.e. introjection of) the other person as a means of keeping out of awareness the anxiety-laden affects that interpersonal closeness stimulates in him (18). And in a paper in 1957 I presented the concept that one significant factor in the causation, and maintenance, of schizophrenia in any given individual consists in the impact upon him of other persons' efforts—largely or wholly unconscious efforts—to drive him "crazy." In support of this concept I presented data from patients' intrafamilial relationships, ward-group relationships, and intensive pychotherapeutic relationships; and I reported the finding that the motivation of the other person, who integrates with the patient in such a fashion, seems most often to consist in an unconscious desire to maintain a symbiotic relatedness with him (20).

CLINICAL MATERIAL

There now follow clinical data illustrative of three different ways in which a patient may respond to the therapist's unconscious processes. The patient may (a) experience the therapist's unconscious processes as being facets of his own personality or (b) experience them in the form of hallucinations or (c) compulsively act them out in behavior that he himself finds incomprehensible.

The Patient's Experiencing the Therapist's Unconscious Processes as Being Facets of His Own Personality

In illustrating this first phenomenon material from only one therapist-patient relationship will be presented, because it is essentially the same phenomenon, I think, as that which one finds so commonly and characteristically in depressive states. I present it here solely because I have realized only recently how frequently this can be detected among schizophrenic patients also. With these latter patients, *projection* is so conspicuous that one may fail to detect the more subtle, but perhaps equally important, place of this type of *introjection* among the patient's psychotic defenses.

Three months ago I began working with a twenty-six–year–old schizophrenic woman whose previous therapist had left the Chestnut Lodge staff. I had seen this woman, in passing, innumerable times in the course of her several years' stay here, and had always thought of her behavior as outstandingly dominated by paranoid projection. She made almost incessant accusations, to myself and other passers-by, of this sort: "I know what you're thinking! You're thinking that I shouldn't have drunk that coffee at 2 P.M. yesterday," or "I know what you're going to say—you're going to say that

I should have visited longer with my aunt over the telephone last week.'' She would go, actually, into endless detail, and with innumerable variations, quite unwittingly displaying before the public eye the most private areas of her own unconscious, in this projected form. And in her psychotherapy with my predecessor, she evidenced projection in a similarly prominent fashion, as I learned from him in my capacity as supervisor during about eighteen months of their work together.

It therefore came as a great surprise to me, when I began having therapeutic sessions with her, to find that although her long-known projection continued to be prominent, there were fascinatingly subtle evidences that introjection was at work with something like equal frequency.

Thus far in the work with her I have not found this operative with respect to truly *unconscious* processes in myself, the kind of processes with which this paper is especially concerned, although I have little doubt that the future course of our work will bring to light such connections. What I have found, rather, have been dozens of evidences of her introjecting aspects of myself that were preconscious in me at the moment and readily accessible to my consciousness. Had they not been so, I could not so quickly have discerned the fact of her introjecting them.

For example, in one of the first week's sessions, as she was prattling on in a self-depreciating and rather absent-minded fashion, I took my ease by tilting my head over, at a sharp angle, against the wall. She continued rambling on, but apparently taking in, with her eyes, this shift in my posture; one of the features of her behavior which had impressed me during these early sessions was her apparently taking sharp visual note of every least little thing about my appearance and bodily movements, but never making any verbal comments about these—never expressing any opinions about, or direct reactions to, them. In this instance, what I heard within a few seconds, in the midst of her prattling, was, ''I know I looked awkward on the tennis court,'' whereupon it occurred to me that this unusual, head-tilted posture of mine might well look awkward to her. In another session soon thereafter, the day was so hot that I removed my coat and loosened my tie; within a few seconds I heard, in the midst of her self-critical prattle, the statement, ''I'm a very slovenly person.'' Thereupon I realized that in the eyes of this woman who had come from a highly genteel background and even in her illness was generally neatly groomed, I might well appear slovenly, sitting there in shirt sleeves and loosened necktie. But the fascinating thing was that she evidently genuinely experienced these traits as being aspects of herself and was quite unable to perceive them as traits of mine. I had already heard from her, within these first few hours, enough about her relationships with her parents to surmise that she had had largely to repress any critical feelings experienced toward either of her parents, both being persons with unresilient and defensive character structures, during her upbringing.

One might look at it that, in each of these instances I have described, this woman reacted, in keeping with her low self-esteem and intense self-criticism, to my actions as being non-verbal communications to her, communications designed to convey to her my opinion that she was awkward and slovenly. This would be a quite-true viewpoint, I think, but would not negate the fact of her genuinely introjecting these behavior traits of mine. Incidentally, it should be noted that what she introjected were, apparently, not only my behavior traits themselves, but, even more clearly, my preconsciously *low opinion* of these behavior traits in myself. This I regard as an example of one of the mechanisms by which the schizophrenic patient expresses his unconscious endeavor to relieve the parent's own anxiety—by, namely, introjecting the parent's intrapsychic conflicts.

In subsequent hours, I found her to be referring to herself variously as "smug," "swaggering," "blah," "sleepy," and so on, at times when, I realized after hearing her say each of these things, I was feeling thus and was no doubt appearing thus to her, but so appearing at a level of perception that was unconscious in her. It was evident that at a conscious level she genuinely perceived only *herself* as being thus-and-so, as, to be sure, she indeed was at times; but she seemed quite unable to perceive, consciously, that *I too* was being smug (or whatnot), and being so, oftentimes, when she showed nothing in her demeanor that would warrant her self-accusation along this line.

Perhaps partly as a result of my perceiving this tendency toward introjection on her part, and my therefore encouraging her to experience, and express, critical feelings to me as these became roused in her by the things I said and did, it required only a few weeks for her to begin expressing annoyance to me about my looking smug, or "blah," or whatnot, at times when I was indeed feeling so. The relative ease with which this introjective mechanism could be relinquished suggests that her perception of these various behavior traits of mine had been taking place at, actually, a preconscious rather than fully unconscious level. And this consideration ties in with my general impression that this particular type of introjective phenomenon, which I have just described, is found in schizophrenic patients whose ego-functioning is at least somewhat more intact than that of the patients who manifest the other two types of introjective phenomena that I shall illustrate. These latter, more deeply disorganized patients leave one with little doubt that these phenomena are taking place in them at a deeply unconscious level—deepest of all, I believe, as regards the third type of phenomenon to be described.

Before going on to the second type of phenomenon, however, let me call attention to the general point, touched upon at the beginning of this paper, that—as can be seen in the brief data already given—introjective phenomena are less easily perceptible, and their detection calls for a higher degree of self-awareness in the therapist, than is the case with projective phenomena. A simple example will point up this contrast. If a patient looks suspiciously at the therapist and says with hostility, "I know what you're thinking— you're just figuring out a way to kill me!", and if this comes at a time when the therapist has no such thought or feeling in his awareness, he is at once alerted to the possibility that the patient is *projecting* some murderous intent upon him. But if a patient says, instead, with the self-disparagement that one finds so frequently among schizophrenic patients, "I'm just a fat slob who can't even speak English!", it takes a bit of doing for the therapist, who probably at the moment is not having the thought that he himself is a fat slob who doesn't speak English in any outstandingly cultured way, to let his own trend of thought open up to just this rather unpleasantly jolting new reflection: namely, that much as he prefers to view himself otherwise, he *is* somewhat corpulent and his use of grammar *isn't* the best. Not until the therapist has traversed this relatively roundabout and difficult path does the thought occur to him, now, that *introjection* may have been involved in the statement the patient has just made.

The Patient's Experiencing the Therapist's Unconscious Processes in the Form of Hallucinations

Until about one year ago I considered hallucinations to be, without exception, essentially projective phenomena. That is, I found that my clinical experience substantiated the usual textbook descriptions of them as being due to projection. I refer, here, to such descriptions as the following one by Fenichel (7): of hallucinations he says that "Inner factors are projected and experienced as if they were external perceptions."[6]

But in the course of my work with a certain schizophrenic man I discovered that, in at least some instances, to understand why a patient is hallucinating we must see this as having to do with not only *projection* but also *intro*jection. To be specific, in this particular instance I found that the patient's evident hallucinating of murderously threatening figures connoted not only his projecting, in the form of hallucinatory figures, his own unconscious murderous impulses, but connoted also his struggle against the introjection of *my* own unconscious murderous impulses toward him.

A thirty-two–year–old man, he had been hospitalized constantly for nearly ten years (including a five-year stay at another hospital prior to his admission to the Lodge), and had had nearly five years of intensive psychotherapy with a succession of therapists, before I undertook therapy with him. He proved, soon after I had begun seeing him, to be a most intensely frustrating and threatening person. For about two and one-half years his behavior during my sessions with him was limited almost exclusively to *(a)* sitting in slovenly torpor, dropping cigarette ashes on my rug, picking his nose and wiping the yield therefrom upon his trousers, and making no sound except for belches and the extremely frequent and quite unrepentantly loud passage of flatus and *(b)* infrequent vitriolic outbursts at me, in which he would give every evidence of being barely able to restrain himself from attacking me physically, and would say such things as, "You black, slimy son of a bitch! Shut up or I'll knock your teeth out!" As the months wore on, I felt under increasing strain because of his massive resistance to psychotherapy, and increasingly afraid of his tenuously controlled rage. There were many evidences, which need not be detailed here, that his rage was largely dissociated; so I had reason to feel that this man, who outweighed me by at least twenty pounds, had a great deal of rage that neither I, nor he himself, could reliably contain.

Meanwhile, he had evidently begun to respond to hallucinatory voices, both in his daily life on the ward and, at times, during his psychotherapeutic sessions. For several months, he gave every indication, in the content and tone of his responses to them, that these were contemptuous, taunting voices; he would talk back to them in a furiously angry way. Only in retrospect did it occur to me that maybe these hallucinations had some connection with the contempt that had developed in me toward him, contempt that in that phase of our work remained in an unconscious, dissociated state in me, erupting into my awareness only at brief moments with an intensity I found shocking. For example, once when I saw him passing through the far end of the corridor I had a startlingly new thought and feeling, about this man whom I had been consciously regarding predominantly as a desperately suffering, psychotic individual, no matter how discouragingly and frighteningly so. My thought was, "There goes that crazy son of a bitch!'', accompanied by a most intense feeling of contempt toward him.

During still later months in this two–and–one-half–year period, it seemed that the hallucinatory figures to which he frequently responded were predominantly frightening ones; his responses to them were not so much angry as frightenedly defiant, as if he were trying to keep his courage mustered in the face of them. In one of the sessions, while I was feeling, as usual, more intensely "strained" than anything else, I noticed that as he came in and sat down he said to himself in a hushed, quavering, very frightened voice, "Careful!'', as if he sensed an ominous presence in the room. It was only a few sessions after this that an incident occurred that showed me how much dissociated rage there had been in me, presumably for a long time, and presumably fostered by my having been laboring under so much discouragement and, still, threat of physical injury for so long. In this particular session to which I now refer, he had been leafing through one of the magazines from a nearby end-table in my office, as he had taken to doing occasionally, with my whole-hearted approval. But after finishing with it he tossed it desultorily toward my couch; it fell short and lay on the floor. At the end of the hour, he left without bothering to pick it up. As he was walking out the door I stooped down to pick up the magazine, still feeling only a sense of great strain. But as I lifted it up I suddenly became overwhelmed with fury, and smashed the magazine down onto the end-table with all my strength, sending a glass ash tray flying. It was at this moment that I realized the probability that he had long been sensing, and responding hallucinatory to, this rage in me, which had been dissociated heretofore.

It required several more months for me to become accustomed to feeling such an intensity of rage toward him; meanwhile, over this several-months' period, this feeling would come into my awareness only fleetingly and then return, presumably, to an unconscious level. One of these subsequent occasions of my momentarily increased awareness involved a magazine again. When, this time, he slung one of my more-prized magazines into a nearby chair, rumpling and tearing it somewhat with the force of the throw, I found myself saying to him in a balefully threatening, even tone, "Go easy on the magazines. You're not in a pig-pen.'' On another occasion when he had been contributing to the session naught but occasional belches and flatus and a kind of insolently contented appearance, and he now took out a cellophane-wrapped package of crackers and ate them, it was at the point when he nonchalantly tossed the cellophane onto the floor that I found myself filled with quick fury and said, "Listen!—Don't do that in my office! Don't throw paper on my floor!'', at which he looked flustered and immediately picked up the cellophane. On another occasion, when I was discussing his psychotherapy with a number of colleagues in a seminar, telling them that I had recently begun sitting over in a corner away from the door so that he would have ready access to the door in case he became terrified of his murderous rage toward me, I realized that I had been unconsciously maneuvering the seating arrangement so that, in case he attacked me physically, I would now have a legitimate excuse—since I would now be unable to get to the door—to enter into a knock-down-drag-out fist fight with him for which, I now knew, I had been yearning for weeks. And it was within a few days of this time that when someone asked me, at lunch, how this patient was getting along, I found myself grating, "Well, he's alive, and that's not doing badly, considering how I feel toward him." More than once I had felt lucky to get out of our sessions alive; but I had not realized before that he could be looked upon as being fortunate in this same sense.

The most memorable of these incidents when this usually dissociated rage came into my awareness was when, one night, I dreamed that he and I were fighting, and I was reacting to him as being—as I in waking life was then considering him to be—a dangerous, uncontrollable person. In the course of this dream-struggle he got his hands on a knifelike letter opener. But what then happened, as I was astonished to recall upon awakening, was that *he* took *me* into custody; he, functioning as a kind of sheriff's deputy, was marching me out to turn me over to the authorities when the dream ended. Upon awakening I realized that my chronic fear of his attacking me was based, in part, upon a fear of my own largely dissociated and therefore poorly controlled rage. On the following day this instructive dream yielded good dividends: when, while sitting in an upholstered chair in my office, he suddenly passed flatus of an unusually gurgling sort, I was able to have, with no attendant anxiety, this furious thought, "You son of a bitch, if you shit in that chair I'll massacre you!"

It was both fascinating to me in a research sense, and deeply gratifying to me as a therapist, to find that, by the end of two and one-half years of both his, and my own, becoming more fully and consistently aware of our respective feelings of intense contempt and rage, his hallucinating had now all but disappeared from our sessions together. One way of describing what had happened is to say that my increasing recognition, and acceptance, of my own feelings of contempt and rage toward him served to arm me sufficiently so that I could step in and interact with him at the furiously vitriolic level at which he had often "interacted" with his hallucinations, previously, while I had sat by, paralyzed with anxiety at the extraordinarily intense rage and contempt his behavior was arousing in me at an unconscious level. I had come to realize that it actually relieved me greatly when he would shunt the most intense portion of his rage, for example, off to one side, toward a hallucinatory figure, and would disclaim that he was having any such feeling toward me. But there came a certain memorable session in which I felt sufficiently furious about what was going on, and sufficiently sure of my ability to meet both my own rage and his, so that I was able to step into the shoes, as it were, of the hallucinatory figure or figures at whom he was directing his greatest fury, and from that day on it was as though there were less and less "need" for these hallucinatory figures in our interaction with one another. What I did, specifically, in that crucial session was to insist, with unyielding fury—despite his enraged threats to assault me—that these vitriolic tirades, such as he had just now been ventilating while denying repeatedly that they were meant for me, were really directed toward me.

Midway in all this long development, it occurred to me that the emotional wavelength, or level of "interaction," upon which he participated with the hallucinatory figure(s) provided me with a clue as to the level at which he needed for *me* as his therapist to be interacting with him; namely, this same level of vitriolic contempt and rage. I still feel that this was true enough, and that this can be looked upon as a valid general principle in one's therapy with a patient who is hallucinating. But during the subsequent months of this development that I have described, I realized in retrospect that I *already had been* participating with him at this emotional level, but had been dissociating my feelings that were invested at this level of interaction.

Subsequent to my experience with this man, I have seen a number of times this same mechanism at work in patients' hallucinatory experiences. I shall mention briefly only two of these additional examples. One of these occurred in the course of my work with a thirty-five–year old–woman suffering from paranoid schizophrenia, a woman who for years—even before I became her therapist—had been indicating, frequently, her involvement in a hallucinatory experience of being raped and impregnated; pregnancy she considered to take place not in the uterus but in the "stomach." I came to see in retrospect, during my own work with her, that this experience of hers bore quite possible correlations with my then-dissociated desires to impregnate her. The likelihood of this came to my attention when the following two events occurred in close sequence: *(a)* In one of our sessions, in which she was not being her usual antagonistic self, but in which there was, rather, predominantly a feeling-tone in the hour that I experienced as mutual, warm friendliness, with considerable sexual undertones, she suddenly looked anxious and demanded, insistently, "Did you just put something from your stomach into my stomach? *Did* you?" I reacted—correctly, I think—to this question as being equivalent to, "Did you just impregnate me?", and her anxiety was so great that, rather than making an analytically investigative response, I assured her flatly and simply that I had not. *(b)* But only a relatively few nights thereafter, I had a dream in which I was impregnating her. Prior to this I had been unaware of this specific desire toward her, although I had felt many times before, in response to her frequently seductive behavior, an erotic urge in which this specifically reproductive aim did not show itself. I can not, of course, prove that her subjective impregnation experience was indeed in part a reaction to such dissociated desires in myself. But it is my impression that there was such a connection, and I am quite ready to believe that her similar experiences in past years, prior to my own work with her, had involved similar links with dissociated processes in other persons who at that time were important to her.

The third, and final, example is from my supervisory work with a therapist who was undergoing personal analysis and who was seeing me for the supervision of his work with a schizophrenic young man. After the therapy —and likewise the supervision—had been under way for several months, I noticed that two new developments had appeared at approximately the same time. First, the patient began showing, in the therapeutic sessions, clear-cut evidence of hallucinatory experiences; specifically, there were strong suggestions, in the way that the patient giggled in a sexually titillated fashion, and murmured verbal responses in the same vein, that he was experiencing some sexually teasing hallucinatory figure in the room. Second, I noticed that the demeanor of the therapist himself had changed very appreciably; he had previously appeared to me to be a quite sexually repressed person, but now was showing many nonverbal indications of seductiveness. He described, at this time, a single instance of his verbally teasing the patient; but I had the impression that the therapist was quite unaware of the probable erotic element in this teasing. My belief was, and is, that the patient was hallucinatorily responding to not only projected desires-to-sexually-tantalize, but also to similar desires in the therapist, which latter desires were being brought toward the surface, but not yet into conscious awareness, by, I thought most likely, his personal analysis. Again, I realize that these data fall far short of constituting solid proof for such a hypothesis. But it is my distinct impression that such was the case; in summary, I found the therapist to be evidencing a newly revealed sexually teasing quality toward me, and there were hints that he was evidencing—unwittingly, as seemed to be the case in his relationship with me—a similar quality toward the newly hallucinating patient.

It is valid, I think, to consider any hallucination as a manifestation of some affect, or combination of affects, that is being warded off from acceptance into the individual's conscious ego. Hence it is indeed correct—no matter how curious it may sound—to look upon the above patients' hallucinations, resultant from both their own and their therapists' dissociated feelings, as representing not only a *projection* of certain feelings of the patient's own, but also a struggle against the *introjection* of the therapist's dissociated feelings of this same variety. A paper by Greenson (9) in 1954, entitled "The Struggle Against Identification," provides clinical data that form an interesting comparison with the data I have just been presenting. Greenson's data were derived from neurotic, rather than psychotic, patients and reveal these persons' struggle against identifications with *parents* from the *past*, whereas my material shows the patient's struggle against identifying with—introjecting—the *therapist*, or more specifically certain unconscious elements in the therapist, in the *present*. A sufficiently searching investigation of the transference connections between the present and past in the experience of the patient would, I feel sure, show how integrally related are Greenson's material and my own; but such an inquiry is beyond the scope of this paper.

One last theoretical point should be made before going on to the third and final, clinical category; this is a point that pertains to each of these three categories of clinical phenomena, but it can be seen most clearly, perhaps, in connection with such hallucinatory phenomena as have been described. That is, one may say in general, I think, that an individual must have a relatively healthy ego in order to remain convinced of the reliability of his preceptions of the other person, in the absence of any *consensual validation* from the latter; validation that, if forthcoming, would reassure him that he is indeed perceiving realistically. A therapist, for instance, must possess a relatively healthy ego to be able to carry on his daily work, relying heavily upon his own perceptions of patients in the usually obtaining absence of much corroboration from the patients, corroboration of, for instance, the therapist's perception of preconscious or unconscious hostility, or guilt, or friendliness, or whatnot in the patient. Therapists can, and much of the time in their daily work do, successfully meet this ego-challenging experience. But the psychotic patient's ego is too weak to meet a similar challenge without his suffering a temporarily increased ego-fragmentation: if he senses that his therapist is murderously inclined, for example, toward him, but if he gets no conscious validation from the therapist that this perception is a correct one, the patient is then likely to experience a hallucination of a murderously inclined figure; since, one might phrase it, the therapist has refused to accept the perception as being truly applicable to himself, as "belonging here upon me."

Acting Out as a Response to, or Vicarious Expression of, The Therapist's Unconscious Processes

For several years I have had the impression that some instances of a patient's acting out may be due partially to the therapist's own unconscious strivings in this same direction; may represent, that is, a vicarious, compulsive expression of, or a response to, the therapist's unconscious desires. Since this general concept has already been described by Schroff (16) and Barchilon (3), and the identical mechanism as taking place in the patient's intrafamilial relationships has been described by Johnson and Szurek (12), Hill (10), Limentani (13), and Bowen (4), I shall give only brief examples of this general mechanism before turning to a more specific type of manifestation of it that, so far as I know, has not been mentioned in the literature.

It was about eight years ago that I discovered evidence, in work with a hebephrenic woman, that the acting out in which one's patient is involved may consist partially in a response to one's own unconscious desires. Relatively early in my work with this woman, she began to evidence, both during her therapeutic sessions and in her daily life on the ward, an intense fear lest she be raped. In the words of her administrative psychiatrist, she was "crawling with terror" in this regard; her life on the ward was largely taken up with her insistently demanding reassurance against this from one and all about her. It was only after several months of this that I became aware, I think very belatedly, of powerful urges to rape her. These urges I found so frighteningly powerful, in fact, that I confided to the Director of Psychotherapy my concern lest I be unable to control them. I might add that he only laughed in mild amusement, a response that I found vaguely belittling; but the life of a director of psychotherapy is doubtless a difficult one. I realized, thus in retrospect, that the patient's anxiety lest she be raped was probably, at least in part, a response to these powerful, and at that time dissociated, desires in me. There was much data at hand to suggest that her transference to me was predominantly colored by her earlier relationship with her father who, her history strongly indicated, had long struggled against just such unconscious desires toward her.

In later months of my work with her she began evidencing a sexually provocative behavior toward various of the male personnel members, and after this had gone on for many weeks, I gained from my personal analysis the realization that erstwhile-unconscious homosexual desires in myself had been quite possibly a factor in this particular acting out; the realization, that is, that she had been vicariously expressing, in her behavior, my unconscious desires to make sexual overtures to these men. And still later on in her therapy I found various clues pointing toward a connection between, on the one hand, her beginning now to set fires on the ward and, on the other hand, largely dissociated urges of a similar kind on my own part. The group of nurses on her ward at this time reacted to me as being quite directly responsible for the patient's fire setting; on one occasion, for example, when I went up to her ward for the therapeutic session, the charge nurse bluntly let me know this. She met me with an accusing, "Edith just set a fire in one of the wastebaskets," and when I protested, "The way you nurses react to me about this sort of thing, anybody would think *I* had set the fire in the wastebasket!", she retorted, *"Well—?"* Later on, as I became more fully conscious of my own similar desires, and of the very probable influence these desires had had upon this phase of the patient's illness, I realized that the nurses' accusations had not been totally unfounded and unfair.

Now I wish to describe, in greater detail, a specific kind of phenomenon of this same general third sort—a specific kind that, as I mentioned, I have not seen described in the literature, and that has come to my attention within the past three years. This phenomenon consists in the (schizophrenic) patient's evidencing, in the therapeutic session itself, pathological and often puzzlingly grotesque behavior that arises partially from this same source; an acted-out behavioral response to, or expression of, unconscious elements in the therapist.

I first became aware of this "introjective acting out" psychodynamic basis of such grotesque behavior in the course of my work with a deeply ego-fragmented schizophrenic woman, twenty-eight years of age at the time when I became her therapist. During the first two years of our work together, she incessantly manifested a striking variety of bizarre, changing physical postures; looking thoroughly bewildered and acting as though the sudden and discoordinate movements of her limbs, head, and torso were taking place via a puppeteer's strings quite outside her control. And such verbalizations as she uttered were, for the most part, similarly discoordinate and confusing to, it appeared, herself as well as to the therapist.

Then, over a subsequent period of approximately six months, a series of incidents suggested to me that a considerable portion, at least, of her strange behavior (as strange in her daily ward life as in her sessions with me) rested partially upon the psychodynamics—the combination of introjection and acting out—that I have described.

One of these incidents occurred during a session in which I was sitting, as I often did, slumped far down in a chair and with my knees crossed in a way which, I realized in retrospect, may well have looked grotesque to an observer. But all I was aware of at the time was that I was feeling comfortably seated and that she, in a nearby chair, began muttering something to the effect that "He comes in here and tears off my arms and legs." She then asked me, twice, to put my leg down, which I declined to do. Then, after a considerable interval she half arose and stood with a leg extended before her, awkwardly crooked and unsupported in the air; the leg gave a peculiar impression of dismemberment from the rest of her body. I asked, astounded at this thought, "Is that the way my leg looks to you?" She agreed, convincingly. I think it valid, too, to look upon such an incident in the following terms: she reacted to my assuming a dismembered-looking posture (a posture I had experienced simply as being a comfortable one) as being my way of serving notice upon her that I intended to dismember her. But I am quite ready to believe, in terms of my long experience with this unusually deeply ill woman, that she may indeed have felt dismembered on the basis of an introjective reaction to my grotesque posture.

My better judgment tells me that, as regards the communicational facet of this incident, what she was responding to, in me, were unconscious desires to dismember her, desires my posture betrayed; but this I can only conjecture, for I have not recognized such desires toward her in our still-continuing work. I have clearly discerned such desires on her part, and have no doubt that *projection*, as well as introjection, was playing a part in this incident as in all these other incidents I have been describing.

By the time this phase in our work had been reached, the patient was now able, as the above material shows, *consciously to let me know* that her bizarre posture was a response to her perception of my own posture. But by now her air of bewilderment had greatly diminished, as had her grosteque and disso-ciated-looking physical movements. My belief is that in this earlier, two-year phase, when her ego-functioning had been clearly more profoundly impaired, she herself had been quite unable to realize that the puzzling movements of her body had any connection with her perceptions of my own movements.

On subsequent occasions she was able to let me know, similarly, that her assuming the posture of a model on a surfboard was her way of showing me how I, draped narcissistically, I now realized, in my chair, appeared to her; and that her (now only occasional) use of verbal gibberish was a representa-tion of the way my own speech often sounded to her. For years she had plucked hair from her scalp and had picked her clothing to pieces, and now, in one of the sessions, as she went through the gestures of pulling the flesh of her hands to pieces, she communicated to me the point that she experi-enced me as picking and pulling her, with horrifying cruelty, into pieces. In each of these instances, I was able, with deep dismay at times, to find a kernel of reality in her perceiving me thus. And when late in one of our sessions I saw a horrid grimace, a grotesquely taut kind of diabolical smile, slowly come over her face as if of its own accord, I was at first baffled, and then reached the jolting realization that this ''smile'' was a representation of the way in which a hypocritical, forced, and undoubtedly rather cruel, smile I had turned on, early in this session, had appeared to her.

In most such instances—and I have found many like examples in my own work with other patients, and in my supervision of other therapists' work with their schizophrenic patients—the patient's response is such a grossly exaggerated caricature of the therapist's actual behavior as to add to the therapist's unreadiness to recognize this connection. That is, the therapist is hampered not only by the fact that he has been manifesting something that he would prefer not to find in himself, but also by the fact of the patient's portraying this in so extremely exaggerated a form. Here it must be remem-bered that the patient's perception is grossly warped by the factors of both projection and transference. But it is very important for the therapist to be able to recognize the nucleus of *reality* perception that lies in the patient's response, for it is by encouraging the growth of such fragments of reality-relatedness that he can be of greatest value to these deeply ill patients.

I shall mention only a second and brief example of this same phenomenon before proceeding to discussion. This example is from my work with the thirty-two–year–old schizophrenic man whose hallucinatory phenomena were described at length in the preceding clinical material. This incident occurred during that phase of our work in which intense rage and contempt toward him had developed within me, but had not yet come fully into my awareness. At the end of one of the very-many sessions throughout which he had remained mute save for belching and the passage of flatus, I said, with forced "friendliness" and "politeness," "Well, the time's up for today." To this he responded with a growlingly hostile, dissociated-sounding, "Go to hell, you son of a bitch!" I recognized this, later on, as constituting not only a presumable expression of the way he felt toward me, but also a quite accurate expression of my own genuine, but repressed or at least heavily suppressed, feeling of rejectingness toward him at this moment.

Eissler (6), in a paper in 1943, made a comment that is relevant to this last-mentioned clinical incident: "The . . . [therapist's] communication, so far as it is verbal, will frequently contain more aggression than the schizophrenic's sensitivity can stand. Actually language contains innumerable terms which have changed their original meaning, so far as they have lost their primary connotations of local or physical reference in favor of a more spiritual meaning. The background of the schizophrenic's language regresses to those original meanings of a cruder, even brutal coloring. Hence, ordinary language tends to hurt the schizophrenic."

But, evidently unlike Eissler, I do not believe that it is simply that the schizophrenic *reads into* the content of the therapist's words an archaic meaning, a brutal meaning that is not at all resident there in actuality. I believe, rather, that here again there is a kernel of reality in the schizophrenic's response; there is genuinely conveyed by the words, in such instances, brutality that is present in the therapist's unconscious, no matter how greatly the patient's response is exaggerated through such mechanisms as projection and transference.

DISCUSSION

This paper does not represent an effort to describe all possible types of introjective manifestations that schizophrenic patients exhibit, but rather to describe only those having to do with *unconscious* processes in the *therapist*. One sometimes finds, for example, a patient expressing the conviction that persons whom he knows or has known in the past, are literally inside him now—in his stomach or in his leg or his foot, or whatnot; or he may be convinced that his bodily parts are those of some other individual.[7] But such material is outside the scope of this particular study.

And I do not mean to imply that the patient introjects only those processes in the therapist that are *unconscious,* or preconscious, in the latter. I surmise that it is indeed such processes in the therapist, or some other person, that the schizophrenic patient is more prone to introjecting, than is the case with the other person's *conscious* affects and ideation—for the reason, having to do with the absence or presence of consensual validation, mentioned earlier. But I consider this particular facet of the matter to be, likewise, beyond the focus of my effort here.

A third point is already implied in this paper, and needs to be made explicit only briefly: the *therapist* not uncommonly has introjective experiences vis-à-vis the *patient.* In my own sessions with schizophrenic patients. I have had, not infrequently, feelings and fantasies that seemed distinctly alien to my usual experience, that I experienced as foreign bodies in my consciousness, and that I regard as instances of introjection on the part of the therapist. And I have heard, many times, fellow therapists describe similar experiences.

This, in turn, brings up the therapeutically *constructive* side of this whole matter. The therapeutic usefulness of these last-mentioned experiences, experiences of introjection by the therapist, is, I believe, very great; they seem to me to constitute the essence of the therapist's empathic sensing of what is transpiring in the patient. And, as I indicated in a paper in 1955, this same process, carried one interpersonal link further, helps the supervisor to sense what is occurring at a deep level in the therapeutic relationship that is being described to him by the therapist in the supervisory session (19).

And, as regards the therapeutic relationship itself, although I have utilized here the frame of reference of the patient's *vulnerability* to the therapist's unconscious processes and, in keeping with this emphasis, have presented examples of disturbances in patients' behavior in this connection, one can see on the other side of the coin an invaluable communicational aspect to this. It is as if the patient were trying to tell the therapist, in all three of the varieties of introjective manifestations I have described, "See, this is the way you look to me," or, "See, this is what is going on between us, below the surface."

I believe that the constructive aspect of these introjective processes in the therapeutic relationship resides not only in this furtherance of *communication,* but resides also in—to present a formulation, now, at which informal discussions with John L. Cameron, a colleague on the Chestnut Lodge staff, have helped me to arrive—a process that is even more directly therapeutic. I refer here to the seeming circumstance that the therapist, at the deepest levels of the therapeutic interaction, temporarily introjects the patient's pathogenic conflicts and deals with them at an intrapsychic, unconscious as well as conscious, level, bringing to bear upon them the capacities of his own relatively strong ego, and then, similarly by introjection, the patient benefits from this intrapsychic therapeutic work that has been accomplished in the therapist. Incidentally, I believe that the patient, on not infrequent occasions, gives the therapist the same kind of therapeutic help with the latter's intra- psychic conflicts. Concerning the benefits that the patient obtains by introjec- tion from the therapist, the following comments by Hill (10) are of interest: "Schizophrenic patients . . . differ conspicuously from hysterical patients in their lack of immoderate admiration, affection, love, and so on, for their physician. . . .

"That the patient does not mention those qualities of his physician which he admires does not mean that he fails to note them. What he does with them is characteristically schizophrenic. *He takes them in as if they were mother's milk, thereby incorporating some of the goodness which comes to be his own and upon which his ego feeds and grows* [italics mine] . . . He is good, and the badness is left with the doctor. . . ."[8]

Wexler (21) and Hoedemaker (11) also have published valuable clinical examples of, and theoretical observations about, schizophrenic patients' re- coveries as being facilitated by introjective responses to the therapist. Both these writers have overlooked, however, the *mutual,* two-directional, nature of this process, and have taken little note of the fact—in my experience—of the therapist's participation here upon unconscious, as well as conscious, levels.

My final observation is directed toward those therapists who do not yet have relatively thoroughgoing personal analysis, and lengthy clinical experi- ence, behind them; to others, this comment will be superfluous. I would regard this paper as having been harmful, rather than helpful, if it accentuated a therapist's irrational feeling of responsibility for what transpires in the therapeutic session, and in the overall course of the patient's illness. The therapist has a responsibility, to be sure, and it is a large one; but it is shared with many other persons, including the patient himself, and it does not extend to the irrational extent of requiring that one be free from the influence of one's own unconscious. I have long ago become convinced that, quite on the contrary, psychotherapy with schizophrenic patients requires that the thera- pist become able to rely, more and more readily, upon his unconscious as being in the nature of a friend, a friend indispensable both to himself and to his patients. Among such clinical incidents that I have described from my own experience, even those that at the moment caused me the greatest dismay proved subsequently to be of inestimable value in illuminating the nature of the transference as well as the countertransference.

NOTES

1. In this paper the terms *incorporation* and *unconscious identification* will be regarded as synonymous with the term *introjection*. If these three terms refer to different psychodynamic processes, I have failed, despite careful perusal of the literature concerning them, to discern any such differences.
2. Reference No. 10, p. 53.
3. Reference No. 10, p. 127.
4. Reference No. 10, p. 156.
5. Reference No. 10, p. 153.
6. Reference No. 7, p. 425.
7. A few days ago, for instance, I read the following item in the daily nurses' report concerning one of my female schizophrenic patients. This item was written by a middle-aged female attendant who has an excellent relationship with the patient: "Called me to rub her back. Says she has my knees. 'Why, Ruth?' 'Because my knees hurt.' 'How did you know my knees hurt, Ruth?' 'Last week you walked funny and this week you don't.' I told her that was because I was wearing my arch supports. 'I'm glad for you; but every time you get a new body they give me your old one, and you change bodies so often.' I told her it was the same old body but just bulged more in some places. She had a good laugh over that one and laid her head over against my arm. Says there are people in her legs and their heads are the hips."
8. Reference No. 10, pp. 205–206.

REFERENCES

1. Abraham, K. A short study of the development of the libido. In *Selected papers*. Institute of Psycho-Analysis and Hogarth Press, London, 1927.
2. Allen, C. Introjection in schizophrenia. Psychoanalyt. Rev., 22: 121–137, 1935.
3. Barchilon, J. On countertransference cures. Unpublished paper presented at the April, 1957 meeting of the Washington Psychoanalytic Society.
4. Bowen, L. M. Quoted in the transcript of the Combined Clinical Staffs of the National Institutes of Health, Clinical Center Auditorium, March 29, 1956; mimeographed by the Department of Health, Education, and Welfare; National Institutes of Health, Bethesda, Maryland.
5. Bychowski, G. A case of oral delusions of persecution. Internat. J. Psycho-Analysis, 11: 332–337, 1930.
6. Eissler, K. R. Limitations to the psycho-therapy of schizophrenia. Psychiatry, 6: 381–391, 1943.
7. Fenichel, O. *The Psychoanalytic Theory of Neurosis*, p. 428. W. W. Norton, New York, 1945.
8. Freud, S. The future prospects of psycho-analytic therapy. In *Collected Papers*, vol. 2. p. 289. Institute of Psycho-Analysis and Hogarth Press, London, 1953.

9. Greenson, R. R. The struggle against identification. J. Am. Psychoanalyt. A., 2: 200–217, 1954.
10. Hill, L. B. *Psychotherapeutic Intervention in Schizophrenia*. Univ. of Chicago Pr., Chicago, 1955.
11. Hoedemaker, E. D. The therapeutic process in the treatment of schizophrenia. J. Am. Psychoanalyt. A., 3: 89–109, 1955.
12. Johnson, A. M., and Szurek, S. A. The genesis of antisocial acting out in children, and adults. Psychoanalyt. Quart., 21: 323–343, 1952.
13. Limentani, D. Symbiotic identification in schizophrenia. Psychiatry, 19: 231–236, 1956.
14. Little, M. Counter-transference and the patient's response to it. Internat. J. Psycho-Analysis, 32: 32–40, 1951.
15. Nunberg, H. The course of the libidinal conflict in a case of schizophrenia. In *The Practice and Theory of Psychoanalysis*. Nervous and Mental Disease Monographs, No. 74, New York, 1948. This paper was first published as: Der Verlauf des Libidokonfliktes in einem Falle von Schizophrenie. Internat. Ztschr. Psychoanal., 7: 301–345, 1921.
16. Schroff, J. Acting out in a patient with a character neurosis. Unpublished paper submitted in 1957 to the Education Committee of the Washington Psychoanalytic Institute.
17. Searles, H. F. Data concerning certain manifestations of incorporation. Psychiatry, 14: 397–413, 1951.
18. Searles, H. F. Dependency process in the psychotherapy of schizophrenia. J. Am. Psychoanalyt. A., 3: 19–66, 1955.
19. Searles, H. F. The informational value of the supervisor's emotional experiences. Psychiatry, 18: 135–146, 1955.
20. Searles, H. F. The effort to drive the other person crazy—an element in the etiology and psychotherapy of schizophrenia. In *Collected Papers on Schizophrenia and Related Subjects*, pp. 254–283. International Universities Pr., New York, 1965.
21. Wexler, M. The structural problem in schizophrenia: the role of the internal object. In *Psychotherapy with Schizophrenics*, Brody, E. B. and Redlich, F. C., eds., pp. 179–201. International Universities Pr., New York, 1952.

13. Observations of Countertransference

Benjamin Wolstein

There is a tendency in the literature to speak of the residual neurotic traits of analysts. This creates the unfortunate impression that these traits are only residuals that either will in time be eliminated, or can or should be restricted to the periphery of the analytic relationship. The better integrated an analyst, of course, the more readily will he approach the patient's problems in a realistic and compassionate manner. But that analyst deceives himself who pretends he has no countertransference.

Since the ideal analyst does not exist, it must, by the same token, be recognized that all analysts have residues of countertransference that remain inalienable if only as a remembrance of things past. In the long run, it may be of greater value to acknowledge this fact once and for all and proceed to make observations and construct operational definitions with due recognition of it. This approach is certainly better than to persist in talking about the qualities of the nonexistent ideal analyst and remaining indifferent and unknowing toward the kinds of personalities actually observed in the analyst-patient field of experience.

Since no two analysts are identical, we are compelled to seek out and make intelligible the differences among them, their modes of experience, value orientations, and styles of therapeutic activity. From even a cursory review of analysts at work, we can set forth some tentative observations. The observations are based on dominant personality traits, and it is quite possible that a specific analyst may fall into more than one category. No analyst has one trait pure and simple, and it is a matter of observation to describe their interpenetration with other traits in an analyst's personality. But we are not writing a novel; we are trying to set forth an interpretive model of analysts at work. Thus, we have to limit ourselves to the predominance of one or two for the purposes of abstraction and presentation. Obviously, these traits have many intermediate shadings of meaning.

These traits are descriptive not only of analysts at work but also in their everyday living. This identity of the person and the practitioner holds as true for those who master the therapeutic art as it does for those who do not happen to engage in the practice of analysis. It may be taken as a truism in all walks of life, and it is mentioned only as a reminder that it is also true for even the seasoned analyst. Moreover, it may make little difference what particular type of patient he works with so long as he is aware of what he is doing. Success or failure ultimately depends on a variety of factors in any given experiential field of therapy, and they cannot all be specified in advance.

It is also important to note that none of these personal traits or qualities necessarily entails a negative therapeutic balance for a particular analyst. We will try to illustrate the constructive as well as the distortive aspects of each of them in the therapeutic process. The qualities are being considered in abstraction here, but the illustrations will be based on their function and consequence within the therapeutic process with different kinds of patients. The emphasis will be on what we may expect to find in concrete experiential fields in which a particular sort of analyst engages.

The illustrations are intended as just that, not to exhaust the possibilities inherent in each instance. As in any attempt at illustration, the purpose will be to discover guiding principles and to generalize what may be expected with greater or lesser probability, not to construct a fixed conceptual scheme that anticipates the occurrence of events with absolute certainty. Not only is absolute certainty unattainable in psychoanalytic inquiry; it is also incompatible with the novelty and freshness in experience that constitute the essence of personality change. Since no interpretive map of the therapeutic field of experience will ever encompass and predict all of the psychological possibilities and emotional nuances in any particular analysis, there will remain artistic elements in the practice of analysis, no matter how refined and precise the scientific formulations ever become.

Of course, no analyst ever possesses a single trait in isolation from any or all others. Personality traits may be conceived along a continuum in which one or another can potentially move to the center of the experiential field. The order in which they will be discussed here is a shorthand way to refer to consecutive stages or epochs in the development of the individual. Analysts, like everyone else, pass through these various stages of development. Just when in the course of his development an analyst encountered the most destructive influences is an entirely individual matter that only he can ascertain. But if he has encountered damaging experience in one or another period of development, and his forward movement is now arrested, it is probable that his predominant countertransference reactions will be conditioned by the maturational obstacles he has encountered.

Even if an analyst attains insight into his particular period of warped development and the significant other people involved in it, he may still not be free to act as if he had overcome its effective results in current experiential fields. Clearly, the historicity of these events cannot be eradicated from his being, though their interpreted meaning can and does change with the unfolding of the present. Were he to present himself in the clinical situation ahistorically and simply as "I am," the experiential field of therapy would deteriorate, and the patient might believe his potential for transference distortion resolved by just learning how to act as "I am," as if his history had never happened to him and no longer even existed.

What has happened in a man's life has happened. To accept the reality of personal history does not entail an enfeebled worship of a disturbed past or a pessimistic fatalism about its effects in the future. Psychological insight is rooted in the temporal dimensions of life; it does not erase the lived past from the matrix of experience, and it has no meaning or penetration apart from the humanly viable future. Though the positive affirmation of "I am" may very neatly cut through the sicklied maze of "to be or not to be," the affirmation is abstracted from the process of becoming and its temporal dimensions. This being so, what the analyst essentially offers his patient is the secure knowledge that psychological insight can have powerful effects on his direction in living, and, of course, his convictions about it are most sound when they are based on first-hand acquaintance.

I

First, there is the analyst who tends to become overprotective in order to nurture the growth of his patients. He is psychologically gifted with an extraordinary ability to establish nurturing contact with them. The reason for this is not difficult to see. Those who seek analysis have deep-seated and unresolved dependency problems, and such dissociated patterns of relatedness will serve them well in response to an analyst who decidedly needs to be nurturing and overprotective. And this analyst wants very much to be needed and desired in this image as the parent he probably thinks the patient did not have in his childhood. That this qualitative need in the analyst fosters infantile omnipotence in his patient has long been recognized, for the nurturing analyst, seeking the image of the good parent, resuscitates these early strivings in the patient that become stabilized and protected in the experiential field of therapy.

In such a turn of events, the patient strives to make a parent out of his analyst, hoping for the support and sustenance he lacked in childhood. Serious dependency problems in patients are usually associated with continually experienced inadequacies in their parents, and they simply have to deny, in their childish helplessness, that there was no one in their immediate environment who was dependable enough to satisfy their childhood needs; they had to fend for themselves, and become, as it were, makeshift parents for themselves and perhaps also for their own parents. And, occasionally, overprotective analysts, impelled by strong maternal feelings, willingly play the supportive role and relate quite easily to the frightened and clinging child in such patients. They have a rather special kind of maternal feeling that requires continued dependency and will not surrender the child.

In the long run, this therapeutic attitude is in for rough sailing on at least two counts: the ambulatory patient, not really as helpless, dependent, or inadequate as this analyst would perceive him, will resent quite early the fact that he is being pampered; or, if he has been taught to be nice and polite and to deny his angry resentment, he will covertly resent such open attacks on his self-esteem. The analyst, in fact doing his best to flood the relationship with tender loving care, will soon find the analysis rather vexing, because his patient does not improve. And if, in his vexation, he is still clear-headed enough to look to himself instead of his patient, he may find that his nurturing motives have, paradoxically enough, caused the impasse. The absence of authoritative firmness on his part has obstructed the progressive unfolding of analytic material.

When the patient has been infantilized by the protective boundaries of the therapeutic situation, he will continue to rely on its shielded quality; and if he feels ''loved'' no matter what he does, he will persistently act out irrational needs for unbounded love. The meaning of what the patient is doing is not easy to understand. He may really have such needs, in which case persistent acting out will not produce insight; or, he may act them out in the hope of trying the analyst to his wit's end, in which case it is a roundabout communication that he resents the analyst's soft solicitousness. But, having assumed that he is dealing with a weak and helpless patient, the analyst, all too humanly, has brought an experiential field of therapy into being where he deals with what he is really most at home with. The patient, who is, by the way, hardly ever as weak or as helpless as the irrational needs of the protective analyst would suggest, may be willing to tolerate, howsoever resentfully, the infantilized image to which the analyst needs to respond if only in the hope that the analyst will be able to help him in this way. It takes the form of a *quid pro quo* arrangement: if the analyst gets what he requires, then he will give the patient what he requires; and there are, of course, a multitude of variations on this theme.

Let us take a closer look at the ramifications of this pattern. At one extreme is the analyst for whom it represents a denial of his fear that he is incapable of love, and, for the analyst at the other extreme, it expresses his poignant awareness of the fact that he would not be plagued with this residue of childhood suffering had he been exposed to the very love that he now expresses to his patient. This is the dual aspect of countertransference that we may expect to find in each of the four remaining illustrations; and it becomes a difficulty when the denial becomes rigid or the compensation is unrelated in the particular experiential field of therapy.

II

A second significant quality to be considered is aggressive dependency or exploitativeness. It differs from overprotective nurture in one major respect but resembles it in another. An aggressive-dependent analyst is remarkably different because he will respond to his patient in a direct and straightforward manner. Without holding back, he calls a spade a spade. And yet, because his own desire for dependency and warmth has not been satisfied, he will falter in his direct, straightforward attitude with his patient when they touch on basic questions of intimacy and warmth. Out of the conditions of his own past, he will lose his firm grasp of the patient's problems and experience, and he will act out in an obstructive manner, hindering the progress of the relationship just because he is anxious and frightened by his patient's require-ments. In becoming anxious, he loses his directness, and he fails to provide the conditions for his patient to experience and explore his dependency more fully in a situation where he might learn why intimacy is so problematic for him. Instead, the analyst who has unresolved dependent needs may deny their existence in himself and brush his patient off with a diversionary ploy, only to leave him in full possession of his own denial of such needs.

We may understand this pattern as follows: The analyst is so frightened of intimacy and warmth that he refuses to note their presence in someone experiencing them before him; and he has rationalized his denial under the guise that he is not going to mother anyone, especially a patient who has probably suffered from too much pseudo-maternal care that substituted for real care anyway. In any event, whether he openly experiences his fear or has a theoretic justification that defends him against it, his patient will be prevented from openly feeling his way through the ins-and-outs of his irrational dependency.

Yet, this quality has a positive as well as a negative aspect. The analyst will be able to deal very directly and very adequately with the patient's defensive organization. Because of his fears, however, he may fail to recognize occasions when support, encouragement, and compassion are appropriate.

When confronted with a frank and perceptive patient, the aggressive-dependent analyst may be compelled to react in a compensatory manner and become overly supportive and warm, even though his patient is not so anxious or distorted that he cannot call a spade a spade. Faced with frank perceptiveness, this analyst may even protest that he is supportive and warm and what not. Contrary to his habitual attitudes, he may even gush over and confuse the patient about the type of person he really is. These intermittent evidences of warmth are inexplicable eruptions through this analyst's defensive system; they are not usually geared to the objective requirements of the therapeutic moment but to intrapersonal ones within his own psychic structure.

When a patient approaches the frightening possibility of intimacy, the most this analyst can do, once the defensive system is engaged, is to face once again his exploitative problem with this particular patient, or simply maintain a detached attitude toward him. In the latter event, he will not overtly interfere with his patient's experienced warmth even though he has placed himself behind the curtain of detachment and can no longer respond in kind. When this analyst assumes the detached attitude, he does so to meet the objective demands of the patient the best way he knows how, because he cannot openly respond to warmth. Yet, detachment is not an authentic response because it is inconsistent with the aggressive-dependent personality. He has introduced a false front into the analytic situation, unless, of course, the patient can perceive its meaning. And, perhaps most unfortunately, he endangers the validity and stability of his excellent work with the defensive system where his straightforwardness was his greatest asset. There are other factors, of course, that will finally determine just how self-destructive he has been; and the most important one is the degree of insight the patient has achieved into himself, for the insightful patient will hold onto his gains regardless of what an analyst is or does.

But detachment is uncomfortable, and it is not his only recourse. To acknowledge the perception of his problem when it is offered without any evident aim of defensive evasion, hostility, or other possible projection would be more therapeutic than to become stuffy and deny the reaction of one man to another. If, in the face of such directness, the analyst becomes wooden and stiltedly professional, the patient may either retire from the experience in an equally wooden and stilted manner or he may stubbornly persist in telling the analyst what he perceives. In the latter event, it is to be hoped that the analyst's scope of awareness and tolerance for anxiety has been sufficiently enlarged to the point where self-analysis in relation to this particular patient will be productive. This certainly does not necessarily entail a full-dress revelation to his patient, not in principle anyway; such a decision cannot be determined in procedural terms since other qualitative factors in the experiential field of therapy are decisive in this matter.

When transference and countertransference are interlocked in this way, the aggressive-dependent analyst is hard put to stay with the data. In retrospect, it would seem that patients deny their dependency in the expectation that the analyst will duplicate the demands of support and sustenance that their inadequate parents originally required of them. And the analyst who has had severe difficulties with intimacy will not be able to sustain an equilibrated relatedness with a patient who requires it. The patient will find himself in a familiar position and may even begin to feel a sense of fated inevitability about the whole thing. His only recourse is to cancel out his demand and withdraw, having learned again from this experience that his demands are excessive. If he perceives that this analyst's reaction is a function of his own personality structure, he will generalize the excessiveness of his demands beyond the limits of the other person in this particular experiential field. One obvious corollary of the fact that the patient's transference experience takes place in the "here and now" is that the analyst must assume personal responsibility for the patterning of that emergent experience until the counter-transference components are clarified, at least to his own satisfaction.

When an aggressive quality emerges in response to an inhibited patient, there is very little apparent difficulty during the opening phases of the analysis. The inhibited obsessional appreciates the analyst's straight-from-the-shoulder quality, even though he may sense and anticipate the intimacy problem that will emerge later on. With deep-seated character disorders where the problem is essentially to untangle a very involved defensive system, this analyst works very well. Because defenses can have such slippery patterns, his straightforwardness will foster a therapeutic attitude that will clear the atmosphere for the consideration of definite, substantive issues, even when he is in error about this or that facet of an interpretation. But when this analyst is faced with a hysteric who openly makes emotional demands, he may try to find another analyst for this patient at the very outset. Such open transference demands call forth countertransference effects the meaning of which is momentarily beyond him. He experiences these countertransference effects as responses to unreasonable demands for the very thing he is incapable of immediately responding to and experiencing directly with another person. He may respond in a manner that appears cruel and harsh to the outsider, but in his own view, he experiences such early demands as the unfounded ones of a comparative stranger.

In such a turn of events, he is anything but the expert. In fact, he has sidestepped this patient's requirements instead of exploring the question of why they are being made. But he demonstrates that he is more simply human than otherwise; he has shut out communicated emotional requirements that are, given his personality structure, impossible to satisfy on demand. Such patients, perhaps more hurt than angered, may also find it more convenient to search further for an analyst. When they stay with this type of analyst, they expose themselves to more of such treatment. If, in spite of their irrationally based needs for attention and affection, they do so, it is because they are vaguely cognizant of the inappropriateness of their demands. And the more perceptive among them may also be vaguely aware of the fact that they touched the sorest of sore spots in the analyst and that it is necessary to create a foundation in the continuity of relatedness for such confrontations.

This is no great cause for concern in itself, so long as a good working relationship exists between them, and by good we mean candid, open, and above-board. The unfortunate possibility here is that the analyst may ultimately have to refer this patient on anyway because of the anxiety he encounters in the face of such hysterical demands, unless, of course, the patient is not essentially manipulative and controlling of the analyst's feelings. In positive circumstances, they may be able to work through this transference-countertransference interlock. When they can arrive at a *modus vivendi* about this crucially difficult convergence of experience, it will signify an enlarged scope of awareness for both analyst and patient.

III

Most contemporary analysts will find some traces of the next quality in themselves. For our purposes, it may be termed other-oriented or narcissistic. It involves elements of charm, and even flattery, a primary interest in putting oneself over. This analyst feels compelled to give the patient something, on occasion without regard for the therapeutic requirements of the experiential field at any given moment. This compulsion has no connection with the standards of his discipline either, because its chief motive is to bolster his own self-esteem in the eyes of the patient. His sense of personal worth is inordinately contingent on the appraisals others make of him, and his professed worth is made up of reflected appraisals.

This analyst, the contemporary man in search of himself, has chosen the field of therapeutic practice as his life's work for various and sundry reasons. When faced with his own inner problems, he did what might be expected of a man with such a personal orientation: he had to choose between an open commitment to struggle with them irrespective of the impression he made on his immediate personal environment or the acquisition of learned behavior designed to make an adjustment in the required fashion; and he consistently made his choice in the latter direction. This is an extreme statement of the alternatives, but its purpose is to put the direction of his choice in sharp relief. Being attached to the opinions of others, he does not dare even temporarily to appear to be a maverick, an unadjusted man in search of self-realization. Though he appears to be perceptive, he is frightened of originality; he even prefers the normally accepted cliche to products of his own direct experience that might be considered odd in some quarters. Usually a knowledgeable person, he has mastered the established patterns of analytic interpretation, and from his store of information and experience, he can readily draw a plausible map of the person before him. This sort of interpretive skill has no bearing on his capacity to relate, however, unless he perceives the supportive acceptance he needs. And when he does not get it, he is alternately angry and cajoling, quite prepared to interpret the patient's character structure in terms of what he, the analyst, requires for the continuing relatedness.

As an observer, this analyst is keenly alerted to the slightest cues emanating from his patient, and he can employ his elaborate interpretive schemes to the full in response to small bits of behavior or slight nuances in mood and feeling. He has confidence in the psychological picture he can draw of the patient simply on the basis of how he lit his cigarette and other incidental items. Not that these items are totally insignificant or escape the notice of any analyst who relates attentively to his patient—in fact, such items often make great claims on the analyst's preconscious attention—but it is certainly foolhardy to proceed directly to a psychological summary solely on the basis of preconscious clues.

This is the man of small personal feeling who finds signs of his intuitive gift in his ability to work out and apply intricate interpretive schemes to such minimal clues. However, if he is also obsessionally oriented, he knows that powers of immediate perception are not his forte and so he tries, by highly systematized interpretations, to create the illusion of perceptive relatedness. This is the alienated man wandering through the world in search of direct relatedness.

Out of this quality there arises his chief asset as a therapist. Compelled to succeed, he is particularly effective in developing a working relationship with his patient. He intrigues the patient with analytic therapy and supports his desires for active collaboration, not with the tender, loving care of the nurturing analyst but, rather, with an overly gracious response to his patient. With cultivated charm and even simulated warmth, he may occasionally encourage the patient to the point of somewhat unrealistic expectations.

But this ability to establish a working relationship with ease has its drawback; it may sometimes blind him to the fact that he needs the patient's response to therapy as confirmation that his search for relatedness has succeeded. That he is compelled to continue searching for it, however, reveals that he does not possess it. And so, as the analysis intensifies and moves to closer quarters, this other-oriented quality moves him further and further away from the actualities of his own immediate experience and obscures his perception of the patient before him.

This brings us to his worst fault: that he can become rather arbitrary and fixed in his need to influence his patient. In his overbearing insistence on the rightness of his view, he considers all evidence to the contrary resistance or evasion—which it may well be, but in the face of his arbitrariness, his patient's resistance is often quite conscious and deliberate. This analyst needs to convince his patient and win him over; and he has developed subtle defenses against the direct expression of such qualities in a clear form. If they were readily detected, he might lose the approval he so deeply craves.

There is no contradiction between being other-oriented and arbitrary. On the contrary, a dynamic tension exists between the two. The more other-oriented he feels himself to be, the more important his need for approval becomes, and the converse is also true. He would not stop at coercing the other's approval, and if his idea of himself is composed of reflected appraisals that others make of him, his arbitrariness and self-centeredness may be understood as representing his failure to develop his own active appraisal of himself. For a persistent and overweening awareness of self, which is what we mean by self-centeredness, actually implies failure in the evolution of the active self.

Thus, with more or less clarity, he can map out the individual's personality as a static conglomeration of psychic blocks. He has very little feeling, on the other hand, for that personality as an integrated organic unity moving toward him and trying to experience him. He deals with the individual as a isolatable entity, which he treats as if it were a closed system working toward self-realization, but he does not deal directly with the convergence of both personalities in the experiential field. To do so would do serious injury to his own self-oriented system. To be sure, a fundamental self-hatred is associated with this style of relatedness, for this analyst believes that nothing he produces is really appreciated and he does not believe it is any good anyway. In his desire to protect himself, he may easily be misled in a reading of a patient he thought had the parataxic disregard for him that he basically has for himself. As a consequence, he may even have destructive effects on the lives of those with whom his contact is avowedly for enlightening and therapeutic purposes.

There are variations in this analyst's attitude to be considered: the too-loud profession of disregard for what his patients think of him; or, in his professed view of himself, his being concerned solely with psychological truth; or, the tendency to jump too quickly to conclusions about his patient's being a charmer or flatterer and then to insist that everything the patient says that does not support his thesis is a defense. Now, we know too well the subtle and ubiquitous quality of the defensive potential of the human personality, and when an analyst becomes doctrinaire, it is reasonable to assume that it is not the patient alone who is trapped in a defense. This is especially true if he tends to ignore, in the face of contrary evidence, that the patient's decision to undertake an analysis and continue in it contains collaborative strivings and growth impulses.

In the therapeutic situation, he stands to lose touch with the patient who may actually stop thinking in response to the projected warmth and willingly "submit to the treatment." But, by this time, this analyst "knows"" what is wrong with the patient; he has become more thinking and less feeling. He is no longer as sensitive and alert to the patient's feelings, and he is forced to become more arbitrary and absolute as he moves further and further away from feeling contact with his patient. The charm was only a "come-on." It was produced by the analyst's compulsion to prove once again to himself and afresh to the patient that he is not as alienated and rootless as he deeply believes himself to be. After he is reassured that he can satisfy this need at his will, he retires from further emotional relatedness; for this was the challenge he experienced with the patient. Once he has used the situation to his satisfaction, he retires from this experiential field of therapy to look again for new fields to conquer. He is restlessly and perpetually dissatisfied with himself, and resolves his insatiable needs through new relationships, searching for reassurance of his potency, warmth, and ability to relate and to do analysis. About all of these he is basically bedeviled.

If the patient accepts this invitation to relate and collaborate at the outset of therapy, if he is blind to the connection of overt charm and covert arbitrariness, he falls into the trap of his own unfulfilled expectations. This analyst cannot come through in the long run, as, for example, the detached analyst usually can, because he lacks emotional staying power. When the emotional chips are down, he will go off into a generally acceptable conceptualization of his patient's problem, with little if any inkling of what his patient is actually feeling at the moment. Paradoxically, he may appear remarkably convincing about the nature of his clinical work to the outsider, but his patients, caught in the throes of a parental transference, will not know what it is all about until after they have had time to evaluate their experience.

This analyst appears to be the most successful when, in actual fact, he is least productive of therapeutic results in the ordinary course of things. He probably does most for patients who suffer from the very same life orientation. Out of an experience with him, any patient, other-oriented or not, will learn the hard way but in a rather final way that, in dealing with other-oriented people, profession far exceeds performance, influence of opinion overshadows productive results, and sustained emotional relatedness is unavailing. The detached patient will also find an experience with such a therapist illuminating, if only to gauge what he might have become if he had mastered the other-oriented style of life.

This is the type of analyst who requires the patient to submit unconscious material to substantiate his favored theoretical conception. And the obliging patient, the helpless person looking for guidance and direction or simply interested in valid psychological understanding will be disappointed. For when this analyst, intrigued with his own interpretations, starts to develop a summary of his clinical findings, the obliging type of patient will readily provide supporting data and suppress contrary data in order to carve out a secure niche for himself in the therapist's experience. As the supporting data are proffered this analyst continues to spin his theories about the patient until neither is sure of what the other is talking about. It is certainly not the live patient, for he has become a kind of sounding board for the analyst's theoretical projects.

The only checks that the analyst now has are within himself. If, in dealing with a variety of patients, he finds that he describes the same sort of personality structure over and over again, the description usually contains a better picture of himself than of the particular patient before him.

In the face of this analyst's arbitrary quality, the excessively dependent patient has, so to speak, gone underground to preserve his sense of integrity the same way he might have had to defend himself against the onslaughts of imperious and ruthless people in his past. His evasiveness, concealed by an appearance of supporting data, is an unconscious maneuver in the interests of preserving his psychological self. This self-protective submissiveness, incidentally not unique to the analytic situation, is the way the patient draws the line with the authoritarian to his face. His manner of doing it is, of course, equally arbitrary, and so the possibilities for rational collaboration are proportionately diminished. For when the authoritarian analyst becomes aware of it, he will do all in his power to reach the frightened patient, who will, in turn, reciprocate with a more complex defense, which causes the analyst to exert himself even more so in this direction, to which the patient responds in an even more complex fashion, and so forth, until for some extraneous reason the situation has to be terminated.

As this interweaving of defenses is drawn tighter and tighter, the patient is left with two possibilities open to him: to evade the analyst or submit to him. Since the patient experiences both possibilities as a violation of his integrity, he will not accede to either. The analyst will, in turn, tolerate nothing else, and here he verges on vindictiveness in his therapeutic attitude: he tends, as we have seen, to generalize elaborate interpretive schemes, his approach is incisive, and he is not afraid to hurt. When these qualities converge in any particular experiential field, he does not maintain responsive contact with the difficulties the patient is experiencing in trying to relate to him. Instead of searching himself, he becomes arrogant and vindictive because he senses his failure to relate to his patient, and direct awareness of this failure threatens his own other-oriented style of relatedness. He will become anxious, act out a whole gamut of feelings, from charm to disdain to indignation, in order to evoke a desired reaction from his patient.

Since he labors under the compulsion to become a special person, it will make little difference whether his patient loves him or hates him, so long as he has the distinct feeling that he plays an important role in the other person's psyche. He leaves no room for choice: accept him or reject him on his, and only his, terms or ignore him. He is as much afraid of rejection as he is of being noticed. This quality drives an analyst into that uncomfortable limbo between the need to be right and the need for the approval of the crowd, and it alienates him from psychological peace. He is caught in an irrational web of his own making. If the patient goes along with his interpretations, he feels that he has won a victory, but when the transference distortions escape his grasp, he is infuriated at what he considers a defeat. On the other hand, when the patient tries to tell him what he thinks or feels as best he can, and if this is not in accord with what the analyst thinks he should be thinking or feeling, he assumes the conventional analytic armor about the father and totem and taboo. And his patient, already frightened at having dared to reveal himself, is confused by it all. He either realizes that this analyst is no one he can really talk to and accepts this experience as a failure or he duplicates something of the analyst's "interpretations" in his behavior to demonstrate their validity in an improved adjustment. And the analyst has suffered his repetition compulsion and is once again in search of relatedness because he will have lost it with this patient.

In aggressive dependency, the analyst gives something to his patient and wants to get something back in return, but the other-oriented analyst believes that he has nothing genuinely worthwhile to offer his patient in the first place. Unlike the analyst who is an obsessional critic out of a profound realization of his many faults and limitations, the narcissist has no faults he is prepared to do anything about—he "loves" himself too much—so when he looks at the patient, he finds everything wrong with him. This analyst would often be correct if the projective element were eliminated, but since he is comparatively oblivious to the immediate experiential field in which he functions, he very frequently fails to discern aspects of his own countertransference potential that evoke the specific forms of his patient's transference manifestations. Thus, relatedness becomes more of a central concept in an overarching theory than a direct experience to be analyzed in the experiential field of therapy.

IV

The next illustration is the obsessional critic, the analyst who strives for perfection and certainty in his formulations because he is so keenly aware of his own personal shortcomings. He adheres quite rigidly to what he construes as the objective data, and then takes the stance of an objective critic toward them. In so doing, he prevents the emergence of an open, two-way relationship in the experiential field of therapy in order to protect himself against the critical insights of his patients that are painfully experienced as reminders of imperfections. It follows, of course, that the "me-you" experience is the most difficult of all for this analyst to work through successfully with his patient. When faced with a straightforward expression of feeling, he becomes edgy and uncomfortable; he would rather deflect his direct response and react from a distance than remain uncomfortable for the duration of that particular session in the hopes of learning something about it.

He seems to resemble the other-oriented analyst in that he will have his own way with his patient, but the psychological roots of his compulsion are decidedly different. Whereas the other-oriented analyst willingly takes the stance of the adjusted model and arrogates an arbitrary interpretive position to himself, the perfectionistic critic, keenly aware of his personal limitations, would prefer to think of analysis solely in technical terms. He takes the impersonal posture in the experiential field of both analytic therapy and everyday life.

Such staunch preference for therapeutic action at a distance is based on his sensitized conviction that he ought to keep his own difficulties out of the patient's way. It is also based on the irrational conviction that technical performance is perfectable, that a finished, self-subsistent, and even immaculate procedure is possible without considering personal variations among analysts. He, therefore, creates what he considers to be a sound, impersonal technique and works, so to speak, from behind it. He professes great disdain for abstract theory as being relatively useless, and he may find it hard even to come to terms with a theoretical approach that does justice to the objective data produced by his technique.

Instead, he substitutes a remarkably one-sided adherence to the infinite multitude of factual details surrounding any particular incident in his patient's life, expecting thereby to eliminate the fact of his own presence. In seeking this goal, however, he runs a double risk: either to follow out all of the details in all of their facets and be swamped with unmanageable data, or to make his suggestions and insinuate his interpretations into his objective questions in such a roundabout way that he can disown responsibility for any of the time-bombs he sets off with the patient.

But he takes this apparent liability and turns it into one of his chief assets as the therapist most suitable for certain patients. He strives to arouse a vital interest in extraordinarily detailed descriptions of events, on the assumption that the significant emotional factors will eventually arise out of this plethora of detailed data and force themselves into awareness. But after an exposure to this rigorous and systematic approach for an extended period of time, the patient learns to present those aspects of himself that an objectified technique is designed to encompass.

It is stipulated, on technical grounds, that the patient's feeling be selectively put aside, and after the seriated data have been exposed to this analytic technique in the required manner, a summary description of what the patient must have felt is then rendered. In such a therapeutic situation, the participants do not talk much with feelings; they talk more about feelings, for the affective domain of the patient's experience is taken as an object of study. Only at rare moments does the technique permit his transformation into an expressive subject. In other words, the obsessional critic severely limits the experiential field of therapy to referential symbols, instead of maintaining a balanced interest in both aspects of the patient's experience, the reflective or referential and the immediate or expressive. To paraphrase the classical maxim, he believes that where expressive symbols were, there referential symbols should be. It is hardly reasonable to expect such an approach to suppress the capacity for direct expression of feeling in anything more than a transitory way. Yet, this approach suffers because of its inflexible delimitation of the experiential field and narrowed scope of therapeutic data.

In this sort of therapeutic setting, when patients are faced with an attack of anxiety, fear, or anger, they readily postpone the expression of feelings and try instead to understand them, as if that were possible or desirable without a full awareness of their extent and depth and reach. There is no *a priori* reason why the patient ought not to express them as they occur in his analysis. The idea that this is a waste of time is only a blind, since the true criterion for judging this or any other question pertaining to therapy is the question of self-realization.

No analytic therapy can call itself adequate that turns psychological life into a pale imitation of what it is or can be, and the analytic field of experience is a slice of life. This imitation of life grows out of recurrent fears that supervisory symbols, as conveyed by the analyst's technique, will not be able to maintain a check on the expressive ones, as conveyed by the patient's feelings, if the latter are not immediately transformed into referential ones, as ordered products of thought. Apparently, a metapsychological issue of considerable importance arises at this point, the issue of how to define the nature of feeling and the nature of thought in their complex relations to each other in the experiential field—important, to be sure, but not entirely relevant.

When the obsessional critic attempts an outward expression of personal feeling, he may feel awkward, gauche, and even grotesque. More often than not, he does not make the feeling fool of himself that he thinks he does, but because he considers his emotional capacities warped in some ways, he will take the unique incident of emotional failure and make a federal case out of it; this is his final proof that he ought to avoid direct expression of feelings. Yet, his studied and resolute decision to repress feelings habitually will only serve to enstate the very situation he believed to be true in the first place: namely, that he really has to persist in his studied demeanor and contain his feelings on the boundaries of the experiential field, for he has lost confidence in his ability to express them appropriately. Occasionally, this sort of analyst will be forced to distort expressions of feelings and turn their meaning into things that were never intended in order to confirm or perhaps to create confirmation of a thesis central to his own therapeutic being. Given these conditions, technical rigidity is an operational imperative.

This type of analyst finds himself in a countertransference mesh of his own making: when he expresses feelings, he expresses them gauchely, and this, in turn, only confirms his original belief that he should remain withheld and stick with the objective details as reported. He can be of greatest service to patients whose security system requires an objective and largely referential attitude toward the feeling psyche, and, yet, what these patients need most is awareness of their expressive potentialities; they need a concerted effort at the creation of a therapeutic atmosphere in which feeling can be fully and freely expressed no matter how "crazy" or disconnected it appears to be. Only in such an atmosphere will they eventually become acquainted with their emotional powers, if that is still possible. Thus, oddly enough, this analyst may be most effective with patients who need his approach least.

But the problem within the experiential field of therapy still remains: how will his patients be able to utilize his therapy if, after they undergo countless transitory attacks of anxiety as new feelings begin to emerge, they are faced by an analyst who has placed himself in the position, through exigencies of his own personality and its required technique, where he cannot listen to open expressions of feeling without a rigorously and critically defined context. And here we see the major weakness of his view of analytic therapy: once the therapeutic context is developed, it requires emotional content, and the patient who finally dares an expression of direct feeling will have to face the emptiness of his analysis when denied an open expression on technical grounds. When inchoate feelings begin to emerge, they fall on deaf ears. No matter how thoroughly the historio-genetic context is built up for qualitative experience, there is no substitute for having qualitative experience. It is like learning how to swim, getting all of the coordinated movements down pat, but never actually getting into the water and doing it.

The obsessional analyst has not faced up to the live possibilities of the analytic field of therapy, for he has been prevented from exploring the depth of his own feelings by fears of basic cynicism and worthlessness and by an untouched core of irrational dependency. Hence, the technical rigidity of his therapeutic attitude toward detailed information from and about his patients that yields a rather one-sided picture of life experience. What also follows from his attitude is intellectualization of the psychic domain, since life in the raw is repugnant to him. When patients who require direct liberation or direct recognition of emotion for psychological growth remain with this type of analyst for any great length of time, they find themselves fumbling about uneasily, repeatedly shifting the context of discussion and slipping from incident to incident without concentration or focus; they hope in some way to find an opening wedge in the analyst's technical facade for a direct act of emotional relatedness. They require a more intimate atmosphere, having touched something in themselves that they would like to get through to the analyst. But this analyst will treat it as just so much more clinical subject matter for detailed interpretive inquiry, instead of taking it simply for what it is and encouraging its expression.

When this analyst is at least consistent and hews the straight line of his approach, which he usually does, the patient's problem is transformed from one of trying to reach something in the analyst to one of learning how to live with him; and if, finally, he cannot even do this, to try, as best he can, to understand why he made his choice, why he remained in the analysis after discovering his mistake, and, perhaps most important of all, what immediate factors in the "me-you" situation eventuated in the experiential results he must now assimilate. If both participants are motivated by a desire for knowledge about the total experiential field, such an inquiry can be truly productive no matter what is ultimately uncovered about that particular convergence of personalities.

There is, of course, the patient who has an overriding need to express his feelings, who cannot or will not suppress them or slide around them in response to the analyst's technical or personal requirements. This type of patient will ultimately get into a struggle over the limits of relatedness, and the analyst will doubtless experience the patient's needs as an unwarranted attempt to change or influence him to be different. And this analyst's position is certainly legitimate from an objective point of view, though the speculation is inescapable that a little unbending might do his work a bit of good, at least with such a patient.

Once such a struggle is seriously engaged, the analyst and the patient have placed themselves in a mutually threatening predicament. As the analyst becomes more rigid, the patient becomes more insistent, and vice versa. There develops a circular tension of technical rigidity and emotional insistence until something gives and the possible termination of the relationship cannot be evaded. The analyst quite rightly wonders why the patient tries to change him, and the patient quite rightly wants to know why direct emotional contact is being denied him. This sort of thing can lead to an interlock of transference and countertransference.

If, therefore, the analyst is not too threatened at least to offer sufficient detachment if nothing more at this juncture, then it is up to him to throw the situation open undefensively in order to learn what the patient is really looking for. Out of this serious attempt at relatedness, a mutual experience of enlarged awareness may and can occur. Otherwise, if nothing gives, the analysis terminates and little more than a zero is chalked up for both participants. They go their own ways and may someday discover in themselves what caused it, but something is inevitably lost if this understanding of what has gone wrong is not arrived at together.

At this point, there is no need to consider the type of analytic attitude that requires the analyst to act as if he did not have the countertransference attitudes he actually does have and to adopt a mechanical mode of behavior detached from his spontaneous responsivity. To put it briefly, this attitude perpetrates an atmosphere of psychological falsehood, and even if the therapist does succeed in some cases, it will delude him into a confusion of his psychological reality when he is confronted by a patient who has seen enough acting in his life and is disgusted with tightly planned behavior. Besides, if the analyst injects this element into the relationship, his patient's planned defensiveness against transference manifestations will escape his notice. By adopting defensiveness as his therapeutic attitude, an analyst may bring an unanalyzable predicament into being, one that is much more complex from a therapeutic standpoint, than an open confrontation of his anxieties.

On the other hand, the compliant patient who seeks direction and guidance from analysis can gain much that is socially useful with this analyst. If he does not want or is not prepared to leave his fairyland of fantasy or under-stand his archaic familial ties but desires, instead, to learn some of the rudiments of acceptable social behavior or if he phrases his adjustment problem in the form "given the component factors of the problem laid out in detail, what is the best strategy to achieve this or that behavioral goal," that is, if he is more interested in what is to be done in terms of the objective requirements of the immediate situation than in what he might judge as the most valuable outcome irrespective of whether it is immediately realizable, this analyst can help him.

There is, however, an unavoidable paradox in the analyst's approach that runs as follows: he attempts in his perfectionistic manner to be considered the specialist in psychic disorder or the expert in interpersonal relations, and in so doing sets for himself unrealizable standards so far as the reality of the psychic domain is concerned. His therapeutic goals are beyond reality just because psychic phenomena cannot be treated as if they were material in fact or idealized entities. It will prove impossible to collate objective data about feelings in order to predict and control their future course until they are simply turned to stone, reduced to neurophysiologic processes or transformed into mathematical symbols.

This analyst will maintain that he is not interested in such larger issues. He is explicitly concerned with the patient before him who is in trouble and whom he would help in the resolution of difficulties in living, even if an outside observer thought his patient adjusted superficially to the objective requirements of the problematic situation in which he is involved. And, in some cases, this is the most appropriate therapeutic response.

An answer to the question of why this analyst clings to his interest in smooth, unexceptionable technique may be found in the process of displace-ment. In every exaggerated type of behavior, it is often interesting to ask what is being so vehemently denied in the affirmation. And exaggerated preference for the perfect, impersonal technique would suggest his serious doubts about the perfectability of man, and perhaps, in a more personal vein, his gnawing doubts about ever confronting deep-seated emotional conflict. In brief, the perfectionist analyst has thus far failed to come to terms with himself; and from this it would follow that he has also failed to come to terms with meaningful conditions of life as actually experienced and lived. He cannot ever say simply that his being is as much a part of the human situation as anyone else's. The tragedy of his world view lies in his blind striving for perfectability that obscures the commonality of the all-too-human experience of guilt, envy, hatred, and destructiveness. These feelings so condemn the obsessional in his own eyes that he overlooks his capabilities of being affectionate, constructive, trustful, and kind as well. He sees himself as such a blackguard because he harbors the former that he runs to high heaven finally to cleanse himself, a cleansing he devoutly wishes but never finds because he does not stay with his experience long enough to come to terms with the total matrix of his experience. So long as he remains unaware of the continuum of his personal qualities, he has thrown out a true appreciation of the good with the negatively judged bad, because awareness of the one entails awareness of the other as well as the whole range of intermediate qualities.

When this analyst does become aware of his positive qualities, he is threatened. And when a patient pointedly calls them to his immediate attention, he will find a way to exclude them from his perceptual consciousness. He will engage in an obscure defensive operation in order to cancel and blot them out of the experiential field of awareness. Then the patient, in turn, becomes confused about the true representation of the analyst's personality. Faced with alternating expressions of warmth and defense, the patient may finally come to realize that some people become so uncomfortable with their basic qualities that they deal with others as if they were yo-yos at the end of a string; for the analyst, when compelled to interfere with a patient's awareness of his warmth, feels guilty and frightened about his compulsion to do this—a cardinal sin in his book—and he will try to retrieve the unkindness. It may eventually dawn upon the patient that if he follows the analyst's unconscious patterns of experiencing warmth, this alternation will persist until he severs the emotional cord that binds him. Or else he will have to accept this analyst's warmth at a distance, since opaque silence will not be as threatening to the analyst as an open confrontation of his capacity for warmth.

Of course, in the obsessional phenomenon, we are dealing with the psychic stuff of which schizoid and schizophrenic processes are made. When the obsessional analyst is too threatened, he may find it necessary to become wooden and stilted, guarded and suspicious, or openly competitive and worse with his patient. He will become desensitized to the real suffering, treat it as if it were really the patient's kettle of fish, and consider it up to the patient to do something about it—which would be all right if he were not dealing with someone in the throes of a transference process. In response to such counter-transference the usual recourse of the patient is to come crawling back to his analyst for relief of his suffering, and this act in itself serves to re-establish the *status quo ante.*

In striving for perfection, this analyst is completely human—it goes back to the ancient Greeks and Hebrews—but if this is all he does, he is also less than human because life cannot be lived in rigid adherence to that goal. By refusing to acknowledge frailties as part of his own self-system, he may produce transference cures because the patient will not have to acknowledge them in himself either. Both participants may actually suppress their short-comings and act as if nothing bothered them, and then proceed to impose the rational measure on all of their experience and to cover up defects.

There is another form of suppressive therapy that is more characteristic of the aggressive analyst. In contradistinction to the perfectionist, he may reveal his frailties and idiosyncracies in order to communicate his rootedness in the all-too-human condition. If done without awareness, however, this can be as suppressive in its own way as the obsessional critic's attitude of denial of imperfection, for though their messages may differ in content—for example, the aggressive's "what are you complaining about, see what I have" versus the obsessional's "what are you complaining about, why don't you act as if you didn't have it either"—their negative therapeutic effects are remarkably similar.

There is always a simple and direct message such as this that an analyst communicates to his patients, no matter how refined his mastery of the analytic craft, how adequate his clinical experience, how elaborate his tech-niques, or how rounded his knowledge of personality theory, dream interpre-tation, and transference analysis. He may, of course, send this message in complicated ways according to the demands of his specific personality struc-ture, but he informs his patient of his responsive feelings. This is true of the analyst regardless of his avowed orientation in theory and practice. Despite the complexities of his rationale, his message is always a simple one as it is felt by his patient; were this not so, and the patient could experience the nuances and variations of the changing nature of the experiential field, he would not be a patient.

This simplicity has nothing to do with what the analyst thinks he is saying because he cannot be absolutely certain that he means what he interprets himself to mean unless he subscribes to a philosophy of absolute voluntarism, in which case he would not be an analyst but an exhortative counselor who prods his patients to willful self-expression as a supreme value, absolute and solus. If, when the analyst looks into what he is doing, he cannot ignore the face value of what he thinks he is trying to do, then it follows that he cannot ignore what his patient thinks he is doing; and there are occasions when the patient is obligated to speak out regardless of whether he is ignored or not. Now, here again, what the patient says may not be an accurate description of what his analyst is doing, just as it may be true that what the analyst says, regardless of his individual personality traits, is also an inaccurate description. But this is the only way to arrive at reliable knowledge in psychoanalytic inquiry: to start from the given, make inferences, check them against accumulated knowledge and against the observable data over and over again, achieving an increased refinement of the description each time around.

V

The detached analyst, our last illustration, resembles the obsessional critic in respect to withholding affective expression, but he does it for different reasons. Unlike disengagement which may be defined as an active process or response to difficult or unintelligible transference material, detachment is considered an ingrained quality of character that appears in the analyst irrespective of the rest of the experiential field. This analyst is the most capable of observation, and it is his greatest asset; but he is also the worst participant, and this may be his waterloo. It would, however, be a mistake to overlook his deep interest in participant observation. On the contrary, this is the analyst who is most self-consciously aware of its importance.

We find this detached mixture of therapeutic participation and nonparticipant observation in Freud's approach: here was the man who believed most staunchly that the analyst must remain an imperceptible *tabula rasa,* a kind of blackboard on which the patient wrote his personal psychography; the analyst had no influence on the course of the patient's associations but merely read back what had been written; and yet this very same analyst conceived the analysis of transference as a "battleground" on which the transference neurosis is fought by every resource the analyst has at his command. That the analyst can do both at the same time is a contradiction on its face; you cannot do battle unless your forces are committed directly in a participant situation. The analyst could not do battle side by side with the patient's mature ego against the regressive aspects of transference if his role were truly that of a nonparticipant observer. This dual conception of the analyst's task has been reconsidered, and it is now acknowledged in all quarters that the analyst's personality plays an active, reciprocal, and mutual role in the therapeutic situation.

One may say in extenuation of Freud's mixed position that he was working with two contradictory perspectives: Locke's mirror psychology and Kant's active theory of mind, that he was struggling with a problem, which had developed in the preceding hundred years, of how to amalgamate the philosophical psychology of British empiricism and continental rationalism with the clinical conceptions he had developed out of his therapeutic investigations. Freud's attempt at synthesis failed, as it was bound to. Had he followed William James's *Principles of Psychology* (1890) more closely, he might have concluded at the outset that a synthesis was fundamentally impossible, and then proceeded to develop a psychopathology based on the James reconstruction that superseded the conflicting psychologies of empiricism and rationalism of the eighteenth and early nineteenth centuries. If Freud had based his theories more firmly on the stream psychology, he might not have been caught in the patently contradictory theories of the analyst's participation in the experiential field of therapy.

Even the detached analyst has since come to recognize his sustained tendencies toward disengagement from active collaboration as one of the factors to be held accountable for the emergence of certain developments between himself and his patient. For instance, there is the compliant patient who always ultimately did the right thing as prescribed by the parental authority even though he may have griped and pulled temper tantrums. He did not go out completely on his own, so that even when he rebelled he secretly required the authorization of one or another of his parents or parental surrogates. Although he seems to tempt the fates, he does not go overboard in any direction except in the one that he believes the analyst, now enstated in the authorizing position, would like to see him go. He runs his course in such extremes, however, in the hope of being able to shake his analyst's involvement in his compliant defense, something that the detached analyst need not, in clear consciousness, ever plead guilty to anyway.

The detached analyst does well with such patients. He actually engages them in a most subtle way that may, at the outset, escape the detection of both participants, for no matter how detached in feeling an analyst may conceive himself to be, he is still trapped in the human predicament of having to make value judgments. The compliant patient has a long history of detecting the most minute clues to the other person's value orientation. Indeed, to compound this complexity, the detached analyst becomes a sort of challenge to the compliant patient's powers of compliance. The charming, compliant, and conciliatory facade is put to the test with the detached analyst who reveals very little of what he really feels about his patient. It takes an expert at compliance to get to know what the expert at detachment really requires of him. And when he finally does find out what the requirements are through subliminal cues, nonverbal communications, or the implicit value judgments contained in therapeutic inquiries, he will also catch on to what the analyst would consider a valid and satisfactory goal for therapy. For this patient remains firm in his belief that he can still be the satisfactory child he had actually been in his childhood.

But there is also the patient who never believed he could actually satisfy anyone, and this patient will give a detached analyst a long and tortuous run for his money, only for both to find at termination that the whole thing seemed in vain. To the very end, this patient is acting out and testing out, leaving this analyst confused and angrily wondering what it is all about. In the abundant wisdom that detachment confers, this analyst will work out an accurate and historically confirmed analysis of this patient's familial anomalies and make a seasoned judgment about genetic sources of difficulty; for he is very observant of data, perceptive and penetrating. Yet, his patient, being rather negativistic in his belief that he is unsatisfactory, just does not seem to change in any fundamental way despite this analyst's best efforts. The beliefs he holds about himself may be irrational, but they are not groundless, and though the detached analyst will be able to spot past difficulties with keen and accurate judgment, he will not be able to engage them.

For reasons of temperament and/or character, he will finally terminate with this noncompliant patient. He may even harbor some resentment at his failure in this case, and may, therefore, proceed to judge the patient as not being good enough for further therapy. This is, of course, a distorted countertransference reaction.

Such an outcome is understandable because the patient required something that the detached analyst was incapable of doing. In this convergence of transference and countertransference, the sore points of both participants were magnified: the analyst who dwells most comfortably on the outskirts of involvement may even become belligerent about the meaning of the term involvement, while the negativistic patient requires an open involvement in order to find something to be negative about. If he finds something central to negate, he creates a potentially therapeutic situation because he will be able to project onto the analyst the very negation he was confronted with in himself and let the analyst experience directly what he had continually experienced in his own past.

But the detached analyst, for no deliberate reasons of his own, does not provide this patient with an experiential backdrop against which to understand himself because implicit value judgments and subliminal cues are not enough to signify involvement. He may complain that his patient is uninteresting and express the wish that he get off his merry-go-round, but this is his own projection. What he must see is that the patient is going around in circles for the chief purpose of maintaining a parody of detachment until his analyst becomes openly involved with him, so that he may deal negatively with him.

Once this happens, the transference-countertransference interlock is broken through. The analyst has stepped out of his splendid detachment and is now open to a complex relationship that has an unpredictable outcome. Having moved out into the center of the experiential field of therapy, he provides his patient with a center of attachment and relatedness, since his true personal qualities, laid open and operant, will now be related to the patient for good or for ill. He no longer complains that the patient is uninteresting because a more genuinely interpersonal type of relatedness has replaced what was formerly, at best, an interlock, a one-way affair at worst. And now, with nothing barred, the analyst engages the negative barrage that will be forthcoming in the hope of discovering why the patient feels so undesirable.

So long as an analyst keeps before him the idea that his patient is trying to resolve something in his own experience, that is, so long as he retains his objectivity and maintains his grasp on the transference qualities of the negativism, he will be able to serve his patient. But if, in the process, the patient touches off a distortion in the analyst and the analyst has to respond this time in a defensive and negative manner before the patient's negativism has run its course, the analytic process will be in for rough sailing and its outcome will be touch and go. If worked through successfully, however, it may turn out to be a mutually rewarding experience for both participants.

The detached analyst runs into therapeutic difficulty when he is confronted with open demands for intimacy, warmth, and affection. And he falls short of the mark when the patient realistically requires warm encouragement to confront half-conscious needs for fundamental change. At such junctures, an analyst has to be prepared to be emotionally present and "there," and this is difficult for the detached analyst.

Of course, detached analysts of the narcissistic stripe willingly act as if they felt warmth and closeness because they think this is what the patient requires of them, but not at all because they truly feel it toward that particular patient. And a patient, who is undiscerningly hungry for intimacy and accepts stilted make-believe for the real thing, will be deeply disappointed and disillusioned. In the end, such an experience will only reinforce his negativism, because he has exposed himself once again to another person who defaulted in his responsibility as others had previously. This is not constructive for any patient, and especially not for such a patient. His true sense of worth has been undermined again, and his angry frustration reinforced. The detached narcissist may rightly observe that this patient has "neurotic" needs for love, but in view of the past experience of such patients, these needs make sense. And in view of his present analytic experience, it makes sense again since his unfulfilled desire for intimacy and his felt lack of warmth was not without foundation in objective fact.

The detached analyst, in sum, has his greatest strength with the compliant patient and runs into his greatest difficulties with the negativistic one; his therapeutic strength is his seemingly uncanny observational power, while his general interpersonal movement in the direction of disengagement will hamper him and prevent the development of direct relatedness in his presence. With the former patient, the detachment of the analyst becomes his most valuable asset when the transference manifestations get thick and sticky, for this is when the compliant patient begins to realize that his integrity is at stake. Unlike the negativist who never knew why he was not good enough, the compliant patient found that it paid off in his childhood with an important adult, or perhaps with a sibling.

Of course, the patient who is deeply negativistic is difficult with anyone. He is usually bright, alert, and penetrating, but he too has to be engaged, like any other patient who seeks therapy. When the transference manifestations of this patient become hazy and heavy, the continued detachment of the anlayst simply means to him that again he is not a satisfactory person to relate to, because his analyst does not even give him a tumble. No matter what he does, it is taken as subject matter for anlaysis. Even when his negativism has been worked through in spots, the detached analyst is in no position to catch hold of the glimmers of intimacy that begin to appear because of his distaste for involvement.

Detachment is not synonymous with objectivity; it is, by and large, a defensive mode of operation. It reveals nothing about the analyst except that he will not or cannot tolerate an open involvement with his patient. The unfortunate thing about it is that he is, in all probability, capable of intimacy a good deal more than he thinks but has come to a fixed decision either through early training or adverse analytic experience that he must assume an uninvolved attitude toward his patients lest he interfere with their growth. Yet, the truth of the matter is that even ambulatory schizophrenics who still have some touch with reality are better off relating to what is real in the detached analyst than to his detached facade. At least, it will be clear that the analyst has no mask; besides, it is self-deceptive for the detached analyst to assume that a perceptive patient will not be able to penetrate this defense and gain a rounded picture of what the analyst is like without his analyzed mask.

To be penetrated by a perceptive patient only creates anxiety in the analyst whose character defense is detachment, and he may even retaliate under the guise of "doing analysis" with petty digs, sarcastic irony, or the exercise of authority, all of which may be directly interpreted by the patient as confirmation of what he initially perceived. The way the detached analyst can experience satisfaction in his work is to take off his mask and relate as he is no matter how he really is. Through an openness to psychological understanding in analysis and in other interpersonal relations, he may grow and possibly change the intrapersonal factors within himself that necessitated the imposition of a detached facade in the first place. Clearly, its continuation not only introduces deceptive operations into the analysis; it also freezes the unacceptable intrapersonal factors in the anlayst's personality and limits his possibilities of movement. True enough, it is not the responsibility of the patient to analyze his analyst, though he may have to try, should the occasion arise, to understand a transference-countertransference interlock. But it is also true that an analyst ought not to be so grandiose as to believe that he cannot be analyzed by a patient.

The facade of detachment signalizes arrested growth. If the analyst cannot find the security in himself to be open and straightforward in his relationship with his patients where his position of authority is reinforced by so many irrational factors from the patient's side, it is doubtful that he will be able to do it elsewhere. An analyst is, of course, enjoined from using patients for his own purposes, but it is, at the same time, useless to transform himself into an unrealistic image of a person. Were this truly necessary he would be perpetrating the greatest deception of all, for this detached analyst, who is usually so skittish about using his patients, is actually using them in a most subtle way: purporting to engage in a therapeutic relationship without actual engagement. By introducing the facade of detachment as a steady attitude, he asserts his claim at the very outset that he has little positive emotion to offer and that the patient must create the entire emotional atmosphere, which is all right when dealing with intrapersonal processes but hardly adequate when dealing with the interpersonal field of experience. The assumption of this attitude is tantamount to resignation, an adjustment to intrapersonal conditions under which a person believes he is compelled to live.

We have already noted the validity of disengagement as a phase of the analyst's therapeutic attitude in the face of an irrational component of the patient's transference relationship. In every analysis, there are occasions of ignorance where empirical forbearance is the only possible or valid response. Aside from its value as a means to engender an inquiring attitude, it is a simple statement of fact. In addition, it will also serve to allay anxiety that is derived from pressures of the patient for immediate gratification of his quest for understanding. For this is not a basically intrapersonal anxiety but a projected interpersonal phenomenon geared to the immediate attainment of that which is not immediately available. If the analyst openly defers his reaction until such time as he gains sufficient confidence in his view, it will not only instruct the patient about the value of a deferred judgment in the face of ignorance, it may lead to a new avenue of investigation, for the patient may then become interested in understanding these anxious pressures for immediate gratification of his wish to know in the face of a paucity of data.

When openly arrived at with the patient, a self-conscious decision such as this is quite different from a deeply ingrained pattern of detachment that is sustained in the analyst without regard to the patient's communications. It is perfectly valid to stay out of the transference manifestations until it is possible to know or at least to have a strong hunch about their direction. It may even prove essential for some patients who become frightened by an irrational emergent and strive to continue the expression of what is, for the moment, so frightening. If the analyst, even though he does not understand this process, can stay with it and not aggravate the fear, he may be detached from the emergent transference but he is quite involved in his patient's striving to discover its meaning at some point after it has moved more clearly into the therapeutic situation. Even under such circumstances, of course, the manner in which an analyst decides to withhold himself will affect the later course of the relationship.

These five qualities—overprotective nurture, aggressive dependency, model adjustment, obsessional criticism, and detachment—lead to countertransference processes in the experiential field of therapy. They represent attitudes that are recurrent and observable in analysts and others as well; and they are present in the analyst not only while he is at work but also in his other relationships. Yet, it is impossible to categorize him once and forever more. His is a continuum of qualitative experience, and with an enlarged perspective in both his life and work, he may move from one quality to another. At any point, however, it should prove feasible to determine which of these qualities predominates in his experiential field.

His freedom is rooted in specific fields of therapy. It is never absolute in kind or function, since he cannot predict, unless he becomes a mechanical robot, what particular response every future patient will evoke from him. An important corollary of this notion is that an analyst, in response to a specific transference manifestation, may find a varied countertransference manifestation emerging in himself that is out of keeping with the predominant way he ordinarily perceives his responsive capacities; and this, of course, requires his concentrated analytic attention.

Since all analysts proceed through various stages of personality development in which the various types of defensive reaction can be evoked and consolidated, no analyst is immune to the whole gamut of reactions. At one time or another while working with one patient or another, any given analyst may retire into one or another qualitative integration that will depend in part on his patient's material and in part on which particular phase of his own development has been most troublesome for him.

The easiest way for an analyst to identify countertransference distortions is his observation of the usual signs of anxiety in himself. They may run the wide gamut from transient anxiety reactions, the continuation of an emotion from one session to another and its recurrence at the end of the day, to the point where his anxiety reactions require serious attention, to acting out and identifying the patient as reminiscent of a particularly difficult or disturbing person in his own personal history, or any other kind of response that he does not ordinarily experience as being part of his customary attitude toward patients, himself, or the therapeutic process. If he has not become too anxious, when involved in a countertransference reaction, to listen to his patient's description of such psychic events, he may at least be able to understand another's description of it even though his own understanding is limited.

Furthermore, it must be emphasized that none of these countertransference possibilities necessarily entails a negative balance for a particular analyst. In the five observations, the constructive as well as the limiting aspects of each were illustrated in the experiential field as constituted by a particular analyst and his patient. These qualities were considered in abstraction from the analyst's and patient's total experience. This was necessary in order to make the illustrations manageable for presentation. Concrete therapeutic situations were described in which a predominant quality of the analyst engages a predominant quality of the patient. It would prove impossible to observe, collate, and interpret all of their functions and consequences. Like any attempt at generalization in psychoanalysis, this is a provisional guide to what may be expected with greater or lesser degrees of probability. It is not a fixed conceptual scheme that anticipates the occurrence of events with absolute certainty. No interpretive map of the experiential field of analytic therapy will ever be constructed that can predict all of the emotional possibilities and nuances of a particular meeting of analyst and patient.

These are some of the complexities of experience that therapeutic work requires the analyst to face, and he has no choice but to open himself to the continual analysis of his personality in order to understand and grow. There is no point in becoming self-conscious because he decides he possesses one quality rather than another, for despite a continuing and painful urge to expand the scope of his awareness, he cannot possibly expect to be able to treat every patient. He will have varying reactions to the wide variety of patients he sees, as they will also have a variety of reactions to him. Yet, he works as best he can with what is given to him in the firm belief that the process of enlarging awareness is infinite, literally unbounded and unending. That this is a difficult enterprise goes without saying; but once he has learned to know who he is, he cannot turn his back on the limitations he brings to the experiential field of therapy.

A discussion of the ideal analyst's qualities has been deliberately omitted simply because he does not exist. There are many texts the reader already knows that contain extensive lists of desirable traits in the analyst's personality, but such lists produce very little in the way of real knowledge about the analyst and his work. If anything, they produce the inescapable impression that the listed traits are considered desirable simply because the particular writer, or other responsible person who made the judgment, felt he possessed them or keenly sensed their absence in himself and was striving to cultivate them. Besides, in trying to outline the traits he would like to see, he has in fact placed himself in the position of describing personifications as opposed to the real people who have chosen theory and practice of analysis as their life's work.

The fact is that an ideal constellation of traits does not add up to a practicing analyst with all of his uniqueness and individuality. The five described qualities of analysts are based on real individuating qualities. These analysts are all capable of practicing analysis so long as they are frank in acknowledging the truth about themselves and are actively engaged in the pursuit of growth.

I have not met the ideal analyst yet, and probably would not take a liking to him if I did, because such an analyst—humans being what they are—would have to be a fraud and a liar to presume the achievement of an ideal state that has so freed him from the pressure of the actual forces with which we live that he can sit in judgment of his peers from the vantage point of the Platonic heavens. Not that any of us can escape the need to make judgments, but the ideal analyst has arrogated to himself the position of judging others to the exclusion of himself.

It would be quite sensible of patients to avoid a pretender to this state of being like a plague, because he will not descend from the Platonic heavens long enough to establish a relationship with a patient in trouble; and, if he did, he would be so rational that he could not know what his patient was talking about with any kind of empathy. The obsessional analyst who strives in the direction of the ideal is a different story, of course; he harbors perfectionistic fantasies that shelter all-too-human limitations: fear of direct contact, low self-esteem, and worthless feelings. Were he ever to attain a sense of having realized his perfectionism in an ideal way, he too would have placed himself beyond the interpersonal pale and would be untouched by anything really human.

Of all the experiences an analyst needs, the most significant is a genuine personal analysis. Regardless of what field his previous training has been in —medicine, clinical psychology, social work or social science, teaching, the arts, law, or philosophy—the difference in personality traits that each of these disciplines reflects is picayune when compared with the necessity for thorough investigation and mastery of his transference potential, his particular value system as it evolved and now develops on the basis of psychological insight, and the enduring effects of his particular sociocultural heritage on his current beliefs about himself and others.

It is strange to look for all kinds of backgrounds and personal experiences to find the distinctive signs of the genuine analyst, instead of looking for the most important experience any analyst could possibly have—the thorough analysis of his own transference potential and its variety of manifestations, for if it is still true that we are all more simply human than otherwise, then the exploration of one human's experience is as useful to the analyst's growth as the exploration of any other. And since, in principle, the range of his perception is conditioned by his self-awareness, it suffices, in practice, to explain why analysis begins at home.

Sometimes the analyst who has gained insight into a deleterious past and has overcome serious personality defects may turn out to be more effective than the analyst with less insight into a more benign history. The former has, through direct experience, acquired rational faith in the powers of psychological insight that the latter has never had to discover. Warranted faith in the powers of psychoanalysis derives from an experience of its effectiveness. Perhaps because of conformist and other less intelligible pressures, analysts have been unusually reticent about the values they have found in psychological insight. This is, in itself, a rather curious reticence, because it is considered valid and necessary to work with the primary subject matter in other domains of human inquiry. If the nature of psychological subject matter is fundamentally uniform, then personal benefits from analysis will increase an analyst's competence and widen his scope in at least the same measure as the productive work he does with others. And his own analysis is the more significant just because the competent scope of his awareness of others is a direct function of his self-awareness.

Regardless of the particularities of his history, the organization of his current existence, or his visions of the future, the analyst has to live his life with vigor and wholeheartedness and try to understand its meaning.

There is no need to look any further for the reason why dominantly destructive people cannot engage in therapy. It is not so much because they would have a directly destructive effect on the other person, though this can happen, but rather because their range of imaginative understanding has been sharply constricted by the limits of their experience. In having denied life, they are people with unlived lives who cannot stand or understand life in others. This is not an invitation to adopt the Pollyanna attitude of "life can be beautiful" or some other trash like that; where not a pose, it is a downright distortion because it leaves out more than it says, for psychological growth involves the experience of pain. But without a larger context for having and undergoing experience, there is nothing to understand, no choices to be made, no positions to be taken, and the destructive individual has placed the stuff of active experience beyond his ken because he has already destroyed it. In some cases, this trait may be analyzed, but one can do little if anything in the furtherance of anyone else's life without overcoming it in his own. To have lived and understood the significance of one's life is not only a matter of living out what is felt and understood, though this is one source of constructive insight, it can also be a matter of imaginative reconstruction of what another must feel. And neither approach to significance is available to the destructive person.

In principle, analysts cannot be destructive of the patient's quest for life. Perhaps because of fear, they may detach themselves and seek to observe and make inferences about the events in the lives of others. They may take the position, with a certain rightness, that these observations and inferences have no relevance to themselves. However, such understanding, based as it is on what others have lived, is superficial, distant, and detached in the sense of hardly getting beyond the dermatology of the patient's experience. To be superficial is to fail to go beyond a description of the overt manifestations of the patient's underlying motivation; to be distant is to fail to recognize that what the patient discusses does not pertain to inhabitants of another planet or a totally distinct plane of life; and to be detached is to fail to allow the patient to come to life in a directly interpersonal situation.

It must be said that the frightened analyst is nothing like the destructive one. He will let his patient live, and even though he cannot participate, he does not, like the destructive analyst, undermine his patient's striving for life.

There are no pure types of analysts. With respect to their constructive desire to understand, they seem to fall into two categories: those who would live and then try to understand what they have lived, and those who stand on the sidelines of life and understand what others have lived. Some may lean more in one direction than in another, but no analyst can avoid the active requisites of life and retain mastery of his professed art. In search for significance in life, he has to live and have something to understand. This is the essential curiosity that motivates the analyst. The possibility must, of course, be considered that more specific factors may yet be isolated that constitute the mark of the analyst's personality.

It remains difficult to ferret out other reasons why an analyst is compelled to work at his craft. To say that the complexity of his own experience has motivated him is not very illuminating, for there are schizophrenics and psychotics whose experience may have been even more complex than that of most analysts without their having been motivated to pursue psychological knowledge. If, in addition to complexity, other factors like sensitivity, interpersonal tact and alertness, and even a keenly discriminating intelligence are cited, they still do not add up to an analyst, for anyone in the creative arts has them. While it is true that these factors are combined in varying degrees in the analyst's experience, the question must still be left open. Meanwhile, the only valid view of the matter is a multifactor one, for these and other factors are found in a variety of dynamic organizations that are equivalent to the variety of personalities in analytic work. Every anlayst must at least learn to recognize his own particular style of integration, because in so doing, he will also discover what particular kinds of people he is best suited for. And this is in the interest of economy of time and energy, which brings us back again to the primacy of personal analysis.

The analyst lives by the primary Aristotelian postulate that all men by nature desire to know. He feels compelled to understand the nature of the human psyche in its many dimensions and variety of manifestations, and his desire to heal is a corollary of this compulsion, not for reasons of primary narcissistic gratification that lead to neither knowledge nor healing, but because the psychic domain constitutes a special interest and challenge. Considerations of status, power, prestige, and money are certainly significant factors to be reckoned with in our culture, but they are in no way distinctive of the science and practice of psychoanalysis. If the analyst shares them with others in our intellectual, economic, and political life, he also has the distinctive residue of interests in psychological knowledge and therapeutic healing. As scientist and healer, he is primarily dedicated to the understanding of psychic life.

It has been said that one outstanding analyst developed a remarkable understanding of clinical data through the observation of friends. But it ought to be added that these observations probably only confirmed hypotheses that had already been arrived at concurrently through intensive personal observation. For an analyst's immediate field of observation is his own experience, and how he relates to it will determine his ability to observe how another person integrates an experiential field with him.

There is no question but that self-analysis has serious limitations. To point up this difficulty, there is the old saw aobut a self-analysis that failed because the countertransference got in the way. The range of perception is limited by the unconscious structure of personality, and another skilled observer can perceive more about that unconscious structure than its possessor, provided, of course, that the observer has a wider scope of awareness. Even Freud, the first self-analyzed analyst, engaged in mutual analysis of countertransference with Ferenczi; he too had to supplement his self-analysis with an interpersonal inquiry. It is still true that a continuous effort on the part of the analyst to understand himself and those around him has to be supplemented with intermittent personal analysis with a competent colleague who is suitable to his personality traits, so that mutual blind spots do not bring the analysis to the dead-end of a transference-countertransference interlock.

However, there is a fundamental truth to be learned from the fact that Freud had undergone a tortuous self-analysis. We ought not to lose sight of some important aspects of this truth, namely, that the final and complete reading on the human personality simply does not exist; that it is impossible to transcend the distinction between conscious and unconscious, and since the experiential field changes from moment to moment, insight is never complete; that it is necessary not only to understand what Freud said about the therapeutic process, but also to attempt what he did with it; and, finally, that there is really no way to avoid the painful struggle involved in self-observation and growth.

A patient's desire to understand his experiential field cannot always be satisfied in a two-way process of interpersonal experience, for his relation to himself is neither identical nor commensurate with his relation to others, even to his analyst. In other words, an intrapersonal process is ultimately not reducible to an interpersonal one; and the converse is also true. The one may be analyzed cognitively and historically into the components of the other, but when this is done the immediate context in which it functions has been transformed into a qualitatively different context. Of course, what is now functioning as an intrapersonal process may once have been interpersonal, but this is not necessarily so because repeated observation confirms the fact that there are some aspects of individual experience that have maintained themselves in potentiality even though they have had no solid chance for actualization in the current life of the patient. This truth is repeatedly affirmed when it is realized that the patient has the last word on the interpretation of his own experience. And yet, self-analysis has, by and large, a very limited chance for success. At one time, this was believed to be a result of the shortcomings of introspection as a technique of psychological inquiry, but clearly a larger issue is involved: the fact that pain accompanies growth and that suffering is a by-product of uncovering distressing unconscious processes. Under the circumstances, it is the rare individual who willingly exposes himself in isolation to such painful suffering when in fact he is able to maintain a reasonably workable place in life without it.

This has important implications for the theory of therapy. The immediate sense of self, as experienced by the individual, is an essential condition for therapy, and it is in no way available directly to the therapist except by way of his own immediate experience. There is nothing in his technical repertoire that will place another person's immediate sense of self under direct observation. It is not objectively available to him, and he has no way of judging its breadth or power except as it is revealed by the patient after the defensive system has been worked through.

The direct experience of two selves in a two-person situation cannot be brought about through an act of will or as a product of technique. Its occurrence cannot be predicted, though its existence in immediate experience may be posited at the outset of therapy by intuition. For example, when the therapist surmises the strength of the ego, this intuitive act is as much an immediate process for the therapist as the sense of self is an immediate experience for the patient. But just as immediate experience is closely joined to the cognitive experience, so this immediate sense of self is intimately intertwined with the defensive system. And even though it is possible to establish the strength of this sense inferentially through the observation of the defensive system, such inference is not equivalent to the first-hand datum.

An inference does not literally provide the givenness of the sense of self. An inference can give us a shorthand symbolic equivalent of what to expect when this sense finally emerges unencumbered by the defensive network. But what it will be when it does emerge is unpredictable, because, being strictly personal, it stands on the boundaries of objective or interpersonal observation.

REFERENCE

James, W. (1890). *Principles of Psychology.* 2 vols. New York: Dover, 1950. Volume 1, Chap. IX.

14. Counter-Transference

D. W. Winnicott

What I want to say can be briefly stated.

I think that the use of this word *counter-transference* should now be brought back to its original use. We can use words as we like, especially artificial words like *counter-transference*. A word like *self* naturally knows more than we do; it uses us, and can command us. But *counter-transference* is a term that we can enslave, and a perusal of the literature makes me think that it is in danger of losing its identity.

There is now quite a literature around the term, and I have tried to study it. In my paper 'Hate in the Counter-transference' (which is chiefly about hate), I said that one use of the word *counter-transference* would be to describe 'abnormality in counter-transference feelings, and set relationships and identifications that are under repression in the analyst. The comment on this is that the analyst needs more analysis. . . .'

For the purposes of that paper I then gave two other possible meanings.

A discussion based on the failures of the analysts' own analyses must be futile. In a sense, this ends the debate.

The meaning of the word *counter-transference* can be extended, however, and I think we have all agreed to extend it a little so that we may take this opportunity to look at our work afresh. I shall return, however, to this idea that I have already expressed. Before I proceed I must go back to a remark made by Michael Fordham at the beginning of his paper, in which he quoted Jung as protesting against the idea that transference was the product of psycho-analytic technique, emphasizing that it was a general transpersonal or social phenomenon. Apart from the fact that I do not know what *transpersonal* means, I think that confusion could arise here by a distortion of the use of the term *transference* as I think Freud introduced it. The characteristic of psycho-analytic technique is this use of transference and of the *transference neurosis*. Transference is not just a matter of rapport, or of relationships. It concerns the way in which a highly subjective phenomenon repeatedly turns up in an analysis. Psycho-analysis very much consists in the arranging of conditions for the development of these phenomena, and in the interpretation of these phenomena at the right moment. The interpretation relates the specific transference phenomenon to a bit of the patient's psychic reality, and this in some cases means at the same time relating it to a bit of the patient's past living.

In a typical example, a patient is gradually working round to suspicion and hate in the relation to the analyst, which can be seen to have a correlation with the danger of meeting another patient, or with the breaks due to week-ends and holidays. In the course of time an interpretation makes sense of all this in terms not of the present but of the dynamic structure of the patient's personality. Following this work the patient loses the specific transference neurosis and begins to boil up for another. (Often the work is not done in such a clear way, but for teaching purposes this might be a fair description of a basic principle.)

Michael Fordham (1960) gave a good example of this in the patient who asked questions. Eventually she said: 'You are like my father, you never answer questions.' Often a patient will have given clues so that the analyst may interpret fruitfully, but here a little bit (but an important bit) of the interpretation was arrived at by the patient, and no doubt the analyst was then able to weigh in with a more complete interpretation.

It is necessary for me to take up time in this way because if we do not agree about the term *transference* we must not start discussing *counter-transference*.

Incidentally, may I remind Dr Fordham that some of the terms he uses are not of any value to me because they belong to the jargon of Jungian conversation. He in turn can tell me which of my words are useless to him. I refer to: *transpersonal, transpersonal unconscious, transpersonal analytic ideal, archetypal, the contra-sexual components of the psyche, the animus and anima, animus-anima conjunction.*

I cannot be communicated with in this language. For some in this hall these are household words, and for the rest they have no precise meaning.

We must also be careful over the use of words that are used in different ways by various groups of workers: *ego, unconscious, illusory, syntonic (react syntonically), analysis,* etc.

I can now return to the subject of transference–counter-transference phenomena and examine what happens in professional work generally. Professional work is quite different from ordinary life, is it not?

All this started up with Hippocrates. He perhaps founded the professional attitude. The medical oath gives a picture of a man or woman who is an idealized version of the ordinary man or woman in the street. Yet *that is how we are* when professionally engaged. Included in the oath is the promise that we do not commit adultery with a patient. Here is a full recognition of one aspect of the transference, the patient's need to idealize the doctor, and to fall in love with him, to dream.

Freud allowed for the development of a full range of subjective phenomena in the professional relationship; the analyst's own analysis was in effect a recognition that the analyst is *under strain in maintaining a professional attitude.* It is on purpose that I use this wording. I am not saying that the analyst's analysis is to free him from neurosis; it is to increase the stability of character and the maturity of the personality of the worker, this being the basis of his or her professional work and of our ability to maintain a professional relationship.

A professional attitude may, of course, be built up on a basis of defences and inhibitions and obsessional orderliness, and I suggest that it is here that the psychotherapist is particularly under strain, because *any structuring of his ego-defences lessens his ability to meet the new situation.* The psychotherapist (analyst, or analytical psychologist) must remain vulnerable, and yet retain his professional role in his actual working hours. I guess that the well-behaving professional analyst is easier to come by than the analyst who (while behaving well) retains the vulnerability that belongs to a flexible defence organization. (Fordham refers to this same idea in his own language.)

There is a much fuller use of transference phenomena in psychoanalysis than in social work, for instance. This gives a therapeutic advantage to the analyst over the social worker, but it is necessary to remember the advantages that remain with the more general caseworker who, working in with the patient's ego functions, is in a better position to relate the individual's ego needs to social provision. As analysts we are often hampered in this which is not our function.

In analysis the transference neurosis is characteristically id-derived. In social work a man may say to the worker, 'You remind me of my mother.' Nothing need be done about this, except for the worker to believe in it. In analysis the analyst will be given the clues so that he can interpret not only the transference of feelings from mother to anlayst, but also the unconscious instinctual elements that underlie this, and the conflicts that are aroused, and the defences that organize. In this way the unconscious begins to have a conscious equivalent and to become a living process involving people, and to be a phenomenon that is acceptable to the patient.

What the patient meets is surely the professional attitude of the analyst, not the unreliable men and women we happen to be in private life.

I want to make this clear observation first, although later I shall modify what I am now saying.

I want to state that the working analyst is in a special state, that is, *his attitude is professional*. The work is done in a professional setting. In this setting we assume a freedom of the analyst from personality and character disorder of such a kind or degree that the professional relationship cannot be maintained, or can only be maintained at great cost involving excessive defences.

The professional attitude is rather like symbolism, in that it assumes a *distance between analyst and patient*. The symbol is in a gap between the subjective object and the object that is perceived objectively.

It will be seen that here I am disagreeing with a statement of Fordham's although a little later I shall agree with him. The statement I am disagreeing with is the following: 'He [Jung] compares the analytic relation to a chemical interaction, and continues that treatment can "by no device . . . be anything but the product of mutual influence, in which the whole being of the doctor as well as the patient plays a part".' Later he is very emphatic that it is futile for the analyst to erect defences of a professional kind against the influence of the patient, and continues: 'By doing so he only denies himself the use of a highly important organ of information.'

I would rather be remembered as maintaining that in between the patient and the analyst is the analyst's professional attitude, his technique, *the work he does with his mind*.

Now I say this without fear because I am not an intellectual and in fact I personally do my work very much from the body ego, so to speak. But I think of myself in my analytic work working with easy but conscious mental effort. Ideas and feelings come to mind, but these are well examined and sifted before an interpretation is made. This is not to say that feelings are not involved. On the one hand I may have stomach ache but this does not usually affect my interpretations; and on the other hand I may have been somewhat stimulated erotically or aggressively by an idea given by the patient, but again this fact does not usually affect my interpretative work, what I say, how I say it, or when I say it.

The analyst is objective and consistent, for the hour, and he is not a rescuer, a teacher, an ally, or a moralist. The important effect of the analyst's own analysis in this connexion is that it has strengthened his own ego so that he can remain *professionally* involved, and this without too much strain.

In so far as all this is true the meaning of the word *counter-transference* can only be the neurotic features *that spoil the professional attitude* and disturb the course of the analytic process as determined by the patient.

In my opinion this holds except insofar as the diagnosis of the patient is of a certain kind, and I now want to describe the kinds of diagnosis that to my mind alter the whole problem and make me wish to agree with the statement that I have just disagreed with. The subject under discussion is now: *the role of the analyst;* and this role must vary according to the diagnosis of the patient. Neither speaker had time to refer more than briefly to the matter of diagnosis (although Fordham quoted Jung: 'It is clear, however, that he is sure the patient can have very drastic effects on the analyst and that this can induce pathological manifestations in him. He states that this is particularly the case when cases of borderline schizophrenia are being treated' and developed the theme in an interesting way.)

I am now, therefore, speaking from a different position, and the change comes from the fact that I now refer to the management and treatment of borderline cases for which the word *psychotic* is more appropriate than the word *neurotic*. But the vast majority of people who may come to us for psychoanalysis are not psychotic and students must be taught first the analysis of non-psychotic cases.

You might expect me to use words like *psychoneurosis, psychosis,* or *hysteria, affective disorder,* and *schizophrenia,* but I shall not do so in classifying cases for our purposes here.

Two types of case seem to me to alter the therapist's professional attitude completely. One is the patient who has *an antisocial tendency,* and the other is the patient *who needs a regression*. The first, the patient with more or less antisocial tendency, is permanently reacting to a deprivation. The therapist is compelled by the patient's illness, or by the hopeful half of the patient's illness, to correct and to go on correcting the failure of ego support that altered the course of the patient's life. The only thing the therapist can do, apart from getting caught up, is to use what happens in an attempt to get down to a precise statement of the original deprivation or deprivations, as perceived and felt by the patient as a child. This may or may not involve work with the patient's unconscious. A therapist wholly engaged in work with patients who display an antisocial tendency would not be in a good position to understand the psychoanalytic technique or the operation of the transference, or the interpretation of the transference neurosis. We try to avoid giving our psychoanalytic students antisocial cases, precisely because we cannot teach psychoanalysis on these cases. They are better dealt with in other ways, though psychoanalysis can sometimes be usefully added. I shall leave aside further consideration of the antisocial tendency.

In the other type of patient to which I refer a regression will be needed. If a signficant change is to be brought about the patient will need to pass through a phase of infantile dependence. Here again psychoanalysis cannot be taught, though it can be practised in modified form. The difficulty here is in diagnosis, in spotting of the falseness of the false personality that hides the immature true self. If the hidden true self is to come into its own in such a case the patient will break down as part of the treatment, and the analyst will need to be able to play the part of mother to the patient's infant. This means giving ego support in a big way. The analyst will need to remain orientated to external reality while in fact being identified with the patient, even merged in with the patient. The patient must become highly dependent, even absolutely dependent, and these words are true even when there is a healthy part of the personality that acts all along as an ally of the analyst and in fact tells the analyst how to behave.

You will note that I am now using phrases that are in line with phrases used by Fordham.

Now here again it can be said that analysts who work chiefly with patients who become very fully dependent in this way can fail to understand and learn the psychoanalytic technique that is based on work with the vast majority of patients, those whose own infantile dependence was successfully managed by their own mothers and fathers. (I cannot too strongly emphasize the fact that most people, if analysed, do need the classical psychoanalytic technique, with the analyst's professional attitude in between the patient and the analyst.)

Per contra, the classical analyst, the one who has learned his job and who is confident in his ability to deal with the transference neurosis as it develops and repeatedly redevelops, has a great deal to learn from those who care for and who attempt to do psychotherapy of the patients who need to go through the stages of emotional development that properly belong to infancy.

From this changed position, therefore, with the patient diagnosed as psychotic or schizophrenic, and the transference dominated by the patient's need to regress to infantile dependence, I find I am able to join up with a whole lot of Dr Fordham's observations, which, however, I think he did not properly link with the classification of the patients because he had not time.

The borderline psychotic gradually breaks through the barriers that I have called the analyst's technique and professional attitude, and forces a direct relationship of a primitive kind, even to the extent of merging. This is done in a gradual and orderly manner, and recovery is correspondingly orderly, except where it is part of the illness that chaos must reign supreme both without and within.

In the training of psychoanalysts and the like we must not place the students in the position of being related to the primitive needs of psychotic patients, because few will be able to stand it, and few will be able to learn anything from the experience. On the other hand, in a properly organized psychoanalytic practice there is room for some patients who force their way across the professional borderline, and who make these special tests and demands that we seem to be including under the term *counter-transference* in this discussion. I could take up the subject of the analyst's responses. In fact I find it difficult to miss this opportunity for discussing all kinds of things that I have experienced and that link up with ideas put forward by Dr Fordham. For instance, I got hit yesterday. What I said is not for publication. It was not an interpretation but a reaction to an event. The patient came across the professional white line and got a little bit of the real me, and I think it felt real to her. But a reaction is not counter-transference.

Would it not be better at this point to *let the term* counter-transference *revert to its meaning* of that which we hope to eliminate by selection and analysis and the training of analysts? This would leave us free to discuss the many interesting things that analysts can do with psychotic patients who are temporarily regressed and dependent for which we could use Margaret Little's term: *the analyst's total response to the patient's needs*. Under this or a similar title there is much to be said about the use that the analyst can make of his or her own conscious and unconscious reactions to the impact of the psychotic patient or the psychotic part of the patient on his or her self, and the effect of this on the analyst's professional attitude. I am one of those who have already written a little and said much on this subject that interests Jungians and Freudians alike. This could form and must indeed form a basis for future discussions, but I think that only muddle can come from stretching to cover all this the word that is in the title of this symposium: *counter-transference*.

REFERENCES

Fordham, Michael. (1960). Counter-transference. *British Journal of Medical Psychology 33* (1): 1–8.

Winnicott, D. W. (1949). Hate in the counter-transference. In *Collected Papers*. London: Tavistock. 1958.

15. The Transference-Countertransference Complex

Leo Stone

Certain specifications as to definition, with a brief re-evaluation of the breadth, depth, and pervasiveness of the transference dynamism, would be relevant to our discussion. First, I should like to state that clarity, both in principle and in everyday communication, is best served by confining the unqualified term *transference* to that aspect or fraction of a relationship which is motivated by persistent unmodified wishes (or other attitudes) toward an actual important personage of the past, which tend to invest a current individual in a sort of misidentification (Nunberg, 1951) with the unconscious image of the past personage. It is essentially inappropriate to the current situation, subjectively ununderstood as to genetic origin until analyzed, and tenaciously resistive to this analysis. I cannot accept the specification of Silverberg (1948) that it is always experienced as disagreeable, although this is often the case, because of conflicts attendant on its separate activation. The opposite quality, pleasure, can also characterize it. Silverberg's specification is connected with his emphasis on the role of the repetition compulsion, a factor that, from Freud onward, has been recognized as important. However, few would assign to this dynamism, strictly interpreted, an exclusive or nearly exclusive role in the transference. See, for example, Nunberg (1951), Lagache (1953), and Loewald (1960).

In daily life and in the early phases of the analysis, the transference is usually integrated with the actual total personal relationship. However, in the sense that I mentioned before, it is better to think of it separately, unless specifically qualified, whether as a latent potentiality, or as an actual emergent ego-dystonic, or objectively inappropriate, phenomenon. (See Anna Freud [1954] in this connection.) For, insofar as the phenomenon is true transference, it retains unmistakably its infantile character. However much the given early relationship may have contributed to the genuinely adult pattern of relationships (via identification, imitation, acceptance of teaching, for example), its transference derivative differs from the latter, approximately in the sense that Breuer and Freud (1895) assigned to the sequelae of the pathogenic traumatic experience, which was neither abreacted as such nor associatively absorbed in the personality. Given an object who has a special transference valence, in a situation that provides a unique mixture of intimacy and deprivation, with (obligatory!) unilateral communicative freedom, minimization of actual observation, and with certain elements of form and mechanics reminiscent of the infantile state, the *tendency* to pristine reemergence of latent transference drives, hitherto incorporated in everyday strivings, in symptoms, or in character structure, is enormously heightened. That the transference is treated in a unique way in the analytic process is assuredly true, and remains of prime significance. However, at one time, this was regarded not only as the unique but as the practically exclusive impingement of the analytic situation on the transference, as if its emergent integrated form in relation to any other physician would be essentially the same phenomenon. Considered as an actual functional phenomenon, as different from a latent potentiality (in a sense, a metapsychological concept), this is rarely the case. The unique emotional vicissitudes of the psychoanalytic situation as well as the de-integrating effect of free association and the interpretative method restore an infantile quality and intensity to the psychoanalytic transference, which lead to the development of the transference neurosis. Thus, to turn Freud's original reservations and admonitions in an affirmative direction: the question of what constitutes the optimum transference neurosis, or whether and how a more nearly optimal type of transference neurosis can be brought about, has always been, and remains, an important and general problem of psychoanalytic technique. This is, to be sure, no simple matter. The modest hope implicit in this presentation is that it may offer a rationale and some suggestions toward the avoidance of spurious and unduly tenacious intensities. The transference neurosis, like other (simpler) elements in the psychoanalytic situation, has an intrinsically dialectical character and position. (Free association, for example, facilitates both exposure and concealment, can occasion either gratification or suffering.) This dialectical quality can *(in part)* be explained by the concept of two separate, although potentially confluent streams of transference origin, to which I call attention elsewhere in this presentation. In relation to the equivocal factor of intensity in the transference neurosis, I suggest that there is a certain *a priori* reasonableness in the conception that the elements of abstinence augmenting transference intensity should derive preponderantly from the formal (i.e., explicitly technical) factors (in which I include nonresponse to primitive transference wishes) rather than from excessively rigorous deficits in human response, which the patient may reasonably expect or require, and where the technical valence of such deprivation may be minimal or altogether dubious as to demonstrability.

It is now all but axiomatic that the transference is the indispensable driving power of the analytic process, and the phenomenon on whose evolution the potentiality for ultimate therapeutic change rests. In analysis, as distinguished from other psychotherapies, the resolution of the transference neurosis, and the dissolution or minimization of the transference(s) as such, is one of the distinctive final goals of the interpretative method. I say "one," because it might be said that insight into dynamic and genetic elements in the unconscious, or the functional extension of the ego's hegemony in relationship to the id and superego, or other germane concepts, are ultimately more important. Actually, however, these are all, certainly in an operational sense, largely if not exclusively, contingent on the thorough analysis of the transference neurosis.

I use the term *minimization of the transference(s),* because I have considerable skepticism regarding the likelihood of complete dissolution or extinction of the transference. The specific personal misidentifications and the specific personally directed wishes and attitudes that usually occupy us in the analytic process (i.e., "the transference") can, in a practical clinical sense, usually be brought to adequate resolution. However, at this point, I should like to emphasize that pathogenic component of the transference complex which underlies and is anterior to these clinical phenomena. The "adequate resolution" of the clinically significant aspect or fraction of the transference frees the basic practically universal element, if it is not itself severely distorted, for integration in socially acceptable enthusiasms held in common with great numbers of other human beings and thus, in a sense, a part of the individual's environmental reality. I have in mind the general latent craving for an omnipotent parent, renewed and specifically colored with, indeed given form by, the conflicts and vicissitudes of each phase of development and developmental separation, a craving of such primitive power that it can produce the profound physiologic alterations of hypnosis, or bring into abeyance an individual's own perceptual capacities or capacities for rational inference, even on the basis of less spectacular vehicles for suggestion. I shall refer to this dynamism, for clarity of statement, as the "primal transference." (This presupposes the accomplished shift to an object, as opposed to Freud's other [germane] use of the term, recently elaborated by Loewald

[1960].) This phenomenon is already dramatically evident in the young (three- to six-month) infant's reaction to any moving bearer of a face as mother (". . . the representative of that infant's security" [Spitz, 1956]). It permeates our whole social organization, is obvious in religious attitudes, in attitudes toward rulers and other powerful political figures, or indeed toward charismatic ideologists of any type. In its narrowest stronghold, in the intellectual avant-garde, it invests questions of scientific validity and rational or empirical demonstration, facilitating irrational and inappropriate attitudes of loyalty or antagonism toward scientific leaders. Human infallibility is attributed to others than the Popes; and the Anti-Christ has parallels in the world of science. Our own field has often been a conspicuous example of this tendency. In the end, scientific perceptual striving, whose autonomy is always relative at best, becomes secondarily burdened, and inevitably suffers, as a result of this type of ambivalent group euphoria.

If it is the entanglement with early objects that elicits the infantile neurosis and lays the ground for its later representation in the transference neurosis, it is the clinical neurosis, the usual motivation for treatment, that lies between them, and is related to both, in a sense a "resistance" both to genetic reconstruction of the former, or to current involvement in the latter. This is, to be sure, a variation of Freud's statement (1914, p. 154) regarding the transference neurosis as an accessible "artificial illness." Perhaps it is not extravagant to suggest that unconscious recognition of the unique transference potentiality of the psychoanalytic situation is intimately connected both with the violent irrational struggle against, and the sometimes fanatical acceptance of, analysis as therapy (i.e., the general and intrinsic fascination of a relationship to "the doctor who gives no medicine") by the patient to whom it is recommended (and by many, prior to the fact). What is *always* fundamentally wanted, in the sense of primal transference, with rare (relative) exceptions, is the original physician, who most closely resembles the parent of earliest infancy. The "doctor who gives no medicine" is in unconscious *a priori* the parent of the repetitive phases of separation. To what extent this unconscious constellation participated in the discovery or creation of psychoanalysis as such would be pure speculation. However, Freud's capacity for transferences in the attachments of daily life was abundantly evident (Freud, 1887–1902; Jones, 1953–1957), and the importance of the relationship with Fliess in his self-analysis was explicitly stated (Freud, 1887–1902, pp. 43, 212). That it plays an important part in the emotional life of many contemporary working analysts is very likely, since all (at this time) have experienced the role of analysand (or analytic patient); the vast majority are physicians; all have been physicians' patients in a traditional sense; and, certainly, all have been dependent and helpless children. Ferenczi (1919) described the evolution of the general psychoanalytic countertransference in terms of initial excessive sympathy, through reactive coldness ("the phase of resistance against the counter-transference"), to mature balance. Lewin (1946a) in referring to this formulation (to contrast it with the sequences of traditional medical training) attributes the first phase to the *fact* of the analyst's having only recently been a patient himself. While Lewin carefully separates the cadaver (the student's first "patient") as an "object" (psychoanalytic sense) from its qualities, we may reasonably speculate that a species of retaliatory mastery of the parental object (perhaps in contrast with the role of helpless child) is sometimes involved in this gratification, and that something of this quality was carried into the dialectic genesis of the psychoanalytic situation. Again, see Freud's contrast between the work of a "man of letters" and his "dissection" of Dora's mental state (although, to be sure, the reference is "surgical" rather than anatomical!) (1905, p. 59). (Also, again, see Fliess's special and interesting elaboration of this theme [1949].) When I refer to the "dialectic genesis" of the psychoanalytic situation, I refer to its genesis largely in the genius of a physician who experienced the training to which Lewin refers. The dialectic is epitomized exquisitely in the role of speech, the bridge for personal separation, rejected or distorted by children in their desperate clinging to more gratifying or more violent object drives, or, on the other hand, sought eagerly as the indispensable vehicle for alternative ego-syntonic developmental aspirations. (See Nunberg [1951] regarding the "Janus" quality of transference.)

The transference neurosis, as distinguished from the initial transference, usually supervenes after the treatment has lasted for a varying length of time. Its emergence depends on the combined stress of the situational dynamics, and the pressure of the interpretative method. The latter tends to close off habitual repetitive avenues of expression, such as new symptom formation, acting out, flight from treatment, etc. The neurosis differs from the initial transference, in the sense that it tends to reproduce in the analytic and germane extra-analytic setting an infantile *dramatis personae,* a complex of transferences, with the various conflicts and anxieties attendant on the restoration of attitudes and wishes paralleling their infantile prototypes. The initial transference (akin to the "floating" transferences of Glover [1955]?) is a relatively integrated phenomenon, allied to character traits, an amalgam or compromise of conflicting forces, that has become established as a habitual attitude, the best resultant of "multiple function" of which the personality is capable, in the general type of relationship that now confronts it. It differs from its everyday counterpart only in its relative separation from its usual everyday context, in the relative lack of tangible provocation, justification, or substantiation, and—sooner or later—in the failure of elicitation of the gratifications or adaptive goals to which it is devoted. As time goes on, varying as to interval before, and character of, emergence, with the nuances of the patient's personality organization and the analyst's technical and personal approach, the unconscious specific transference attitudes will press for expression against the defenses with which they have been hitherto integrated, in varying mixtures of associational derivatives, symptomatic acts, dreams, often "acting out," and manifest feelings. At this point (or better, in this zone of a continuum), conflict involving the psychoanalytic situation becomes quasi-manifest, and the transference neurosis as such is incipient. If I offer a brief and oversimple outline illustration it is only because there are various interpretations of these terms, and I should like to make clear my own rather simple usage.

A male patient may adopt a characteristically obsequious although subtly sarcastic attitude toward his older male analyst, quite inappropriate to the situation, but thoroughly habitual in all relations with older men. As time goes on, his wife and business partner become connected in his dreams with the analytic situation, his wife in the role of mother, the analyst as father, his business partner as older brother, with corresponding and related anxieties and fluctuations of function, in his business and sexual life. Violently hostile or sexually submissive or guilty attitudes may appear in direct or indirect relation to the analyst, in the patient's manifest activities, or in the analytic material, in dynamic and economic connection with changes in the patient's other relationships. The entire development is not seldom first announced in diffuse resistance phenomena in the analytic situation and processes (Glover, 1955). The transference neurosis as such can, of course, be endlessly elaborated; when extended beyond the point of effectively demonstrable relevance to the central transference, its resistance function may well be in the foreground. It must be remembered that the whole array of strongly cathected persons in the individual's development, as well as the related variety of attitudes, are all distributed, so to speak, from a single original relationship, the relationship with a mother in earliest infancy. In all of them, there are elements of "transference" from this relationship, most conspicuously and decisively, of course, the shifting of hostile or erotic drives from the mother to the father. In a sense, then, the entire complex of the transference neurosis is a direct, although paradoxically opposed derivative of the basic attachment and unrenounced craving, which arises in relation to the primal object, the more complicated drama having a relation to the original object attachment somewhat like that which Lewin (1946b) assigns to the elements of the manifest dream in relation to the dream screen. (This is, of course, not unrelated to Lewin's interpretation [1955] of the analytic situation in terms of dream psychology.) I stress this, because in the analytic situation, the patient is again confronted with a unique relationship on which, via the instrumentality of communication by speech, all other relationships and experiences tend to converge, emotionally and intellectually. In this convergence, however, there is a conspicuous differential, due to the intellectual or cognitive lag. In the latter sphere, the analyst's autonomous ego functions play a decisive operational role, via his interpretations. In the genesis of this lag, an important role must be assigned to the original (reverse) differential, which may establish itself between the centrifugal distribution of primal object libido and aggression and the relatively autonomous energies of perception (the ego's "activity"). The detachment of libido and aggression from the primal object will of course be contingent not only on their original intensities but on the special vicissitudes of early gratifications. If we consider the limitless panpsychic scope and potentiality of free association, we must assume that some shaping tendency gives the associations a form or pattern reasonably accessible to our perceptive and interpretative skill. It would seem likely that this is the latent inner preoccupation with the elements of the transference neurosis, the original transferences of which it is in itself composed, and finally the derivative vicissitudes of the primal object relationship itself, the primal transference.

Insofar as an individual has achieved more than a physical-perceptual-linguistic separation from the primal object, the latter elements (i.e., the actual manifestations of primal transference) may play little or no important role in the empirical realities of a given analysis. Except in certain "borderline" (and allied) problems, they are of metapsychological importance. It is the problems of the derivative phase and structural conflicts that largely occupy us in the analysis of the neuroses. In an individual of unusually fortunate neurosis (!), the transference neurosis (thus the analysis) may not require deeper penetration than the relatively integrated conflict phenomena of the Oedipus complex. In speech, of course, there is at one time a powerful and versatile vehicle of direct object relationship, and at the same time the marvelously elaborate communicative-referential instrumentality that can convey from one individual to another the subjectively experienced parts or whole of an inner and outer world of endlessly multiplied things, persons, qualities, and relationships, in intelligible code. This code, furthermore, is one whose mastery was originally of profound importance (in conjunction with other crucial maturational phenomena, such as independent locomotion) in enabling the physical separation from the first object (in continuing relationship), and the gradual physical and mental mastery of the rest of the environment.

With regard to the countertransference, I believe that the same important and narrowing distinction from the other aspects of the current relationship should be made as in the case of the patient's transference; for here, too, an individual is involved in a complicated relationship with another human being in which three separate but constantly interacting and sometimes integrated modalities can be discerned. In a sense, since the patient has at least a considerable freedom of verbal and emotional expression, the analyst's emotional burden is a heavier one. This, however, is like saying that the patient's responsibility is greater than the child's, or (to turn back to an earlier page!) that the surgeon carries a greater burden than his comfortably anesthetized patient. The analyst is, or should be, better prepared for this burden than his patient. Still, if we remove this entire question from the realm of professional moralism, self-debasement, or self-pity, we can all the more genuinely appreciate the essential message of the frequent contributions on the countertransference in recent years, i.e., the reminder that no one is "completely" (or, as Freud [1937] preferred, "perfectly") analyzed, that even those who may have approximated this as closely as may reasonably be expected, have certain specific vulnerabilities to certain individuals or situations, that these may appear in milder form or ephemerally, but nevertheless importantly, with others; that, in fact, self-analysis for the specific "countertransference neurosis" (Tower, 1956) with each case is, to varying degrees, as silent counterpoint, an integral part of all good analytic work. This would be true whether the countertransference played its traditional impeding role or its more subtle favorable (i.e., "catalytic") role (Tower, 1956) in a given analysis. One never knows where the usefulness of an unanalyzed reaction may end, and difficulties begin. Another important contribution, not separate, except in terms of emphasis, is the growing appreciation of the countertransference as an affirmative instrument facilitating perception, whereby a sensitive awareness of one's incipient reactions to the patient, fully controlled, and appropriately analyzed in an immediate sense, leads to a richer and more subtle understanding of the patient's transference striving (Racker, 1957; Weigert, 1954). This would be opposite yet cognate to the understanding by transitory empathic identification (Reich, 1960). There is also the important attention (Money-Kyrle, 1956) to the specific vicissitudes of the analyst's peculiarly constricted and emotionally inhibited therapeutic effort, and the mutual projective and introjective identifications that may occur between analyst and patient in crises of technical frustration, i.e., frustration of the analyst's understanding. The operational primacy of the latter function must be stressed. As I see it, this function and the germane emotional attitude constitute central and essential "gratifications" for the patient's "mature transference" strivings, enabling his toleration, even positive utilization of the principle of abstinence, in relation to primitive transference demands. Loewald's views (1960) are importantly related to these, perhaps, in a sense, complementary to them. An important connotation of these countertransference studies is the diminution of the rigid status barrier between analyst and analysand. They point to the patient in the physician, the child in the parent (a sort of latent or potential "seesaw," to modify Phyllis Greenacre's [1954] "tilted relationship"!). This intellectual tendency can be, and often is, overdone, just as the magical power of the countertransference to determine the course of treatment has become an almost euphoric overwrought mystical belief among certain younger therapists, and, as a concept, a formidable source of resistance in the technically informed patient. Such exaggerated views, when not of specific and immediate emotional genesis, or due to ignorance, may be connected with a general lack of conviction regarding the efficacy of the therapist's own analysis, or of the effectiveness of the interpretative method. There may indeed be a general lack of awareness or acceptance of the power that the original "tilt" lends to the patient's transference. In the final analysis it is this "tilt" in the situation, and also (very importantly) the actuality of its representation in the respective emotional and intellectual states of the participants, on which we must rely. If temperately considered, a view of the relationship that gives great weight to the countertransference, is productively important. It places the operational attitude and technique of the analyst in better perspective, as an integration of several important factors that *always include* the countertransference, and it permits an examination of nuances of technical decision on a much more illuminating and genuinely dependable basis than *pure* precedent, or rule-of-thumb, or pseudo-mathematical certainty. Thus, to give a patient in pain some aspirin or not, to inspect his eye for a foreign body or not, to tell him promptly where one is going on vacation or not, may be right or wrong in either alternative, depending on the analyst's own specific motivation or anxiety, as against the patient's actual need, or the objective clinical indications of the moment, weighed against the continuing and rationally interpreted conventions of technique. It is less likely that *any* maneuver, assuming the adherence to basic broad technical principles, will create significant analytic distortion, if executed with genuine and exclusive therapeutic intentions appropriate to the need, than a maneuver or *default of maneuver*, based entirely or largely on exhibitionistic or seductive or anxious or compulsive reasons, however respectable the latter may seem. These principles, of course, assume the general analytic framework, and the maintenance of the principle of abstinence, insofar as it does not conflict with overriding human requirements, or does not reach beyond the subtle limits that I have sought to discuss earlier. (See Scheunert's interesting examples [1961], in both directions.) The issue of the increment of unanswered innocuous questions, of injudiciously withheld expressions of reasonable human interest, where the human relationship requires them, I have dealt with as a matter of general and objective technical principle. Still it is not unrelated to the emotional position of the analyst; for a "rule" obviously has a different meaning to an anxious or sadistic or compulsive person than to an individual not thus burdened. The general problem is germane to the perennial interest in why (beyond the usual verities or clichés) an individual becomes a physician, and specifically why he then chooses this physically and emotionally inhibited specialty, which depends so largely on benignly purposive frustration of the patient, on occasional informed talking, and possibly even more on extended and perceptive listening. It is not unreasonable to assume that, with the myriad individual factors, some general or common countertransference element enters the overdetermination both of choice of the medical profession and of the specialty that holds a unique position in the minds of medical men and patients alike. The uniqueness of this position is perhaps best suggested by the remarkably frequent query of the naive patient: "Are you *really* an M.D.?" or "Are you a *medical* doctor too?" This is in a different intellectual realm, but surely related to the more informed discussions as to whether analysis is a branch of medicine, or a special development in psychology, or an entirely independent discipline. I would suggest that, apart from more usual considerations, the fascination and strain of analytic work are related to the same phenomenon which evokes the *a priori* patient reaction to it. I have in mind the state of separation and of infantile deprivation that are integral in the situation, and the effort to utilize these toward solutions more favorable than those originally evolved. Setting aside the specific *phase* problems and other qualitative aspects of individual countertransference, there will still be quantitative individual variations, tending toward excessive deprivation or overindulgence (for example), revolving about the central and necessary principle of abstinence in the psychoanalytic situation, whose skillful administration is a part of the basic occupational commitment. Insofar as "weaning" is the great focal prototype of abstinence or deprivation, I call attention to the historical vicissitudes of the word *wean* (*Oxford English Dictionary,* Vol. 12 [1933]) in which even a secondary (nonetymologic) development of the affirmative meaning "wean to" has become obsolete. This is no doubt intertwined with cultural considerations far beyond our present scope of interest. However, it is also symbolically related to the (obsolescent?) technical mood, which I feel can be restored to analytic work, with advantage.

REFERENCES

Breuer, J. and Freud, S. (1895). Studies on Hysteria. *Standard Edition, 2.* London: Hogarth Press, 1955.

Ferenczi, S. (1919). On the Technique of Psychoanalysis (Part IV—The Control of the Counter-Transference). In: *Further Contributions to the Theory and Technique of Psycho-Analysis.* London: Hogarth Press, 1926, pp. 177–188.

Fliess, R. (1949). Silence and Verbalization: A Supplement to the Theory of the Analytic Rule. *International Journal of Psycho-Analysis, 30:* 21–30.

Freud, A. (1954). The Widening Scope of Indications for Psychoanalysis, Discussion. *Journal of the American Psychoanalytic Association, 2:* 607–620.

Freud, S. (1887–1902). *The Origins of Psychoanalysis.* New York: Basic Books, 1954.

———. (1905). Fragment of an Analysis of a Case of Hysteria. *Standard Edition, 7:* 3–122. London: Hogarth Press, 1953.

———. (1914). Remembering, Repeating and Working-Through. *Standard Edition, 12:* 145–156. London: Hogarth Press, 1958.

———. (1937). Analysis Terminable and Interminable. *Collected Papers, 5:* 316–357. London: Hogarth Press, 1950.

Glover, E. (1928 [1938, 1955]). *The Technique of Psychoanalysis.* New York: International Universities Press (Part II, Questionnaire, 1938, pp. 259–350), new rev. ed., 1955.

Greenacre, P. (1954). The Role of Transference. *Journal of the American Psychoanalytic Association, 2:* 671–684.

Jones, E. (1953–1957). *The Life and Work of Sigmund Freud,* 3 vols. New York: Basic Books.

Lagache, D. (1953). Some Aspects of Transference. *International Journal of Psycho-Analysis, 34:* 1–10.

Lewin, B. D. (1946a). Counter-transference in the Technique of Medical Practice. *Psychosomatic Medicine, 8:* 195–199.

————. (1946b). Sleep, the Mouth, and the Dream Screen. *Psychoanalytic Quarterly, 15:* 419–434.

————. (1955). Dream Psychology and the Analytic Situation. *Psychoanalytic Quarterly, 23:* 487–510.

Loewald, H. W. (1960). On the Therapeutic Action of Psycho-Analysis. *International Journal of Psycho-Analysis, 41:* 1–18.

Money-Kyrle, R. E. (1956). Normal Counter-Transference and Some of Its Deviations. *International Journal of Psycho-Analysis, 37:* 360–366.

Nunberg, H. (1951). Transference and Reality. *International Journal of Psycho-Analysis, 32:* 1–9.

Racker, H. (1957). The Meanings and Uses of Countertransference. *Psychoanalytic Quarterly, 26:* 303–357.

Reich, A. (1960). Further Remarks on Counter-Transference. *International Journal of Psycho-Analysis, 41:* 389–395.

Scheunert, G. (1961). Die Abstinenzregel in der Psychoanalyse. *Psyche, 15:* 105–123.

Silverberg, W. V. (1948). The Concept of Transference. *Psychoanalytic Quarterly, 17:* 303–321.

Spitz, R. A. (1956). Transference: The Analytical Setting and Its Prototype. *International Journal of Psycho-Analysis, 37:* 380–385.

Tower, L. E. (1956). Countertransference. *Journal of the American Psychoanalytic Association, 4:* 224–255.

Weigert, E. (1954). Counter-Transference and Self-Analysis of the Psycho-Analyst. *International Journal of Psycho-Analysis, 35:* 242–246.

16. Countertransference: The Therapist's Contribution to Treatment

Lawrence Epstein and Arthur H. Feiner

AN OVERVIEW

In this paper there is no intention to offer a complete review of the literature on the topic of countertransference. Langs (1976) has already published comprehensive and scholarly chapters that review the literature on countertransference from the time of Freud's earliest statement on the phenomenon (Freud 1910), to the significant papers published as late as 1976. We are interested here in tracing the development of the key themes and issues from their inception to their current status in contemporary psychoanalytic thinking.

One must start with a recognition of the incisiveness of Freud's thought. His earliest remarks on the identification of countertransference, in that famous paragraph whose second sentence begins with, "We have become aware of the 'countertransference' which arises in the physician as a result of the patient's influence on his unconscious feelings . . . ," also contains the phrase "he shall begin his activity with a self-analysis and continually carry it deeper while he is making his observations on his patients" (Freud 1910). And two years later Freud (1912) wrote that the analyst "must turn his own unconscious like a receptive organ towards the transmitting unconscious of the patient. . . . [So] the doctor's unconscious mind is able . . . to reconstruct [the patient's unconscious] . . ." (Freud 1912). These two thematic constructs, countertransference as a hindrance, and the doctor's use of his own unconscious to understand the patient, have intertwined, like a double helix, throughout the historical development of psychoanalytic conceptions of countertransference. And we might add, the theory of treatment, itself.

Racker (1953), in Argentina; Winnicott (1949), Heimann (1950), and Little (1951), in England; in the United States Fromm-Reichmann (1950), Mable Blake Cohen (1952), Thompson, Crowley, and Tauber (1952) and Tauber (1954) have made several significant contributions to the issue. These analysts turned to the *data* of countertransference to seek a better understanding of the patient in the ongoing process of psychoanalysis. We specifically focus in this paper on the seminal contributions of Heimann (1950), Little (1951), Winnicott (1949), and Racker (1953). True, the Balints (1939) had commented on the analyst's subtle influence on the patient's transference; Horney (1939) had earlier likened the countertransference to an aspect of the analyst's characterology, and Sharpe (1947) had mentioned both conscious and unconscious aspects of countertransference. But it was Heimann (1950), Little (1951, 1957), Winnicott (1949), and Racker (1953) who actually broke through the barrier of the prevailing classical view that countertransference was simply a hindrance to effective psycho-analytic work. Their ideas concerning the therapeutic usefulness of countertransference data have foreshadowed all subsequent developments, and their papers are even today the most widely quoted in the literature. In fact, Racker's elaboration of countertransference theory, and of the use to which countertransference data may be put in clinical practice, remains probably the most comprehensive and original contribution by any single author.

We will consider also the polar classical position of Annie Reich (1951, 1960, 1966), who holds to the viewpoint that ultimately, countertransference is a hindrance to the analysis. Finally we will consider some of the bases for resistance to the continued scientific study of the use of countertransference in both the classical and the interpersonal schools.

Note that more than thirty years passed before Freud's position that countertransference was little more than a hindrance was effectively challenged. It remained for the late forties and early fifties before marked interest in countertransference emerged throughout the psychoanalytic community. The challenge took the form of respecting the anti-therapeutic aspects of countertransference, while sensing the possibility that by its study analysts could derive and formulate interventions that might enhance the therapeutic process. We shall return to this issue when we discuss the possible reasons why the challenge and reformulation of the classical concept of countertransference had to wait this long. First let us review the ideas of the seminal quartet.

Paula Heimann:

Heimann in her brief paper "On Countertransference" (1950) offered several revisions of the concept. First, she extended the term to include *all* of the feelings that the therapist experiences toward his patient, no longer restricting it, as did Freud to the pathological components of the therapist's response. She went on to remark that

The aim of the analyst's own analysis . . . is not to turn him into a mechanical brain which can produce interpretations on the basis of a purely intellectual procedure, but to enable him, to *sustain* the feelings which are stirred in him as opposed to discharging them (as does the patient), in order to *subordinate* them to the analytic task in which he functions as the patient's mirror reflection [p. 82].

She considered "the analyst's emotional response to his patient within the analytic situation . . . one of the most important tools for his work. The analyst's countertransference is an instrument of research into the patient's unconscious" (p. 81).

She therefore recommended that the analyst's evenly hovering, freely working attention to the patient's associations be extended as well to the doctor's own emotional responses. Echoing Freud (1912), she wrote pointedly:

Our basic assumption is that the analyst's unconscious understands that of his patient. This rapport on the deep level comes to the surface in the form of feelings which the analyst notices in response to his patient, in his 'counter-transference'.

Thus Heimann, freeing himself of the popular view of countertransference as "bad" and consequently a barrier to understanding, turned her attention to its potential value in furthering the analytic work.

While most analysts would reject Heimann's perhaps overstated conclusion that the countertransference is "the patient's *creation*" and "part of the patient's personality," there are those who describe typical clinical situations in which this may be nearly true. Spotnitz (1979), discussing the "narcissistic countertransference" writes:

A severely disturbed patient may appear to be totally unaware of the therapist's presence and totally preoccupied with himself. The therapist may then tend to focus on himself and become totally unaware of the patient. . . . When a very depressed patient talks repetitively about committing suicide, I suddenly experience strong anger. I become aware of urges to get out of the office for the day, or get rid of the case. Schizophrenic patients early in treatment characteristically verbalize feelings of emptiness, strangeness, confusion, and hopelessness. The therapist may then be assailed by feelings of helplessness and hopelessness.

Grinberg (1979), elaborating on projective counter-identification points out that the unconscious content rejected by the analysand may be violently projected onto the analyst who, as the recipient of such projective identifications, will suffer their effects and react as if he had acquired and assimilated the parts projected onto him in a "real and concrete way."

Finally, when it came to what the therapist should *do* with his countertransference, Heimann was quite explicit. It should not be communicated to the patient, she advised, but should be *used* as a source of insight into the patient's conflicts and defenses. This remains the widespread view among analysts of almost all schools, especially when working with the more integrated patient (Langs 1976, Sandler 1976).

Margaret Little:

In her 1951 paper as well as in another appearing in 1957, Little placed the analyst's countertransference at the center of the therapeutic work with severely disturbed patients. It is the countertransference, she wrote, that often has to do the work.

She observed that these patients are often successfully treated by beginning therapists who are not afraid to allow their unconscious impulses a considerable degree of freedom, and by experienced analysts who trust their unconscious impulses. She recommended that when an interpretation has been mistimed or wrongly emphasized, the analyst should admit his error to the patient and—unless this is contraindicated—explain its origin in his unconscious countertransference. And, she commented, this is essential for the progress of the analysis and contributes to the patient's developing a confidence in the honesty and good will of an analyst who is also seen as having the right to make mistakes. Furthermore, it demonstrates the universality of transference in all relationships.

Little suggested that not only does the therapist hold up a "mirror" to the patient, but the patient also holds one up to the therapist. In addition to his fantasies about the analyst, the patient often becomes aware of real feelings in the analyst even before the analyst himself is fully aware of them himself. She noted that, "What comes [from the patient] may on occasion be a piece of real counter-transference interpretation for the analyst" (1951, p. 39).

Thus in her (1951) paper Little extended the Balints' suggestion (1939) as to the analyst's influence on the patient's transference, and introduced a view that subsequently has been elaborated by Langs (1976). That view is that the patient is indeed exquisitely sensitive to, and influenced by the therapist's unconscious countertransference as well as his deliberate interventions. Harold Searles has also developed this theme throughout his writings (1958, 1978).

Little also noted that the act of interpreting transference actually contains an implicit denial that the analyst is indeed behaving as had the earlier parental figure.

In her 1957 paper, Little commented that the severely disturbed patient constantly tests the analyst to see whether he has sufficient ego strength to deal with his own instinct tensions. If this reveals that the analyst cannot successfully manage his own tensions, the patient will be shattered. This statement presaged Bion's view (1962, 1963, 1970) that the analyst must function as an active container and metabolizer of the patient's projective identifications and projected inner contents. This view has also influenced Kernberg (1965) and several others in particular, Issacharoff (1979), Langs (1976), Feiner (1979), Grinberg (1979), McDougall (1979), Epstein (1979b), and Fordham (1979).

In this paper, Little went even farther in her recommendations for the communication of the therapist's countertransference reactions to severely disturbed patients. She wrote that the analyst must feel free to react, even primitively and spontaneously at times, since this type of patient needs to experience the analyst as one human being with whom it is possible to have genuine contact. It is essential therefore that this patient discover that the analyst can bear the patient's tensions as well as their discharge, and that there are some things that even the analyst cannot stand. A patient's paranoid anxiety, Little advised, can be relieved only in a direct way through the experience of the analyst as a human, that is, a limited being. This point is further elaborated by Epstein (1979b). In this connection, Spotnitz (1969, 1976) and Searles (1958, 1978) also have recommended that therapists selectively communicate feelings induced in them by schizophrenic and borderline patients.

D. W. Winnicott:

Winnicott's pithy ''Hate in the Countertransference'' (1949) dealt with several core issues. He distinguished the idiosyncratic from the therapeutically useful countertransference, in classifying its phenomena as follows:

1. Abnormality in countertransference, and set relationships and identifications that are under repression in the analyst. . . .
   It is evident here, that the analyst needs more analysis. . . .
2. The identifications and tendencies belonging to an analyst's personal experiences

and personal development which provide the positive setting for his analytic work and make his work different in quality from that of any other analyst

3. the truly objective countertransference, (or . . .) the analyst's love and hate in reaction to the actual personality and behavior of the patient based on objective observation [p. 195].

Winnicott then suggested, anticipating Little (1951):

that if an analyst is to analyze psychotics or antisocials, he must be able to be so thoroughly aware of the countertransference that he can sort out and study his *objective* reactions to the patient. These will include hate. Countertransference phenomena will at times be the important things in the analysis (p. 195).

"A main task of the analyst is to maintain objectivity," he stressed, adding that "a special case of this is to hate the patient objectively" (p. 196). He then went on to discuss how certain patients repeatedly arouse intense hate in the analyst and to indicate that for these patients the evocation of hatred in the other is part of a maturational process. As was characteristic of him, Winnicott made his point succinctly: "If the patient seeks objective or justified hate he must be able to reach it, else he cannot feel he can reach objective love" (p. 199).

In this essay Winnicott did the following:

1. He went far beyond the traditional view of countertransference as hindrance and taboo, making an excellent case for its therapeutic usefulness.

2. He indicated that countertransference was useful as a source of information not only about the patient, but about the ongoing process of the analysis as well.

3. He emphasized that the analyst's intense countertransference feelings, when "objectively" evoked by the patient, may be needed as feedback, and that this need for feedback is nothing less than a maturational need.

4. He noted the analyst's necessity to detoxify intense countertransference feelings so as to be able to continue functioning constructively with his patient.

Winnicott's schema of the objective and subjective components of the countertransference has been utilized by Spotnitz (1979), Marshall (1979), and Epstein (1979a). An elaboration of the therapeutic usefulness of hate appears in the paper by Epstein (1979a).

Heinrich Racker:

Racker's papers concerning countertransference appeared in English language psychoanalytic journals between 1953 and 1958 (The Spanish originals had begun to appear somewhat earlier) and were collected in his *Transference and Countertransference* (1968). In these papers, more completely than any other writer in the psychoanalytic literature, Racker addressed himself to a full study of the issue.[1] He attempted to penetrate the countertransference experience to its depths, illuminating its meanings in detailed patient-therapist transactions, and formulating interpretations based on his understanding. He delineated the *normal* predispositions shared by analysts, any of whom under certain conditions can find themselves in the emotional position of the child vis-à-vis the patient-parent. Racker termed this complex of predispositions and its manifestations the countertransference neurosis, implying that it is as natural and normal a development in the analyst in response to his patient as is the transference neurosis in the patient. Feiner (1979) and Issacharoff (1979) have developed this theme. In 1949, when Racker presented his paper on the countertransference neurosis (Racker 1953) and for many years after, the popularly accepted conception among classical analysts (e.g. Reich 1951)[2] was that the normal ego state of the analyst should be hovering, and contemplative and emotionally neutral. The occurrence of strong emotions in response to a patient would be considered, according to this position, an aberration, signifying a pathological problem within the analyst. Racker's notion of countertransference neurosis rejects this view. To him the countertransference neurosis is inevitable and, once understood and accepted as such, yields easily to self analysis.

Even those instances in which the analyst finds himself in the child position can illuminate the patient's ongoing transference. Once the analyst has identified his own emotional state, he is able to consider the questions "Why have I fallen into this position now?", "What has this to do with the analytic process?", "What internal self and object relations might the patient be enacting with me?", "Do my feelings indicate that he needs my love, or that he wants to triumph over me?", "Is the patient from the position of his child-self relating to me as if I were his superego?", and "Do my feelings indicate that he wants me to punish or criticize or demean him?" Thus, to Racker, the totality of the therapist's countertransference, even though it may be dominated by idiosyncratic or even pathological components, is likely to yield significant information about the patient's immediate ego state.

Unfortunately Racker did not present his ideas as clearly as we have stated them here. He wrote in a Freudian-Kleinian metapsychological framework that does not make for easy reading (Hunt and Issacharoff 1977). We believe, however, that our translation of Racker's *experience-distant* terminology into *experience-near* language (Kohut 1978) accurately reflects his thought.

Racker's classification of countertransference reactions is systematic, pre-cise, and, above all, clinically useful. He distinguishes between the *direct* and the *indirect* countertransference. Direct countertransference is a response *to the patient*. Indirect countertransference is a response to an emotionally significant other person outside the therapeutic setting. This might for ex-ample, be anyone whose good opinion of the therapist's work with the patient the therapist might be concerned about. It might be someone in the profes-sional community, a referral source, a supervisor, or a training committee at a psychoanalytic training institute. It could be anyone who knows the patient, colleague, relative, or friend.

Racker further differentiated direct countertransference into two processes: *concordant identifications* and *complementary identifications*. Concordant identifications are empathic responses to the patient's thoughts and feelings. In Racker's language they are identifications with the patient's ego or id. In the case of complementary identifications, the analyst finds himself in the emotional position of some projected (unwanted) part of the patient's self or superego. For example, the therapist might find himself in an adversary position vis-à-vis the patient. He might experience himself as persecuted by the patient or he might even feel punitive toward the patient, which is typical with the violent-prone (King 1976). Racker uses Klein's theory of projective identification to account for complementary identifications in the therapist. Projective identification is an unconscious primitive, aggressively, self-preservative operation, involving two stages, splitting and projection. In this way, according to the theory the patient rids himself of either a toxic introject or some unwanted part of himself, and then identifies the therapist with the split off aspect of his personality. The therapist may then experience these feelings and impulses toward the patient. He is likely also to feel pressured to engage in counterprojective processes toward the patient. If, for instance, the therapist is made to feel like a bad person, his normal inclination will be to see the patient as bad. Racker remarks that such reactions follow the *lex talionis* ("eye for an eye, tooth for a tooth"). By restraining his own inclination to follow the talionic principle, *containing* the patient's projected impulses and feelings, and then addressing these contents analytically, the therapist will be in a favorable position to understand the transference-countertransference matrix and formulate an interpretative intervention. Racker assumes the universality of the talionic principle as well as of projective identification, thereby linking the unconscious processes in the patient with those in the therapist. As such they become fundamental to his understanding of countertransference processes and his conceptualization of countertransference theory. Projective identification has been used to account for a variety of countertransference phenomena in papers by Issacharoff (1979), McDougall (1979), Grinberg (1979), Meltzer (1979), Epstein (1979a and 1979b), Boyer (1979), and Kernberg (1965).

With numerous clinical vignettes Racker illustrates how the analyst's concordant and complementary identifications with the patient may be addressed as data providing important clues concerning the self experience of the patient, and his experience of his internal and early objects. According to Racker, therefore, countertransference is the most reliable guide to knowing what, in the patient's communications or behavior, the analyst should respond to at any given moment. Even countertransference reactions of great intensity may serve as aids to understanding. While Little and Winnicott have underscored the inevitability of such intense reactions in response to disturbed patients and even recommended the selective communication of such reactions, it was Racker who first showed how these reactions may be used as tools to develop a more trenchant understanding of the patient. This view is radically at odds with the conventional orthodox emphasis on the therapist's intense emotional reactions as pathological, and has been developed by Kernberg (1965) with borderline patients, and by Searles (1978) and Spotnitz (1969, 1976) with both psychotic and borderline patients.

A careful scrutiny of Racker's work reveals the caution in his recommendations concerning what the therapist should *do* with his countertransference reactions. He recommended that the analyst first develop an understanding of the patient's internal processes in the here and now, and that he then use the countertransference as an aid in formulating appropriate interpretations. Racker was cautious concerning the direct communication of countertransference reactions, but did not rule it out. He advised, however, that ''we need extensive and detailed study of the inherent problems of communication of countertransference.'' Gitelson (1952) too recommended communicating countertransference only when necessary to further the analysis.

We turn now to one classical position on countertransference, most eloquently represented by Annie Reich (1951), a position decidedly at odds with those we have discussed.

Reich (1951, 1960, 1966) sharply rejects the notion that countertransference can in any way be used as a therapeutic tool, either as data for understanding the patient or for communication. The second of her three papers on countertransference (1960), ''Further Remarks on Counter-Transference,'' is a strong polemic against the position advanced by Heimann, Little, and Racker. Reich states that to use the analyst's emotional responses and countertransference manifestations to understand the patient is really ''a substitute for empathy.'' In her 1950 paper, Heimann had presented a clinical example of how she came to understand her countertransference reaction of worry and anxiety in response to a patient. Her eventual formulation was that this was the counterpart of the patient's sadistically tinged fantasies about the analyst who was seen as a defective object. To this Reich comments that

Something interfered with the process of immediate, intuitive understanding. The analyst reacted to the patient's striving with an emotional response of her own. She did not just 'know' that the patient was involved in an acting out of his transference, since she failed to identify with him and to detach herself again from such trial identification. For this process she substituted a *retranslation* of her own feelings into those of the patient [Reich's italics].

To Reich, then, Heimann is converting a fault into a virtue. She does not however, consider the possibility that Heimann's understanding of her countertransference might have enhanced the therapeutic process.

Reich stands on firmer ground when she attacks Little's recommendations for the free expression of countertransference feelings with disturbed patients.

But such therapeutic endeavors are not psychoanalysis, even though they may be based on the fundamental insights of analytic psychology. . . . Any differentiated subtle understanding of the interaction of the various psychic structures; any detailed careful analysis of defenses; any effort to analyze ego pathology and correct it is left behind. Instead, there is an attempt to work directly with the id and to exert immediate influence upon the object relations. Such an approach disregards Freud's most important formulation concerning the therapeutic aim of analysis: 'Where id was, ego shall be.' Therefore, no lasting effect can be expected from these methods (pp. 393–394).

However, her argument is arbitrary and mechanistic, omitting any consideration of a possible integration of the two positions. In fact, Little carefully detailed the usefulness not only of the communication of countertransference reactions but of interpretations as well, and stressed that countertransference revelation or the direct impact of the analyst's emotions can break ''through the wall of resistance when interpretation is to no avail.'' Tauber (1954, 1979) has elaborated this position.

While Reich writes of countertransference as a ''prerequisite'' of psychoanalysis, her attack on the therapeutic usefulness does not distinguish between countertransference as an inner experience, to be digested, scrutinized, clarified, understood, and subsequently harnessed for therapeutic understanding, and countertransference as directly, impulsively enacted or discharged. She rejects intense countertransference experience as *ipso facto* pathological. She states patently,

A neutralized cathexis of the patient is *never* relinquished. Thus, the analyst *never* loses sight of the patient as a separate being and at no time feels his own identity changes. This enables him to remain *uninvolved*, [p. 391, our italics].

Thus, the analyst is simply not supposed to have intense emotional reactions to the patient, and must remain, *uninvolved*. This disregards Freud's recognition that the psychoanalyst has feelings toward his patients and conflicts aroused by them (Sandler et al. 1973). Though respectful of Heimann's "honesty" about countertransference, Reich acerbically comments that countertransference "as such is not helpful." She then remarks, "But the readiness to acknowledge its existence and the ability to overcome it is."

Reich firmly rejects Racker's conjecture that the countertransference is dominated by the *lex talionis*, as well as the idea that typical countertransference reactions may arise *in response to* a patient's covert processes. She states that "all such notions about a typical content of counter-transference represent schematizations and a narrowing down of the beautiful variety of psychic functioning." The usefulness of what Reich calls "free countertransference" as a tool for understanding the patient is arbitrarily dismissed.

Reich's arguments are not based on empirical considerations, nor does she recommend any further scientific study of countertransference for its potential therapeutic uses. We do not believe that Reich's views are currently shared by a majority of classical analysts. Those who hold that strong emotional reactions are necessarily due to empathic failures based on the therapist's psychopathology are far fewer now than there were in 1960. The view that countertransference reactions can be useful for understanding the patient seems to be gaining acceptance, especially in working with psychotic and borderline patients, among analysts of various orientations. Tauber (1979) considers the classical "anticountertransference" position to be an unconscious countertransference reaction. Yet it is true that techniques involving the direct communication of countertransference reactions continue to be widely rejected or, at best, viewed with considerable skepticism (Langs 1976).

During the last few years interest in countertransference as a valuable component in psychoanalysis and psychoanalytic psychotherapy has risen with increasing spirit and vitality among the various psychoanalytic schools. Professional journals abound in papers on the subject. Definitions, however, still vary, with at least three conceptions currently in use: (1) the *totalistic conception*, in which *all* feelings and attitudes of the therapist toward the patient are considered countertransference; (2) the *classical conception*, in which countertransference is viewed as the unconscious resistive reaction of the analyst to the transference of the patient, or parts of the patient, and as containing both neurotic and nonneurotic elements; and, (3) the view of countertransference as the natural, role-responsive, necessary *complement* or *counterpart* to the transference of the patient, or to his style of relatedness.

Furthermore, we can identify four working orientations to countertransference, that is, the way in which countertransference is actually used by different therapists:

1. Countertransference is attended to when "difficulties arise," when the therapist experiences emotional disturbances, or disturbances of attention or concentration. Such interferences are then subjected to self-analysis.

2. Interferences in the analyst's efforts caused by disturbances in the analyst's emotional state are studied primarily in order to gain an understanding of the patient's contribution.

3. The totality of the countertransference is used as essential data for understanding the patient in the here and now. Accordingly the countertransference is frequently considered when formulating interventions and strategies. Interventions may be restricted to interpretations; countertransference fantasies may be directly communicated to the patient, or induced countertransference feelings may be communicated "as needed" by the patient. This orientation usually includes the view that the therapist's internal silent processing of countertransferential disturbances is essential to the further integration of the patient. This is especially important with the more disturbed patient.

4. Countertransference inevitably infiltrates the patient's unconscious process. Such infiltrations must be constantly monitored by studying the patient's associations and responses, and subsequently interpreted.

Considering the career of countertransference throughout psychoanalytic history we note two nodal points: the flurry of interest surfacing in the late forties and early fifties, and now its resurgence in the seventies. The question naturally occurs to us, "Why the long and almost unbroken history of resistance among psychoanalysts to the study of countertransference?" Although Freud initially treated transference as an obstacle to treatment he then shifted his view to involve it as a useful tool in the psychoanalytic effort. He never did this with countertransference. Bird (1972) reminds us that Freud considered transference "a mental structure of the greatest magnitude." In "An Autobiographical Study" (1925), Freud wrote that transference "is a universal phenomenon of the human mind . . . and in fact dominates the whole of each person's relations to his human environment" (p. 42). But, Bird writes sadly, Freud never followed this idea up, an idea he had in fact introduced as early as his postscript to the case of Dora (1905). Bird points out that Freud in his "Analysis Terminable and Interminable" (1937) "in an otherwise masterful discussion of difficulties contributed by the individuality of the analyst, . . . fails almost completely to direct these difficulties to their most obvious source, the countertransference" (p. 275). For thirty years Freud toyed with but never thoroughly worked through his own conception of transference-countertransference phenomena. Yet despite his never changing his mind about countertransference being a hindrance, requiring mastery through analysis on the part of the analyst, he did as we have remarked, offer at various times, those subtle and exciting suggestions concerning the value of the analyst's unconscious processes to analytic work. Hence his statement (Freud 1912) that the analyst:

must turn his own unconscious like a receptive organ toward the transmitting unconscious of the patient . . . adjust himself to the patient as a telephone receiver is adjusted to the transmitting microphone. Just as the receiver converts back into sound waves the electric oscillations . . . , so the doctor's unconscious is able, from the derivatives of the unconscious which are communicated to him, to reconstruct that unconscious, which has determined the patient's free associations [Freud 1912, pp. 115–116].

And again: ". . . everyone possesses in his own unconscious an instrument with which he can interpret the utterances of the unconscious in other people" (Freud 1913, p. 320).

These are typical of the ways Freud hinted at what might be a fruitful area for discovery. And so again we must ask why, from 1912 to 1950, did interest in these kinds of complex processes lag, and why did it take another twenty years before it resurfaced? Racker (1953) provides some insight here.

The lack of scientific investigation of countertransference must be due to rejection by analysts of their own countertransferences—a rejection that represents unresolved struggles with their own primitive anxiety and guilt. These struggles are closely connected with those infantile ideals that survive because of deficiencies in the personal analysis of just those transference problems that later affect the analyst's countertransference. These deficiencies in the training analysis are in turn partly due to countertransference problems insufficiently solved in the training analyst. . . . Thus we are in a vicious circle but we can see where a breach must be made. We must begin by revision of our feelings about our own countertransference and try to overcome our own infantile ideals more thoroughly, accepting more fully the fact that we are still children and neurotics even when we are adults and analysts. Only in this way—by better overcoming our rejection of countertransference—can we achieve the same result in candidates.

The insufficient dissolution of these idealizations and underlying anxieties and guilt-feelings leads to special difficulties when the child becomes an adult and the analysand an analyst, for the analyst unconsciously requires of himself that he be fully identified with these ideals. I think that it is at least partly for this reason that the Oepidus complex of the child toward his parents, and of the patient toward his analyst, has been so much more fully considered than that of the parents towards their children and of the analyst towards the analysand. For the same basic reason transference has been dealt with much more than countertransference. . . .

The repression of countertransference (and other pathological fates that it may meet) necessarily leads to deficiencies in the analysis of transference, which in turn lead to the repression and other mishandling of countertransference as soon as the candidate becomes an analyst. It is a heritage from generation to generation, similar to the heritage of idealizations and denials concerning the imagos of the parents, which continue working even when the child becomes a father or mother. The child's mythology is prolonged in the mythology of the analytic situation, the analyst himself being partially subject to it and collaborating unconsciously in its maintenance in the candidate. . . .

No one, of course, denies the existence of subjective factors in the analyst and of countertransference in itself; but there seems to exist an important difference between what is generally acknowledged in practice and the real state of affairs. The first distortion of truth in the 'myth of the analytic situation' is that analysis is an interaction between a sick person and a healthy one. The truth is that it is in interaction between two personalities, in both of which the ego is under pressure from the id, the superego, and the external world; each personality has its internal and external dependencies, anxieties, and pathological defenses; each is also a child with his internal parents; and each of these whole personalities—that of the analysand and that of the analyst—responds to every event of the analytic situation. Besides these similarities between the personalities of analyst and analysand, there also exist differences, and one of these is in 'objectivity.' The analyst's objectivity consists mainly in a certain attitude toward his own subjectivity and countertransference. The neurotic (obsessive) ideal of objectivity leads to repression and blocking of subjectivity and so to the apparent fulfillment of the myth of the 'analyst without anxiety or anger.' The other neurotic extreme is that of 'drowning' in the countertransference. True objectivity is based upon a form of internal division that enables the analyst to make himself (his own countertransference and subjectivity) the object of his continuous observation and analysis. This position also enables him to be relatively 'objective' towards the analysand [Racker 1953, pp. 130–135].

Racker's analysis of the unconscious resistance to an evolving understanding of countertransference data may be more generally applicable to classical analysts than to those analysts of the less orthodox schools.

Racker's contributions have been late in reaching a substantial number of psychoanalysts in the United States. One reason for Racker's not being studied until lately in the United States is that he wrote in a Kleinian metaphor that is uncongenial to a large sector of the psychoanalytic community (Hunt and Issacharoff 1977). Furthermore the fact is, as we have stated, that Racker is difficult to read.

Harry Stack Sullivan (1953) and Erich Fromm (1947), stressed as early as the late thirties and early forties the limits and fallibility of the analyst in his participation with his patient. What is important to grasp is that the so-called egalitarian attitudes of the neofreudians, the "democratizing" of the analytic situation by members of the interpersonal and other less orthodox schools, did not have their origins simply in the ideologies and value systems of the theoreticians. The "political" overtones of typically American antiauthoritarian attitudes in the consulting rooms were actually less relevant than the epistemological ones.

When Sullivan (1953) introduced the concept of participant observation in the late thirties, he was already paying homage to the ubiquitous influences of other scientific disciplines on his thinking. Einstein's notion of the significance of the position of the observer (that it influences the nature of the data), Heisenberg's principle of indeterminacy (the act of observation influences the data), the operationalism of American pragmatism, to all of which Sullivan had been exposed, funneled into his one-genus hypothesis; that is, that we are all more simply human than otherwise. The impinging demands of his therapeutic work with schizophrenics was still another important factor. Sullivan (1953), together with Fromm-Reichmann (1950) "humanized" the therapist. That is, they pointed to the significance of the analyst as a real object. They rejected the orthodox "mirror" concept as the analyst's *only* function, not because it was based on an inadequate theory of technique, but because they believed that the opacity of the mirror-analyst and the separation of the patient's affectivity from the analyst's were impossible to maintain in light of the recognition of a field of forces in the consulting room. The idea, was also advanced, that awareness and confrontation of the myth of the analysts' anonymity actually furthered the work (Fromm-Reichmann 1950, Cohen 1952).

Accordingly, Fromm (1947), for whom the analyst was a "rational authority," rejected the idea that anyone, simply by virtue of being an analyst and having undergone a training analysis, is therefore the possessor of superior mental health. Freud had touched on this in his "Analysis Terminable and Interminable" (1937, p. 247). In supervision and in seminars Fromm repeatedly stressed that the temptation to believe the fiction of the analyst's superiority could only lead the analyst into the major pitfall of the profession, that is, unconscious despair. Fromm believed that psychoanalysts must face endlessly in themselves the same regressive forces others are heir to, and he therefore advised that analysts engage in lifelong self-analysis. This was the same advice that Freud offered in 1910 (and later in 1937), but Fromm went beyond the need to gain mastery over "complexes," or the "abrasiveness" of the derepressed. He was concerned lest those forces insidiously erode an analyst's potential for growing and living fully.

Candidates in training at the William Alanson White Institute and elsewhere, have traditionally been encouraged to scrutinize and discuss openly their countertransference reactions in seminars and in supervision. This kind of openness to countertransference perhaps approaches the monitoring function originally recommended by Freud (1910). But this reasonable concern with the protection of the patient from the potentially damaging effects of the analyst's inner processes and their products, a concern shared by all serious analysts, lends itself, unfortunately, to restricting the aim of studying countertransference to a simple uncovering of the analyst's residual pathology. We view this tendency as the "rational factor" that has impeded research into the data of countertransference. It has been extremely difficult to make the shift from regarding the analyst's emotional or affective reactions as errors from which the patient naturally needs to be protected, to regarding these responses as significant data with a potential for illuminating the therapeutic situation. And Freud's ambivalence on this point certainly did not help.

Some of the factors that have reawakened the profession's interest following the period of dormancy from the fifties to the seventies, have been neatly and tersely commented on by Witenberg (1979). He writes: "As one views society as a whole, one sees increasing openness and candor in all sectors . . . a diminution in the power of authority—whether it be religious or secular. . . . The breakdown of institutions such as the family . . . has been accompanied by a spate of literature that analyzes authority roles." And he further credits the "growing maturity of psychoanalysis" as well as "the widespread acceptance in the field of the fact that each of us can potentially be the other."

What impresses us here is Witenberg's easy, relaxed use of the phrase "the growing maturity of psychoanalysis." For it was not too long ago that the death knell was being tolled for psychoanalysis. Long considered an inadequate form of psychotherapy for schizophrenics and other patients with primitively, poorly organized personality structures such as the borderline and the narcissistic character disorders, psychoanalysis (and psychoanalytic psychotherapy) has had to struggle to maintain its position as treatment of choice for the neuroses and the more moderate character disabilities. Its protracted and sometimes virtually interminable treatment situations with sometimes limited but costly results, has occasioned disillusionment and cynicism among therapists and patients alike. Young therapists and their patients were increasingly attracted to the human potential movement and to the more abreactive forms of therapy, encouraged by the movement's popularity. These therapists provoked an intensity of affective experiences and hence held out the promise of quick and easy cure. As Freud had predicted (1910) such hopes and promises of quick and lasting results were bound to prove illusory. Despite the growth during the sixties and seventies of these forms of treatment, many new, younger therapists are turning again to the hard work of psychoanalysis and psychoanalytic psychotherapy for training, and many patients are returning for treatment. In addition, psychoanalysis and psychoanalytic psychotherapy have been emerging more and more strongly as the treatments of choice for those very patients for whom it was so long considered ineffectual, that is, patients with poorly organized personality structures. Almost everything that has been written about the treatment of such patients includes much on the subject of countertransference itself.

It is hardly surprising that this has happened. Throughout the history of psychoanalysis analysts have addressed themselves to the question of what is curative in the process. Friedman (1978) has delineated the continuing development of the analytic theory of treatment and the analytic concept of curative factors, a history that is ongoing. The two milestones of this history, as Friedman writes (1978), are the Marienbad Conference of 1936 and the Edinburgh Conference of 1961. Both meetings focused on elucidating the curative factors. These were assumed to be (1) *introjection,* which is concerned with the taking in from the analyst and the analytic process the necessary healthy replacements for old and now unhealthy aspects of experience; (2) *attachment,* which refers to the quality of the analytic relationship, the medium in which introjection and all other analytic procedures take place; and (3) *insight* via interpretation, by which unconscious processes are made conscious so that mastery over them can be achieved. Interest in countertransference is kindled whenever analysts turn their attention to the relationship between themselves and their patients and begin to notice what the patient receives and takes in. With the new scientific emphasis on fields of forces, interpretation taken alone, which reflects a dichotomous subject-object conception, is devalued. This is not to demean the importance of interpretation and interpretative intervention, but as analysts turn to the question of *what* is being interpreted, under what *conditions,* and by *whom* and *how* it is being received, the issue of countertransference becomes of paramount importance. Not simply a misplaced "empathy" or "trial identification" as A. Reich (1966) would have it, countertransference plays the same role in the attachment of analyst to patient as transference does in the attachment of patient to analyst. The fulfillment of the promise implicit in Freud's Dora postscript (1905) requires that countertransference be studied scientifically as the effective ally in the analytic process it can become when recognized for what it is. And so the double helix of Freud's views of the analyst's complexes inhibiting his effectiveness, and the necessary use of the analyst's available unconscious forces for understanding the unconscious of the patient (Freud 1910, 1912) forces itself upon us today, more insistently than ever.

In general, then, we seem to have become more receptive to the idea that in relation to our patients we are more similar than different in kind, (Sullivan 1953). We have also been made aware of the fact that our more intense countertransference reactions are usually generated by the more severely disturbed type of patient. Thus, countertransference is now seen as a normal, natural interpersonal event, rather than an idiosyncratic pathological phenomenon. This has contributed to a heightening of our psychoanalytic consciousness, facilitating the shift from viewing countertransference reactions solely as a hindrance to the possibility of grasping the data of countertransference for their potential value in understanding the patient, and the therapeutic relationship, and in formulating interventions that deepen and intensify the psychoanalytic process.

The question of what is most useful about countertransference seems to us to pose one of the more interesting challenges in psychoanalysis today

(Sandler 1976, Moeller 1977, Feiner 1979). As a radical and refreshing change of orientation in the performance of our task, it stimulates us intellectually as well as technically. The implications are far-reaching. Today's emphasis has shifted from the therapist's suppression of self in the clinical situation to his viewing himself as a genuine coparticipant in an ongoing process (Wolstein 1959, 1973). This enables us to be more vivacious and less elitist in our work with our patients and furthermore promises better therapeutic results, all of which makes our work not only more exciting, but more exacting and gratifying as well. Despite the history of internecine warfare among the various schools, psychoanalysts by and large are arriving at a consensus regarding their own contributions in the consulting room.

We see, for instance, an increasing convergence and integration of the intrapsychic and interpersonal field orientations, points of view that were, some years back, evidently polarized. Freud alluded to such an integration in 1912, but only today are the internal processes of patients and analysts being examined for the impact each has on the other. The main thrust today is to examine various aspects of countertransference and develop the role these have come to play in our work with patients.

Among the themes and issues addressed currently are the following:

1. How to differentiate those components of the patient's reactions resulting from the impact of the analyst's unconscious countertransference; and how to recognize those conditions under which infiltrations may likely occur.
2. How to differentiate components of the countertransference that derive directly from the patient's contribution from those which emerge from the idiosyncratic and/or pathological features of the analyst.
3. Theories of the role that ego-splitting and unconscious projective and introjective processes play in transference and countertransference reactions.
4. The therapeutic functions of the analyst-as-"container" (not "receptacle") of the patient's projections, and of the analyst's resistances to the patient's unconscious efforts to nullify the bipersonal situation by means of penetration, fusion, incorporation, or modification of the field.
5. The therapeutic function of the patient as "container" of the analyst's unconscious countertransference projections.
6. Countertransference data as the basis for understanding the patient's unconscious communication of impulses, affects, fantasies, and conflicts.
7. Countertransference data as the key to understanding ongoing resistances and split-self, split-object relationships.
8. The phenomenology, theory, and management of the average, expectable variations in countertransference reactions, including those disturbances in attention and concentration which may be generated by different personality organizations of the patient, specifically the borderline, narcissistic, and psychotic states and organizations, and the structural neuroses.

9. The integration of countertransference data in the formulation of interventions and strategies, for example, interpretation, confrontation, interpersonal transactions, joining techniques, the judicious sharing of countertransference reactions, emotional communications, and so on.

10. How countertransference might be most meaningfully defined or redefined. There have been challenges, from a field-theoretical point of view, to the utility of a concept that separates transference as something emanating from the patient and something counter to it emanating from the therapist.

We assume that this paper is not the last statement in this area. In fact, we see it serving as a stimulus for further research. Furthermore, we trust others will be encouraged to write about countertransference with even greater precision and in a way that will broaden our understanding.

NOTES

1. For a complete review of Racker's work, from which some of this material was derived, see Hunt and Issacharoff (1977).
2. We discuss Reich's position later in this essay.

REFERENCES

Balint, A., and Balint, M. (1939). On transference and countertransference. *International Journal of Psycho-Analysis* 20: 223–230.

Bion, W. (1962). *Learning from Experience*. New York: Basic Books.

Bion, W. (1963). *Elements of Psychoanalysis*. New York: Basic Books.

Bion, W. (1970). *Attention and Interpretation*. London: Tavistock.

Bird, B. (1972). Notes on transference: Universal phenomenon and hardest part of analysis. *Journal of the American Psychoanalytic Association* 20: 267–301.

Boyer, L. B. (1979). Countertransference with severely regressed patients. In: *Countertransference: The Therapist's Contribution to Treatment.* Ed. by L. Epstein and A. H. Feiner. New York: Jason Aronson, Inc. 1979.

Cohen, M. B. (1952). Countertransference and anxiety. *Psychiatry* 15: 231–243.

Epstein, L. (1979a). The therapeutic function of hate in the countertransference. In: *Countertransference: The Therapist's Contribution to Treatment.* Ed. by L. Epstein and A. H. Feiner. New York: Jason Aronson, Inc. 1979.

Epstein, L. (1979b). Countertransference with borderline patients. In: *Countertransference: The Therapist's Contribution to Treatment.* Ed. by L. Epstein and A. H. Feiner. New York: Jason Aronson, Inc. 1979.

Epstein, L., and Feiner, A. H. (1979). *Countertransference: The Therapist's Contribution to Treatment.* New York: Jason Aronson, Inc.

Feiner, A. H. (1979). The anxiety of influence and countertransference. In: *Countertransference: The Therapist's Contribution to Treatment.* Ed. by L. Epstein and A. H. Feiner. New York: Jason Aronson, Inc. 1979.

Fordham, M. (1979). Analytical psychology and countertransference. In: *Countertransference: The Therapist's Contribution to Treatment.* Ed. by L. Epstein and A. H. Feiner. New York: Jason Aronson, Inc. 1979.

Freud, S. (1905). Fragment of an analysis of a case of hysteria. *Standard Edition* 7: 3–122. London: Hogarth Press. 1957.

Freud, S. (1910). The future prospects of psycho-analytic therapy. *Standard Edition* 11: 139–152. London: Hogarth Press. 1957.

Freud, S. (1912). Recommendations for physicians practising psychoanalysis. *Standard Edition* 12: 109–120. London: Hogarth Press. 1957.

Freud, S. (1913). The disposition to obsessional neurosis. *Standard Edition* 12: 313–326. London: Hogarth Press. 1957.

Freud, S. (1925). An autobiographical study. *Standard Edition* 20: 3–74. London: Hogarth Press. 1957.

Freud, S. (1937). Analysis terminable and interminable. *Standard Edition* 23: 209–253. London: Hogarth Press. 1957.

Friedman, L. (1978). Trends in the psychoanalytic theory of treatment. *The Psychoanalytic Quarterly* 47: 524–567.

Fromm, E. (1947). *Man For Himself.* New York: Holt, Rinehart and Winston.

Fromm-Reichmann, F. (1950). *Principles of Intensive Psychotherapy.* Chicago: University of Chicago Press.

Gitelson, M. (1952). The emotional position of the analyst in the psycho-analytic situation. *International Journal of Psycho-Analysis* 33: 1–10.

Grinberg, L. (1979). Projective counteridentification and countertransference. In: *Countertransference: The Therapist's Contribution to Treatment.* Ed. by L. Epstein and A. H. Feiner. New York: Jason Aronson, Inc. 1979.

Heimann, P. (1950). On countertransference. *International Journal of Psycho-Analysis* 31: 81–84.

Horney, K. (1939). *New Ways in Psychoanalysis.* New York: W. W. Norton.

Hunt, W., and Issacharoff, A. (1977). Heinrich Racker and countertransference theory. *Journal of the American Academy of Psychoanalysis* 5: 95–105.

Issacharoff, A. (1979). Barriers to knowing. In: *Countertransference: The Therapist's Contribution to Treatment.* Ed. L. Epstein and A. H. Feiner. New York: Jason Aronson, Inc. 1979.

Kernberg, O. (1965). Notes on countertransference. *Journal of the American Psychoanalytic Association* 13: 38–56.

King, C. (1976). Counter-transference and counter-experience in the treatment of violence prone youth. *American Journal of Orthopsychiatry* 46: 43–52.

Kohut, H. (1978). *The Restoration of the Self.* New York: International Universities Press.

Langs, R. (1976). *The Therapeutic Interaction,* volume 2. New York: Jason Aronson, Inc.

Little, M. (1951). Countertransference and the patient's response to it. *International Journal of Psycho-Analysis* 32: 32–40.

Little, M. (1957). 'R'—The analyst's response to his patient's needs. *International Journal of Psycho-Analysis* 38: 240–254.

Marshall, R. (1979). Countertransference with children and adolescents. In: *Countertransference: The Therapist's Contribution to Treatment.* Ed. by L. Epstein and A. H. Feiner. New York: Jason Aronson, Inc. 1979.

McDougall, J. (1979). Primitive communication and the use of countertransference. In: *Countertransference: The Therapist's Contribution to Treatment.* Ed. by L. Epstein and A. H. Feiner. New York: Jason Aronson, Inc. 1979.

Meltzer, D. (1979). Routine and inspired interpretations. In: *Countertransference: The Therapist's Contribution to Treatment.* Ed. by L. Epstein and A. H. Feiner. New York: Jason Aronson, Inc. 1979.

Moeller, M. L. (1977). Self and object in countertransference. *International Journal of Psycho-Analysis* 58: 365–374.

Racker, H. (1953). The countertransference neurosis. *International Journal of Psycho-Analysis* 34: 313–324. Reprinted in H. Racker, *Transference and Countertransference.* New York: International Universities Press. 1968.

Racker, H. (1957). The meanings and uses of countertransference. *Psychoanalytic Quarterly* 26: 303–357. Reprinted in H. Racker *Transference and Countertransference.* New York: International Universities Press. 1968.

Racker, H. (1968). *Transference and Countertransference.* New York: International Universities Press.

Reich, A. (1951). On countertransference. *International Journal of Psycho-Analysis* 32: 25–31.

Reich, A. (1960). Further remarks on countertransference. *International Journal of Psycho-Analysis* 41: 389–395.

Reich, A. (1966). Empathy and countertransference. In: Annie Reich, *Psychoanalytic Contributions.* New York: International Universities Press. 1973.

Sandler, J. (1976). Countertransference and role-responsiveness. *International Review of Psycho-Analysis* 3: 43–47.

Sandler, J., Dare, C., and Holder, A. (1973). *The Patient and the Analyst.* New York: International Universities Press.

Searles, H. (1958). The schizophrenic's vulnerability to the therapist's unconscious processes. *Journal of Nervous and Mental Diseases* 127: 247–262.

Searles, H. (1978). Psychoanalytic therapy with the borderline adult. In: *New Perspectives on Psychotherapy with the Borderline Adult.* Ed. J. Masterson. New York: Brunner/Mazel.

Sharpe, E. (1947). The psychoanalyst. *International Journal of Psycho-Analysis* 28: 1–60.

Spotnitz, H. (1969). *Modern Psychoanalysis of the Schizophrenic Patient.* New York: Grune and Stratton.

Spotnitz, H. (1976). *Psychotherapy of Preoedipal Conditions.* New York: Jason Aronson, Inc.

Spotnitz, H. (1979). Narcissistic countertransference. In: *Countertransference: The Therapist's Contribution to Treatment.* Ed. by L. Epstein and A. H. Feiner. New York: Jason Aronson, Inc. 1979.

Sullivan, H. S. (1953). *The Interpersonal Theory of Psychiatry.* New York: W. W. Norton.

Tauber, E. (1954). Exploring the therapeutic use of countertransference data. *Psychiatry* 17: 331–336.

Tauber, E. (1979). Countertransference re-examined. In: *Countertransference: The Therapist's Contribution to Treatment.* Ed. by L. Epstein and A. H. Feiner. New York: Jason Aronson Inc. 1979.

Thompson, C., Crowley, R., and Tauber, E. (1952). Symposium on countertransference. *Samiksa* 6: 205–228.

Winnicott, D. (1949). Hate in the countertransference. *International Journal of Psycho-Analysis* 30: 69–75. In D. W. Winnicott, *Through Paediatrics to Psychoanalysis.* New York: Basic Books. 1958.

Witenberg, E. (1979). The inner experience of the psychoanalyst. In: *Countertransference: The Therapist's Contribution to Treatment.* Ed. by L. Epstein and A. H. Feiner. New York: Jason Aronson, Inc. 1979.

Wolstein, B. (1959). *Countertransference.* New York: Grune and Stratton.

Wolstein, B. (1973). The new significance of psychoanalytic structure. In: *Interpersonal Explorations in Psychoanalysis.* Ed. by E. G. Witenberg. New York: Basic Books.

17. The Interpersonal Paradigm and the Degree of the Therapist's Involvement

Merton M. Gill

I will begin with a brief account of the history of this paper because I believe that will make it more understandable. During the past few years when I have presented my views on the centrality of the analysis of transference and especially on the participation of the analyst in determining how the transference is expressed I have on occasion been asked what was the relation between my ideas and those of Sullivan and later interpersonalists. The question usually implied that there was a strong similarity. Having been reared as a proper Freudian with a more or less unthinking dismissal of Sullivan and interpersonal writings, I was unable to answer. I told myself that I should study these writings, even if I had to risk losing illusions of originality.

What finally forced me to take the question of the relation between my ideas and interpersonal writings seriously was the invitation to present a paper to you. Indeed the invitation referred to a compatibility between my ideas on transference and your views. So I began to read your writings, especially the journal *Contemporary Psychoanalysis,* but also books by Chrzanowski (1977), Levenson (1972), Singer (1965), and Wolstein (1959). What follows is the partial result of reflection on this reading, which naturally was in the context of how it related to my ideas on transference.

I became progressively aware of an important distinction between two cleavages in psychoanalytic thought that had been more or less fused in my mind. It may be that the clarification of this distinction is especially newsworthy for someone trained in the Freudian tradition like myself. Nevertheless I believe it will be worthwhile to state it sharply for this audience too because although it is referred to in various ways in the interpersonal litera-

Revised from a presentation to the William Alanson White Psychoanalytic Society, April 2, 1982.

ture I am not aware that it has been explicitly focused upon as a major issue. In any case my experience was that I had to dig it out for myself.

I refer to the distinction between two major cleavages in psychoanalytic thought: One cleavage is between the interpersonal paradigm and the drive-discharge paradigm. The other cleavage is between those who believe the analyst inevitably participates in a major way in the analytic situation and those who do not. I came to realize that I had assumed that these two cleavages run parallel to each other, or at least that those who adhered to the interpersonal paradigm would also ascribe to the analyst's major participation in the analytic situation.

That I had made this assumption implied an intrinsic connection between the interpersonal paradigm and a major participation on the one hand and the drive-discharge paradigm and a minor involvement on the other.

To attempt to discover whether the assumption of such intrinsic connections is justified would require an examination and comparison of the interpersonal and drive-discharge paradigms. That is an important and difficult task that I am not attempting in this paper. I should say however that I believe it can be demonstrated that there is no such intrinsic connection. I will also say that I suspect that in the course of such an examination it will turn out that the cleavage between interpersonal and drive-discharge paradigms will be paralleled by the current controversy between the hermeneutic and metapsychological positions in psychoanalytic theory with the hermeneutic position allied to the interpersonal paradigm and the metapsychological to the drive-discharge paradigm. Such a discussion would also have to distinguish between Freud's theories about object relations and an interpersonal paradigm. It would furthermore have to take account of Kernberg's views that the two paradigms are not incompatible (1980). I also suggest that the participant-observation theorem may not necessarily imply the interpersonal-relations paradigm. I mean that it may be that one can agree that any psychological observation is influenced by the position of the observer without necessarily agreeing that all psychological observations must have interpersonal relations as their basic organizing framework.

My goals in this paper are much more modest than the comparison of the paradigms. I wish to demonstrate first that the cleavages are indeed not parallel in our literature, that is that an adherent of the interpersonal paradigm need not ascribe a major-participant role to the analyst and that an adherent of the drive-discharge pattern may ascribe a major-participant role to the analyst. Then I will outline some of the implications for technique that I believe follow if one accepts the interpersonal paradigm. I emphasize that I am explicitly distinguishing between the interpersonal paradigm and object-relations theory.

First I will show that the paradigms and the quality of participation do not run parallel. The demonstration depends on yet further assumptions, namely that an analyst who calls himself Freudian adheres to the drive-discharge paradigm while an analyst who considers himself a Sullivanian adheres to the interpersonal paradigm. I realize that these assumptions may not hold. Indeed it is my hope that the very discrepancies among avowed allegiance to a particular school of psychoanalysis, a particular paradigm, and a particular view of the analyst's participation will suggest that functional groupings that cross cut avowed allegiances tell more about how an analyst works than allegiances do.

I will first quote a statement by Abrams and Shengold (1978, p. 402), two staunch Freudians, to show that they distinguish between themselves and those who ascribe a major-participant role to the analyst. The statement occurs in a paper summing up the International Psychoanalytic Congress of 1977. After sketching what would be generally accepted as the Freudian model they say that

clinical investigation and theory building over the past fifty years have tested and challenged much of this with the result that some analysts have developed substantially different views of the psychoanalytic situation . . . in the new model . . . the psychoanalytic situation is seen primarily as an *encounter* between two people, rather than as a setting whose purpose is the examination of the intrapsychic processes of one of them.

It was made in a context that implied that the new model is the Kleinian. I leave aside for now the question of whether the Kleinian theory is based on a drive-discharge or an interpersonal paradigm. My point here is that these representatives of the Freudian position believe there is a cleavage between themselves and those who see the analytic situation as an encounter, that is, that the latter see the analyst as appropriately significantly involved as a participant in the analytic situation whereas they do not.

My next illustration is an example of a Freudian, presumably an adherent of the drive-discharge paradigm, who ascribes a major role to the analyst. James McLaughlin (1981, p. 652) sufficiently respected and trusted by his colleagues that he was chosen to give the final summing up statement at the meeting of the International Psychoanalytic Association (1981) has written recently that several analysts from quite different operational positions, have provided rich data to demonstrate that both parties are caught up in a communicative field of incredible sensitivity and subtlety, with transferential-countertransferential shadings constantly at play in enormous affective intensities—a field in which the possibility of a neutral or catalytic comment, given or received, is remote indeed.

The theme of the paper in which this remark occurs is that it is a mistake to have different terms for the patient's and the analyst's participations in the analytic situation, that is, to distinguish between them by calling them transference and countertransference because such a distinction implies that the two phenomena are significantly different. It is suggested that we therefore should refer to both of them as transference. There is evidence that McLaughlin assumes that his ascription of this major participation to the analyst will be considered to justify classifying him as an adherent of the interpersonal school since he is moved to disavow such adherence explicitly. He writes: "I am not referring to the ever-present alternative of interpersonal psychology, but rather to a closer scrutiny of the verbal intervention-response sequence and patterning of classical technique" (p. 652).

My next illustration comes from Kohut. I believe it can be shown that his self psychology is a significant, though not complete, abandonment of the drive paradigm in favor of an interpersonal paradigm but I am not attempting such a demonstration here. Making that assumption, however, I wish to show that his view of the analyst's participation is that it is a minor one, thus again contradicting the assumption that the interpersonal paradigm is paralleled by the ascription of major participation to the analyst. Kohut writes that in the transference neurosis "the analyst, to the extent that he is a transference figure, is not experienced in the framework of an interpersonal relationship" while in the narcissistic disorders the analyst is "introspectively experienced within the framework of an archaic interpersonal relationship." (1959)

One might think that with this view Kohut would see the analyst as making a relatively minor contribution to the interpersonal relationship in the transference neuroses and a relatively major one in the narcissistic personality disorders. One would be right about the former but only partially right about the latter. He writes that in true transference there is "an amalgamation of repressed infantile object strivings with (in the present reality, insignificant) aspects of the analyst" (Kohut, 1959). But in describing a schizophrenic patient who comes to the session in a cold and withdrawn state he says: "the patient's emotional coldness and his dream are found to be a reaction to an apparently minute, but in reality significant, rejection of the patient by the analyst'' (Kohut, 1959). I interpret the distinction between ''apparently minute'' and ''in reality significant'' to mean that from the point of view of the analyst or an external observer the involvement is in fact minimal even though to the patient it is significant. I suggest that the position that the contribution is a significant one only from the point of view of the patient, not that of an external observer, is consistent with the position that the contribution of the analyst is minor. In this sense it is wrong to consider that Kohut believes the analyst makes a relatively major contribution to the patient's pathological experience of the relationship in the narcissistic personality disorders. On the other hand Kohut argues in the concept of transmuting internalization that the analyst does play a major role in the ''restoration'' of a cohesive self.

One of the most illuminating and unexpected jolts I got to my assumption that the interpersonal paradigm goes parallel with the ascription of major participation to the analyst was the complaint by some interpersonalists that Sullivan's concept of participant observation does not make of the analyst as much of a participant as they think he is and should be.

Chrzanowski (1977, pp. 150–151) for example, expresses his dissatisfaction with Sullivan's concept of participant observation by saying that ''it is difficult to include the phenomenon of countertransference into the formulation of participant observation because the term does not address itself to emotional components.'' And

the emotional components of rational and irrational responses to the patient's transferential and actual attitudes to the analyst require broader representation than is possible within the instrumental model of participant observation. My clinical preference is for a different role definition of the analyst, which emphasizes the role reciprocity between patient and analyst while focusing on the analyst's self monitoring and self revealing attitudes.

Levenson (1972, p. 215) also feels that the Sullivanian concept of participant observer is not adequate. He writes: ''the therapist, as an extension of Sullivan's participant observer, becomes a total participant and an observer of his own *experience* of participation.'' While Sullivan did stress the importance of the analyst's being aware of his participation, what Levenson proposes in addition is that the therapist becomes a ''total participant.''

Greenberg (1981) explicitly contrasts the view of analysts of what he calls the ''British school'' on the analyst's participation with that of what he calls American interpersonalists. He says that the former see the analyst not only as *participating with* the patient but as, inevitably *participating in* the patient's illness but then says that the latter view would be considered neurotically determined countertransference by Sullivan (p. 252). The complexity of the possible combinations of views on the paradigm and views on the analyst's participation may be seen in the fact that in referring to the British school Greenberg includes Sandler and Khan, who are not usually considered Kleinians, and Racker and Grinberg, who are. While Racker, a Kleinian, considers the analyst's participation to be a constant co-determinant of the patient's experience of the relationship to varying degrees, the Kleinians are generally criticized for failing to consider the analyst to be a participant as evidenced by their lack of attention to the role he plays in the here-and-now in determining the nature of the transference. Bird (1972), a Freudian, also suggests that a countertransference neurosis may also be a regular phenomenon, at least in an analysis of significant depth. His paper reveals a striking vacillation in the participation he ascribes to the analyst.

My last quotation in this series is from Levenson (1981) again. He writes:

To give a quick example: that the patient thinks that you are poisoning his soup, the Freudian sees some small and trivial event as having set off a paranoid mechanism of projection. The interpersonalist wonders, what did he *really* do with the patient which cannot be identified or responded to and is therefore amplified in this way? Did he, in the previous session, in some real way, rebuff the patient? For him, the therapy lies in the patient's being able to establish the interrupted threads of connection between the event (unattended) and the symbolism. I consider this to be an absolutely vital distinction, certainly deserving more elaborate documentation (p. 488).

So Levenson here considers the difference between the Freudian and the interpersonalist to be that the interpersonalist sees the analyst as significantly involved while the Freudian does not. Indeed when he says the Freudian sees some small and trivial event as having set off a paranoid projection he does not even specify that this small and trivial event is something the analyst did. So again, there is an assumption that the interpersonal paradigm is paralleled by significant participation.

THE FREUDIAN POSITION

An important gain in stating the distinction between a major and a minor participation by the analyst in the analytic situation is that it will focus on a genuine difference of opinion that is now obscured by a caricature of the position of those who consider that appropriate participation to be minor. I mean the attribution to them of the blank screen or mirror view of the analyst.

If there is any statement that appears in the remarks of almost every author in the symposium on participant observation in *Contemporary Psychoanalysis* in 1977 it is to refer to and reject Freud's famous remark that "the doctor should be opaque to his patients and, like a mirror, should show them nothing but what is shown to him" (Standard Edition 12, p. 118). I believe the remark has been seriously misinterpreted. Certainly Freud didn't behave that way. The remark is made directly after Freud suggests that the analyst might understandably think it might be useful to give the patient "a glimpse of his own mental defects and conflicts and, by giving him intimate information about his own life, enable him to put himself on an equal footing. One confidence deserves another, and any one who demands intimacy from someone else must be prepared to give it in return" (Standard Edition 12, p. 117–118). It is only as a dramatic antithesis to this understandable but to-be-resisted temptation that Freud makes the mirror remark.

The Freudian considers the attack on the blank screen concept to be directed at a straw man. His rebuttal might run as follows:

Of course I know that the analytic situation is an interpersonal one, he is likely to say. Isn't the definition of transference that it's a distortion of a real situation? Of course I know that there is a real relationship between patient and analyst but if the patient is not experiencing a transference and the analyst is not involved in a countertransference the relationship is realistic and adapted to the current reality. But when he is expressing a transference the patient is incorrectly attributing his experience to the real situation. Indeed it is my experience that if I emphasize what the patient incorrectly considers to be the reality justification for his transference I merely confirm him in his view that it is not transference.

Freud actually cautioned against underinvolvement on the analyst's part. It is true that this caution is not to be found in his published writings but in a letter he wrote to Oskar Pfister on October 22, 1927;

On the question of therapeutic technique I must express myself plainly. You as a minister naturally have the right to call on all the reinforcements that you can command, while we as analysts must be more reserved, and must lay the chief accent on the effort to make the patient independent, which often works out to the disadvantage of the therapy. Apart from that, I am not so far from your point of view as you think. You know the human propensity to take precepts literally or exaggerate them. I know very well that in the matter of analytic passivity that is what some of my pupils do. Of H. in particular I am willing to believe that he spoils the effect of analysis by a certain listless indifference, and then neglects to lay bare the resistance which he thereby awakens in his patients. It should not be concluded from this instance that analysis should be followed by a synthesis, but rather that thorough analysis of the transference situation is of special importance. What then remains of the transference may, indeed should, have the character of a cordial human relationship'' (Freud, 1927, p. 113).

Yet it remains true that Freud's primary concern about the participation of the analyst is the danger of becoming over-involved. The late essay "Analysis Terminable and Interminable" is ordinarily looked upon as relating to the terminability of a patient's analysis, but it includes a sentence that makes clear that the entire essay applies to analyst as well as analysand. He wrote: "This would mean, then, that not only the therapeutic analysis of patients but his own analysis would change from terminable into an interminable task" (Standard Edition 23, p. 249). Nor does Freud believe that self analysis alone will do the job. He suggested that "Every analyst should periodically—at intervals of five years or so—submit himself to analysis once more, without feeling ashamed of taking this step" (p. 249). The recommendation might seem to be at odds with the spirit of the essay, for Freud made clear that a latent conflict cannot be analyzed except intellectually. What then would be the use of an analyst's entering analysis every five years unless he felt actively conflicted? Perhaps there is a resolution of the apparent paradox that Freud did not make explicit, that is, that a practicing analyst should always be aware that he has active conflicts. The nature of his work will stir up these conflicts in a way that need not be true for persons who are not engaged in daily intense interpersonal interactions. Freud said in the same essay: "It would scarcely be surprising if constant preoccupation with all the repressed impulses which struggle for freedom in the human mind sometimes cause all the instinctual demands which have hitherto been restrained to be violently awakened in the analyst himself" (p. 267). But one must note that Freud spoke of the awakening of instinctual demands, not explicitly about how the analyst would be influenced in his interaction with the patient.

If it is thought that I am being unfair and Freud obviously meant the interpersonal interaction in what I have just quoted I add these sentences, which he wrote in the same year (1937):

The danger of our leading a patient astray by suggestion, be persuading him to accept things which we ourselves believe but which he ought not to, has certainly been enormously exaggerated. An analyst would have had to behave very incorrectly before such a misfortune could overtake him, above all he would have to blame himself with not allowing his patients to have their say. I can assert without boasting that such an abuse of "suggestion" has never occurred in my practice (Standard Edition 23, p. 262).

I conclude that the attitude betrayed in this last remark suggests that Freud did not consider that the "instinctual demands" which are "violently awakened" inevitably find expression in the analyst's behavior.

Despite recent emphasis on the real relationship and the various alliances there is no doubt that insofar as there is an official Freudian position, it is to advocate a lesser participation by the analyst than Freud did. Freud is frequently criticized by Freudian analysts for having been as interactive with his patients as he was. Lipton (1977) agrees that Freud was more manifestly interactive than contemporary Freudian technique would permit but he considers Freud's technique to be preferable. He argues that in addition to his technical relation to the patient an analyst should have a personal relation with his patient too. While his personal relation shoud be relatively circumscribed, its limits cannot be prescribed. Lipton is careful to emphasize that what one does in this relationship may very well have repercussions on the transference, which need then to be drawn into the technical activity of the analyst.

In addition to the blank-screen accusation, Freudians believe their position on the participation of the analyst is caricatured as though they do not recognize the importance of object relations. I believe it will be clarifying to distinguish between the drive paradigm within which object relations are important and an interpersonal paradigm. Of course Freud makes much of object relations. Transference and the Oedipus complex are about object relations. It is one of the interesting ironies of psychoanalysis that Freud saw transference as the clinching validation for the drive-discharge paradigm. In the Introductory Lectures he writes: "It may be said that our conviction of the significance of symptoms as substitutive satisfactions of the libido only received its final confirmation after the enlistment of the transference" (Standard Edition 16, p. 445).

Chrzanowski has repeatedly called attention to Freud's statement in the introduction to "Group Psychology and the Analysis of the Ego" from which one would be hard put to deduce exactly how Freud conceived of the connection between object relations and the satisfaction of instinctual impulses, close though the connection must be. Freud wrote:

The contrast between individual psychology and social or group psychology, which at first glance may seem to be full of significance, loses a great deal of its sharpness when it is examined more closely. It is true that individual psychology is concerned with the individual man and explores the paths by which he seeks to find satisfaction for his instinctual impulses; but only rarely and under certain exceptional conditions is individual psychology in a position to disregard the relations of this individual to others. In the individual's mental life someone else is invariably involved, as a model, as an object, as a helper, as an opponent; and so from the very first individual psychology, in this extended but entirely justifiable sense of the words, is at the same time social psychology as well (Standard Edition 18, p. 69).

The difference between a psychoanalytic theory that includes theories about object relations and a psychoanalytic theory built on an interpersonal paradigm can be illustrated by the juxtaposition of the following quotations from Stone and Sullivan. Stone (1981, p. 716) writes: "whether or not one is an enthusiastic proponent of 'object relations theory' in any of its elaborate forms, it seems self evident that all major developmental vicissitudes and conflicts have occurred in the context of important relations with important objects, and that they or their effects continue to be reflected in relationships with current persons of similar or parallel importance." The reader may not have noticed that the author says that major developmental vicissitudes and conflicts have occurred in the *context* of important relations with important objects. He does not say that major developmental vicissitudes *are* matters of important relations with important objects. I believe that he, wittingly or not, inserts the phrase "in the context of" because he wishes to avoid the implication that the field of psychoanalysis is the field of interpersonal relations. That is, in his view, interpersonal relationships are important in psychoanalysis but they do not constitute the field of psychoanalysis.

Sullivan on the other hand (1954) writes: "The psychiatrist should never lose track of the fact that all the processes of the patient are more or less exactly addressed at him and that all that he offers—his experience—is more or less accurately aimed at the patient with a resulting wonderful interplay (pp. 19–20)."

I summarize then that while it is a caricature of the Freudian view to say that the analyst is a blank screen or a mirror, it is true that the Freudian view sees the analyst as appropriately participating in only a minor way. I allow myself a verbal play by calling the analyst who is considered to be a participant in only a minor way the precipitant observer rather than the participant observer.

I am indebted to Irwin Hoffman for the crucial clarification that the foregoing discussion does not grapple with the distinction between the analyst as a growth-promoting participant as in Strachey, Loewald, and Kohut and as implicated in the formation of neurotic transferences. He discusses the issue in an important as yet unpublished paper (1983) in terms of the distinction between "conservative" and "radical" critiques of the blank-screen view.

SULLIVAN'S POSITION ON THE ANALYST'S PARTICIPATION

Does Sullivan anywhere suggest that a major involvement with the analyst is a necessary part of the interpersonal view? In fact the theorem of participant observation asserts only that there must be *some* involvement. Sullivan (1954) says this. "There are no psychiatric data that can be observed from a detached position by a person in no way involved in the operation. All psychiatric data arise from participation in the situation that is observed—in other words by participant observation" (p. 57).

The Sullivanian statement, which would seem to bespeak the inevitability of a major participation, is not the interpersonal paradigm but the one-genus statement : " . . . we are all much more simply human than otherwise, be we happy and successful, contented and detached, miserable and mentally disordered or whatever" (1940, p. 7). McLaughlin's (1981) statement quoted above implies the same view of human beings. So does Racker's (1968) statement that " . . . 'the myth of the analytic situation' is that analysis is an interaction between a sick person and a healthy one" (p. 132).

Sullivan speaks of the degree of involvement only in a descriptive sense. He alludes to varying degrees of involvement. He says that an inexperienced interviewer may well be more anxious than the patient, that even an experienced interviewer will certainly, particularly if he interviews incipient psychotics, be very acutely anxious in his work now and then and that "in almost everyone, a great deal of anxiety occurs of which the person concerned has no clear awareness" (1954, p. 135). When he asks whether a really skillful psychiatrist "knows just what role to take or just how to behave" he answers' "yes, *but with very great qualifications*. It is more accurate to say that the experience of the psychiatrist is synthesized into *an aptitude to do nothing exterior to his awareness* which will greatly handicap the interview situation, or which will direct its development in an unnecessarily obscure way" (1954, pp. 68–69). The emphasis falls on being aware of what one is doing rather than on what to do. This passage also subtly reveals Sullivan's attitude about what even the skillful psychoanalyst is likely to do and is one of the reasons it is so often a pleasure to read him. It is a variant of "we are all much more simply human than otherwise." He doesn't say "will handicap"; he says "will greatly handicap." He doesn't say "in an obscure way''; he says in an ''unnecessarily obscure way.'' He takes it for granted that there will be handicapping and obscurity. It is true that Sullivan thereby implies that the involvement is unlikely to be merely trivial but he does not make that his explicit and central point.

PRESCRIPTION VERSUS DESCRIPTION

It is important to distinguish between the concepts of how much the analyst ought to be involved and how much he is inevitably involved. This subject has been discussed by Greenberg (1981) in terms of a felicitous distinction between prescription and description. The prescription relates to what is thought to be appropriate whereas the description relates to what is fact. Greenberg correctly says that too much attention to prescription has detracted attention from description and of course that an analyst's concern about conforming to what he considers the proper prescription may be so great that he seriously distorts what is his actual participation, that is to say, the description.

The primary current Freudian position on the analyst's participation is in the prescriptive mode. The analyst is warned against too great participation. The Freudians believe it is important to struggle against involvement and to render it as minimal as possible. Tarachow's (1963) distinction between psychoanalysis and psychotherapy argues, for example, that both participants in the therapeutic situation are constantly tempted to engage in an interaction and that a therapy is psychoanalytic rather than psychotherapeutic only to the extent to which the analyst successfully resists this temptation.

Sullivan's position on the analyst's participation is contradictory. As I have mentioned, and as Greenberg said, he would have regarded a major participation as a pathological countertransference rather than the average expectable variations in countertransference reactions, to use Epstein's and Feiner's (1979, p. 20) phrase. That is a prescriptive view. On the other hand the one-genus theorem is a descriptive statement about the nature of human beings. It implies that the analyst's *participation* cannot be minor.[1]

Sullivan's position should not be confused with statements by interpersonalists and others that are prescriptive. I refer to the idea that the analyst *ought* to be involved with his patients. A common rationale for this prescription is that one cannot understand another human being unless one is involved to some unspecified degree. Such involvement is sometimes characterized as normal countertransference. There are other prescriptive statements as to the analyst's participation that are based on a conviction that the analyst's participation in a more than trivial way is crucial in bringing about change. Levenson (1972, p. 214) writes for example: "If the therapist can be loving, because the patient does not impinge on his life in any long-standing meaningful way, is that love worth very much? . . . This willingness to risk his own identity, to "trip" with the patient, is the keystone of helpers from shamans to psychoanalysts." I will return to this point when I discuss the implications for technique of the interpersonal paradigm.

It would seem obvious that even within a major or a minor participation the degree to which an analyst participates varies widely. This is true not only as between one analyst and another but also in the different way in which an analyst treats his different patients as well as differences in the analyst's involvement with his patient in different phases of the analysis or on different issues that come up in the analysis.

It would also seem obvious that the analyst's participation is a function not only of his personality but also of the kind of patient he is treating. This is usually formulated in terms of the increasing difficulty of avoiding countertransference concomitant with the increasing pathology of the patient one is treating. In this connection the following admittedly somewhat-mocking formulation of analyzability has occurred to me: An analyzable patient is a patient with whom the analyst can maintain the illusion of neutrality. It is important to recognize therefore that the emphasis on inevitable major participation in treating patients with severe pathology can be used to sidestep the question of the average expectable participation in treating the average expectable neurosis—the patient who meets the ordinary criteria for a classical analysis.

It is also worth pointing out that one's view of the countertransference will differ depending on whether one examines an analysis microscopically in isolated sessions or macroscopically in broad longitudinal trends. Presumably a countertransference neurosis will take the form of an organized psychic position over time.

It is also not necessary to assume that a significant participation on the analyst's part will be discernible in any random segment of an analysis and irrespective of the issue under consideration. The analyst's participation will likely wax and wane as the process touches to a greater or lesser extent on issues central in his own psychodynamics.

HOW TO STATE THE DEGREE OF PARTICIPATION

I realize that I have contrasted major with minor participation without indicating how one can judge or measure degrees of participation. We have no measures nor are we likely to get any. The terms are qualitative and have only operational significance.

The words employed in discussions of the degree of participation are not only qualitative but their implications are also not usually focused upon. In the example I quoted from Levenson of the patient who says the analyst is poisoning his soup, Levenson asks what the analyst *really* did do with the patient. The word *really* is clearly meant to imply a significant involvement. In discussing a similar issue in another context he uses the word *precipitant* for an unimportant involvement and *genuine* to connote what he considers a significant and appropriate involvement of the analyst (p. 143).

One of the major stimuli that led me to focus as sharply as I have on the distinction between the paradigm and the degree of involvement and that led me to see that I had condensed them is the criticism of my writing on transference for using the words *co-determination* by the analyst and *plausibility* of the patient's experience to refer to the transference because of their connotation of a degree of involvement greater than many analysts consider inevitable or desirable. Clearly my choice of words reflects a belief in the inevitability of significant involvement but that is the very point in question.

Perhaps the decisive question is this: Might the patient attribute something to the analyst that is entirely imaginary, that has no basis in anything the analyst has said or done? Does the Freudian conception of transference imply such a possibility?

A Freudian could reply to Levenson's illustration of the patient who thinks the therapist is poisoning his soup on the basis of some "trivial" action on the therapist's part that the patient is responding to something "real," albeit trivial. In discussing ideas of reference Freud states that "sufferers from persecutory paranoia . . . cannot regard anything in other people as indifferent, and they, too, take up minute indications with which these other, unknown people present them, and use them in their delusions of reference." Again " . . . they do not project it into the blue, so to speak, where there is nothing of the sort already" (Standard Edition 18, p. 226). More generally Freud spoke of the nucleus of truth in a delusion.

The paranoid patient will very likely say that the analyst has said or done something, which is his justification for the accusation. Must it be true then that the analyst has said or done that of which he is accused? Is it enough to find something he has said or done that can be misinterpreted to mean what the patient takes it to mean? Does there have to be a meaningful connection between what the analyst has said or done and the patient's interpretation of it? What does it mean in this connection to say "a meaningful connection"? At least part of the answer lies in considering the range of unconscious meanings that any particular action may have—including, of course, the analyst's actions. The very concept of meaning in this connection relates to the hermeneutic position and the interpersonal paradigm.

I would like to mention a few other words that are used to refer to the analyst's participation to look at this connotation. I have already referred to the word *precipitant*. A colleague of mine is willing to go only so far as to say the patient "has a point." Levenson's conviction that the analyst's participation must be more than trivial leads him to reject several terms sometimes used to describe the analyst's participation. He writes: "The therapist does not, as in the machine paradigm, act as the 'servant of the process' as Masud Kahn puts it. Nor is he midwife at a delivery" (1972, p. 214).

Levenson's effort to answer this question leads him to use several words in addition to *really* that are worth looking at. One is *relevant*. He says: "Thus, from the most benign neurotic 'distortions' to the outrageous misrepresentations of the paranoid, one could say that the perception, albeit not literally correct, is a *relevant* conception of the therapist" (p. 151). Another word he uses in the same paragraph for the same phenomenon is to call the patient's perception "aesthetically" true.

A clarification of this issue lies in what Levenson calls the perspectivist view. That is, from the patient's perspective the observation is relevant. This may even be a perspective that the patient himself disavows. The disavowal may or may not be conscious. He may recognize that it will not sustain the conclusion he draws, or he may be too distressed to acknowledge what he believes he has seen, or he may feel the analyst would be unwilling or unable to acknowledge what the patient believes he has seen or the conclusion he draws from it. Here perhaps is a place where a distinction between the concepts of participant observer and that of a field constituted by the interpersonal relation—a distinction I earlier alluded to—may have merit. Even if an external observer were to agree with the analyst that what he had done does not justify the patient's conclusion, the fact remains that the patient's organization of the field includes attributing something to the therapist that is relevant to the conclusion, again even if the patient himself does not believe it justifies the conclusion. The event that for the patient is relevant to his conclusion will necessarily be an integral part of an organized position on the patient's part, that is to say, his perspective.

It is now possible to understand the word *relevant* better. It is relevant even if at first the analyst does not recognize that it is. Is this any different from saying that the patient is distorting something because of his own projection? It is because it states the interpersonal paradigm. It changes the question from whether the analyst did anything to justify the patient's experience to the recognition that the patient's perspective always illuminates at least a possible meaning of the analyst's participation, no matter how far-fetched an observer, including the patient in his role of observing participant, may consider this meaning to be. You note that the phrase *observing participant* for the patient rings another change on the phrase *participant observer* in addition to Wolstein's (1960) observed participant. Wolstein meant the phrase *observed participant* to refer to the analyst but it could refer to the patient as well. Wolstein (1981) indicates the analyst's major participation by calling him a co-participant.

THE TRANSFERENCE-COUNTERTRANSFERENCE TRANSACTION

I believe the distinction between the degree of the analyst's participation and the interpersonal paradigm will help to clarify a conceptualization and definition of *transference* and *countertransference* significantly different from the more generally accepted one, at least in the Freudian literature.

In a research on transference in which Irwin Hoffman and I are engaged (Gill and Hoffman, 1982) we have come to the conclusion that the concept of a dichotomy between transference as distortion and nontransference as realistic does violence to the actual nature of the relationship between patient and analyst. Even Langs (1978), whose concept of the bipersonal field places great emphasis on the interpersonal interaction still does not employ the interpersonal paradigm, for he insists that a dichotomy be drawn between transference as distortion and non-transference as realistic, as well as similarly between countertransference and non-countertransference, and between all the other dimensions based on fact and those based on fantasy. Langs's illustrations of analytic material invariably includes a major participation by the analyst but it is not clear whether he considers such involvement to be inevitable. Even if he did, that does not constitute the interpersonal paradigm.

Wachtel (1980), who also rejects the dichotomy, has attempted to state a different model by using Piaget's concept of the inevitable coexistence of assimilation and accomodation in the functioning of a schema—in this instance a schema of interpersonal relationship—in however differing proportions. In a recent statement of the issue Hoffman and I argued that interpersonal reality is of such a nature that a person's interpersonal motives must always have a degree of ambiguity (Gill and Hoffman, 1982). Given that this is the fact, the ascription of a particular motive to an analyst by a patient might rest on some subtle item that only the patient, because of his vested interest in seeing the situation in a particular way, would notice and make much of. We concluded that the patient's experience of the relationship was always plausible in this sense and that we therefore could not accept the view that the patient was distorting the "reality" as perceived by the analyst.

We emphasized that the patient's experience was still transference because it was his past that led him to organize the field as he did, to single out, for example, the particular item that others ignored but to which he attributed an idiosyncratic significance. We recognized that the patient and analyst could differ on their assessment of the situation. We reject the argument that the analyst's view is necessarily the correct one because we reject the view that the analyst can be the arbiter of reality, to use a phrase fairly commonly employed in the analytic literature by those who take the same position. I believe Sullivan's concept of "consensual validation" (1950, pp. 212–214) stems from a similar rejection of the analyst as the sole judge of external reality. Bromberg (1980, p. 237) has noted that Rapaport pointed out that Sullivan was one of the very few who emphasized the interpersonal context of reality testing.

Our argument in effect rests on the ambiguity and relativity of interpersonal reality. We continue to distinguish between transference and nontransference but the distinction is not between realistic and distorted but rather between rigidity and flexibility of an interpersonal attitude, that is, whether it is susceptible to influence from the outside. While we distinguish between the degree of involvement and the interpersonal paradigm we think it likely that any analyst who accepts the interpersonal paradigm is likely to consider the average expectable and acceptable involvement of an analyst to be greater than does an analyst who does not accept that paradigm.

If one holds to the interpersonal paradigm one will hold that transference and countertransference do indeed constitute a transaction rather than countertransference's being an occasional regrettable, even if in some ways, useful intrusion into a field essentially determined by the patient's realistic and transferential reactions. The recent book on countertransference edited by Epstein and Feiner (1979) shows a strong contemporary movement among those who call themselves interpersonalists toward such a transactional view of transference and countertransference.

I suggest that the various efforts to spell out a relationship between patient and analyst in addition to transference and countertransference such as a reality relationship and the variously proposed alliances are abortive movements toward the concept of a continuing transference-countertransference transaction.

Because *transference* continues to be defined by most people apart from the analyst's contribution, anyone who uses the term is considered to be restricting himself to the patient's contribution. I believe this is the reason for example that Chrzanowski (1980) believes he is differing with me when he advocates "an exploration of the personal relationship along with the transferential aspects of it rather than primarily in the service of the transference." He is ascribing to me the usual definition of *transference* and *countertransference* according to which they are distortions and in which the analyst's appropriate contribution is considered to be only a realistic alliance. I believe on the contrary that the attitudes and responses of each participant are complex unities arising from the transaction, each with its own plausibility. My suggestion that the transference be focused upon includes therefore what Chrzanowski feels is left out if one focuses only on transference.

It may be that here indeed lies a justification for coining a term like *parataxis* to substitute for the term *transference*. It is not uncommon to hear the two concepts referred to as different names for the same phenomenon. Aside from other differences however, I believe the true distinction between them lies in Sullivan's use of the concept parataxis to refer to the interpersonal field. He wrote for example: " . . . *parataxic;* that is, when, besides the interpersonal situation as defined within the awareness of the speaker, there is a concomitant interpersonal situation quite different as to its principal integrating tendencies, of which the speaker is more or less completely unaware" (1940, p. 92). I realize that Freud spoke of "situation" too, but he spoke of the analytic situation, while Sullivan spoke of the interpersonal situation. The difference is not merely verbal. Because parataxis is a concept in the framework of the interpersonal field, while transference is not unless it is redefined as in this paper, the concepts are indeed different, despite the fact that both Freud and Sullivan spoke of the patient's distortion of the situation.

THE ANALYST'S PARTICIPATION AND TECHNIQUE

Levenson has said that "proponents of Sullivan encounter some considerable difficulty, not in explicating the theoretical differences between Freud and Sullivan but in demonstrating the practical consequences for therapy" (1972, p. 181). I believe there are important consequences for therapy and that the difficulty in recognizing them is related to the failure to see clearly the distinction, which is the burden of this essay, that is between the therapist's participation and the interpersonal paradigm.

An important reason that it is difficult to spell out the technical implications of the interpersonal paradigm is that the paradigm does not have unequivocal implications for technique. I became most clearly aware of this when I realized that the implications Sullivan draws from it are very different from the ones I draw from it. Before I was clearly aware that I was working with the interpersonal paradigm I had come to the conclusion that transference, defined as I just have defined it, has to be the primary concern of technique and that therefore the first step in technique should be to clarify the patient's experience of the relationship, while the second should be to discover what is the patient's justification in the analyst's behavior or attitude or even just in a plausible conjecture as to the analyst's subjective feeling for the construction the patient makes of the field. But to clarify the patient's experience and to seek his justification for it means to make the interpersonal interaction in the analytic situation as the patient sees it as explicit as possible.

I turn first to Sullivan's views on the subject. There is no doubt about his belief that the patterns of interpersonal relation need to be made explicit. He said that "one achieves mental health to the extent that one becomes aware of one's interpersonal relations" (1940, p. 102). At the same time he clearly believed there were serious obstacles to doing so in the analytic situation itself, at least for some time. He wrote:

In general, in the treatment of personality there are three fields of events which are of very great relevance. First of these is the field of current events in the patient's life outside the treatment situation. . . . The second is his current relations in the treatment situation—that is, his relations with the psychiatrist. And the third field of relevant data is the events of the patient's past.

It is difficult for most people to be straightforward and forthright in discussing their feelings, thoughts, impulses, and so on, with respect to a person with whom they are in the peculiar relationship of patient to a psychiatrist. For a fairly long time at the start of all therapeutic work, most of our field of investigation is concerned with current events outside the treatment situation. . . . It is from current events that we move into the current therapeutic relationship between doctor and patient, uncovering both the noted and unnoted emotional problems which constitute the patient's difficulties in living (1954, p. 174, ftn.).

In fact there is abundant evidence in case material, both his own and supervised, that Sullivan did very little in the way of making the relationship in the analytic situation explicit, preferring to deal with it implicitly. This tendency is so marked that a careful study of his work led Havens (1976) to conclude that Sullivan essentially employed a counter-projective technique, that is, "the patient's surmises about the therapist's attitudes, his projections onto the therapist are actively combatted" (p. 15), and I add—by means other than interpretation. An example from Sullivan: The patient hints about thoughts he expects the therapist to find horrible. After eliciting them, Sullivan writes: "One has to be prepared for an eruption of this sort of thing, and probably my response would be, 'well, hell, you must have felt terribly *sore* sometimes in the past.' That proves that I am not horrified and I don't get in too deep. I have tossed out a lifeline, the awful stuff is before us, and we are still there" (Mullahy, 1952, p. 147).

Havens approves and says that Sullivan "has abandoned the parental authoritative position doctors so easily assume" and done something better than saying "I am not one of those who disapprove" (1976, p. 15). An alternative not taken by Sullivan would have been to make the patient's fear explicit and say: "you are afraid I will disapprove."

But that is not Sullivan's way. In fact as a second major difference between interpersonal psychiatry and psychoanalysis, in addition to the idea that transference does not only develop but is present from the start, Havens (1976) concludes that transference cannot always be effectively interpreted, but must often be acted against (p. 25, ftn.).

Mary White's (1952) discussion of Sullivan's technique and a review of Sullivan's supervisory work in detail in the recent report edited by Kvarnes and Parloff (1976), as well as more globally in the cases treated by Tower (1947) and Cohen (1947), make clear how thoroughly Sullivan avoided making the relationship in the analytic situation explicit. In the case treated by Kvarnes, the rare instances in which the therapist did make the transference explicit were essentially ignored.

Perhaps the extent to which he was involved with sicker patients is responsible for Sullivan's reluctance to make the interaction explicit. Perhaps it reflected his general aversion to interpretation, of which he caustically said the supply far outweighs the demand. Perhaps it was because of his distrust of the magic of words. In the vignette I referred to, for example, he did much more than say that the patient must have been terribly sore. When he suspected that the patient was struggling with the ideas he considered horrible, Sullivan indicated his disrespect for such things by saying for example, "God help us, why must we have this hokum when we are doing useful work most of the time? I know something bothers you but does it have to be disguised as a catastrophe?" and so on. His whole attitude was designed to demonstrate that he was not horrified. In his general discussions of communication in *The Psychiatric Interview* (1954) he lays much stress on non-verbal communication. Yet it remains true that he did very little by way of making the interaction explicit, in words at any rate.

In this respect there is an irony in the difference between Sullivan and Freud. Sullivan made the interpersonal paradigm explicit while Freud did not, but Sullivan did much less to make the transference in the analytic relationship explicit than did Freud.

But what was true of Sullivan is not true of present-day interpersonalists insofar as I can judge current practice from the literature. Analysis of the transference clearly plays an important role in neo-Sullivanian technique. Even so I believe that a more explicit spelling out of the implications for technique of the interpersonal paradigm would be useful. I will state some of these implications and will illustrate their application by vignettes drawn largely from papers published in *Contemporary Psychoanalysis*.

Before doing so however I want to comment generally on the spirit in which I present this and other vignettes. I ran across a remark by Antonovsky (1980) that almost made me laugh out loud: " . . . when it comes to clinical examples, anyone courageous or foolhardy enough to tell what [she] did invites in a horde of critics eager to explain to the reporting therapist what instead she could have done, should have done, or, worse yet, what she "really" did do" (p. 208). I am not implying some ideal in which no mistakes are made. I do suggest however that the more clearly and explicitly a principle is stated the more does one increase the likelihood that it will be applied more consistently.

In line with the distinction that is the theme of this paper I emphasize that the implications I draw for technique are based on the interpersonal paradigm and not on the assumption of a major participation on the analyst's part.

(1) The first principle I propose is that because the presenting manifestation of psychopathology lies in the immediate interpersonal interaction, the therapist should be ever ready to inquire into the patient's experience of the relationship. Sullivan said that "The psychiatrist . . . plays a very active role in introducing interrogations, not to show that he is smart or that he is skeptical, but literally to make sure that he knows what he is being told" (1954, p. 21). The statement does not refer to what he is being told about the patient's experience of the relationship. Indeed one could see the principle that a therapist should make sure that he knows what he is being told as antecedent to the principle that he should make sure that he knows what he is being told about the patient's experience of the relationship.

I will give two examples, one from Levenson and one from Chrzanowski of what I consider to be insufficient inquiry into the patient's experience of the relationship.

The illustration from Levenson occurs in a paper entitled "Facts or Fantasies" (1981) the central thrust of which is to argue that the "data of psychoanalysis are disguised reality, and not autonomous fantasy" (pp. 494–495). Criticizing a vignette offered by Greenson (1976) Levenson writes: "The patient points out that when he expresses political opinions that match the therapist's he gets marginal cues of approval; when he doesn't he is subjected to masked hostile analysis . . . [The analyst, that is, Greenson] validates the patient's perception, admits his fault and then asks, why do you feel obliged to satisfy my political views." Levenson assesses this remark by the analyst as playing out exactly the kind of authoritarian inquiry of which the patient complains and recommends instead that patient and analyst should talk about their mutual experience rather than "analyze" the patient's distortions.

I will later refer approvingly to Levenson's application of structuralist thinking to the analytic situation in his emphasis on the isomorphic transformation that leads the patient to hear what the analyst says as though it confirmed his preexisting expectations—in this instance that the analyst is authoritarian. But here Levenson overgeneralizes the principle.

My own criticism of Greenson's question would take a different tack and illustrates a third approach to the issue involved. Not only would it not assume that one knew how the patient experienced this exchange but it would also focus on the most immediate aspect of the patient's experience of it.

Does it not seem plausible that if the patient has finally plucked up the courage to complain, the most immediately significant aspect of the exchange to him would be that Greenson validated his perception? Should Greenson not have looked for direct or indirect indications of the patient's response to the fact that the analyst validated his observation?

The illustration points up that one cannot assume that one's view of what is the most immediate here-and-now is the same as the patient's experience of the matter. One might consider it to be why the patient feels obliged to satisfy the analyst's views, or even their mutual experience, meaning by that how it came about that they interacted as they did about their political views. Or as I suggest, that it is the complaint and its validation in this instance. One must also recognize that unless one concedes that there is often a time lag between the time something happens in the interaction and when it gets talked about, the patient would face a barrage of inquiry and would be unable to develop a theme.

To take another example of inadequate inquiry, Chrzanowski (1980) tells a vignette of a patient who suggested that the analyst's mind was not functioning well as a result of a recent illness. The analyst called this a crude attack on his mental faculties, a formulation that suggests to me his feelings were hurt, all the more so perhaps because the patient had expressed solicitude by sending him a get-well card when he was in the hospital. The analyst responded by saying that for all he knew his mind was working well and then he interpreted that perhaps the patient was feeling cut off from him and concealing an element of compassion by his criticism. The patient responded with tears and thanked the analyst the next day, which the analyst clearly took as validation of his interpretation, (pp. 363–364).

Chrzanowski does tell us that the patient felt the analyst was not paying close attention and that he had changed the subject when the patient was in the midst of something he was explaining. I suggest that it is a reasonable hypothesis that the analyst made the interpretation he did to overcome his distress at the patient's criticism and that only further inquiry into the patient's experience would have clarified what was going on.

Chrzanowski uses the vignette as a basis for his argument that there is relational participation as well as transference and countertransference. He calls the former non-technical and the latter technical. I agree that the analyst does much that is not intended as technical but I also suggest that a split between transference-countertransference and participation-relation increases the likelihood that a situation such as the one I described will be dealt with by conjecture rather than inquiry. Levenson correctly says that the "attribution of meaning to behavior is a highly arbitrary business" (1981, p. 197). All the more reason that we should do more inquiring and less interpreting.

(2) The second principle I offer is that the analyst should always be ready to consider that associations not explicitly about the relationship may nevertheless be disguised allusions to it. The centrality of the interpersonal relationship and the reluctance to be clearly aware of many aspects of it on the part of both participants—although in this connection I am emphasizing the analyst's participation—is such that there will be ubiquitously present disguised allusions to the relationship in the patient's associations.

I offer a vignette from Chrzanowski (1980) which I think illustrates the failure to employ this principle though I assume that it is a principle he accepts. Chrzanowski tells of a situation with a patient who was in serious conflict as to whether to marry a girl from a markedly different background. He feared his loneliness and despair were he not to marry her. At this point he turned to the analyst and asked his opinion. The analyst replied that he was not in a position to tell him what to do but made it clear that he understood his predicament and felt sympathy for his reluctance to get married under the prevailing conditions. Chrzanowski summarizes that he found it compatible with his position as an analyst to show the patient where he stood despite strong emphasis on the subjectivity of his support. Chrzanowski refers to his stance as being a relational participant rather than simply a participant observer. I suggest that the technical implication of the interpersonal paradigm would rather have been to investigate the possibility that the conflict about his relation with the girl—important and even crucial though it was in the patient's life—was being used in the analysis as a disguised allusion to a conflict about his relation with the analyst and that the investigation of this conflict in the transference-countertransference situation would have been more valuable than the stance the analyst took.[2]

Levenson (1972, p. 189) criticizes this view that the patient's associations can be understood as disguised allusions to the transference as subject to the caricataure of becoming a therapeutic gimmick in the hands of what he calls "here-and-now" oriented psychoanalytic therapists. That can happen but not for the reason he proposes. It can become a gimmick if the analyst mechanically assumes that anything said must relate to the interaction without making such a hypothesis plausible by relating it to something the analyst has said or done. Levenson says that after all the patient may be talking about an outside relationship, using the analyst as medium. My rejoinder would be that what the patient is talking about is meaningful for *both* his outside relationship and his relationship with the analyst. To focus on the meaning in the analytic interaction is not to deny the significance of the outside meaning but to deal with the interaction in the analytic situation on the assumption that the outside and inside meanings are parallel and that the progress of the analysis is best served by giving priority to clarifying that interaction rather than priority to the interaction in outside relationships. This is not to deny the value in showing the connection between the two.

(3) My third and last implication for technique, one that follows only somewhat indirectly from the interpersonal paradigm because it makes an assumption about involvement as well, is that the analyst will inevitably to a greater or lesser degree fall in with the patient's prior expectations. It is well stated in Levenson's (1972) book *The Fallacy of Understanding*. He says that what makes the therapy is the therapist's "ability to be trapped, immersed and participating in the system and then to work his way out" (1972, p. 174). I had an interesting experience with Levenson's book. It seemed clearly important and insightful to me, so much so that I began recommending it to colleagues. But I kept feeling that some important issue in it was eluding me. I could not clearly understand exactly why he called it *The Fallacy of Understanding*. I think I understand now. As I see it the book makes three main points that are not separated as sharply as they might be. One, which is structuralism applied to the analytic exchange, says that the same theme will be expressed in varied guises in the interaction between the two participants, most notably in the content of their exchange and in the meaning of their behavioral interaction. Two is the analyst always succumbs to a greater or lesser but significant degree to the patient's pressure to experience the interaction according to the patient's prior neurotic expectations. Sandler (1976) calls this the analyst's role responsiveness. Three is the patient interprets whatever the analyst does as evidence for his prior neurotic expectations. Levenson's wish to emphasize this last point leads him to deemphasize insight and to speak of the fallacy of understanding. He pushes the point so far as to call the therapist and patient "each other's creations" (p. 185). He makes what I consider to be the contradictory statements that on the one hand the analyst has to resist transformation and on the other hand that he "acts from within the structure of the patient's transactional field" (p. 214), that he becomes "a total participant" (p. 215), and that intent lies in effect (pp. 76 and 203). Hence the "fallacy of understanding." Hence the description of therapy as though it were a matter of the "aesthetics of

experience . . . rather than content and meaning'' (p. 211). Hence the conclusion that ''neither insight, clarification, nor novel experience will make the difference'' (p. 213).

Levenson recognizes that if he leaves his argument at that point, there is no room for the analyst to have an influence on the patient. He makes various attempts to extricate himself from this dilemma in his book. In later papers however he makes what I consider a more balanced formulation. It is that the therapeutic process is both participation and understanding, that is, that the therapist inevitably participates and works his way out of that participation by progressive understanding of the interaction, at the same time communicating that understanding to the patient, who of course plays a role in reaching that understanding too, at least in what he says in response to the therapist's effort to understand what the patient is experiencing and how he accounts for that experience. It is the idea that understanding alone will suffice that is the fallacy because it fails to take account of the inevitable participation on the analyst's part. In a paper published recently (1982) Levenson achieves a view that takes both insight and experience into account. He writes: *"The power of psychoanalysis may well depend on what is said about what is done* as a continuous, integral part of the therapy'' (p. 101).[3]

Levenson offers several good examples of the analyst's role responsiveness in his discussion of the case of a young woman he treated (1972). I will give one illustration. She had come home from college because of a sudden panic despite being in supportive psychotherapy. After three apparently good sessions the patient made an abortive suicide attempt. When she came for her next interview she was shockingly changed, apparently in a paranoid state. Instead of making the easy assumption that this was a natural progression of her disorder the analyst searched for how he might have been responsible and made a suggestion about that, which led to a marked improvement in her state. The suggestion was that he was so pleased with her cooperativeness and apparent cheerfulness because it was easier to deal with than to recognize how terribly upset she was. He fulfilled her expectation that, like her parents, he would prefer not to have to deal with her serious distress (pp. 167–169).

In this instance the analyst was sharp enough to deduce what had happened, but what if he could not come up with a suggestion and still held fast to the assumption I have stated as the third principle that he must be contributing to what is happening? The answer would lie in the first two principles I described. He would try to understand her experience of the relationship by careful inquiry and he would assume that associations that were not manifestly about the relationship were nevertheless probably disguised allusions to it.

SHOULD THE ANALYST REVEAL HIS FEELINGS?

The conviction that the transference-countertransference interaction is a transaction raises the difficult question of how explicit the analyst should be in revealing how he experiences his own participation. It is clear that there is a major difference of opinion between those who advocate a significant degree of self revelation and those who oppose it. Chrzanowski refers to an atmosphere of "exchanging and documenting mutual impressions, emotions, and observations" (1980, p. 354). Levenson (1972) suggests that one facilitates a shift in the patient's structure "not by interpreting the patient's resistance to one's truth but by reporting one's *own* experience of the transaction" (p. 211). I do not think it is always wrong to report one's own experience though I believe that when one does so one must be especially alert to how the patient experiences such a report. I realize that often the very inquiry into a particular exchange may be so revealing of something the analyst is experiencing that it would be fatuous to pretend one has not revealed it. Nevertheless, I think it best to be quite chary with such revelations. I believe they have a tendency to shut off further inquiry into the patient's experience, not least because such inquiry might lead to the exposure of something on the analyst's part that he would rather not know about. Furthermore the analyst must recognize that his subjective experience may be as defensive on his own part as he believes the patient's conscious attitudes are. He cannot therefore assume that if he reports his own experience that is the end of the story. But the pursuit of the possible hidden implications of his experience would change the analysis of the patient into a mutual analysis of patient and analyst. Some therapists advocate just that. I assume it is clear that I do not. The position that the analyst makes a major contribution to the transaction does not necessarily mean that a mutual analysis is desirable or perhaps even possible.

My emphasis on the significant role of the analyst in the interaction can be misunderstood to imply a failure to attribute enough importance to the role of fixed patterns of behavior in the patient. I do not intend such an implication. That I may seem to be doing so is an unfortunate result of my emphasis on what I believe is usually not emphasized. The ultimate goal is indeed the exploration and change of the patient's patterns of relationship. The exploration of the analyst's contribution is a prior and necessary means to that end. Such exploration changes the atmosphere of the analysis from one in which the patient is wrong to one in which the patient's point of view gets more respectful hearing. As the patient sees that he is rigidly prone to evaluate and create situations in predetermined terms he can come to see that other evaluations of reality and ways of relating are also possible and is thus embarked on the road to change in his patterns of interpersonal interaction.

THE EXPLORATION OF THE PAST

The great emphasis on the here-and-now, which inevitably accompanies the suggestions I have made for the technical implications of the interpersonal paradigm with the possibility of a substantial contribution by the analyst to the transference-countertransference transaction, may also seem to imply an underemphasis on the role of the exploration of the patient's past in the analytic process.

Despite wise injunctions to distribute one's attention evenly between past and present there is a reciprocal relationship between emphasis on one or the other, and, as I said, it is inevitable that one will emphasize what one considers to be generally underemphasized. Sullivan (1954) like most Freudians, emphasizes the recovery of the past. He wrote somewhat ambivalently:

When we locate a problem, identifying something that is impractical, inefficient, and definitely contrary to the achievement of the patient's idealized goals, we have every reason to return to the third field of greatly relevant data—the distant past in which this particular emotional difficulty had its beginning. It is important to notice that finding out how things start often provides a great deal of information as to what they represent, whereas their more sophisticated, more mature manifestations may be very obscure indeed. However, some patients, as I have already said, have a distinct tendency to alter history to suit their wishes or needs; to them, the present has the virtue of being capable of at least some investigation, whereas the past is apt to be pretty heavily colored. From this general standpoint, what is currently going on has a very special significance (p. 174, ftn.).

In another remark he emphasizes the importance of seeing the connection between the past and the present:

Until a patient has seen clearly and unmistakably a concrete example of the way in which unresolved situations from the distant past color the perception of present situations and over-complicate actions in them, there can be no material reorganization of personality, no therapeutically satisfactory expansion of the self, no significant insight into the complexities of one's performances or into the unexpected and often disconcerting behavior of others concerned'' (1940, p. 101).

I am not sure that this last is true. In any case I believe the relative importance of present and past and their connection that can best serve an analysis will vary among patients, analysts, and patient-analyst pairs.

THE RELATIONSHIP AS A FACTOR IN BRINGING ABOUT CHANGE

I turn to the question of whether the interpersonal paradigm and the view that the analyst may play a substantial role in the transference-countertransference transaction has necessary consequences for the role of the interpersonal relationship between patient and analyst in bringing about change. The question as I have just put it must be differentiated into the role of new experience as such and the role of new experience that is examined and reflected upon.[4] The former may well be relatively ineffective and the latter of central consequence. Without this distinction one could easily misunderstand Levenson, for example, to deny the role of new experience when he writes, as I have already quoted in part: "The therapist's 'new' experience will emerge as stale as yesterday's insight. From the organismic perspective neither insight, clarification nor novel experience will make the difference.'' One might think that Levenson is even attempting to shame a therapist who believes that new experience in a therapeutic relationship makes a difference by saying that: "the idea that the therapist 'cured' through his kindness, respect for the patient, love, is an incredible conceit considering both the complexity of the patient's needs and the emotional capacity of most psychoanalysts, which largely are no better or worse than most men's'' (1972, pp. 213–214).

Levenson perhaps overstates this point. Schafer (1983) has suggested that the analyst, in his role as analyst, is very often able to behave with much more consideration and tact than he is in his life outside, though I realize there are limits to how different he can be. From his writings in general, notably in the concept of resisting transformation, it is clear that Levenson ascribes crucial importance to new experience, but both the old and the new patterns must be explicitly examined.

The distinction I have just offered is ordinarily not made. Instead interpersonalists and Freudians are described as differing sharply in the role ascribed to new experience, with Freudians insisting that insight is the only truly mutative agent.

Greenberg (1981), for example, suggests that despite their differences, Sullivan and Fairbairn agree that "change comes about as a result of the analyst's use of himself as a new person to break into the closed inner world of the patient" (p. 249). He refers to Valenstein's (1980) position that insofar as the *"real* relationship to the analyst as a *real* person is considered to be pivotal" this leads to what Valenstein calls "interpersonally promoted experiential effects," that is, to "not-real-psychoanalysis" (pp. 117–118). Once again there is the implied condensation of degree of involvement and interpersonal paradigm in referring to "real" and "pivotal" effects as "interpersonally promoted."

One can find here and there in the writing of Freudian analysts references to the significant role of the relationship in bringing about change (Loewald, 1960; Dewald, 1976). But as Greenberg points out these views may be accomodations made by the Freudian paradigm and not a significant change in paradigm.

In addition to the distinction between new experience that is and is not explicitly examined, a discussion of the role of experience in analysis can be clarified by a related distinction between advertent and inadvertent interpersonal influence exerted by the analyst in his interaction with the patient (Gill, 1979b and Reppen, 1982).

I believe the failure to make this distinction leads Greenberg to the mistaken conclusion that there is a contradiction between Loewald's earlier (1960) depiction of psychoanalysis as a developmental experience and his insistence in a recent statement that encouragement and reassurance are not analytic.

By an inadvertent interpersonal effect I mean, for example, an analyst's making an interpretation that the patient experiences as a criticism when, so far as the analyst was aware, the analyst had no such intent. An advertent interpersonal intervention would be one in which he encouraged, reassured, scolded, or whatever knowing that he was doing something intended to have such an effect. Even then I would say that what is unanalytic would not be that the analyst engaged in such an intervention but only if he failed to look for and make explicit the interpersonal significance to the patient of his intervention.

Here perhaps we come upon a genuine difference of opinion as to what is analytic. I define a non-analytic behavior as one in which the therapist fails to make explicit an interpersonal experience that he knows the patient is having and that he knows the patient would be unable to speak about freely.

That means that I would say that if Sullivan attempted to bring about an interpersonal effect knowingly and did not make that interaction explicit in the relationship even if he realized that the patient would resist recognizing what had happened, he was being non-analytic. I do not mean to imply that the analyst would have to interpret his view of how the patient had experienced his intervention as soon as the analyst realized what happened but that his ultimate aim would be to bring inadvertent effects of the interaction to awareness as much as possible.

Greenberg (1981) is of the opinion that my recent paper (1979a) on the analysis of transference remains in the drive paradigm and that, in common with other Freudians who ascribe some significance to the relationship in bringing about change, I assume that ultimately "analytic change derives from interpretation, from some version of making the unconscious conscious, rather than from an aspect of the actual encounter with the analyst" (pp. 253–254).

That is not my view (see Gill and Hoffman, 1982). I believe that Greenberg's position is too dichotomous. Greenberg refers approvingly to Fairbairn's position that every interpretation is really an intervention. I would alter that to read that every interpretation is *also* an intervention. I might note in passing that Kernberg (1980) considers the difference between borderline personalities and transference neurotics to be that the former take an interpretation to be a personal intervention whereas the latter do not. Kernberg therefore advises that the interpersonal significance of interpretation has to be interpreted in borderline personalities. I assume that we would agree that the interpersonal significance of an interpretation would have to be interpreted in the whole range of patients. That is, the interpersonal significance of an interpretation will require an interpretation if there is evidence that the patient experiences it in a way that he is unable either to be conscious of or to tell the analyst freely if he is conscious of it. In that case it is the analyst's job to look for allusions to the interpersonal significance of the interpretation to the patient.

I believe that both insight and new experience play a role in bringing about change in psychoanalysis. I do not believe that the relative roles of the two are the same for all analyses. I suspect that the more a result is dependent upon insight alone rather than a new experience as well the less is it likely that it will be maintained in the face of life's vicissitudes. Most of all I believe that the insight into one's patterns of interpersonal relationship at the same time that one is being exposed to a new pattern of interpersonal relationship is the most mutative of all. Especially is this true if the insight is into the comparison between the old and the new at the very moment that the inclination to behave according to the old pattern is being met by an opportunity to relate in a new way.

CONCLUDING STATEMENT

I have argued that the interpersonal paradigm does not necessarily imply a conviction that the analyst plays a major role in the analytic interaction even though there is considerable evidence in both Freudian and interpersonal literature that the two are often considered to go together. I have discussed the difficulty one encounters in stating how important a role one is ascribing to the analyst in the interaction and have catalogued a number of terms employed to connote the nature of that ascription. On the basis of a conviction that the interpersonal paradigm is the appropriate one for the therapeutic situation, I have suggested a redefinition of *transference*. The definition would change from the customary one of transference as a distortion of a reality defined by the analyst to a conception of a transference-countertransference transaction in which from the differing perspectives of patient and analyst each has a view that has its plausibility. I discussed a number of implications of the interpersonal paradigm for psychoanalytic technique. They are: increased attention to the here-and-now patient-analyst transaction including increased attention to the patient's experience of the relationship, to disguised allusions to the transaction in the patient's associations and to the basis in the therapist's behavior on which the patient justifies his experiences, including the assumption that the analyst inevitably responds to a greater or lesser degree to the patient's pressure on him to behave in ways that conform to the patient's prior expectations. I conclude with some comments on the relative roles of the here-and-now and the exploration of the past history and on the relative roles of insight and new experience in bringing about change.

A last word: A response to the idea that the analyst often plays a significantly participant role could well be that it has merit but is overblown. I mean that it could be argued that I have emphasized only the extreme of a continuum of degrees of involvement. It could be conceded that the attitude toward a substantial involvement might well be changed from a rebuke to the analyst for his countertransference to a more relaxed acceptance of our common humanity with the advice to try to work one's way out of the involvement. As matters now stand one's position on the frequency of major involvement is a matter of one's own experience and one's general view of human nature. Only an examination by an external observer of the details of what actually goes on in any particular analysis would show what the analyst's involvement is. I suspect it would very often be significantly greater than he thought it was. One might require a span of sessions to detect the involvement in any particular instance because silence on the analyst's part can hide many qualities and intensities of feelings.

NOTES

1. Commenting on this paper Hoffman (1983) wrote: "The term 'participation' is ambiguous throughout. It's not clear whether it refers to external *behavior* or to internal emotional *states*. They may correlate but behavior *can* be controlled more than internal states, so behavior can be more readily 'prescribed' although not entirely, of course."
2. If it is countered that one is entitled to conclude only that the patient's manner of relating to the analyst is the issue rather than that there is a specific connection between the *content* of the patient's associations and his relation to the analyst I reply that in principle they are the same.
3. Compare this statement by Sullivan (1950): "No great progress can be made in this field of study [psychiatry] until it is realized that the field of observation is what people do with each other, what they can communicate to each other about what they do with each other (pp. 220–221).
4. I realize this may seem to threaten an infinite regress. I believe the escape from that conceptual possibility is that it is not necessary for the patient to examine and reflect upon his experience in the relationship unless there is an obstacle to his becoming aware of that experience.

REFERENCES

Abrams, S. and Shengold, L. (1978) Some reflexions on the topic of the 30th congress: "Affects and the psychoanalytic situation." *International Journal of Psychoanalysis*, 59: 395–407.

Antonovsky, A. (1980) Object relationship or object relations? *Contemporary Psychoanalysis*, 16: 203–210.

Bird, B. (1972) Notes on transference. *Journal of the American Psychoanalytic Association*, 20: 267–301.

Bromberg, P. (1980) Sullivan's concept of "consensual validation." *Contemporary Psychoanalysis*, 16: 237–248.

Chrzanowski, G. (1977) *Interpersonal Approach to Psychoanalysis*. New York: Gardner Press.

Chrzanowski, G. (1980) Collaborative inquiry, affirmation, and neutrality in the psychoanalytic situation. *Contemporary Psychoanalysis*, 16: 348–366.

Cohen, M. (1947) The management of anxiety in a case of paranoid schizophrenia. *Psychiatry*, 10: 143–157.

Dewald, P. (1976) Transference regression and real experience in the psychoanalytic process. *The Psychoanalytic Quarterly*, 43: 213–230.

Epstein, L. and Feiner, A. (1979) *Countertransference*. New York: Jason Aronson, Inc.

Freud, S. (1912) Recommendations to physicians practicing psychoanalysis. *Standard Edition*, 12: 111–120. London: Hogarth Press, 1958.

Freud, S. (1916–1917) Introductory lectures on psychoanalysis. *Standard Edition*, 16: 243–496. London: Hogarth Press, 1963.

Freud, S. (1921) Group psychology and the analysis of the ego. *Standard Edition*, 18: 67–143. London: Hogarth Press, 1955.

Freud, S. (1922) Some neurotic mechanisms in jealousy, paranoia, and homosexuality. *Standard Edition*, 18: 223–232. London: Hogarth Press, 1955.

Freud, S. (1927) Letter to Oskar Pfister. In *Sigmund Freud: Psychoanalysis and Faith*. H. Meng and E. Freud, eds. New York: Basic Books, 1963.

Freud, S. (1937) Analysis terminable and interminable. *Standard Edition*, 23: 216–253. London: Hogarth Press, 1964.

Freud, S. (1937) Constructions in analysis. *Standard Edition*, 23: 257–269. London: Hogarth Press, 1964.

Gill, M. (1979a) The analysis of transference. *Journal of the American Psychoanalytic Association*, 27 Supplement: 263–288.

Gill, M. (1979b) Psychoanalysis and Psychotherapy—1954–1979. Symposium on psychoanalysis and psychotherapy—Similarities and differences—a 25 year perspective. Atlanta, October 20. (Unpublished.)

Gill, M. and Hoffman, I. (1980) A contribution to: Some views on effective principles of psychotherapy. *Cognitive Therapy and Research* (Special issue: *Psychotherapy Process*), 4: 271–306. Reprinted in *Converging Themes in Psychotherapy*. M. Goldfried, ed., 155–190. New York: Springer, 1982.

Gill, M. and Hoffman, I. (1982) A method for studying the analysis of aspects of the patient's experience of the relationship in psychoanalysis and psychotherapy. *Journal of the American Psychoanalytic Association*, 30: 137–168.

Greenberg, J. (1981) Prescription or description: therapeutic action of psychoanalysis. *Contemporary Psychoanalysis*, 17: 239–257.

Greenson, R. (1976) *The Technique and Practice of Psychoanalysis*. New York: International Universities Press.

Grinberg, L. (1979) Projective counteridentification and countertransference. In: *Countertransference*, L. Epstein and A. Feiner, eds. New York: Jason Aronson, Inc., 169–191.

Havens, L. (1976) *Participant Observation*. New York: Jason Aronson, Inc.

Hoffman, I. (1983) The patient as interpreter of the analyst's experience. *Contemporary Psychoanalysis*, 19: 389–422.

Kernberg, O. (1980) *Internal World and External Reality*. New York: Jason Aronson, Inc.

Khan, M. (1972) On Freud's provision of the therapeutic frame. In: M. Khan, *The Privacy of the Self*. New York: International Universities Press, 129–135.

Kohut, H. (1959) Introspection, empathy, and psychoanalysis. *Journal of the American Psychoanalytic Association*, 7: 459–483.

Kvarnes, R. and Parloff, G., eds. (1976) *A Harry Stack Sullivan Case Seminar*. New York: W. W. Norton and Co.

Langs, R. (1978) The adaptational-interactional dimension of countertransference. *Contemporary Psychoanalysis*, 14: 502–533. And: *Technique in Transition*. New York: Jason Aronson, Inc.

Levenson, E. (1972) *The Fallacy of Understanding*. New York: Basic Books.

Levenson, E. (1981) Facts or fantasies: The nature of psychoanalytic data. *Contemporary Psychoanalysis*, 17: 486–500.

Levenson, E. (1982) Language and healing. In: *Curative Factors in Dynamic Psychotherapy*. S. Slipp, ed. New York: McGraw-Hill, pp. 91–103.

Lipton, S. (1977) The advantages of Freud's technique as shown in his analysis of the Rat Man. *International Journal of Psycho-Analysis*, 58: 255–274.

Loewald, H. (1960) On the therapeutic action of psychoanalysis. *International Journal of Psycho-Analysis*, 41: 16–33.

McLaughlin, J. (1981) Transference, psychic reality, and countertransference. *The Psychoanalytic Quarterly*, 50: 639–664.

Mullahy, P., ed. (1952) *The Contributions of Harry Stack Sullivan*. New York: Hermitage House.

Racker, H. (1968) *Transference and Countertransference*. New York: International Universities Press.

Reppen, J. (1982) Merton Gill: An interview. *Psychoanalytic Review*, 69: 167–190.

Sandler, J. (1976) Countertransference and role responsiveness. *International Review of Psycho-Analysis*, 3: 43–47.

Schafer, R. (1983) *The Analytic Attitude*. New York: Basic Books.

Scharfman, M. (1979) Panel discussion: Conceptualizing the nature of the therapeutic action of psychoanalysis. *Journal of the American Psychoanalytic Association*, 27: 627–642.

Singer, E. (1965) *Key Concepts in Psychotherapy*. New York: Random House.

Stone, L. (1981) Some thoughts on the "here and now" in psychoanalytic technique and process. *The Psychoanalytic Quarterly*, 50: 709–733.

Sullivan, H. (1940) *Conceptions of Modern Psychiatry*. New York: W. W. Norton and Co.

Sullivan, H. (1950) The illusion of personal individuality. In: *The Fusion of Psychiatry and Social Science*. New York: W. W. Norton and Co., 1964, 198–226.

Sullivan, H. (1954) *The Psychiatric Interview*. H. Perry and M. Gawel, eds. New York: W. W. Norton and Co.

Sullivan's concept of participant observation (a symposium). (1977) *Contemporary Psychoanalysis*, 13: 347–386.

Tarachow, S. (1963) *An Introduction to Psychotherapy*. New York: International Universities Press.

Tower, S. (1947) Management of paranoid trends in treatment of a post-psychotic obsessional condition. *Psychiatry*, 10: 137–141.

Valenstein, A. (1980) The concept of "classical" psychoanalysis. In: *Psychoanalytic Explorations of Technique*. H. Blum, ed. New York: International Universities Press, 113–136.

Wachtel, P. (1980) The relevance of Piaget to the psychoanalytic theory of transference. *The Annual of Psychoanalysis*, 8: 59–76. New York: International Universities Press.

White, M. (1952) Sullivan and treatment. *Contemporary Psychoanalysis*, 1977, 13: 317–346.

Wolstein, B. (1959) *Countertransference*. New York: Grune and Stratton.

Wolstein, B. (1960) Transference: historical roots and current concepts in psychoanalytic theory and practice. *Psychiatry*, 23: 159–172.

Wolstein, B. (1981) The psychic realism of psychoanalytic inquiry. *Contemporary Psychoanalysis*, 17: 399–412.

18. The Pluralism of Perspectives on Countertransference

Benjamin Wolstein

Much historical research is required now for developing a fuller knowledge of the current psychoanalytic situation of the 1980s, as it both derives and differs from that of the 1930s. Almost half a century has already passed and we are, culturally speaking, light years away from a uniform, unqualified, and unquestioning belief in the necessary determinism of biology or the relational conditioning of sociology. Neither "environment" of the psyche is absolute. Such a research effort will, therefore, essentially be philosophical in content and reconstructive in scope. Of special interest are two questions. First, from within the standpoint of the ego-interpersonal perspectives, where do such environmentalist psychoanalysts as Sullivan and Hartmann, among others, find the logical and empirical grounds even to create their personal perspectives, let alone account for the uniquely individual, selfic resources from which they derive their own distinctly innovative directions? That of course, is a perspectival question concerning the overall construction of their special points of view. The second question concerns the clinical interaction. Does their systematic exclusion of the patient's uniquely individual, first-personal processes from the structure of psychoanalytic inquiry, in practical terms, also extend the psychoanalyst's authority unilaterally, and reinforce it for managing the procedures and for selecting the goals of the therapeutic inquiry? In other words: Does this exclusion of their own and their patient's immediate experience of first-personal processes mainly appeal to psychoanalysts who believe that it is they, of themselves, who control the conditions under which their patients appear to change? I shall not, of course, attempt to develop the clinical and speculative implications of these themes in exhaustive detail here. But my comments, below, on the radical individuation

Read in part, with changes, at the Annual Week-End Meeting of the W. A. White Psychoanalytic Society, Walker Valley, New York, April 1982.

of psychoanalytic metapsychologies are, as we shall see, also suggestive of ways to address them.

I

As background for this discussion, it is useful to introduce a closely related theme. Let us consider in some detail why we are, at present, witness in clinical psychoanalytic inquiry to the increasing reports of evidence for the psychology of the self and for its origins in the immediate experience of first-personal processes. I trace its beginnings to the direct clinical work with countertransference and, later, with counterresistance and counteranxiety, undertaken as a serious effort for the psychoanalytic field of inquiry in which that work is done. It begins to occur during those phases of the inquiry, especially, in which both the psychoanalyst undergoing counterresistance and counteranxiety, and the patient in the analysis of transference, undergoing resistance and anxiety, cooperate to explore the interlocking of their unconscious and preconscious experience.

For this sort of exploratory inquiry to take hold, the two coparticipants must, without serious reservation, be open to seeking their own particular contributions to that interlocking. They cannot, in any case, work through their interlocking of transference and countertransference with a reasonable degree of adequacy until, in some measure, either or both are accorded the psychic space in the experiential field of therapy to stand behind what they each, in their own special ways, feel and think, desire and imagine, believe and realize. To take such a stand, they soon discover, requires a point of psychic origin from within the experience of its possessor, unsupported from without by the ego-interpersonal other in their shared field of inquiry. Now literally undefended, they must, on their own, fend for themselves. Whence, in their direct experience of this transaction, the observable rise of first-personal processes. It falls into the format, to both their own. In other words: Who, finally, generates "my" transference, the patient asks? or who generates "my" countertransference, the psychoanalyst asks?—to which each coparticipant must, eventually, give a uniquely personal answer. On taking personal responsibility, their response, "I" do, given during the actual working through of transference interlocked with countertransference, is, for the ego-interpersonal model, the major point of breakthrough into this new direction in psychoanalytic thought.

But still another, perhaps less obvious source of this increasing evidence for the psychology of the self may be found stored away in the 1930s ego-interpersonal model. There it was to remain long hidden and waiting, until the new clinical exploration of the immediate experience of first-personal processes brought it to the surface. It came out into the open in the following way: As a logical step beyond the id model, the patient's ego or interpersona was admitted to full participation during the actual therapeutic inquiry. That clinical change Ferenczi and Rank and Reich began in the 1920s; A. Freud and Hartmann and Sullivan and Thompson, among others, completed it in the 1930s. So now, in the context of this new ego-interpersonal experience, the patient, after undergoing the lengthy and arduous procedures of clarifying some central irrational distortions of transference, may therefore come to perceive and understand self and others more directly, more clearly, more openly. What, then, is more natural and expectable than for the patient, in turn, to exercise this fresh sense of clarity in the very field of psychoanalytic inquiry in which, for the first time, the patient attains it, and, of course, with the ego-interpersonal other in relation to whom this significant psychic change first takes place? But now, where the patient perceives aspects of the psychoanalyst's ego-interpersonality that the psychoanalyst, adapting to peer consensus, has already learned to accept as rational, objective, and realistic about relating and communicating with patients, there no problem arises for their inquiry. The patient is observing only what others, including the psychoanalyst, have grown accustomed to observe about how that particular psychoanalyst relates and communicates. So far does the ego-interpersonal model go, but no further.

However, the psychoanalyst, possessing a total psyche, is not only present as conscious (that is, adaptive and consensual) in a particular field of psychoanalytic inquiry, but, accept it or not, also as unconscious and preconscious (that is, unadaptive and unisensual) in that same field of therapy. Consider what happens next. Suppose the patient, here, is able to turn some newly found psychoanalyzed clarity to a deeper perceptiveness, even to a unique understanding of the psychoanalyst, especially concerning one or another aspect this time beyond the fringes of the psychoanalyst's conscious awareness. The patient, it appears, begins to experience distinct cues arising from the unconscious and the preconscious processes and patterns of countertransference and counterresistance. By virtue of reporting them, the patient is calling for clinical notice to be taken of some aspect or other of the psychoanalyst's ego or interpersona that in origin or effect, or both, persists beyond the psychoanalyst's awareness, no matter whether they help or hinder the movement of the inquiry. For, in part or whole, the psychoanalyst's unconscious psyche most likely escapes the patient's immediate attention, interest, and concern, before the patient's own resolution of critical aspects of transference, resistance, and anxiety. However, now that the two are well enough along in the inquiry together, the patient sees some aspect of countertransference; the psychoanalyst doesn't.

Even with the most cooperative of conscious intentions, no psychoanalyst can do more, obviously, than say, not clear. For the psychoanalyst does not perceive or understand the way the patient does, the patient's experience of some unconscious dimension of countertransference, and so on. Or, if the patient touches the nub of some painful blindspot, the psychoanalyst may actively, even angrily, counter it in defense for security. So now, whatever else may happen, the patient stands alone in the midst of that experience, it is clear, with no choice but to draw conclusions about that perception and that understanding of the psychoanalyst from within the patient's own psychic resources, unsupported from without. There is no longer any ego-interpersonal ground for continuing.

It is during such particular phases of the inquiry that, hidden and waiting, the direct sense of psychic self becomes the major point of breakthrough beyond the confines of the ego-interpersonal model. For the patient, thrown back on psychic resources outside that model, has to generate the self-supporting subjectivity for those perceptions from those inner resources. That is, thrown back on the psychic point of origin in immediate experience from which the first-personal processes arise. What else can a patient do in this circumstance now, except make some private judgment of the understanding presented to the blocked psychoanalyst. Of no help, here, is the psychoanalyst whose adaptive ego or consensual interpersona cannot, as defined, work itself into this phase of the clinical psychoanalytic inquiry. It doesn't have what is required: namely, the immediate experience of first-personal processes, which are, in fact, no different in psychic kind from the first-personal processes that the ego-interpersonal psychoanalyst must bring, undefined and unacknowledged, to those earlier phases of the inquiry in which unconscious and preconscious aspects of the patient's transference are, instead, the major focus of the inquiry. For then, no matter how cooperative a patient may be, or wish to become, no patient can help but be aware of, and resistive to, the observations and inferences, or the insights and intuitions that the psychoanalyst may offer about the unconscious and preconscious aspects of the patient's own psyche.

As further clinical background for this proposed point of view, consider, in brief sketch, how the field of psychoanalytic inquiry changed from the earlier id model to the later ego-interpersonal model. Not from 1915 to 1917, we know, but only during the 1930s did the clinical psychoanalyst first take therapeutic cognizance of the patient's ego or interpersona as it was actually present and functioning in the psychoanalytic inquiry. Never before was the ego or the interpersona treated as psychoanalyzable, nor was it, therefore, even noticed as present and functioning in the field of clinical inquiry marked out by the previous id model. That creative breakthrough was, of course, brought about through the collaboration of many post-Freudian workers, and its landmark effects may be identified at many levels of modern psychoanalytic knowledge. I mention but two here, one because of its enduring historical interest, the other because it leads into our theme. Interest in that 1930s breakthrough endures because it was a first in historical fact. Not since Freud's postscript on transference in the case study of Dora, in 1905, had the practice of psychoanalysis, from its earliest beginnings in the 1880s hypnocathartic and autohypnotic therapies, undergone so radical a change in clinical direction. Not in Freud's lifetime, moreover, had so radical a change ever been brought about before, without his own contributed view taking the lead. Thus, Hartmann's ego with autonomous functions is, for example, not id-ego bound; Sullivan's interpersonal self is, by the same token, wholly made up of reflected appraisals, which means that from then on the working model of psychoanalytic inquiry could again be changed and, as necessary, be further extended by those who follow the post-Freudians, but who modify their social and cultural perspective in turn. That is, of course, by the post-post-Freudians (including, under this rubric, the post-Sullivanians and the post-Hartmannians) and their psychic-experiential model of therapy. But closer to our present theme is the second effect. For that movement from the id to the ego-interpersonal model brought into direct clinical view new possibilities of therapeutic inquiry, distinct from the derivatives of the patient's instincts, libido, or biology in general, undreamed and unpsychoanalyzed from the standpoint of the id model.

II

How, though still unnamed and unaccepted, do the first-personal processes first emerge during ego-interpersonal therapy? This question leads directly to the point of our present theme, the radical individuation of psychoanalytic metapsychologies. To provide one approach to this question, I discuss some clinical aspects of how this change in the direction of psychoanalytic inquiry came about. Once the patient's egoic mechanisms or interpersonal operations are psychoanalyzed with a reasonable degree of clarity, and when the psychoanalyst is satisfied that this is actually the case, what remains, here, to be done about the ego or the interpersona in the patient's psychic structure? Nothing more, I am suggesting, than that the patient use it. But, now, with whom? With none other, obviously, than the ego-interpersonal other who is, at that point, sharing that immediate field of experience with that patient— which means, therefore, looking somewhat more closely at the other person in that inquiry, and, if nothing more, at least to see some strengths and limitations of the psychoanalyst's ego or interpersona as well. This sort of direct activity, it seems to me, is a natural and valuable extension of the patient's increased self-awareness, to be greeted and respected quite as un-self-consciously as it arises. Why not, now, also expect the patient to turn to the coparticipant other in the inquiry, the psychoanalyst, with whose coparticipating agency the patient gets into and works through some significantly distorted patterns of ego-interpersonality? Or, if blocked by countertransference and frustrated by counterresistance in the actual field of inquiry, the patient may have to leave, so as to check out the undergone experience as a private effort, but without the active coparticipation of the psychoanalyst with whom it first took place. Now that is, of course, a matter for a particular psychoanalyst's or patient's own personal choice, judgment, and decision. The point is, it is no longer a rule of procedure fixed in accordance with the prevailing model of psychoanalytic inquiry. But the requirement that the patient leave without doing it, on the other hand, is a matter of policy for the procedure in ego-interpersonal psychoanalysis. In that frame of reference, nothing more remains to be done.

Suppose, instead, that the patient does not leave, and the ego-interpersonal psychoanalyst, out of personal and scientific curiosity, becomes actively interested in the patient's perceptions of countertransference, and so on. Something new and unprecedented is happening, for which no established and reliable guidelines are laid down in ego-interpersonal therapy. In this circumstance, what the psychoanalyst knows and accepts as adaptive or consensual about his/her personality—which is to say, what the psychoanalyst, as ego-interpersonal other, sees and understands about him/herself as a participant observer and/or interpreter—is, of course, what a group of ego-interpersonal peers, including the psychoanalyst, appraises and judges to be the case. Without reservation, here, the psychoanalyst can most easily agree with the patient. The two are, after all, still working together in an ego-interpersonal frame of reference, aren't they? No problem, yet, for the psychoanalyst working in this model of therapeutic inquiry.

Where, on the other hand, the two coparticipants have no such consensus or adaptive agreement about the psychoanalyst's personality to fall back upon, there is nothing further ego-interpersonal for them to do. The clinical psychoanalytic inquiry is, practically speaking, now over. But, consider the alternative: Where, especially, the patient sees the psychoanalyst in some unwonted, even novel way—distorted or not, but beyond the psychoanalyst's ego-interpersonal scope of awareness—the psychoanalyst may, at first, counterresist, and, of course, also undergo the experience of counteranxiety as well. If, however, the patient doesn't back off from the presented counterresistance, and even stays close enough to it to see the counteranxiety emerging, something new begins to happen in that particular phase of their psychoanalytic inquiry. As a direct result, something new also happens to the overall structure of the ego-interpersonal model. It changes, fundamentally and irreversibly. For the patient is not only observing some aspect of countertransference, adaptive and consensual, to which the psychoanalyst may respond in counterresistance and counteranxiety, but the patient is, now alone and unsupported, also coparticipating with the psychoanalyst in that further effort at inquiry with some new input. No one else's psychic resources to rely on, the patient can move forward only from within.

Opposed by the personal psychoanalyst who is counterresistive and counteranxious, unassisted by a consultant or supervising psychoanalyst whom, as a rule, the patient doesn't call upon (as a treating psychoanalyst may, especially when working through distortions about self and other beyond their interlocked awareness), and, finally, without the unspoken edge of the psychoanalyst's position for, as some phrase it, managing the therapeutic situation—because of all such prescribed limits of the ego-interpersonal model, partly inbuilt, partly conventional—the patient still interested in doing something constructive about some deeper perception and understanding of the psychoanalyst, must face that experience of the psychoanalyst alone, fairly unsupported, and without ego-interpersonal expectancy. The patient is no longer defended, but must, as we say, fend for him/herself.

The psychoanalyst, too, is moving into a fresh, unprecedented situation. That is, of course, most expectable. For the patient, in some sense capable of uniquely individual differences, is bound to see something uniquely individual, something different about the way in which the particular psychoanalyst faces the new perception being presented. Whether, now, the psychoanalyst works as the mirror of the id model, or as the participant observer and/ or interpreter of the ego-interpersonal model, is of little consequence here. That is to say, whether the psychoanalyst chooses to respond to the patient openly or indirectly or not at all, as part of some established rule of therapeutic procedure, the choice to be made, now, is critical, decisive, individuating, uniquely differentiated, and it usually has irreversible consequences for their future work. It can't, in any case, be erased from the cumulative record of their coparticipant experience. But there is no way for the psychoanalyst to get off that spot, whatever a psychoanalyst feels or thinks about it: it's yes or no (silence, here, is also no). Yes: to engage the new line of inquiry with the patient who introduces it, aware enough of what the patient is talking about, and open enough to invite the patient to continue, even though it pushes beyond the psychoanalyst's customary scope of conscious awareness. Or no: to declare openly, or in unremitting silence, that the patient's new perceptions of the psychoanalyst are out of clinical bounds, and therefore unworkable within the defined limits of established psychoanalytic inquiry.

This latter choice of procedure originates, of course, in the id model, but it derives, for us, directly from the ego-interpersonal point of view. To round out our discussion, its rationale may briefly be sketched: All the patient's new perceptions of the psychoanalyst's conscious and unconscious psychic experience, whether true or false, belong to the psychoanalyst's but not to the patient's personal therapeutic work. Hardly shared is the ego-interpersonal definition of its boundaries here, for the psychoanalyst alone takes the position to define them. That is the ego-interpersonal, as derived from the id, rule of procedure, and there is no getting around it. Such deferment of consideration of the patient's perception of the psychoanalyst, of course, any serious psychoanalyst can readily obtain simply for the noting, or, in any case, by reminding the patient, by spoken word, or with steady silence, that the standards of clinical inquiry are so constructed as to exclude the psychoanalyst's psychic structure from the conditions of the inquiry. The id or the ego-interpersonal psychoanalyst, at that point, by that means, forecloses the possibility of a two-way exploration of countertransference, counterresistance, and counteranxiety, and, as a close consequence, also discontinues the work with relevant aspects of transference, resistance, and anxiety.

That is to say, only the outer exploration stops; the inner experience goes on. As set in motion by the patient's direct observation, the inner sequence of psychic process and pattern about that observation of the psychoanalyst's unconscious psychology continues to have effect in the experience of both coparticipants. And that, of course, is not so easily turned off. So much easier is it, by way of contrast, to turn off the patient's overt discussion with some arbitrary statement of the limits of the standard procedure. The sequences of inner experience continue unobstructed by it, however, not only for the patient but also for the psychoanalyst. After being eliminated from the working context of the ego-interpersonal field of inquiry, the inner experience may surface outside that field, at the least expected times, in the least predictable places. But it can't surface openly and naturally for a full and first-hand exploration in the ego-interpersonal inquiry in which it first arises.

III

At such points as these in psychoanalytic therapy ego-interpersonally defined, some ego-interpersonal psychoanalysts, howsoever quietly, privately, even painfully listening to their patient's voices of truth about countertransference, counterresistance, or counteranxiety, begin to hear the possibilities of new experimental procedures from within. They feel them, they follow them, they map them. They begin to look out, as well, to discover a new basis for furthering their coparticipation in the psychoanalytic inquiry. Toward that end, they search about for a new major empirical observation with the comparable power of, and as a worthy addition to, those already defined in the structure of psychoanalysis, such as transference and countertransference, resistance and counterresistance, anxiety and counteranxiety. They have, now, to work out some new empirical observation as fundamentally important for the conduct of clinical psychoanalytic inquiry, as these three pairs of defined observations already proved themselves to be, all three mutually consistent, yet each pair uniquely forward-moving. They had to find the relevance of some previously unexplored psychic process and pattern in order to accomplish at least two things during the actual inquiry.

First, and more relevant to personal experience, to make possible a direct and self-supporting release from their deep and painful sufferings of counteranxiety, and that, clearly, was the more immediate objective for obvious personal reasons. And second, but more relevant to procedural decisions, to make possible a forthcoming clinical acknowledgment of unconscious and preconscious aspects of countertransference, and so on, for further psychoanalytic inquiry, so that the patient, on clarifying some owned ego-interpersonal distortions, may now look more closely at the psychoanalyst's ego-interpersonal psychology, and address new, perhaps highly individual perceptions of the psychoanalyst, with or without the psychoanalyst's cooperation, no matter whether these perceptions prove, by the end of the inquiry, to be true or false. Here, the process of inquiry into psychic experience is all important.

This new mode of empirical psychoanalytic inquiry had, furthermore, to tap new psychic resources previously overlooked by, or expressly omitted from, both the id and the ego-interpersonal models of therapy. In other words, and in terms of an altogether new approach to metapsychology, it was necessary to discover a basis in the human psyche that stood in a dialectical and transforming relation to both the patient's anxieties and the psychoanalyst's counteranxieties arising in the course of their shared clinical inquiry into their resistances and counterresistances—which are: in the ego perspective, the Hartmann adaptive, defense mechanisms; in the interpersonal perspective, the Sullivan consensual, security operations. That is to say: from one side, to discover a psychic base in the patient's direct experience of anxiety about standing alone and unsupported, and from which, nonetheless, to continue offering some direct observations of the psychoanalyst, especially to indicate some unconscious and preconscious dimensions of countertransference, counterresistance, and counteranxiety; and, from the other side, to discover a psychic base in the psychoanalyst's direct experience of counteranxiety about some disturbed and failing counterresistance in the face of the patient's perception of some aspect of countertransference, or anything else about the psychoanalyst's psychic structure beyond the conscious awareness of the other coparticipant in the inquiry, namely the patient.

It is at such junctures of experience that the id and/or the ego-interpersonal psychoanalyst, following the lead of the standard procedure, can follow the lead of the inquiry no further. Psychoanalysis itself, it becomes clear, needs new theory and new practice. Lest, otherwise, the therapeutic quest for psychological change come to a standstill. There is, of course, nothing more in the id canon of psychoanalysis for the ego-interpersonal psychoanalyst to fall back upon, because the id model is constructed expressly in the absence of extended inquiry into the mechanisms of the ego or the operations of the interpersona. Nor, in addition, is there anything in the ego-interpersonal canon for us to fall back upon, because the notion of anxiety and its correlatives of transference and resistance represent the innermost workable limits of the therapeutic inquiry. As already indicated, there is nothing more that the id or the ego-interpersonal psychoanalyst could possibly do, not in empirical observation and definition, nor in metaphorical interpretation and speculation, to account for these newly emergent possibilities of further therapeutic inquiry. Nothing more that these psychoanalysts could do, and still remain consistent with their professed models of therapeutic inquiry.

It is for this clinical purpose, I am suggesting, that the old and many-faceted notion of the self, very hard to define, yet even harder to ignore, long explored in classical philosophical psychology but scarcely noticed in previous psychoanalytic inquiry, is now being brought into the field of therapy as comparatively new psychoanalytic psychology. The introduction of the clinical experience of the self, the psychoanalyst's as well as the patient's, provides the psychic counterpoint from which to study both the counteranxiety and the anxiety that the two coparticipants each directly experience from within, at first hand, and unmediated by the other, for working through the analysis of "me-you" relations. The immediate experience of the self in the first person, singular and active, is being brought into the clinical focus of psychoanalytic inquiry, I am also suggesting, for the unsuppressible reason that it proves, finally, to be ineluctable and ineradicable in human-psychic life. The development of new procedures for psychoanalytic inquiry into the psychology of that immediate experience, of course, still requires much empirical and systematic, clinical work. But the first step is, however, already underway in the making of a new psychoanalytic psychology of the first-personal self, providing, as it does, for the active processes of unique individuality that hold the experiential and dialectical counterpoint to the patient's processes and patterns of anxiety in transforming relation to those of the psychoanalyst's counteranxiety, as they each suffer and undergo their own from within.

This brings us to the center of my theme, and entitles the point of this paper: pluralism in perspectives on countertransference. For the new direction in contemporary psychoanalytic inquiry is the radical individuation of its metapsychologies. Once the psychology of the self, the patient's now, as well as the psychoanalyst's, is seriously taken into empirical and systematic account, and once it is fully admitted into the field of clinical psychoanalytic inquiry, the working perspective that the two adopt for the interpretive metapsychology of their work, then, no longer remains the province and prerogative of the psychoanalyst only. That, so far, is clear beyond question. The two coparticipants in the psychoanalytic inquiry may, now, each offer

elements of their own personal perspectives on interpretive metapsychology
—with neither one, however, held back by the reservations and caveats of
the antecedently established id and ego-interpersonal standards of procedure,
nor, of course, by the private and cherished commitments, of the other.

The immediate experience of first-personal processes, singular and active,
from its psychological origins to its logical functions, augurs well for this
entirely new approach to the clinical working out of psychoanalytic metapsychology. Unacknowledged though the inbuilt psychic resources to do this
were, they, in any case, still remained present and functioning in the previous
id and ego-interpersonal models. But they, nonetheless, remained dormant.
Now, however, every psychoanalyst and every patient engaging in clinical
psychoanalytic inquiry also has this new freedom in the new psychic-experiential model, explicitly encompassing the experience of inbuilt psychic
resources of both coparticipants. Every patient and every psychoanalyst is,
now, free to pursue any interpretive and speculative outlook on metapsychology, old or new, that interests either or both of them. They may, for the first
time, freely open the field and turn the procedure to the psychic uniqueness
of their respective first-personal resources, arising from their unalienable
experience of the self in the active singular, private and public. In this
coparticipant effort, especially to cope with both their anxieties and their
counteranxieties, they may, now, acknowledge the individuating resources
of the psychic self, newly admitted into therapeutic awareness of that purpose. Unexceptionably, it applies to all.

Once emerged into the therapeutic field and finally engaged in the therapeutic inquiry, not only is there no turning back from the psychic movement
of the first-personal self. It is, also, free to do other things in the psychoanalyzable field as well. Especially may the first-personal self do such things in
the psychoanalytic situation that, before its being admitted, once were, and
that, even after its being admitted, still are ordinarily considered its customary province in the quotidian conduct of living. Such things as, that is,
holding beliefs worth nurturing, deciding values worth striving for, cherish-
ing ideals worth consummating—in short, seeking the psychic realizations
of experience and the ego-interpersonal fulfillments of behavior. In fact now,
without both coparticipants, at some point, expressing some uniquely individual slant on beliefs, values, and ideals, no psychoanalytic inquiry really
takes hold.

In sum, and this is the compelling direction in contemporary psychoanalytic inquiry, both coparticipants may suggest some uniquely individual
emphasis in perspective on metapsychology, and select the particular myth

and metaphor to depict their own private and closely held part in the clinical psychoanalytic inquiry. From this the following hypothesis emerges: that the number of uniquely individual perspectives now possible for interpretive usage in psychoanalytic metapsychology is practically infinite, no more, no less than the practically infinite number of coparticipants in the inquiry. Hence, the radical individuation of its metapsychologies. In other words: no uniquely individual emphasis on beliefs, values, and ideals; no genuine therapeutic inquiry.

The undertaking of the actual psychoanalytic inquiry, we now know in practice, generates a far deeper and more intensive experience of the relativity of transference and countertransference than workers in the earlier id and ego-interpersonal models ever acknowledged in theory. This inquiry into the unconscious dimensions of transference converging with those of countertransference can be done within the shared field of their occurrence. It doesn't have to be done, but it can be. It cuts across metapsychological lines, and focuses on what is variously termed the transference-countertransference neurosis, the transference-countertransference situation, or the interlocking of transference and countertransference. Regardless of differences in terminology, however, the relativity of transference and countertransference is defined by the fact that these observable processes and patterns, in so far as they are human-psychic, are interchangeable without altering their essential character. Composed of the same psychic substance, they are symmetrical in value, and may be so considered during actual psychoanalytic inquiry (Wolstein 1953, 1954).

"Doctor" and "patient" designate the, so to speak, extra-psychic activities that derive from the hierarchical aspects of societal roles, and all that playing them entails—but are not, as such, indigenous to the psychic reality of the experience they both undergo together. For the clinical psychoanalytic inquiry into transference and countertransference, as well as both resistance and counterresistance, and anxiety and counteranxiety, also brings the two coparticipants face-to-face with the sense of self. An autogenerative point of origin from within the psyche, this sense of self is uniquely individual. With it, the two may, in their separate ways, each establish ownership of, responsibility for, choice among these processes and patterns as these emerge for possible reconstructive change. The classic discussion of the self in American psychology is W. James's *Principles of Psychology* (New York: Holt, 1890), volume I, chapter 10; see also, G. Mead, *Mind, Self, and Society* (Chicago: University of Chicago Press, 1934).

From the 1930s onward, colleagues and students of Reich, A. Freud, and

Hartmann in the id-ego wing, and Fromm-Reichmann, Sullivan, and Thompson in the interpersonal-cultural wing, have been psychoanalyzing the character armoring, defense mechanisms, and security operations. To study this sector of personality, they have developed therapeutic formulations in their diverse approaches to cover the adaptive and consensual side of the self. As Sullivan (1940) succinctly put it: "The self is made up of reflected appraisals" (Sullivan, H. [1940]. *Conceptions of Modern Psychiatry*. Washington, D.C.: W.A. White Psychiatric Foundation [1947], 10). This statement holds, however, only as long as the patient is treated in disjunction from the psychoanalyst, and the model of therapeutic inquiry is managerial. But a view of the patient as interacting with the psychoanalyst in a shared experience of the inquiry indicates the need for a larger conception of the self. That is to say, in addition to the self as adaptive, environed, and objective, what's needed is the subjective, spontaneous, and autogenerative side of the self. Sullivan, as is clear from the above citation, concerns himself with the objective side. Though he is, by standard scholarship, placed in the tradition of James, Dewey, and Mead (especially Mead, because of Sullivan's Chicago period), it is clear, now, that he emphasizes the objective side of the self (which they, of course, also do), but he leaves out the subjective side of the self (which they, especially James and Mead, do not). He is, I think, most fully in accord with Dewey (Wolstein, 1949).

Some current work in the philosophical psychology of the self delineates the self in the first person ("I") as both distinct from, and as related to, the interpersona ("me") even more sharply. And more comprehensively also, in my opinion, than James or Dewey or Mead. Among recent contributions to this emphasis in the psychology of the self, which I find interesting and useful, are R. Chisholm, *The First Person* (Minneapolis: University of Minnesota Press, 1981) and P. Weiss, *You, I, and the Others* (Carbondale: Southern Illinois University Press, 1980).[1] Although both Chisholm and Weiss develop the structural elements of their themes from different philosophical and psychological points of view, their works converge in focusing on both the language and the experience of the self as origin, as self-moving, and as first person, singular and active. Other recent items of interest are: E. Anscombe, "The First Person," in S. Guttenplan (ed.), *Mind and Language* (Oxford: The Clarendon Press, 1975), pages 45–65; F. Brentano, *Psychology from an Empirical Standpoint* (London: Routledge and Kegan Paul, 1973); K. Popper and J. Eccles, *The Self and Its Brain* (New York: Springer International, 1977); and P. Strawson, *Individuals* (London: Methuen, 1959).

NOTE

1. For a more detailed discussion of these two works, see my review essay, "The First Person in Interpersonal Relations," *Contemporary Psychoanalysis* (1983) 19: 522–535. There consider, especially, the notion of "privilege of direct access," which gives psychological support to the generic distinction of first-personal from ego-interpersonal relations. The first person singular active, so privileged, is, therefore, both individual and unique. But this individuality, if not psychic, is resourceless, and this uniqueness, if not ego-interpersonal, is anonymous.

   First-personal relations, singular and active, supply the ego-interpersonal relations of their possessor with an inbuilt and induplicable opening to the domain of immediate experience. That is, literally, experience unmediated by the environing media of relatedness and communication. The inclusion of such experience within the structure of psychoanalytic knowledge extends the field of therapeutic inquiry through the patterned foreground of ego-interpersonal relations into its background of process in psychic origins. And how, in short, does acknowledging the "privilege of direct access" affect such perspectives as character structure, ego psychology, interpersonal and object relations? It brings irreversible changes into the metaphors of character adjustment, ego adaptation, and interpersonal or object-relational consensus. For it makes them directly responsive to the uniquely individual, first-personal experience of the subject, to whom, finally, the structure, psychology, and relations belong.

REFERENCES

Wolstein, B. (1949), Dewey's theory of human nature, *Psychiatry* 12: 77–85.

Wolstein, B. (1953), The field of psychotherapeutic inquiry, *American Journal of Psychotherapy* 7: 503–514.

Wolstein, B. (1954; 2nd ed., 1964), *Transference*. New York: Grune & Stratton.

Name Index

Subject Index